Computational Science: Concepts and Applications

Computational Science: Concepts and Applications

Edited by Rushel Davis

CLANRYE INTERNATIONAL
www.clanryeinternational.com

Clanrye International,
750 Third Avenue, 9th Floor,
New York, NY 10017, USA

ISBN: 978-1-63240-825-9

Cataloging-in-Publication Data

Computational science : concepts and applications / edited by Rushel Davis.
    p. cm.
Includes bibliographical references and index.
ISBN 978-1-63240-825-9
1. Computer science. 2. Computational complexity. 3. Computational intelligence.
I. Davis, Rushel.
QA76 .C66 2019
004--dc23

For information on all Clanrye International publications
visit our website at www.clanryeinternational.com

Contents

Permissions

List of Contributors

Index

Preface

Computational science is a multidisciplinary field that applies computer simulation and advanced computation to develop solutions for complex problems. The core functional areas of this field are recognizing complex problems, conceptualizing the system, designing a simulation for studying the system, choosing an appropriate computing infrastructure, etc. Some of the commonly applied methods include numerical analysis, finite element methods, Monte Carlo methods, numerical linear algebra, etc. The applications of the computational models and simulations developed in computational science are in the fields of urban complex systems, computational finance, computational biology and computational engineering. It is an upcoming field of science that has undergone rapid development over the past few decades. This book elucidates the concepts and innovative models around prospective developments with respect to computational science. It will help the readers in keeping pace with the rapid changes in this field.

The information shared in this book is based on empirical researches made by veterans in this field of study. The elaborative information provided in this book will help the readers further their scope of knowledge leading to advancements in this field.

Finally, I would like to thank my fellow researchers who gave constructive feedback and my family members who supported me at every step of my research.

Editor

Application of the Recursive Finite Element Approach on 2D Periodic Structures under Harmonic Vibrations

Reem Yassine [1], **Faten Salman** [1], **Ali Al Shaer** [1], **Mohammad Hammoud** [1,*] and **Denis Duhamel** [2]

[1]   Department of Mechanical Engineering, Lebanese International University, 146404 Mazraa, Beirut, Lebanon; reem.yassine@liu.edu.lb (R.Y.); 11030164@students.liu.edu.lb (F.S.); ali.alshaer@liu.edu.lb (A.A.S.)

[2]   Laboratoire Navier—UMR 8205 (Ecole des Ponts Paris Tech—IFSTTAR—CNRS), Cité Descartes—Champs-sur-Marne, Université Paris-Est, 77455 Marne-la-Vallée Cedex 2, France; denis.duhamel@enpc.fr

*   Correspondence: mohamad.hammoud@liu.edu.lb

Academic Editor: Demos T. Tsahalis

Abstract: The frequency response function is a quantitative measure used in structural analysis and engineering design; hence, it is targeted for accuracy. For a large structure, a high number of substructures, also called cells, must be considered, which will lead to a high amount of computational time. In this paper, the recursive method, a finite element method, is used for computing the frequency response function, independent of the number of cells with much lesser time costs. The fundamental principle is eliminating the internal degrees of freedom that are at the interface between a cell and its succeeding one. The method is applied solely for free (no load) nodes. Based on the boundary and interior degrees of freedom, the global dynamic stiffness matrix is computed by means of products and inverses resulting with a dimension the same as that for one cell. The recursive method is demonstrated on periodic structures (cranes and buildings) under harmonic vibrations. The method yielded a satisfying time decrease with a maximum time ratio of $\frac{1}{18}$ and a percentage difference of 19%, in comparison with the conventional finite element method. Close values were attained at low and very high frequencies; the analysis is supported for two types of materials (steel and plastic). The method maintained its efficiency with a high number of forces, excluding the case when all of the nodes are under loads.

Keywords: finite element analysis; recursive method; periodic structures; harmonic vibrations

---

1. Introduction

The study of structural dynamics is essential for understanding and evaluating the performance of any engineering structure. Most structures vibrate. In operation, all machines, vehicles and buildings are subjected to dynamic forces that cause vibrations. Very often, the vibrations have to be investigated because they may cause an immediate problem. Whatever the reason, we need to quantify the structural response in some way, so that its implication on factors such as performance and fatigue can be evaluated. The frequency response function (FRF) will then be considered. These structures may have a uniform geometry or a periodic one. The frequency response function has acquired much consideration for high frequencies, since at small values, the system can be analyzed statically. Getting this function for the structures and system mentioned under a high range of angular frequencies will lead to a large amount of computation time, since solving for the displacement vector requires inversing the dynamic stiffness matrix at each angular frequency. As the number of substructures, also called cells, increases the computational cost increases. Hence, the approach emphasized in this research presents a solution for this time issue.

Various methods were inspected to determine the frequency response for one-dimensional structures and their behavior as assembled for a two-dimensional element as a truss or frame. Original numerical approaches were done by Dong and Aalami [1,2] to estimate the deformations on each point on the cross-section by finite element analysis (conventional FEM).

One approach for structural analysis is the spectral finite element method (SFEM) that was mainly used by Finnveden [3,4]. It considers general uniform structures with complex cross-sections and handles all types of boundary conditions. The displacements in the cross-section are described by the finite element method (FEM), while ordinary differential equations for 2D structures will express the variation along the axis of symmetry (x-axis) with a solution of the form $e^{jkx}U(y,z)$, where y and z are cross-sectional coordinates. A similar approach as SFEM called the dynamic stiffness method (DSM) is notably efficient for the study of excited structures under high frequencies [5]. It provides an economical solution with a much higher accuracy, since it divides the member into distinct elements. Both methods include similar steps till the extent of obtaining the dynamic stiffness matrix. DSM defines a relationship between the nodal displacement and forces of the element using shape functions, in order to derive the dynamic stiffness matrix; whereas the SFEM uses the virtual work method to obtain the stiffness matrix, and the dynamic matrix will have a more laborious presentation, being a function of the wave number. Structures made of plates and shells were examined by the SFEM approach by Nilsson [6]. Birgersson [7–9] studied plane wave and fluid structure interaction. Gry and Gavric [10,11] applied similar approaches for the detection of wave propagation on rails, where they calculated the relative dispersion relations. Similar techniques were interpreted by Bartoli and Marzani [12,13] for the purpose of computing the dispersion relations for damped structures of arbitrary cross-sections and with symmetric elements.

Duhamel et al. [14] established a combined method between wave and finite element approaches for investigating periodic structures; it has an advantage over the SFEM by its ease of operations for complex geometries and scattered materials. Lee et al. [15] utilized a compounded method using finite element and boundary element (FEBE) methods for studying periodic structures meshed non-periodically.

Reduced order models (ROMs) are mainly mathematically-inexpensive methods for solving complex and large-scale dynamic problems by decreasing the model's degrees of freedom. It gathers the system's responses under excitations, providing near real-life analysis, however with low accuracy. ROM was applied on mistuned bladed disks by Castanier et al. [16] for capturing localized modes and producing low order models with modest memory storage; it calculated relatively acceptable results in comparison with FEM. The method was later improved by employing the Craig–Bampton component mode synthesis (CMS), which is an ROM-based technique yielding better mode accuracy; it required that at least one subspace iteration is executed (Bathe et al. [17]). CMS was then applied by Zhou et al. [18] on dynamics analysis using non-uniform rational B-spline (NURBS) finite elements to generate appropriate constructions of interfaced substructures. The method obtained a complete structural model consistent with the original model.

Duhamel [19,20] analyzed the frequency response by the recursive method (RM), on waveguide structures, as beams, plates and tires. The beam was divided into two substructures. As the division number increases, a higher accuracy in the frequency response is obtained. He also studied some plates excited in the mid x and y positions. A simply supported plate is meshed, and then, its mass and stiffness matrices are extracted from ABAQUS and then inserted in MATLAB to obtain the frequency response using the method studied. A similar method aiming to reduce the number of degrees of freedom under zero forces called the Guyan method is commonly used; however, it had been employed mainly for static analysis. Further, it neglects the inertia at the omitted DOF, hence being obsolete for structures of high mass to stiffness ratios [21].

The paper provides a computational solving method for periodic structures that cannot be designed as waveguides, where the recursive method is studied for its efficiency. The recursive method tends to ease the study of finite element analysis for complex structures. It is a computational method that computes the global dynamic stiffness matrix by products and inverses of matrices, resulting with the same dimension as that of one cell. For a complex cross-section, the structure is sectioned and modeled in the conventional finite element software and then post-processed in MATLAB. RM tends to eliminate any degrees of freedom (DOF) on the nodes that are not under study. Thus, a structure of two elements can be examined as one, on account of omitting the DOF at the boundaries between two consecutive cells, if there were no internal loads.

Two applications were examined under the illustrated method. The first application is where the RM is applied on 1D bar structures and demonstrating their manner as assembled in a crane under harmonic and seismic loadings. The crane will be dealt with as a truss. A real-life example will be considered, with a conservative number of elements. For the second application, the RM will be applied on a building modeled as a frame. The seismic load will be designed as harmonic displacement at its base end. The truss and the frame are considered as 2D periodic structures.

Modal analysis is used to assess the dynamic properties of a structure by assessing the natural frequencies and their corresponding mode shapes. It was employed to determine the range of frequencies to be examined. FEM works on the full modes when computing the FRF, while RM will only work on the modes that include the studied nodes. For example, in the presented study, the structure has no internal nodes for examination; hence, RM will consider the first mode only with the two end nodes. Using the recursive method, a few computations are needed for finding a close response compared to the number of computations used in the finite element analysis.

2. Recursive Method

2.1. Review

The recursive method is used to calculate the forced response of various types of structures, which might lead to a high consumption of computation. This method is used to compute the general dynamic stiffness matrix with a much lower amount of computational time. Generally, the recursive method is a purely computational method, which computes the global dynamic stiffness matrix by products and inverses of matrices with the same dimensions as the dynamic stiffness matrix of a cell.

For a complex cross-section, the structure is sectioned and modeled in the conventional finite element software (ANSYS). Then, the mass, stiffness and damping matrices are extracted from ANSYS.

These matrices will be post-processed to give the dynamic stiffness matrix of the section under study, after which, the global dynamic stiffness matrix of the whole structure will be figured from the recursive method. It will be obtained by means of products and inverses of the matrices with the dimension equal to that of the dynamic stiffness matrix of the section. This method tends to eliminate any degrees of freedom (DOF) on the nodes that are not under study. Thus, a structure of two elements can be examined as one, on account of omitting the DOF at the boundaries between two consecutive cells, if there were no internal loads. In general, this method is applicable and effective when the structure is not under a large number of forces.

The periodic structure that is divided into N cells is considered. The problem studied is under a point force excitation, having a response u. Following is a demonstration for the recursive method, numerically [14].

2.2. Behavior of One Cell

First, consider a one-cell element. The discrete dynamic stiffness matrix of a cell for a time-dependent $e^{-i\omega t}$ is given by:

$$\left(K - i\omega C - \omega^2 M\right)q = f, \tag{1}$$

where $i = \sqrt{-1}$, ω is the angular frequency, K is the stiffness matrix, C is the damping matrix, M is the mass matrix, q is the displacement vector and f is the loading vector.

Thus, the dynamic stiffness matrix is:

$$\tilde{D} = K - i\omega C - \omega^2 M. \tag{2}$$

Decomposing the degrees of freedom into the boundary (B) and interior (I), the resulting dynamic equation is:

$$\begin{bmatrix} \tilde{D}_{BB} & \tilde{D}_{BI} \\ \tilde{D}_{IB} & \tilde{D}_{II} \end{bmatrix} \begin{bmatrix} q_B \\ q_I \end{bmatrix} = \begin{bmatrix} f_B \\ 0 \end{bmatrix}. \tag{3}$$

Then, eliminate the second row of Equation (3):

$$\begin{aligned} \tilde{D}_{IB}q_B + \tilde{D}_{II}q_I &= 0, \\ q_I &= -\tilde{D}_{II}^{-1}\tilde{D}_{IB}q_B. \end{aligned} \tag{4}$$

The first row in Equation (3) will be:

$$f_B = (\tilde{D}_{BB} - \tilde{D}_{BI}\tilde{D}_{II}^{-1}\tilde{D}_{IB})q_B. \tag{5}$$

Thus, boundary conditions are only considered in the study. These conditions can be decomposed into left (L) and right (R) for the relative nodes.

Equation (5) becomes:

$$\begin{bmatrix} f_L \\ f_R \end{bmatrix} = \begin{bmatrix} D_{LL}^{(1)} & D_{LR}^{(1)} \\ D_{RL}^{(1)} & D_{RR}^{(1)} \end{bmatrix} \begin{bmatrix} q_L \\ q_R \end{bmatrix} = D^{(1)} \begin{bmatrix} q_L \\ q_R \end{bmatrix}, \tag{6}$$

where $D^{(1)}$ is the dynamic stiffness matrix of a single cell.

Since matrices K, C and M are symmetric, matrix $D^{(1)}$ will also be symmetric.

2.3. Behavior of Two Cells

For the assembly of two cells, consider the dynamic stiffness matrices A and B for Cell 1 and Cell 2, respectively, as shown in Figure 1. The dynamic stiffness matrix is now denoted with $D^{(2)}$, which relates the DOF between the two sides (left and right). The dynamic stiffness matrix of the structure is calculated using:

$$\begin{bmatrix} f_1 \\ f_2 \\ f_3 \end{bmatrix} = \begin{bmatrix} A_{LL} & A_{LR} & 0 \\ A_{RL} & A_{RR} + B_{LL} & B_{LR} \\ 0 & B_{RL} & B_{RR} \end{bmatrix} \begin{bmatrix} q_1 \\ q_2 \\ q_3 \end{bmatrix}, \tag{7}$$

since the interior side is taken with free loading $f_2 = 0$. Thus, solving for the second row in the matrix:

$$q_2 = -(A_{RR} + B_{LL})^{-1}(A_{RL}q_1 + B_{LR}q_3). \tag{8}$$

The global dynamic stiffness matrix will then be:

$$\begin{aligned} \begin{bmatrix} f_1 \\ f_3 \end{bmatrix} &= \begin{bmatrix} A_{LL} - (A_{RR} + B_{LL})^{-1}A_{RL} & -A_{LR}(A_{RR} + B_{LL})^{-1}B_{LR} \\ -B_{RL}(A_{RR} + B_{LL})^{-1}A_{RL} & B_{RR} - B_{RL}(A_{RR} + B_{LL})^{-1}B_{RL} \end{bmatrix} \\ \begin{bmatrix} q_1 \\ q_3 \end{bmatrix} &= \begin{bmatrix} D_{LL}^{(2)} & D_{LR}^{(2)} \\ D_{RL}^{(2)} & D_{RR}^{(2)} \end{bmatrix} \begin{bmatrix} q_1 \\ q_3 \end{bmatrix} = D^{(2)} \begin{bmatrix} q_1 \\ q_3 \end{bmatrix}, \end{aligned} \tag{9}$$

where $D^{(2)}$ is the dynamic stiffness matrix of the two cells' structure.

Since matrices A and B are symmetric, matrix $D^{(2)}$ will also be symmetric. Therefore, we can write:

$$D^{(2)} = \{A, B\}. \tag{10}$$

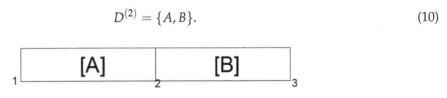

Figure 1. Two-cell element.

2.4. General Case

Consider now a general case of a structure made of N cells, where it is under no load at its internal nodes. Denote its total dynamic stiffness matrix as $D^{(N)}$. Note that the structure is periodic and is isotropic. Firstly, consider a structure with identical cells; omit the internal degrees of freedom that are under no load. As stated in the foregoing method, the element of two cells is subsequently modeled as one cell. Hence, the current one-cell element will be assembled with a one-cell element that was previously a two-cell element. Proceeding with the N-cell structure, the outcome is a one-cell element that holds the nodes that are of interest for the assessment. For no restriction on the number of cells, the procedure is computed for $log_2 N$ steps. This accustomed number of steps will have a high effectiveness on saving the number of computations, when comparing with the conventional finite element analysis; since it is no longer required for the global assembly of the whole structure. The complete analysis is reviewed in Figure 2.

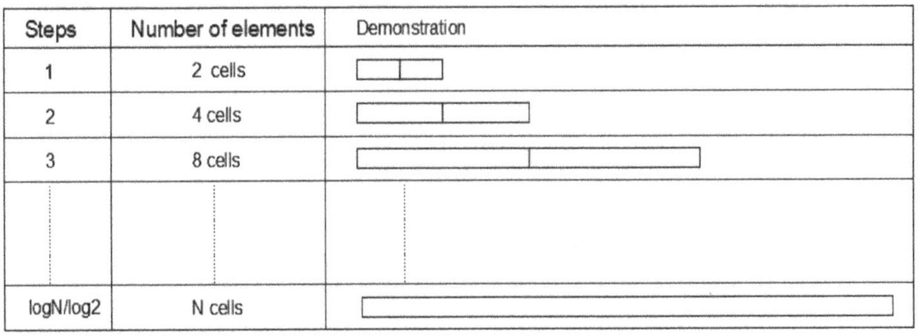

Steps	Number of elements	Demonstration
1	2 cells	
2	4 cells	
3	8 cells	
logN/log2	N cells	

Figure 2. Element assembly in the recursive method.

In case the number of cells was not as a power of two, a binary representation will be used to model the system. For example, for N number of cells where N is not equal to a number with a power of two, it can be written in binary representation as $N = 11 = 1011_b$.

The system is solved as follows:

- Calculate the dynamic stiffness matrix for a structure of eight cells, decomposing them into four of two cells each.
- The studied structure is then assembled with a structure of two cells, studied previously.
- The resulting matrix is assembled with a structure of one cell.

This approach can be resumed by:

$$D^{(11)} = \left\{ \left\{ D^{(8)}, D^{(2)} \right\}, D^{(1)} \right\}. \tag{11}$$

This method provides an easy approach for the computations of a structure with a large number of cells under harmonic vibrations. After applying the force and displacement boundary conditions, the response for the node subjected to forced vibrations is studied and detected for the frequency response function.

3. Applications

Periodic structures were examined in this paper. For the first application, 1D bar structures are assembled in a crane. Excitation and seismic loading will be examined on cranes, where it will be dealt with as a truss. On the other hand, the application of the recursive method will be on 2D frame, where a harmonic displacement is loaded at its base nodes (model of seismic load). The frame is considered as a 2D periodic structure.

After computing the FRF conventionally (using harmonic analysis in ANSYS), the response will be compared to that determined from the recursive method. Note that a FULL analysis method was used in ANSYS, where it uses the full system's matrices for computing the response; this will lead to a more comprehensive and detailed approach. RM is defined by a self-written MATLAB code where it takes the K, M and C matrices of a one cell from ANSYS for the frame structure. However, these matrices will be calculated manually for the truss application. Then, the matrices will be assembled reaching N cells, recursively. The dynamic stiffness matrix will be obtained by products and inverses of matrices with the same dimension as the dynamic stiffness matrix of one cell. Nodes that are under no load or not under study will be omitted using this method. Hence, internal degrees of freedom between the adjacent cells will be removed using the RM.

3.1. Truss Application

A truss is an element structure consisting of two or more bar elements, connected to each other by pins, by which each pin will support rotations around its axis only. Cranes are modeled as a truss, where this will be studied under forced vibrations and seismic loading. A freestanding crane is considered as a periodic structure where the repeated cell is shown in Figure 3. The global nodes are numbered as in the displayed order in ANSYS.

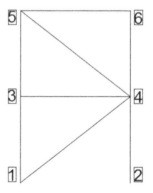

Figure 3. Repeated cell in the truss.

The bar elements will differ by their cross-sectional areas, since the vertical bars hold larger loads; then, its cross-sectional area is larger than those of the horizontal and inclined bars. Hence, each element is oriented differently relative to the global coordinate system.

The element equation is expressed as:

$$[\overline{K}^e + i\omega\overline{C}^e - \omega^2\overline{M}^e]\,[\overline{\Delta}^e] = [\overline{F}^e], \tag{12}$$

where $i = \sqrt{-1}$, ω is the angular velocity, $\overline{K}^e$ is the local stiffness matrix, $\overline{C}^e$ is the local damping matrix, $\overline{M}^e$ is the local mass matrix, $\overline{\Delta}^e$ is the local displacement vector and $\overline{F}^e$ is the local loading vector.

The truss element will have two degrees of freedom (DOF) at each node: translations in the nodal x and y directions.

The bar element under study is a steel bar with characteristics represented in Table 1.

Table 1. Bar element characteristics.

Young's Modulus of Elasticity	$E = 200$ GPa
Density	$\rho = 7800\ \frac{kg}{m^3}$
Damping Ratio	$\zeta = 0.004$ [22]
Larger Cross-Sectional Area	$A1 = 0.001175$ m^2
Smaller Cross-Sectional Area	$A2 = 2.91 \times 10^{-4}$ m^2
Length for the Vertical and Horizontal Bars, Respectively	$l = 1.5 - 2$ m

Referenced to real-life applications, freestanding tower cranes with fixed foundations and no undercarriage supports are modeled as cranes with the repeated cell mentioned before, and they are only repeated 16 times with a total length of 53.65 m, including the foundation height. All dimensions are assumed relative to actual values.

Both types of loadings will be applied to the same crane structure presented, with the same repeated cell and type of material employed. Hence, the structures relative to the two different loadings will have equal stiffness, mass and damping matrices. The dynamic stiffness matrix is obtained due to the discussed approach, without the need for global assembly.

3.1.1. Truss under Forced Vibration at the Last Node

$\overline{C}^e$ is taken for two different types of damping:

- Rayleigh damping:

$$\overline{C}^e = \alpha \overline{K}^e + \beta \overline{M}^e,$$ (13)

where α and β are calculated from the natural frequencies and the relative damping ratio. The natural frequencies taken are the first two natural frequencies, with their relative mode shapes shown in Figure 4; determined by modal analysis. The damping ratio for steel material used in a footbridge damping is $\zeta = 0.004$ [22].

- Hysteretic damping:

The dynamic stiffness matrix is demonstrated as:

$$D^e = (1 + 0.01 * i)K^e - \omega^2 M^e.$$ (14)

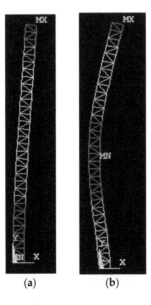

(a)   (b)

Figure 4. Mode shapes for the natural frequencies. (a) The first mode shape with a modal frequency of $fn_1 = 1.0235$ Hz; (b) the second mode shape with a modal frequency of $fn_2 = 5.7271$ Hz .

The crane interpreted is illustrated in Figure 5. The last nodes of interest are under harmonic vibrations for $F = F_0 e^{-i\omega t}$, where $F_0 = 1$ N. The fixed foundation will remove the degrees of freedom on the first two nodes in the global system, and the matrix is assembled upon a relationship between a cell and its consecutive one. The periodic structure is computed under a range of driving frequencies, for the purpose of estimating the frequency response function at the excited node.

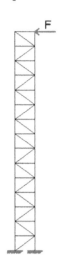

Figure 5. Crane under forced excitation.

3.1.2. Truss under Seismic Load

The truss application is applied under a second type of loading for the investigation of the frequency response function under a range of frequencies. The crane structure will be studied under hysteretic damping solely, represented by the previously shown dynamic stiffness matrix (14). The first two nodes are subjected to seismic load, which is modeled as a harmonic displacement of $d = d_0 e^{-i\omega t}$, where $d_0 = 0.01$ m on the base of the structure, as shown in Figure 6.

Figure 6. Crane under seismic load.

3.2. Frame Application under Seismic Load

Frames are structures that have a combination of beams resisting loads. Such structures are modeled to overcome large moments developed due to the applied loading. The connected node acquires three DOF, preventing displacement in the y-direction and rotations in the x- and z-direction. A building under seismic load is modeled as a frame. Timoshenko beams will be studied, having four degrees of freedom. The cross-sectional dimensions of all frame elements and the repeated cell are illustrated in Figures 7 and 8, respectively. The cell will be repeated 16 times with a total length of 48 m.

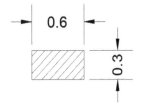

Figure 7. Cross-section of the frame; dimensions are in meters.

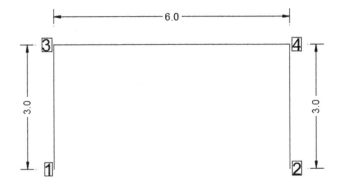

Figure 8. Repeated cell in the frame; dimensions are in meters.

Frame analysis for the local element is similar to the truss element. Stiffness and mass matrices ($\overline{K}^e$ and $\overline{M}^e$) are found from the ANSYS program, and the damping matrix ($\overline{C}^e$) is established using hysteretic damping, as mentioned for the truss; where the dynamic stiffness matrix is represented as:

$$D^e = (1 + 0.01 * i)K^e - \omega^2 M^e \tag{15}$$

The beam used is made up of steel with a modulus of elasticity and density similar to that of the bar element; where Young's modulus of elasticity is $E = 200$ GPa and the density is $\rho = 7800 \frac{\text{kg}}{\text{m}^3}$. The nodes at the base are under a harmonic displacement of $d = d_0 e^{-i\omega t}$, where $d_0 = 0.01$ m, as shown in Figure 9. The periodic structure will be examined for a range of frequencies for computing the frequency response function.

Figure 9. Frame model under seismic load.

4. Results

The FRF obtained from the recursive method will be compared to that using a conventional finite element program (ANSYS). The elapsed time for each application is measured and collated between the FEM and RM. The PC machine utilized for finite element analysis runs on an Intel Core i7-4500U with a clk (clock) speed of 2.40 GHz and 8.00 GB of RAM.

4.1. Truss Application under Forced Vibration

The results for the crane structure made up of 16 repeated cells under Rayleigh damping is demonstrated in Figure 10, and a zoomed-in presentation was done to illustrate the difference in achieving close results between low and high frequencies. The results represent the variation of the modulus of displacement logarithmically with respect to the range of frequencies for the last node, excited under harmonic forced vibration.

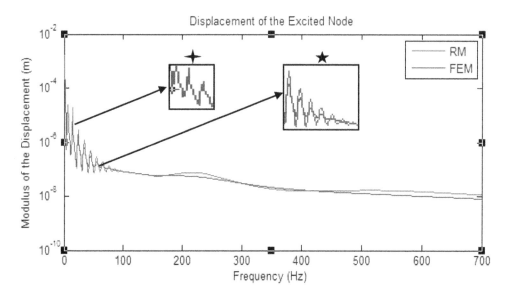

Figure 10. Displacement of the excited node under Rayleigh damping for the truss application that is applied to forced vibration. The graph is logarithmically scaled. ✛: low frequencies; ★: high frequencies. RM, recursive method.

Figure 11 illustrates the normalized percentage error between the RM and FEM methods in the low and high frequencies domains, evaluating approximate low frequencies as values less than 50 Hz. In the low frequency domain, the structure most likely behaves as in the static equilibrium, where the effect of the driving frequencies is still minimal on the response (low effect as if $\omega = 0$). The evaluated percentages were very small for $f < 50$ Hz. However, for $f > 50$ Hz, the structure is most likely showing dynamic behavior. High frequencies will estimate a larger percentage range since then, the effect of ω^2 becomes recognizable and influential, increasing the mass effect $K^e - \omega^2 M^e$. Very high frequencies estimated better results since beyond that for cases where the structure's properties (mass and stiffness) are high (complete structure estimated recursively), the inverse of the dynamic stiffness matrix will result in closer FRF. The response under hysteretic damping is shown in Figure 12.

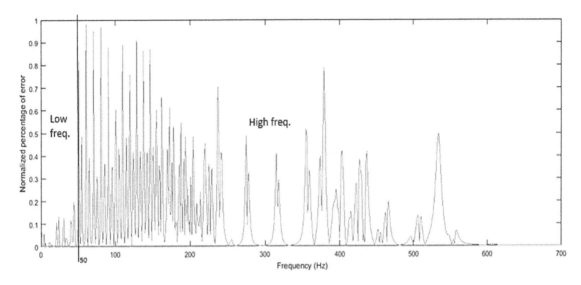

Figure 11. Normalized percentage of error between FEM and RM for a range of frequencies.

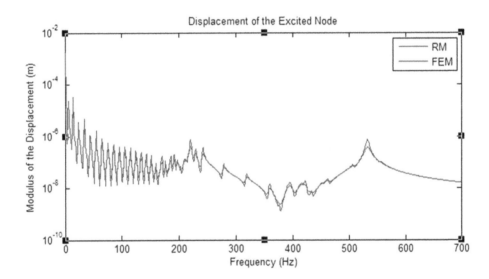

Figure 12. Displacement of the excited node under hysteretic damping for the truss application that is applied to forced vibration. The graph is logarithmically scaled.

The difference in the elapsed time for each method is presented in Table 2. The time elapsed for getting the frequency response in both damping cases is much higher using the finite element method than that of the recursive method. The finite element analysis took approximately 18-times more than the recursive method. Larger time differences between the two damping types are anticipated to be calculated for more complex structures where the number of DOF is very large.

Table 2. Time comparison between the two methods, for the truss application under forced vibrations.

Method	Elapsed Time (s)		Time Ratio
	Rayleigh Damping	**Hysteretic Damping**	
RM	0.618	0.638	$\frac{t_{RM}}{t_{FEM}} \simeq \frac{1}{18}$
FEM	11.26	11.43	

More high frequency peaks are shown for hysteretic damping, due to its complete material dependency. The peaks are caused by imperfections in material elasticity, in which the reaction of the material to changes is dependent on its past reactions to change.

4.2. Truss Application under Seismic Load

The frequency response function found from the recursive method using hysteretic damping will be compared to that using the conventional finite element program (ANSYS), and the results are shown in Figure 13. The values calculated demonstrate the variation of the displacement under a range of frequencies for the first node that is applied to harmonic displacement. Hysteretic damping is known to be completely material dependent. This is due to some imperfection of the elasticity of the material, in which the reaction of the material to changes is dependent on its past reactions to change.

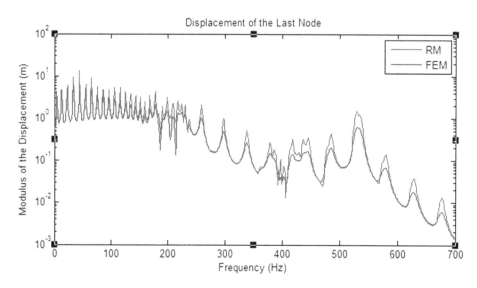

Figure 13. Displacement of the last top node of the truss structure under seismic load, applied to hysteretic damping. The graph is logarithmically scaled.

The time ratio calculated between the two methods is approximately 1:22, as in Table 3. The calculated elapsed time shows that the finite element method took approximately 22-times more than the recursive method to compute the FRF for the crane structure under hysteretic damping.

Table 3. Time comparison between the two methods, for the truss application under seismic load.

Method	Elapsed Time (s)	Time Ratio
RM	0.505	$\frac{t_{RM}}{t_{FEM}} \simeq \frac{1}{22}$
FEM	11.08	

4.3. Frame Application under Seismic Load

The results found using the recursive method and the conventional finite element software (ANSYS) for determining the frequency response function are presented in Figure 14. It displays the logarithmic varying displacement of the first bottom node that is excited under harmonic displacement. The modulus of displacement is studied for a range of frequencies.

The time ratio calculated between two methods is approximately 1/31.6, as shown in Table 4. The measured time elapsed for the two comparing methods reveals that the FEM took approximately 32-times more than the RM to compute the FRF for the frame structure under seismic load.

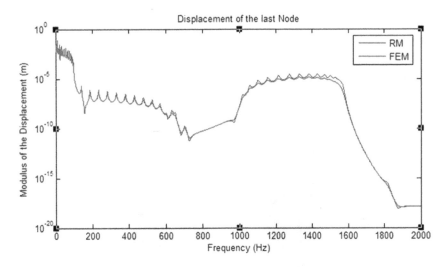

Figure 14. Displacement of the last top node for the frame application under seismic loading, applied to hysteretic damping. The graph is logarithmically scaled.

Table 4. Time comparison between the two methods for the frame application.

Method	Elapsed Time (s)	Time Ratio
RM	2.078	$\frac{t_{RM}}{t_{FEM}} \simeq \frac{1}{31.6}$
FEM	65.80	

4.4. Analysis

4.4.1. Periodic Structures Having Steel Material

The results for the two different applications under harmonic vibrations showed that RM calculated values are close, but slightly higher than the values of the FEM. For low and high frequencies, the modulus of displacement of the RM showed nearer values than at frequencies that cannot be considered as high. Note that the finite element analysis was taken as the reference method. The percentage difference between the two approaches for the two applications is established in Table 5.

Rayleigh damping is defined as the type of damping that is frequency dependent, and it depends on the natural frequencies for defining its equation. However, hysteretic damping is a material-dependent type of damping; thus, it has the advantage of minimizing the effect of the driving frequency on the response. These two types of damping were studied on the truss application under forced excitations, solely. The graph relative to the Rayleigh damping demonstrates that the response was damped at lower frequency than that of the other type of damping.

Table 5. Percentage difference.

Type of Application	Type of Loading	Type of Damping	Range of Frequency Studied	Percentage Difference
Crane	Forced vibrations	Rayleigh damping	1:1:700	17.519%
		Hysteretic damping	1:1:700	11.783%
	Harmonic displacement	Hysteretic damping	1:1:700	12.544%
Building	Harmonic displacement	Hysteretic damping	1:1:2000	18.920%

The maximum natural frequency is defined as the greatest value of the frequency that can illustrate a physical understanding of the structure's response via the mode shape demonstrated by modal analysis. Further, this value of the natural frequency will determine the maximum range of frequencies to be examined. Concerning the truss structure, for natural frequencies greater than

$fn_T = 133.63$ Hz, the crane structure could not be interpreted physically. Nevertheless, for the frame structure, the maximum natural frequency was $fn_F = 33.135$ Hz, beyond which it will not acquire major interest. The mode shapes relative to these frequencies are observed in Figure 15. Hence, the range of frequencies considered for both applications compensates for this frequency and beyond.

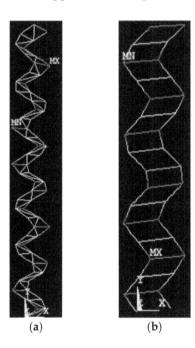

(a)   (b)

Figure 15. Mode shapes for the natural frequencies. (a) The mode shapes relative to the modal frequency for the truss application of $fn_T = 133.63$ Hz; (b) the mode shape for the frame application of $fn_F = 33.135$ Hz .

The modulus of displacement at the excited node for the truss application under forced vibrations was examined upon altering the repeated cell, leading to a change in the total number of cells used. RM was studied when enlarging the repeated cell, by making the new total number of cells as $N_{new} = \frac{N_{old}}{2}$, where N_{old} is the total number of cells in the previous step. Hence, N_{new} will initially be 16. The study was done at the most critical case, resonance, where the driving frequencies are equal to the natural frequencies of the structure. This is demonstrated in Figure 16, and the results are presented in Table 6, where it represents the modulus of displacement in the x-direction for the studied node. This test was applied on the two applications (truss and frame) under the studied types of loadings, and they all evaluated the same analysis. The table showed that the response is not affected by the number of cells used, as long as the same structure is studied. The structure is the same when changing the repeated cell, since the total number of the cells was modified correspondingly.

Table 6. The modulus of displacement in the x-direction for the excited node under three different natural frequencies, for a truss application under forced vibrations.

# of Repeating Times	Mode Shape #3 $f = 13.994$ Hz		Mode Shape #7 $f = 44.4651$ Hz		Mode Shape #14 $f = 105.294$ Hz	
	Displacement (m)	Elapsed Time (s)	Displacement (m)	Elapsed Time (s)	Displacement (m)	Elapsed Time (s)
16	3.29×10^{-5}	0.008694	2.63×10^{-6}	0.008967	4.50×10^{-7}	0.008403
8	3.29×10^{-5}	0.008946	2.63×10^{-6}	0.008710	4.50×10^{-7}	0.008837
4	3.29×10^{-5}	0.008666	2.63×10^{-6}	0.009064	4.50×10^{-7}	0.008530
2	3.29×10^{-5}	0.008368	2.63×10^{-6}	0.008437	4.50×10^{-7}	0.008868

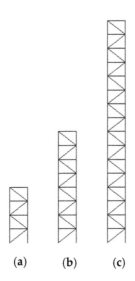

Figure 16. The repeated cells are presented where: (**a**) the new repeated cell is double the previous one and it is repeated eight times; (**b**) the new repeated cell consists of four-times the old cell, and it is repeated four times; (**c**) the cell will be repeated two times.

4.4.2. Periodic Structures Having Plastic Material

This was also investigated for a plastic material (PVC: polyvinyl chloride) having Young's modulus of elasticity of $E = 3.4$ GPa and a density of $\rho = 1330 \frac{\text{kg}}{\text{m}^3}$ for the two applications under forced excitation and seismic loading. The results are shown in Table 7. The values measured had the same inspection, determining the acceptance of the analysis deduced, by which for low and high driving frequencies, the response was more acceptable than intermediate frequencies in comparison with FEM. The percentage difference between the two approaches for the two applications when PVC material is assigned are established in Table 8. The table shows that the measured elapsed time for the FEM took approximately $22\times$ more time than the RM to compute the FRF for the truss structure under the two types of loadings. Moreover, FEM consumed a high amount of time in the computations during the implementations of the frame structure under seismic load, where it took $150\times$ more time than the RM to compute the FRF.

Table 7. The modulus of displacement in the x-direction for the excited node under three different natural frequencies, for a truss application under forced vibrations, upon assignment of PVC.

# of Repeating Times	Mode Shape #3 $f = 4.4185$ Hz		Mode Shape #7 $f = 14.0399$ Hz		Mode Shape #14 $f = 33.2466$ Hz	
	Displacement (m)	Elapsed Time (s)	Displacement (m)	Elapsed Time (s)	Displacement (m)	Elapsed Time (s)
16	1.94×10^{-3}	0.008859	1.55×10^{-4}	0.009104	2.65×10^{-5}	0.009558
8	1.94×10^{-3}	0.008405	1.55×10^{-4}	0.009659	2.65×10^{-5}	0.010223
4	1.94×10^{-3}	0.008891	1.55×10^{-4}	0.008590	2.65×10^{-5}	0.013492
2	1.94×10^{-3}	0.008651	1.55×10^{-4}	0.008518	2.65×10^{-5}	0.008253

Table 8. Percentage difference for the PVC material.

Type of Application	Type of Loading	Type of Damping	Time Elapsed (s)		Time Ratio ($\frac{t_{RM}}{t_{FEM}}$)	Range of Frequency Studied (Hz)	Percentage Difference
			FEM	RM			
Crane	Forced vibrations	Hysteretic damping	12.64	0.572	$\cong \frac{1}{22}$	1:700	3.3584%
	Harmonic displacement	Hysteretic damping	11.03	0.509	$\cong \frac{1}{22}$	1:700	17.4930%
Building	Harmonic displacement	Hysteretic damping	86.34	0.575	$\cong \frac{1}{151}$	1:800	14.3027%

4.4.3. The Effect of the Number of Forces Applied

The first study on the crane included behavioral examination of the excited node under forced vibrations. Loads were applied on one node exclusively. This section includes studying the effectiveness of this approach for periodic structures under a large number of forces. The effect of the number of forces is investigated in three different cases, in an increasing order of multiplying by two. A force is added at the mid-span of the truss structure in addition to the load exerted at its top. Then, the number of loads increases to four, after applying two excitations at $\frac{1}{4}L$ and $\frac{3}{4}L$. Further increasing includes the addition of four more forces, resulting in a periodic structure applied to eight loads that are equal in magnitude and uniformly distanced. Table 9 presents the resultant outcomes for the relevant test.

Table 9. Results upon adding different numbers of forces distributed equally over the periodic structure.

# of Forces Added	Elapsed Time (s)		Time Ratio $\frac{t_{RM}}{t_{FEM}}$	Range of Frequency Studied (Hz)	Range of Percentage Difference
	FEM	RM			
2	70.70	0.6680	$\cong \frac{1}{106}$	1:1:700	$9 \leq \%E \leq 12$
4	84.46	0.4909	$\cong \frac{1}{172}$	1:1:700	$8 \leq \%E \leq 10$
8	73.85	0.6727	$\cong \frac{1}{110}$	1:1:700	$9 \leq \%E \leq 11$

The elapsed times consumed by the FEM and the RM are displayed and compared; the time ratio shows the high efficacy of applying this method on a high number of forces. The percentage difference was measured at each excited node, and the results show a low difference between the two methods. However, there were two excited nodes that showed a high difference upon interpretations. The two nodes are the last excited node when four forces were applied, and the other is the mid-excited node upon eight force excitations, where the percentage difference exceeded 50%. Farther studies should be employed to illustrate a relation between the numbers of forces that can be applied with the length of the periodic structure, while maintaining significant effectiveness. Supplementary expectations are that when the forces are engaged with every node, the method will not be feasible for calculating the frequency response function, since the advantage of removing the internal nodes recursively will be obsolete.

5. Conclusions

In this paper, a further study was done on structures that cannot be designed as waveguides. Cranes and buildings were modeled as trusses and frames, respectively, under various loading. Trusses and frames have in their structural composition the inability to guide waves along their longitudinal axis. Waveguides are used in various types of applications and have different methods for accurate computations. However, structures that are not considered as waveguides consume various applications, as well, but there are no different numerical methods for easier, faster and precise computations.

The recursive method is an approach used for calculating the frequency response function of general periodic structures. In spite of the element's complexity, a recursive method can be employed on all types of periodic structures, as long as the internal nodes are under no load. For finding a satisfying result, a high number of cells must be considered, which will lead to a large number of computations. This method provides a solution close to that obtained from the reference method (FEM), and it decreases the time consumption. The time consumed for a steel material was observed to a have a range of ratios between 1:18 and 1:31, depending on the type of cells and the load exerted. Displacement values were nearer to that of the finite element method at low and very high frequencies. The percentage difference for the structures studied under various types of loading does not exceed 19%. Nevertheless, different materials were studied to have further support of the analysis. The plastic material had much lower time ratios, in the range between 1:22 and 1:151, while the relative percentage difference did not exceed 17%. This difference is due to the inverse of the dynamic stiffness matrix, which will lead to a slight numerical difference between the finite element method and the recursive method. Upon varying the number of forces, the time ratio lied in the range of 1:106 till 1:172, with a low percentage difference.

Future examinations include studying the effectiveness of this approach for periodic structures under a large number of forces. Expectations are that when the forces are engaged with every node, the method will not be feasible for calculating the frequency response function, since the advantage of removing the internal nodes recursively will be obsolete. Further studies include the types of cells to be repeated and the effect on the frequency response function. Moreover, a more applicable solution may be calculated by changing the type of element from linear to quadratic; therefore, vibrations at internal nodes can be computed. Otherwise, an element with a greater mesh size should be examined, since the increase in the mesh size will display the response for the internal nodes. The effect of the frequency on the modulus of displacement will be also inspected, and more complex periodic structures will be interpreted. Unsteady states in heat transfer problems may be evaluated for complex fin geometries.

Author Contributions: Reem Yassine and Faten Salman wrote most of this paper. Ali Al Shaer and Mohammad Hammoud contributed to the numerical simulations. Denis Duhamel contributed to the finalizing of the paper and the reviewing process.

References

1. Dong, S.B.; Nelson, R.B. On natural vibrations and waves in laminated orthotropic plates. *J. Appl. Mech.* **1972**, *39*, 739–745. [CrossRef]
2. Aalami, B. Waves in prismatic guides of arbitrary cross section. *J. Appl. Mech.* **1973**, *40*, 1067–1072. [CrossRef]
3. Finnveden, S. Finite Element Techniques for the Evaluation of Energy Flow Parameters: Keynote Lecture. In Proceedings of the Novem2000 Conference, Lyon, France, 2–4 November 2000.
4. Finnveden, S. Evaluation of modal density and group velocity by a finite element method. *J. Sound Vib.* **2004**, *273*, 51–75. [CrossRef]
5. Yu, C.P.; Roesset, J.M. Dynamic stiffness matrices for linear members with distributed mass. *J. Appl. Sci. Eng.* **2001**, *4*, 253–264.
6. Nilsson, C.M. Waveguide Finite Elements for Thin-Waled Structures. Licentiate Thesis, KTH Royal Institute of Technology, Stockholm, Sweden, 2002.
7. Birgersson, F. Prediction of Random Vibration Using Spectral Methods. Ph.D. Thesis, KTH Royal Institute of Technology, TRITA-AVE, Stockholm, Sweden, 2003; p. 30.
8. Birgersson, F.; Finnveden, S.; Nilsson, C.M. A spectral super element for modelling of plate vibration. Part 1: General theory. *J. Sound Vib.* **2005**, *287*, 297–314. [CrossRef]
9. Birgersson, F.; Finnveden, S. A spectral super element for modelling of plate vibration. Part 2: Turbulence excitation. *J. Sound Vib.* **2005**, *287*, 315–328. [CrossRef]
10. Gry, L. Dynamic modelling of railway track based on wave propagation. *J. Sound Vib.* **1996**, *195*, 477–505. [CrossRef]

11. Gavric, L. Computation of propagative waves in free rail using finite element technique. *J. Sound Vib.* **1995**, *185*, 531–543. [CrossRef]

12. Bartoli, I.; Marzani, A.; Lanza di Scalea, F.; Viola, E. Modelling wave propagation in damed waveguide of arbitrary cross-section. *J. Sound Vib.* **2006**, *295*, 685–707. [CrossRef]

13. Marzani, A.; Viola, E.; Bartoli, I.; Lanza di Scalea, F.; Rizzo, P. A semi-analytical finite element formulation for modelling stress wave propagation in axisymmertic damped waveguides. *J. Sound Vib.* **2008**, *318*, 488–505. [CrossRef]

14. Duhamel, D.; Mace, B.R.; Brennan, M.J. Finite element analysis of the vibrations of waveguides and periodic structures. *J. Sound Vib.* **2004**, *294*, 205–220. [CrossRef]

15. Lee, S.C.; Rawatt, V.; Lee, J.F. A hybrid finite/boundary element method for periodic structures on non-periodic meshes using an interior penalty formulation for Maxwell's equations. *J. Comput. Phys.* **2010**, *229*, 4934–4951. [CrossRef]

16. Castanier, M.P.; Ottarsson, G.; Pierre, C. A Reduced Order Modeling Technique for Mistuned Bladed Disks. *J. Vib. Acoust.* **1997**, *119*, 439–447. [CrossRef]

17. Bathe, K.J.; Dong, J. Component mode synthesis with subspace iterations for controlled accuracy of frequency and mode shape solutions. *Comput. Struct.* **2014**, *139*, 28–32. [CrossRef]

18. Zhou, K.; Liang, G.; Tang, J. Component mode synthesis order-reduction for dynamic analysis of structure modeled with NURBS finite element. *J. Vib. Acoust.* **2016**, *138*, 021016. [CrossRef]

19. Duhamel, D. A recursive approach for the finite element computation of waveguides. *J. Sound Vib.* **2009**, *323*, 163–172. [CrossRef]

20. Duhamel, D.; Erlicher, S.; Nguyen, H.H. A recursive finite element method for comuting tyre vibrations. *Eur. J. Comput. Mech.* **2011**, *20*, 9–27.

21. Guyan, R.J. Reduction of stiffness and mass matrices. *AIAA J.* **1965**, *3*, 380–387. [CrossRef]

22. Bachmann, H.; Ammann, W.J.; Deischl, F.; Eisenmann, J.; Floegl, J.; Hirsch, G.H.; Klein, G.K.; Lande, G.J.; Mahrenholtz, O.; Natke, H.G.; et al. *Vibration Problems in Structures: Practical Guidelines*; Institut für Baustatik und Konstruktion (IBK): Basel, Switzerland, 1995.

2

Excitons in Solids from Time-Dependent Density-Functional Theory: Assessing the Tamm-Dancoff Approximation

Young-Moo Byun and Carsten A. Ullrich *

Department of Physics and Astronomy, University of Missouri, Columbia, MO 65211, USA;
byuny@missouri.edu
* Correspondence: ullrichc@missouri.edu

Academic Editor: Jianmin Tao

Abstract: Excitonic effects in solids can be calculated using the Bethe-Salpeter equation (BSE) or the Casida equation of time-dependent density-functional theory (TDDFT). In both methods, the Tamm-Dancoff approximation (TDA), which decouples excitations and de-excitations, is widely used to reduce computational cost. Here, we study the effect of the TDA on exciton binding energies of solids obtained from the Casida equation using long-range-corrected (LRC) exchange-correlation kernels. We find that the TDA underestimates TDDFT-LRC exciton binding energies of semiconductors slightly, but those of insulators significantly (i.e., by more than 100%), and thus it is essential to solve the full Casida equation to describe strongly bound excitons. These findings are relevant in the ongoing search for accurate and efficient TDDFT approaches for excitons.

Keywords: excitons; time-dependent density-functional theory; Tamm-Dancoff approximation

1. Introduction

Excitons are bound electron-hole pairs arising in optically excited finite and extended systems. Understanding and predicting excitonic properties is important for the design of novel photovoltaic materials. For example, low exciton binding energies in perovskite solar cells promote the electron-hole separation and thereby enhance power conversion efficiencies [1].

Many-body perturbation theory is a standard method to calculate excitonic properties of solids: one obtains accurate exciton binding energies E_b and optical absorption spectra of semiconductors and insulators by solving the Bethe-Salpeter equation (BSE) [2]. However, the BSE is computationally expensive and cannot be applied to large systems.

Time-dependent density-functional theory (TDDFT) is a computationally cheaper alternative to the BSE [3], but its application to the study of excitonic effects in solids depends on finding good approximations to the unknown exchange-correlation (xc) kernel f_{xc}. The random-phase approximation (RPA) (i.e., $f_{xc} = 0$), the local-density approximation (LDA), as well as any standard gradient-corrected semilocal approximation fail to capture excitonic properties of solids due to their inadequate long-range behavior. A very accurate xc kernel can be derived by reverse-engineering the BSE [2,4], but it is computationally as expensive. A drastic simplification, known as the long-range-corrected (LRC) kernel,

$$f_{xc}^{LRC} = -\frac{\alpha}{\mathbf{q}^2},$$

(1)

where $\mathbf{q}$ is a momentum transfer in the first Brillouin zone (BZ), accounts for bound excitons in solids, but it requires a material-dependent parameter α, a positive scalar. Inspired by the simple form (1), a whole family of LRC-type kernels have been proposed in the literature [5–9].

The performance of LRC-type kernels is typically judged by how well they appear to reproduce experimental optical absorption spectra. The quality of a spectrum is usually assessed by inspection, and it depends strongly on the underlying band structure and on the numerical broadening. A better quantitative measure are exciton binding energies, which are defined as the energetic separation between the exciton and the band gap, and can hence be precisely quantified (to within experimental and numerical error bars). Furthermore, there is no numerical broadening in our scheme (see below), and the dependence on the choice of band structure is much weaker.

Experimentally, E_b can be directly extracted from the optical absorption spectra for the case of strongly bound excitons in insulators; for semiconductors, E_b can be obtained from photoluminescence data. The direct calculation of exciton binding energies can be achieved by solving the so-called Casida equation of TDDFT [10–12]. This approach is sometimes referred to as "diagonalizing the exciton Hamiltonian", and is formally similar in BSE and TDDFT. Usually, this is done within the Tamm-Dancoff approximation (TDA), which neglects the coupling between resonant and anti-resonant excitations. There are some recent studies investigating the performance of the TDA for the BSE [13,14]; however, the extent to which the TDA affects the solution of the excitonic Casida equation has not been studied in detail.

Let us remark here that the TDA is a popular method in computational chemistry, see e.g., [15]. Because it is formally simpler than the full Casida formalism, it can save computer time, and it has been used in the literature for conceptual analysis of excitation processes (for instance, in the so-called single-pole approximation [16]). Another benefit of the TDA is that there are situations where it is better behaved than the full Casida formalism, for example for open-shell systems away from the ground-state equilibrium geometry, where the TDA avoids so-called triplet instabilities [17].

In this paper, we assess the TDA for TDDFT-LRC exciton binding energies of solids. First, we introduce the various LRC-type kernels to be used in this work and examine the effect of the LRC kernel on excitonic properties of solids. Next, we compare LRC exciton binding energies E_b^{LRC} of solids obtained from the Casida equation within and beyond the TDA. We discover that the TDA makes very little difference in semiconductors, but has a significant impact in insulators. We discuss the origins, practical implications, and limitations of our findings.

2. Theoretical Background

2.1. Dyson Equation

In linear-response TDDFT, there are two ways of calculating optical absorption spectra of periodic systems [3]. One way is to use the interacting response function $\chi(\mathbf{q}, \omega)$, which is obtained from the Dyson equation (all quantities are matrices depending on reciprocal lattice vectors $\mathbf{G}, \mathbf{G}'$):

$$\chi(\mathbf{q}, \omega) = \chi_0(\mathbf{q}, \omega) + \chi_0(\mathbf{q}, \omega)\{v(\mathbf{q}) + f_{xc}(\mathbf{q}, \omega)\}\chi(\mathbf{q}, \omega), \tag{2}$$

where $v = v_0 + \bar{v} = 4\pi\delta_{\mathbf{GG}'}/|\mathbf{q} + \mathbf{G}|^2$ is the Coulomb interaction, and χ_0 is the noninteracting response function. v_0 is the long-range ($\mathbf{G} = 0$) part of the Coulomb interaction, and $\bar{v}$ is the Coulomb interaction without the long-range part. In the optical limit ($\mathbf{q} \to 0$), the head ($\mathbf{G} = \mathbf{G}' = 0$) of χ_0 is given by [18]

$$\chi_0(\mathbf{q}) = -\frac{4\mathbf{q}^2}{(2\pi)^3}\sum_{vc}\int_{BZ} d\mathbf{k}\frac{|\langle c\mathbf{k}|\hat{p} + i[V_{NL}, \hat{r}]|v\mathbf{k}\rangle|^2}{(E_{c\mathbf{k}} - E_{v\mathbf{k}})^3}, \tag{3}$$

where v and c are valence and conduction band indices, respectively, $E_{c,v\mathbf{k}}$ denotes Kohn-Sham single-particle energies, $\hat{p}$ is the momentum operator, $\hat{r}$ is the position operator, and V_{NL} is the non-local part of the pseudopotential. The optical spectrum is obtained from the macroscopic dielectric function ϵ_M:

$$\epsilon_M(\omega) = \lim_{\mathbf{q}\to 0} \frac{1}{\epsilon_{\mathbf{G}=\mathbf{G}'=0}^{-1}(\mathbf{q},\omega)}$$

$$= \lim_{\mathbf{q}\to 0} \frac{1}{1+v_{\mathbf{G}=0}(\mathbf{q})\chi_{\mathbf{G}=\mathbf{G}'=0}(\mathbf{q},\omega)}, \tag{4}$$

where ϵ^{-1} is the inverse dielectric function. The Dyson-equation approach is computationally relatively cheap, and thus it is the method of choice of most excitonic calculations. However, the method does not allow the precise determination of exciton binding energies, especially if the excitons are weakly bound. The reason is that, in practice, calculations are done with an artificial broadening of several tens of meV, in order to produce spectra that can be compared to experiment. This broadening will completely wash out any excitonic peaks that are on the order of a few tens of meV, which is the case for semiconductors. On the other hand, for insulators, where exciton binding energies are of order 1 eV or more, the peaks are sharp enough to allow exciton binding energies to be read off.

2.2. Casida Equation

Alternatively, both optical spectra and exciton binding energies can be obtained from the Casida equation [10]:

$$\begin{pmatrix} \mathbf{A} & \mathbf{B} \\ \mathbf{B}^* & \mathbf{A}^* \end{pmatrix} \begin{pmatrix} X_n \\ Y_n \end{pmatrix} = \omega_n \begin{pmatrix} -\mathbf{1} & 0 \\ 0 & \mathbf{1} \end{pmatrix} \begin{pmatrix} X_n \\ Y_n \end{pmatrix}, \tag{5}$$

where $\mathbf{A}$ and $\mathbf{B}$ are excitation and de-excitation matrices, respectively, X_n and Y_n are nth eigenvectors, and ω_n is the nth eigenvalue. The matrix elements of $\mathbf{A}$ and $\mathbf{B}$ are

$$A_{v\mathbf{ck},v'c'\mathbf{k}'} = (E_{c\mathbf{k}} - E_{v\mathbf{k}})\delta_{vv'}\delta_{cc'}\delta_{\mathbf{kk}'} + F^{Hxc}_{v\mathbf{ck},v'c'\mathbf{k}'} \tag{6}$$

$$B_{v\mathbf{ck},v'c'\mathbf{k}'} = F^{Hxc}_{v\mathbf{ck},v'c'\mathbf{k}'} \tag{7}$$

where $F^{Hxc} = F^H + F^{xc}$ is the Hartree-exchange-correlation (Hxc) matrix. In the optical limit, the matrix elements of F^{Hxc} using the LRC kernel are given by

$$F^{Hxc}_{v\mathbf{ck},v'c'\mathbf{k}'} = \frac{2}{V}\left(\sum_{\mathbf{G}\neq 0} \frac{4\pi-\bar{\alpha}}{|\mathbf{G}|^2} \langle c\mathbf{k}|e^{i\mathbf{G}\cdot\mathbf{r}}|v\mathbf{k}\rangle \langle v'\mathbf{k}'|e^{-i\mathbf{G}\cdot\mathbf{r}}|c'\mathbf{k}'\rangle \right.$$

$$\left. -\alpha_0 \frac{\langle c\mathbf{k}|\hat{p}+i[V_{NL},\hat{r}]|v\mathbf{k}\rangle}{E_{c\mathbf{k}}-E_{v\mathbf{k}}} \frac{\langle c'\mathbf{k}'|\hat{p}+i[V_{NL},\hat{r}]|v'\mathbf{k}'\rangle^*}{E_{c'\mathbf{k}'}-E_{v'\mathbf{k}'}} \right). \tag{8}$$

Here, V is the crystal volume, $\alpha = \alpha_0 \neq \bar{\alpha} = 0$ for $f^{LRC}_{xc} = -(\alpha/4\pi)v_0$ (head-only), and $\alpha = \alpha_0 = \bar{\alpha} \neq 0$ for $f^{LRC}_{xc} = -(\alpha/4\pi)v$ (diagonal).

Solving the Casida Equation (5) gives a continuous distribution of energy eigenvalues that lie above the band gap (this is the renormalized single-particle spectrum), and an isolated eigenvalue whose energy is less than the gap (note that this is because we are using a frequency-independent xc kernel, which yields only a single bound exciton [19]). The exciton binding energy is obtained as the difference between the band gap and the lowest, isolated eigenvalue.

Thus, the eigenvalues of the Casida equation yield exciton binding energies in principle with arbitrary precision, in contrast with the Dyson-equation approach, which includes an artificial broadening, as discussed above. In addition, from the eigenvectors of the Casida equations one can obtain oscillator strengths, which can then be used to generate optical spectra. Therefore, the Dyson and Casida approaches are in principle equivalent, but differ in their practical implementation. Furthermore, the Casida approach is computationally significantly more expensive because it requires building and diagonalizing a large matrix.

2.3. Local-Field Effect

The local-field effect (LFE) has different meanings in Dyson and Casida equations. In the Dyson equation, the LFE means that $\epsilon^{-1} \neq 1/\epsilon$. The Dyson equation is used to calculate optical spectra and Bootstrap-type kernels, which will be explained in Section 4.1. In the Dyson equation for optical spectra, the LFE is not a matter of choice and should be included. However, in the definition of Bootstrap-type kernels, we have the freedom of whether or not to include the LFE, because Bootstrap-type kernels are not constrained by formal derivations. In the following, we chose to include the LFE when calculating Bootstrap-type kernels to be consistent and focus on the TDA.

In the Casida equation, the LFE means that not only the head (i.e., $\mathbf{G} = \mathbf{G}' = 0$) term, but also other terms are included in the summation of F_{Hxc} matrix elements in Equation (8). In the Casida equation, the LFE is not a matter of choice and should be included.

2.4. LRC Kernel: Head-Only vs. Diagonal

Head-only and diagonal LRC kernels, with $f_{\text{xc}}^{\text{LRC}} = -(\alpha/4\pi)v_0$ and $f_{\text{xc}}^{\text{LRC}} = -(\alpha/4\pi)v$, respectively, have been used interchangeably because (i) the form of the LRC kernel is not dictated by a rigorous formal derivation, so the two LRC kernels are largely a matter of choice; (ii) the two LRC kernels cause negligible differences in optical spectra of semiconductors such as Si (because $\bar{\alpha} \approx 0.2 \ll 4\pi$ in Equation (8)) [5]. However, as we will report elsewhere [20], we found that the two kernels yield very different results for exciton binding energies of insulators, so it is important to state clearly which version is used. We used the head-only LRC kernel in this work; however, our findings concerning the performance of the TDA hold for both types of LRC kernels. Note that the head-only LRC kernel can be viewed as the diagonal one without the LFE.

2.5. Tamm-Dancoff Approximation

The TDA decouples excitations and de-excitations by setting $\mathbf{B}$ to zero in Equation (5). The TDA is widely used in the BSE and the Casida equation because it cuts the computational cost significantly by reducing the size of the exciton Hamiltonian matrix by a factor of two and changing a non-Hermitian eigenvalue problem to a Hermitian one. However, it turns out that the full Casida equation can be solved at the same computational cost as the TDA one [13] using a transformation that is well known from computational chemistry [10]. Making use of time-reversal symmetry, Equation (5) can be transformed to a Hermitian eigenvalue equation:

$$\mathbf{C}Z_n = \omega_n^2 Z_n, \tag{9}$$

where

$$\begin{aligned} \mathbf{C} &= (\mathbf{A} - \mathbf{B})^{1/2}(\mathbf{A} + \mathbf{B})(\mathbf{A} - \mathbf{B})^{1/2}, \\ Z_n &= (\mathbf{A} - \mathbf{B})^{1/2}(X_n - Y_n). \end{aligned} \tag{10}$$

2.6. Band-Gap Corrections: LDA vs. Scissors Shift

A standard method of producing band structures with the correct band gap is to use so-called scissors operators. There are many ways of applying the scissors shift to Dyson and Casida equations in Equations (3) and (8) and LRC-type kernels. The scissors shift can be applied to only conduction bands (i.e., replacing $E_{c\mathbf{k}}$ by $E_{c\mathbf{k}} + \Delta$) or to the momentum operator (i.e., replacing $\hat{p}$ by $\{(E_{c\mathbf{k}} + \Delta - E_{v\mathbf{k}})/(E_{c\mathbf{k}} - E_{v\mathbf{k}})\}\hat{p}$) as well [21], where Δ is the difference between experimental (or GW) and DFT bandgaps.

Due to the many choices involved and the high sensitivity of the LRC kernel, the scissors shift can cause some ambiguities (we will address these issues elsewhere in more detail [20]). In this paper our focus is on the performance of the TDA; we wish to avoid any unnecessary distractions and therefore simply work with uncorrected LDA band structures in both Dyson and Casida equations and in the construction of all xc kernels. This impacts the exciton binding energies calculated with and without TDA in the same way (both are calculated relative to the LDA gap), so a meaningful assessment of the TDA is possible. On the other hand, to compare optical spectra with experiment, we simply shift them rigidly by the difference between the LDA gap and the experimental band gap.

3. Computational Details

We used the Abinit code for norm-conserving pseudopotentials, Kohn-Sham eigenvectors and eigenvalues, and GW bandgaps within the LDA [22]. We wrote our own TDDFT code for calculating exciton binding energies, and used the dp code for optical spectra [23]. We used experimental lattice parameters and align the optical spectra of GaAs and solid Ne with the experimental band gaps.

In the Dyson equation for optical spectra, we used a $16 \times 16 \times 16$ Monkhorst-Pack **k**-point mesh, 4 valence bands, and 20 conduction bands for GaAs and solid Ne. In the Dyson equation for Bootstrap-type kernels, we used a $20 \times 20 \times 20$ $(20 \times 20 \times 10)$ Γ-centered **k**-point mesh, 4 (8) valence bands, 20 (20) conduction bands, and 59 (73) **G** vectors for GaAs, β-GaN, MgO, LiF, solid Ar, and solid Ne (α-GaN and AlN). In the Casida equation, we used a $28 \times 28 \times 28$ $(16 \times 16 \times 16)$ $\{16 \times 16 \times 8\}$ $[8 \times 8 \times 8]$ Γ-centered **k**-point mesh, 3 (3) {6} [3] valence bands, 2 (6) {9} [24] conduction bands, and 59 (59) {73} [59] **G** vectors for GaAs (β-GaN and MgO) {α-GaN and AlN} [LiF, solid Ar, and solid Ne]. Convergence was carefully tested throughout.

4. Results and Discussion

4.1. Overview of LRC-Type Kernels

We begin by listing five static LRC-type kernels (empirical LRC, Bootstrap, 0-Bootstrap, RPA-Bootstrap, and JGM kernels) which were used in this work.

The empirical LRC kernel ($\alpha = 4.615\epsilon_\infty^{-1} - 0.213$, where ϵ_∞ is the high-frequency dielectric constant) is the first LRC-type kernel for optical spectra of semiconductors [5]. Note that we used the calculated ϵ_{RPA}^{-1} instead of experimental ϵ_∞^{-1}; further, ϵ_{RPA}^{-1} is greater than ϵ_∞^{-1} by $\sim 10\%$.

The Bootstrap kernel $f_{xc}^{Boot} = \epsilon^{-1}/\chi_0$, where ϵ^{-1} is the self-consistent ("bootstrapped") inverse dielectric function and Boot represents Bootstrap, is a parameter-free kernel for optical spectra of semiconductors and insulators [6].

The 0-Bootstrap kernel ($f_{xc}^{0-Boot} = \epsilon_{RPA}^{-1}/\chi_0$) is the Bootstrap kernel without bootstrapping (i.e., only the first cycle of the self-consistent iteration is carried out). Note that α_{0-Boot} is greater than α_{Boot} by $\sim 10\%$ because ϵ_{RPA}^{-1} is greater than ϵ^{-1} by $\sim 10\%$.

The RPA-Bootstrap kernel $f_{xc}^{RPA-Boot} = \epsilon_{RPA}^{-1}/\tilde{\chi}_{RPA}$, where $\tilde{\chi}_{RPA}$ is obtained from $\bar{v}$, is a parameter-free kernel for exciton binding energies of insulators [7]. Note that $\alpha_{RPA-Boot}$ is greater than α_{0-Boot} by $\sim 10\%$ because $|\tilde{\chi}_{RPA}|$ is smaller than $|\chi_0|$ by $\sim 10\%$.

Lastly, the jellium-with-gap-model (JGM) kernel, $\alpha_{JGM} \approx E_g^2/n$, where E_g is the band gap and n is the electron density, is a parameter-free kernel for optical spectra of semiconductors and insulators [9]. Whereas other LRC-type kernels depend on dielectric constants, the JGM kernel depends on band gaps.

We point out again that we used LDA band gaps for all kernels instead of experimental (or GW) band gaps, which affects exciton binding energies of insulators significantly, because our aim is not to test the accuracy of kernels, but to study the effect of the TDA on LRC exciton binding energies. Figure 1 shows the α values of all kernels for different materials. We see that the strength α varies from ~ 0.1 ($\alpha_{RPA-Boot}$ for GaAs) to ~ 30 ($\alpha_{RPA-Boot}$ for solid Ne).

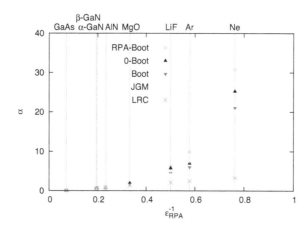

Figure 1. Long-range-corrected (LRC) kernel strengths α (see Equation (1)) of LRC-type kernels for various materials.

4.2. Effect of the LRC Kernel on Optical Spectra

Next, we examine the effect of the LRC kernel on optical spectra of solids. Figure 2 shows calculated optical spectra of GaAs and solid Ne obtained from the Dyson equation using $f_{xc}^{LRC} = -\alpha/\mathbf{q}^2$ ($\alpha = A\alpha_{0-Boot}$, where A is a scaling factor) and compares them with experimental ones. We chose GaAs and solid Ne because they are extreme examples of semiconductors with weakly bound excitons (Wannier-Mott type) and insulators with strongly bound excitons (Frenkel type), respectively.

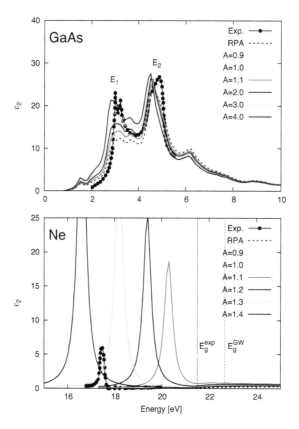

Figure 2. Experimental [24,25] and calculated optical absorption spectra of GaAs (**top**) and solid Ne (**bottom**). For the LRC kernel, $\alpha = A\alpha_{0-Boot}$ is used, where $\alpha_{0-Boot} = 0.064$ (25.3) for GaAs (solid Ne). The spectra are shifted to align the LDA gap with the experimental gap E_g^{exp}; the GW gap E_g^{GW} is shown only for comparison. A Lorentzian broadening of 0.15 eV (0.2 eV) is used for GaAs (solid Ne). Note that $A = 0.9$ and 1.1 approximately correspond to Bootstrap and RPA-Bootstrap kernels, respectively.

There are important differences between semiconductors and insulators. First, exciton binding energies cannot be easily read off of the optical spectra of semiconductors since the exciton peaks are too close to the gap, and the binding energies tend to be smaller than the spectral broadening; by contrast, the binding energies can be quite accurately obtained from the spacings between experimental gaps and excitonic peaks in the optical spectra of insulators.

Second, LRC spectra of semiconductors are insensitive to α (e.g., a 10% change in α has little effect on the LRC spectrum of GaAs), whereas LRC spectra of insulators are highly sensitive to α (e.g., a 10% change in α shifts excitonic peaks by $\sim$1 eV in the spectrum of solid Ne). These different effects of the LRC kernel on optical spectra of semiconductors and insulators are important because they are related to different effects of the TDA on LRC exciton binding energies of semiconductors and insulators, which will be shown later. Note that we neglected the effect of the LRC kernel on oscillator strengths or spectral weights (i.e., excitonic peak heights and widths) to focus on excitonic peak positions. We also point out that, whereas we focus here on the two materials GaAs and solid Ne, we have confirmed the generality of our conclusions for many other materials with various degrees of exciton binding strength (see Table 1).

4.3. TDA and Exciton Binding Energies

Next, we explore the effect of the TDA on exciton binding energies. Table 1 shows exciton binding energies of different materials obtained from the full and TDA Casida equation using LRC-type kernels. The calculated binding energies are significantly below the experimental results. This is typical for the performance of the different LRC kernels; in a forthcoming publication, we shall analyze this in detail and propose a new LRC kernel which agrees well with experiment [20]. In the present study, our aim is to reveal the differences between the TDA and the full calculation as clearly as possible, rather than reproducing experimental data; therefore, we chose to limit our analysis to the existing unoptimized LRC kernels, and to use LDA gaps instead of scissors corrected gaps.

Table 1. Calculated exciton binding energies (in meV) obtained from Tamm-Dancoff approximation (TDA) and full Casida equations. Experimental exciton binding energies (in meV) are taken from Refs. [26–33] and shown only for comparison.

	Casida Equation	GaAs	α-GaN	β-GaN	AlN	MgO	LiF	Ar	Ne
Exp.		**3.27**	**20.4**	**26.0**	**48.0**	**80.0**	**1600**	**1900**	**4080**
RPA-Boot	TDA	0.334	0.927	0.875	0.00	1.72	33.3	37.7	666
0-Boot	TDA	0.285	0.811	0.720	0.00	1.43	22.4	10.8	128
Boot	TDA	0.267	0.651	0.562	0.00	1.03	10.7	7.70	39.7
JGM	TDA	0.137	0.387	0.226	0.00	0.348	9.12	12.9	5.30
LRC	TDA	0.636	1.16	1.14	0.00	0.747	1.61	1.46	1.01
RPA-Boot	Full	0.344	1.06	1.01	0.00	2.12	94.7	96.0	2400
0-Boot	Full	0.293	0.919	0.829	0.00	1.72	43.2	13.7	612
Boot	Full	0.278	0.735	0.649	0.00	1.20	14.8	9.14	101
JGM	Full	0.141	0.438	0.279	0.00	0.397	12.1	17.1	5.96
LRC	Full	0.670	1.33	1.32	0.00	0.855	1.89	1.54	1.06

We find that the TDA consistently underestimates the exciton binding energies compared to the full calculation. This is consistent with the known fact that the TDA overestimates BSE eigenvalues [14]. Secondly, the magnitude of the E_b underestimation by the TDA is small for semiconductors, but large for insulators. For instance, full and TDA E_b^{LRC} for GaAS differ by 0.034 meV (a 5% decrease), whereas full and TDA $E_b^{RPA-Boot}$ of solid Ne differ by 1734 meV (a 72% decrease).

There are two possible causes for the large E_b underestimation by the TDA for insulators: (i) large band gaps (e.g., $E_g^{exp} = 1.43$ and 21.5 eV for GaAs and solid Ne, respectively) or (ii) large α values (e.g., $\alpha_{RPA-Boot} = 0.12$ and 31 for GaAs and solid Ne, respectively). The large E_b

underestimation by the TDA for insulators vanishes when small α values are used. For example, full and TDA E_b^{LRC} of solid Ne differ by 0.05 meV (a 5% decrease) because $\alpha_{LRC} = 3.3$ for solid Ne. This indicates that the large E_b underestimation by the TDA for insulators is solely due to large α values. The large E_b underestimation by the TDA (i.e., a $\sim$50% decrease) starts to appear when $\alpha \approx 10$.

The general trend is thus that the TDA performs well as long as E_b is small compared to the gap (as is the case for semiconductors), but fails when E_b becomes comparable to the gap (as is the case for insulators). (Interestingly, this argument can also be used to rationalize the failure of the TDA to describe plasmons in simple metals, where the gap is zero.) These findings are consistent with the original formulation of TDDFT for excitation energies by Petersilka et al. [16], where the dynamical TDDFT correction to the Kohn-Sham single-particle excitation energies is expressed as a Laurent expansion around individual poles in the response function; as long as the correction to the single-particle spectrum is small, the lowest term in this expansion (which is the TDA) will be appropriate.

4.4. Comparison of Dyson and Full Casida Equations

Next, we verify our finding above from the Casida equation using the Dyson equation. In principle, Dyson and Casida equations are equivalent, so they should result in the same exciton binding energy when they use the same kernel. Figure 3 shows exciton binding energies of solid Ne from the Dyson equation (i.e., from Figure 2) and the full and TDA Casida equation as a function of scaling factor A.

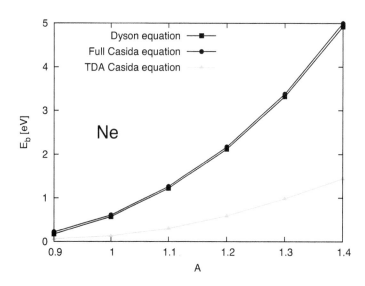

Figure 3. Calculated exciton binding energies E_b of solid Ne as a function of scaling factor A. For the LRC kernel, $\alpha = A\alpha_{0-Boot}$ is used, where $\alpha_{0-Boot} = 25.3$.

We find at all A values considered that the Dyson and full Casida equations indeed produce almost identical exciton binding energies, and that the TDA underestimates E_b^{LRC} of solid Ne by a factor of $\sim$3. This indicates that it is essential to solve the full Casida equation instead of the TDA one when testing whether LRC-type kernels designed for Dyson-equation optical spectra can produce correct and accurate exciton binding energies of insulators.

4.5. Limitations of Our Findings

Finally, we discuss the limitations of our findings. First, our conclusions hold only for LRC-type kernels designed for solids. We did not check the effect of the TDA on other types of methods that account for bound excitons in solids (such as the reverse-engineered BSE kernel [2,4], meta-generalized gradient approximations (meta-GGAs) [34] or hybrid xc kernels [12,35–38]) or are designed for atoms and molecules (some discussion of the TDA in the latter case can be found in Ref. [39]).

The large E_b underestimation by the TDA for insulators is partly due to the high sensitivity of the LRC kernel, which is a unique property of the LRC kernel. Hence, it may not be as pronounced in non-LRC-type kernels.

Secondly, we studied only eigenvalues (i.e., exciton energies), not eigenvectors (i.e., exciton states). The impact of the TDA on oscillator strengths in optical spectra and exciton wavefunctions in real space, which are obtained from eigenvectors, remains to be investigated. Third, we studied only the optical limit ($\mathbf{q} \to 0$); the effect of the TDA on finite $\mathbf{q}$ values remains to be tested [13]. Lastly, we studied the TDA only for excitons in the optical spectra of bulk materials; in nanoscale systems, additional complications for the TDA can arise [40].

5. Conclusions

In summary, we investigated the effect of the TDA on TDDFT-LRC exciton binding energies of solids. We found that the TDA overestimates LRC eigenvalues and thereby underestimates LRC exciton binding energies. This is consistent with the effect of TDA on E_b^{BSE}. We also found that the magnitude of the E_b^{LRC} underestimation by the TDA depends on the material: it is negligible for semiconductors with small α values, but significant for insulators with large α values. This behavior of the E_b^{LRC} underestimation by the TDA is similar to that of the f_{xc}^{LRC} sensitivity: LRC excitonic properties of semiconductors are rather insensitive to α, whereas those of insulators are highly sensitive to α.

We quantitatively verified that Dyson and full Casida equations produce identical exciton binding energies. This indicates that it is crucial to solve the full Casida equation instead of the TDA one when studying excitonic properties of insulators using LRC-type kernels.

For now, our conclusions hold only for LRC exciton binding energies of semiconductors and insulators. It will be of interest to study the effect of the TDA for non-LRC-type kernels, and on spectral properties such as oscillator strengths and exciton momentum dispersions.

Acknowledgments: This work was supported by National Science Foundation Grant No. DMR-1408904. The computation for this work was performed on the high performance computing infrastructure provided by Research Computing Support Services at the University of Missouri, Columbia MO.

Author Contributions: Both authors conceived and designed the study; Y.-M.B. performed the numerical calculations; both authors analyzed the data and wrote the paper.

References

1. Miyata, A.; Mitioglu, A.; Plochocka, P.; Portugall, O.; Wang, J.T.W.; Stranks, S.D.; Snaith, H.J.; Nicholas, R.J. Direct measurement of the exciton binding energy and effective masses for charge carriers in organic–inorganic tri-halide perovskites. *Nat. Phys.* **2015**, *11*, 582–587.

2. Onida, G.; Reining, L.; Rubio, A. Electronic excitations: Density-functional versus many-body Green's-function approaches. *Rev. Mod. Phys.* **2002**, *74*, 601.

3. Ullrich, C.A.; Yang, Z.H. Excitons in time-dependent density-functional theory. In *Density-Functional Methods for Excited States*; Ferré, N., Filatov, M., Huix-Rotllant, M., Eds.; Springer: Berlin, Germany, 2015; Volume 368.

4. Reining, L.; Olevano, V.; Rubio, A.; Onida, G. Excitonic effects in solids described by time-dependent density-functional theory. *Phys. Rev. Lett.* **2002**, *88*, 066404.

5. Botti, S.; Sottile, F.; Vast, N.; Olevano, V.; Reining, L.; Weissker, H.C.; Rubio, A.; Onida, G.; del Sole, R.; Godby, R.W. Long-range contribution to the exchange-correlation kernel of time-dependent density functional theory. *Phys. Rev. B* **2004**, *69*, 155112–155114.

6. Sharma, S.; Dewhurst, J.K.; Sanna, A.; Gross, E.K.U. Bootstrap approximation for the exchange-correlation kernel of time-dependent density-functional theory. *Phys. Rev. Lett.* **2011**, *107*, 186401.

7. Rigamonti, S.; Botti, S.; Veniard, V.; Draxl, C.; Reining, L.; Sottile, F. Estimating excitonic effects in the absorption spectra of solids: Problems and insight from a guided iteration scheme. *Phys. Rev. Lett.* **2015**, *114*, 146402.

8. Berger, J.A. Fully parameter-free calculation of optical spectra for insulators, semiconductors, and metals from a simple polarization functional. *Phys. Rev. Lett.* **2015**, *115*, 137402.

9. Trevisanutto, P.E.; Terentjevs, A.; Constantin, L.A.; Olevano, V.; Sala, F.D. Optical spectra of solids obtained by time-dependent density functional theory with the jellium-with-gap-model exchange-correlation kernel. *Phys. Rev. B* **2013**, *87*, 205143.

10. Casida, M.E. Time-dependent density functional response theory for molecules. In *Recent Advances in Density Functional Methods*; Chong, D.E., Ed.; World Scientific: Singapore, 1995; Volume 1, pp. 155–192.

11. Yang, Z.H.; Ullrich, C.A. Direct calculation of exciton binding energies with time-dependent density-functional theory. *Phys. Rev. B* **2013**, *87*, 195204.

12. Yang, Z.H.; Sottile, F.; Ullrich, C.A. A simple screened exact-exchange approach for excitonic properties in solids. *Phys. Rev. B* **2015**, *92*, 035202.

13. Sander, T.; Maggio, E.; Kresse, G. Beyond the Tamm-Dancoff approximation for extended systems using exact diagonalization. *Phys. Rev. B* **2015**, *92*, 045209.

14. Shao, M.; da Jornada, F.H.; Yang, C.; Deslippe, J.; Louie, S.G. Structure preserving parallel algorithms for solving the Bethe–Salpeter eigenvalue problem. *Linear Algebra Its Appl.* **2016**, *488*, 148–167.

15. Dreuw, A.; Head-Gordon, M. Single-reference ab initio methods for the calculation of excited states of large molecules. *Chem. Rev.* **2005**, *105*, 4009–4037.

16. Petersilka, M.; Gossmann, U.J.; Gross, E.K.U. Excitation energies from time-dependent density-functional theory. *Phys. Rev. Lett.* **1996**, *76*, 1212–1215.

17. Casida, M.E.; Gutierrez, F.; Guan, J.; Cadea, F.X.; Salahub, D.; Daudey, J.P. Charge-transfer correction for improved time-dependent local density approximation excited-state potential energy curves: Analysis within the two-level model with illustration for H_2 and LiH. *J. Chem. Phys.* **2000**, *113*, 7062–7071.

18. Baroni, S.; Resta, R. Ab initio calculation of the macroscopic dielectric constant in silicon. *Phys. Rev. B* **1986**, *33*, 7017.

19. Yang, Z.H.; Li, Y.; Ullrich, C.A. A minimal model for excitons within time-dependent density-functional theory. *J. Chem. Phys.* **2012**, *137*, 014513.

20. Byun, Y.M.; Ullrich, C.A. Systematic assessment of long-range-corrected exchange-correlation kernels for solids: Accurate excitonic properties via a nonuniformly scaled Bootstrap kernel. *Phys. Rev. B* **2017**, In preparation.

21. Levine, Z.H.; Allan, D.C. Linear optical response in silicon and germanium including self-energy effects. *Phys. Rev. Lett.* **1989**, *63*, 1719.

22. Gonze, X.; Amadon, B.; Anglade, P.M.; Beuken, J.M.; Bottin, F.; Boulanger, P.; Bruneval, F.; Caliste, D.; Caracas, R.; Côté, M.; et al. ABINIT: First-principles approach to material and nanosystem properties. *Comput. Phys. Commun.* **2009**, *180*, 2582–2615.

23. Olevano, V.; Reining, L.; Sottile, F. The Dp Code 1997. Available online: http://www.dp-code.org/ (accessed on 25 January 2017).

24. Lautenschlager, P.; Garriga, M.; Logothetidis, S.; Cardona, M. Interband critical points of GaAs and their temperature dependence. *Phys. Rev. B* **1987**, *35*, 9174.

25. Sonntag, B. Dielectric and optical properties. In *Rare Gas Solids*; Klein, M.L., Venables, J.A., Eds.; Academic Press: London, UK, 1976; Volume II, p. 1021.

26. Parenteau, M.; Carlone, C.; Khanna, S.M. Damage coefficient associated with free exciton lifetime in GaAs irradiated with neutrons and electrons. *J. Appl. Phys.* **1992**, *71*, 3747.

27. As, D.J.; Schmilgus, F.; Wang, C.; Schöttker, B.; Schikora, D.; Lischka, K. The near band edge photoluminescence of cubic GaN epilayers. *Appl. Phys. Lett.* **1997**, *70*, 1311.

28. Muth, J.F.; Lee, J.H.; Shmagin, I.K.; Kolbas, R.M.; Casey, H.C.; Keller, B.P.; Mishra, U.K.; DenBaars, S.P. Absorption coefficient, energy gap, exciton binding energy, and recombination lifetime of GaN obtained from transmission measurements. *Appl. Phys. Lett.* **1997**, *71*, 2572.

29. Haensel, R.; Keitel, G.; Koch, E.E.; Skibowski, M.; Schreiber, P. Reflection spectrum of solid argon in the vacuum ultraviolet. *Phys. Rev. Lett.* **1969**, *23*, 1160.

30. Roessler, D.M.; Walker, W.C. Optical constants of magnesium oxide and lithium fluoride in the far ultraviolet. *J. Opt. Soc. Am.* **1967**, *57*, 835–836.

31. Saile, V.; Koch, E.E. Bulk and surface excitons in solid neon. *Phys. Rev. B* **1979**, *20*, 784.

32. Leute, R.A.R.; Feneberg, M.; Sauer, R.; Thonke, K.; Thapa, S.B.; Scholz, F.; Taniyasu, Y.; Kasu, M. Photoluminescence of highly excited AlN: Biexcitons and exciton-exciton scattering. *Appl. Phys. Lett.* **2009**, *95*, 031903.

33. Roessler, D.M.; Walker, W.C. Electronic Spectrum and Ultraviolet Optical Properties of Crystalline MgO. *Phys. Rev.* **1967**, *159*, 733.

34. Nazarov, V.U.; Vignale, G. Optics of semiconductors from meta-generalized-gradient approximation based time-dependent density-functional theory. *Phys. Rev. Lett.* **2011**, *107*, 216402.

35. Stephens, P.J.; Devlin, F.J.; Chabalowski, C.F.; Frisch, M.J. Ab initio calculation of vibrational absorption and circular dichroism spectra using density functional force fields. *J. Phys. Chem.* **1994**, *98*, 11623.

36. Bernasconi, L.; Tomić, S.; Ferrero, M.; Rérat, M.; Orlando, R.; Dovesi, R.; Harrison, N.M. First-principles optical response of semiconductors and oxide materials. *Phys. Rev. B* **2011**, *83*, 195325.

37. Tomić, S.; Bernasconi, L.; Searle, B.G.; Harrison, N.M. Electronic and Optical Structure of Wurtzite $CuInS_2$. *J. Phys. Chem. C* **2014**, *118*, 14478–14484.

38. Refaely-Abramson, S.; Jain, M.; Sharifzadeh, S.; Neaton, J.B.; Kronik, L. Solid-state optical absorption from optimally tuned time-dependent range-separated hybrid density functional theory. *Phys. Rev. B* **2015**, *92*, 081204.

39. Ullrich, C.A. *Time-Dependent Density-Functional Theory: Concepts and Applications*; Oxford University Press: Oxford, UK, 2012.

40. Grüning, M.; Marini, A.; Gonze, X. Exciton-plasmon states in nanoscale materials: Breakdown of the Tamm-Dancoff approximation. *Nano Lett.* **2009**, *9*, 2820–2824.

3

Numerical Modelling of Double-Steel Plate Composite Shear Walls

Michaela Elmatzoglou and Aris Avdelas *

School of Civil Engineering, Aristotle University, GR-541 24 Thessaloniki, Greece; emichael@civil.auth.gr
* Correspondence: avdelas@civil.auth.gr

Academic Editor: Demos T. Tsahalis

Abstract: Double-steel plate concrete composite shear walls are being used for nuclear plants and high-rise buildings. They consist of thick concrete walls, exterior steel faceplates serving as reinforcement and shear connectors, which guarantee the composite action between the two different materials. Several researchers have used the Finite Element Method to investigate the behaviour of double-steel plate concrete walls. The majority of them model every element explicitly leading to a rather time-consuming solution, which cannot be easily used for design purposes. In the present paper, the main objective is the introduction of a three-dimensional finite element model, which can efficiently predict the overall performance of a double-steel plate concrete wall in terms of accuracy and time saving. At first, empirical formulations and design relations established in current design codes for shear connectors are evaluated. Then, a simplified finite element model is used to investigate the nonlinear response of composite walls. The developed model is validated using results from tests reported in the literature in terms of axial compression and monotonic, cyclic in-plane shear loading. Several finite element modelling issues related to potential convergence problems, loading strategies and computer efficiency are also discussed. The accuracy and simplicity of the proposed model make it suitable for further numerical studies on the shear connection behaviour at the steel-concrete interface.

Keywords: steel-plate composite shear wall; shear connectors; infill concrete; steel faceplate; finite element modelling; ANSYS

1. Introduction

Composite construction is more and more frequently implemented in building structures and especially in shear walls, which are undoubtedly one of the most critical elements in a high-rise structural system. Double-steel plate concrete composite walls are composed of steel plates anchored to the infill concrete using welded stud shear connectors. Although steel plate and reinforced concrete shear walls are traditionally used as axial and seismic load-resisting systems, composite wall construction can offer a wide range of benefits. Double-steel plate concrete walls allow for modular construction leading to important cost and time saving. Steel faceplates can be fabricated offsite and then assembled and filled with concrete onsite. Steel faceplates serve both as concrete formwork and as primary reinforcement. In addition, this system has superior blast and impact resistance.

The two major fields on which this system can be widely used are multi-storey buildings and nuclear facilities. Design requirements differ for each case. Applications of double-steel plate concrete walls to the containment of internal structures (enclosures around a nuclear reactor to confine fission products that might be released to the atmosphere if an accident occurred) and shield building in nuclear facilities have begun in the United States and China, based on the work of Varma and his partners at Purdue University [1–4]. Additionally, based on the experimental and numerical work of Varma, Appendix 9, which refers to composite construction, has been added to the existing US standards (ANSI/AISC N690) [5,6]. In contrast, as refers to the design of building structures, a double-steel plate concrete wall should not only be designed to work over the elastic limit, but also to obtain a significant amount of ductility during the post-elastic stage. Consequently, it is evident that the focus of the accomplished research was the elastic response and further investigation is needed regarding nonlinear response and seismic behaviour of double-steel plate concrete walls.

1.1. Numerical Literature Overview

Vecchio and McQuade [7] adapted the Distributed Stress Field Model, a smeared rotating crack model for reinforced concrete based on the Modified Compression Field Theory, to the analysis of steel and concrete wall elements under axial and shear loads. The computational model was then incorporated into a two-dimensional nonlinear finite element analysis algorithm using the two-dimensional nonlinear finite element analysis program Vector2 [8]. A perfect bond was assumed between the steel faceplates and infill concrete. The critical buckling stress proposed by Usami et al. [9] has been adopted. The accuracy of the model was proved using experimental results reported in the literature [9–11]. In all cases, the analysis model was found to provide accurate calculations of shearing strength, but the stiffness at displacements lower than those associated with peak strength was significantly overestimated [7]. Additionally, deficiencies were found in terms of faceplate buckling and interfacial slip between steel and concrete.

Zhou et al. [12] developed a 2D finite element model to simulate the cyclic response of double-steel plate concrete walls. They used membrane elements with plane stress behaviour to model the infill concrete and the steel faceplates. The finite element model did not include the connectors and the steel faceplates were tied to the infill concrete. The Cyclic-Softened-Membrane-Model developed by Mansour et al. [13,14] has been validated using experimental data of a reinforced concrete (RC) shear wall [15] and then it was used to model the infill concrete in combination with a plasticity model for steel faceplates. The numerical model was not validated. The parameters considered in the investigation were wall thickness and faceplate slenderness ratio.

Ma et al. [16] conducted a numerical study on double-steel plate concrete walls under axial compressive and cyclic lateral loadings to investigate the effects of the axial force and steel faceplate thickness on the response of double-steel plate concrete walls. Concrete was modelled with smeared-crack solid elements, whereas steel faceplates were simulated with piece-wise-linear plastic shell elements with isotropic hardening. Hard interfacial contact was assumed to avoid penetration of the steel faceplates into the infill concrete. The skeleton curve obtained from the predicted hysteretic curve was divided into three stages, namely elastic, elastic-plastic (cracking of the concrete core and yielding of steel faceplates) and hardening (buckling of steel faceplates). Post-peak strength response has not been considered. The proposed model successfully predicted the shear strength of the walls but underestimated the displacement at peak force.

Rafiei et al. [17] used ABAQUS [18] to simulate the behaviour of a composite shear wall system consisting of profiled steel sheeting and a concrete core under in-plane monotonic loading. They conducted a parametric study to investigate the effects of the configuration of the intermediate fasteners along the height and width of the wall, the steel yield and the concrete compressive strength. They developed a detailed and a simplified numerical model and proved that the simplified numerical model was more efficient in terms of computation time and accuracy.

Ali et al. [19] developed an ABAQUS model [18] to simulate the response of four I-shaped (walls with flanges) double-steel plate concrete walls with varying steel plate thickness in the web and flanges. In order to model the infill concrete and the steel faceplates, concrete damage plasticity (CDP) and bilinear kinematic hardening models were used respectively. The concrete core and the steel plates were modelled using solid elements. The nodes of the flange wall were tied to the nodes of the web. The numerical results matched the experimental behaviour with reasonable accuracy in the pre-peak stage of response.

Varma et al. [3] developed a simple mechanistic representation of the in-plane shear behaviour of double-steel plate concrete walls and a design equation for calculating their in-plane stiffness and strength. The model was verified using experimental results reported in the literature [11] and a large-scale in-plane shear test conducted by Varma et al. [3]. Nevertheless, the numerical model had important limitations. It did not include concrete cracking and post-cracking behaviour in tension. In addition, it did not directly account for concrete inelasticity in compression and the analysis was terminated if the minimum principal concrete compressive stress exceeded 70% of the compressive strength. Finally, a fully bonded interaction between steel and concrete was assumed. To overcome these limitations, Varma et al. [4] developed a layered composite shell finite element model using ABAQUS [18]. However, the numerical peak shear strength predicted by both models was less than the experimental peak shear strength of the composite walls. Analytical and numerical models have been used to generate in-plane force and out-of-plane moment interaction curves. However, in order to use this approach, the wall cross-section should be detailed with adequate shear connectors and transverse tie bars so as to prevent brittle failure modes like local buckling of the faceplates before yielding, out-of-plane shear failure and interfacial shear failure.

Kurt et al. [20] developed a finite element model using explicit analysis [21] to study the monotonic in-plane shear behaviour of double-steel plate concrete walls. Afterwards, they conducted a parametric study to study the influence of wall thickness and aspect ratio on the response of composite walls. Epackachi et al. [22] also used LS-DYNA [21] to develop a numerical model and simulate the nonlinear cyclic response of composite shear walls. They used 2-node beam elements to model each shear connector and coupled one of the nodes to concrete elements. The assumption of a perfect bond between the faceplates and infill concrete resulted in a conservative prediction of the post-peak resistance of the composite walls. However, it may also affect the pre-peak response for different faceplate slenderness ratios, defined as the spacing of the connectors to the thickness of the faceplates.

Vazouras and Avdelas [23] studied the behaviour of double-steel plate concrete walls under monotonic and cyclic horizontal loading using the ANSYS Mechanical finite element package [24]. The objective of the research was to evaluate the influence of fundamental parameters of its response, such as aspect ratio and thickness of steel plates and to study the behavioural curve, the capacity under both compressive and bending conditions, the ductility and the failure process. Shear connectors have not been modelled. Therefore, the numerical model assumed a perfect bond between the faceplates and infill concrete using tie constraints. Since the focus of the investigation was not the behaviour of shear connectors, the model provided reasonable results for composite walls designed using a dense spacing of shear connectors.

In conclusion, the majority of the aforementioned numerical studies focused on the behaviour of composite walls before achieving the peak load. Furthermore, the majority of them assumed the steel nodes tied to the concrete nodes and did not address the effects of steel faceplate buckling and spacing of connectors on the in-plane response.

1.2. Objectives and Scope of Work

This paper proposes a new three-dimensional finite element model, developed using the software ANSYS 15.0 [24], incorporating a detailed description of the modelling process, material properties, element types, boundary conditions and application of loads. The most important aspect of this model is that although it uses low order elements, it can result in an accurate prediction of the structural elastic and post-elastic response of a double-steel plate concrete wall.

Two cases have been identified in terms of loading types imposed on composite walls, namely axial compression loading and monotonic, cyclic in-plane shear loading. The first loading case is critical for the relative motion between faceplates and infill concrete, whereas the second one is significant to investigate the seismic behaviour of double-steel plate concrete walls. Different modelling assumptions are adopted in each case in order to maintain reasonable accuracy in predicting the response of double-steel plate concrete walls. This approach resulted in a numerical model that can effectively describe the major loading conditions on composite walls in a reasonable time and with significant accuracy.

The numerical model generally accounted for the nonlinear monotonic and cyclic responses of the steel faceplates and the infill concrete, friction between the two materials and presence of connectors (studs and possible steel side plates). The inclusion of shear connectors, contact elements and friction in the steel-concrete interface was necessary to accurately simulate the behaviour of double-steel plate concrete walls. Furthermore, the numerical model addressed the effect of modelling the foundation of a composite wall, since its flexibility could considerably influence global response.

The accuracy of the numerical model was verified using data from tests of six experimental programs reported in the literature [9,11,22,25–27]. The cases listed above were selected because they not only describe comprehensively geometric, material and structural response details, but also four of them examined compression loading, whereas the rest accounted for in-plane shear loading. Considering the analysis results, the developed finite element model is proposed as being suitable for design purposes and further parametric studies.

Finally, it should be noted that the focus of this research is the description of a structural system for building construction which consists of prefabricated steel plates serving as permanent concrete formwork and filled with concrete. Other possible configurations such as two thin steel faceplates connected through the concrete infill (which are impractical for building construction due to the need for thermal insulation etc.) are out of the scope of this research. Furthermore, the effect of concrete reinforcement may be beneficial, but it provokes other construction problems, which can be easily solved with the use of shear connectors. Additionally, steel plates serve as reinforcement. Positioning the faceplates at the extreme fibre of the cross-section not only maximises their influence on flexural resistance but also provides tension reinforcement in all directions. This cannot be achieved in reinforced concrete walls due to clear cover requirements. Thus, for the same section depth, the moment capacity and flexural rigidity are inherently larger and simultaneously the resulting deflections are smaller for a composite wall than in a reinforced concrete one of the same thickness. Alternatively, it is evident that the required capacities for building construction are easily achieved with this wall type without adopting large section thickness. Even in the case of double-steel plate concrete walls used in nuclear facilities [1–4,20,27], where a larger wall thickness is needed due to the need for radiation shielding and where transverse tie bars instead of reinforcing bars are being used to join the steel plates, their role is to enhance the structural integrity of the cross-section and not the capacity. As a result, providing further reinforcement in a concrete core to enhance the capacity of a double-steel plate concrete wall is out of the scope of this research.

2. Numerical Model Formulation

The numerical study was undertaken using the ANSYS 15 finite element analysis program [24]. The following sections briefly describe the modelling properties and assumptions. The finite element model accounted for the nonlinear behaviour of materials, the nonlinear interfacial shear force-slip behaviour of shear studs, the local buckling of the steel plates associated with geometrical nonlinearity and was capable of nonlinear static and dynamic analysis so as to capture the effects of concrete cracking and crushing.

2.1. Analysis Method

Overall, two major analysis finite element analysis methods can be used: implicit or explicit. The majority of the researchers used explicit analysis to model the behaviour of composite walls, due to the difficulty in modelling the nonlinear behaviour of concrete. Bruhl et al. [1], Sener et al. [2] and Varma et al. [3,4] used explicit analyses for the analysis of double-steel plate concrete walls used in nuclear facilities. Epackachi et al. [22] also used explicit analyses for the analysis of composite walls used in multi-storey buildings. In contrast, Vazouras and Avdelas [23] used implicit analyses to analyse the behaviour of composite walls, assuming tied connection between steel and concrete nodes.

In the case of an implicit analysis, the calculation of current quantities in one time-step is based on the quantities calculated during the previous time step. This procedure is called Euler Time Integration Scheme. In this scheme even if large time steps are chosen, the solution remains stable. In contrast, an explicit solution is unstable as it does not utilise the Euler Time Integration Scheme. The use of very small time steps is needed to overpass this problem. Another difference is that the implicit algorithm requires the calculation of the inverse of the stiffness matrix, whereas the explicit algorithm requires the inversion of the mass matrix, which can be diagonal if lower order elements are used. As a result, in a static loading case, it is preferable to use implicit analysis, in which big time steps can be used and the solution can be obtained in a few iterations. For these reasons, implicit analysis has been used in this research for the investigation of the performance of double-steel plate concrete walls.

Additionally, it should be noted that in an implicit analysis nonlinearities can be modelled even better than in explicit analysis because every parameter of the material behaviour and every property of the contact model can be controlled. As a result, the nonlinear behaviour of concrete has been represented accordingly. Furthermore, convergence in an implicit analysis is rather difficult (this is one of the reasons why many researchers choose explicit analysis), but when it is achieved the accuracy of the results is better. In general, this analysis method was considered ideal to study the general behaviour of a composite wall. On the other hand, explicit analysis can be used to focus on the behaviour of shear connectors. The results of this research will be presented in the future.

2.2. Element Types and Material Properties

2.2.1. Concrete Infill

Two concrete types were used in this research depending on the configuration of the cross-section: fully confined and partially confined. In the case of the composite wall, concrete has been considered as properly confined when steel side plates were welded to the faceplates to form a closed-formed rectangular steel section infilled with concrete as shown in Figure 1. Overall, the configuration of a composite wall depends on the existence or absence of boundary elements or the type of the building's structural system. Consequently, although the existence of steel side plates may be beneficial to the performance of double-steel plate concrete, placing concrete in a triaxial stress state and providing structural integrity, their application may not be always feasible. As a result, concrete behaviour has been categorised into two groups namely confined (Figure 1) and partially confined (Figure 2). Different modelling strategies have been used for each case.

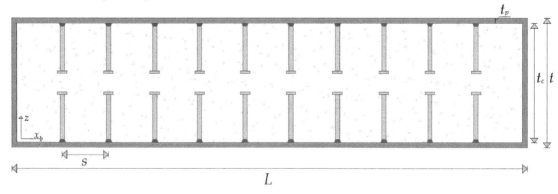

Figure 1. Cross-section of a double-steel plate concrete wall with confined concrete.

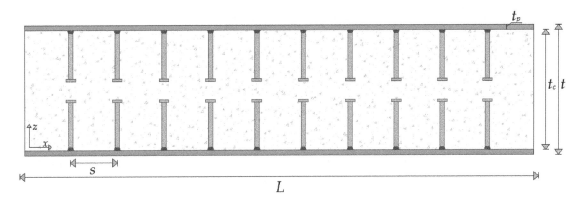

Figure 2. Cross-section of a double-steel plate concrete wall with partially confined concrete.

This approach came up during the validation procedure due to the different behaviour of concrete in the composite wall configurations exhibited in Figures 1 and 2. This modelling approach has been validated using experimental results reported in the literature. To be more specific, wall specimens tested by Epackachi et al. [22], Ozaki et al. [11], Choi et al. [26] and Zhang [27] did not include side plates resulting in a partially confined concrete model, whereas specimens tested by Akiyama et al. [25] and Usami et al. [9] included side plates resulting in a fully confined concrete model. Additionally, it has been assumed that the confinement provided by the steel plates exceeds by far the confinement provided by the shear connectors and as a result, the latter has been neglected. This assumption has been proved during the validation procedure.

In general, modelling concrete behaviour was of great concern not only due to its different behaviour in tension and compression but also due to convergence difficulties in an implicit analysis procedure caused when concrete is not properly confined.

An eight-node 3D solid element (SOLID65) was used to properly model concrete behaviour. This element has three degrees of freedom at each node (translations in the nodal x, y and z directions) [28]. It is capable of plastic deformation, creep, cracking in the three orthogonal directions and crushing. The William-Warnke criterion [29] has been used as failure criterion due to multiaxial stress state. When concrete fails, the software sets the stiffness of the failed element to zero and proceeds to the next sub-step. This would eventually result in a non-convergence state meaning that the concrete has completely failed. Several trials have been made and it has been concluded that crushing of concrete in the first configuration provided accurate results, while it may lead to premature failure in the second configuration. Barbosa et al. [30] also reported premature indications of failure due to crushing, when the Solid65 crushing capability was turned on. They reported that the failure occurred due to concrete crushing, before reaching the experimental ultimate load. In this research, the same behaviour was observed for unconfined concrete.

As refers to confined concrete, the presence, at an integration point, of a crack has been represented through modification of the stress-strain relations. This has been done by the introduction of a weakness plane in a direction normal to the crack face [24]. Further, a shear transfer coefficient β_t was introduced representing a reduction factor of shear strength that accounts for sliding (shear) across the crack face induced by subsequent loading. If the crack closes, then all compressive stresses normal to the crack plane are transmitted across the crack and only a shear transfer coefficient β_c for a closed crack is introduced. If the material at an integration point fails in uniaxial, biaxial, or triaxial compression, then it is assumed that the material crushes at that point, with crushing defined as the case in which the structural integrity of the material deteriorates completely. Finally, the failure surface of the concrete has been defined by five strength input parameters. The shear transfer coefficients for an open and closed crack were 0.3 and 0.7, respectively. The stress relaxation coefficient was equal to the default value of 0.6. The characteristic yield stress in compression was determined based on either experimental data for the validation studies or on nominal material properties [31]. The ultimate tensile stress was determined based on Eurocode 2 (EC2) provisions [31].

Considering partially confined concrete, the crushing capability of element Solid65 has been turned off. Two alternative methods have been developed to define the concrete crushing failure using strains developed in concrete. The first method uses the maximum strain as an indication of failure. In general, the maximum strain is not a reliable measure for assessing the concrete crushing mode of failure since, although the capacity of the section is large enough to carry loads till crushing, strains propagate completely in the wall section. This causes certain points to experience high strains under the concentrated pressures, even when the wall is still in its elastic state limit. To eliminate this effect, the top endplates of each specimen need to be modelled in order to transfer the load to the composite section progressively, instead of omitting their existence and apply the pressure directly to the concrete elements. According to the second method, the concrete crushing is considered when the first contour line of a strain equal or larger than 0.0035 (value proposed by EC2 [31] and achieving the best correlation with experimental results) is formed all through the concrete width. Although both methods ended up to similar results regarding failure due to the crushing of the concrete infill, the first method has been adopted in order to explore the effects of modelling endplates on the general structural behaviour.

In all specimens, concrete reached its ultimate strength after 28 days. However, curves derived from compression tests were not available for these cases. As a result, each stress-strain curve was calculated separately for the ultimate compressive strength of every specimen. The nonlinear behaviour of concrete depicted in Figure 3 by an equivalent uniaxial stress-strain curve developed according to EC2 [31] has been adopted. This figure indicates the behaviour of concrete in tension and compression. As regards concrete in compression, the first part of the curve and until the proportional limit stress, was initially assumed to be in the elastic range. The proportional limit stress value was taken as equal to $0.4f_c$, where f_c is the ultimate compressive cylinder strength of concrete. The strain ε_{c1} associated with f_c was equal to 0.0022. The Poisson ratio v of the concrete was taken as equal to 0.2.

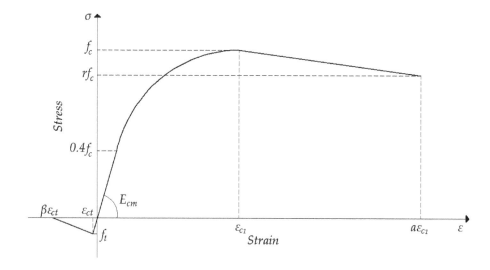

Figure 3. The concrete stress-strain model.

The second part of the curve is a nonlinear parabolic curve starting from $0.4f_c$ and reaching to the concrete compressive strength f_c. This part of the curve can be determined from Equation (1) given by EC2 [31], where σ_c is the stress at any strain ε_c, f_c is the characteristic cylinder compressive strength of concrete, n is the ratio of the strain ε_c at stress σ_c to the strain ε_{c1}. At the peak compressive stress f_c is equal to 0.0022 and k is a parameter equal to $1.1E_{cm}\varepsilon_{c1}/f_c$

$$\sigma_c = \left[\left(kn - n^2\right)/(1 + (k-2)n)\right]f_c \tag{1}$$

The third part of the stress-strain curve is a descending part from f_c to a value of $r f_c$ lower than or equal to f_c, where r is a reduction factor referred from the study of Ellobody et al. [32]. This factor varies from 1 to 0.5 corresponding to concrete cube strength from 30 to 100 MPa. In this study, r was taken as equal to a constant value of 0.85. The ultimate strain ε_{cu} of concrete at failure was equal to $a\, \varepsilon_{c1}$. According to EC2 [31], ε_{cu} is equal to 0.0035 ($a = 1.59$). Ellobody et al. [32] considered a equal to 11 in a confined concrete model. In the present study, an ultimate strain of 0.0035 ($a = 1.59$) has been considered. As regards specimens with side plates, a higher value of a has been assumed since concrete was under a triaxial state of stresses and its performance was enhanced.

2.2.2. Steel Plates

Due to the fact that steel plate thickness is rather small compared to its other dimensions, they have been considered as thin-walled elements [24,33]. This was a decisive fact for the selection of the appropriate finite element. A four node structural shell element (SHELL181) was used to represent the steel faceplates and possible side plates. Side plates are used only in specimens fabricated by Akiyama et al. [25] and Usami et al. [9] and this is another reason why these specimens were selected for this validation study. SHELL181 is suitable for analysing thin to moderately thick shell structures. It has six degrees of freedom at each node: translations in the x, y, z directions and rotations about the x, y, z-axes [28]. Additionally, it is well-suited for linear, large rotation and large strain nonlinear applications. Although the default option for this element is reduced integration with hourglass control, full integration with incompatible modes has been used in this study so as to achieve the best simulation of the deformed shape of a double-steel plate concrete wall due to buckling.

The constitutive material law selected to represent monotonic steel behaviour used the von Mises yield criterion with kinematic hardening rule. The Poisson ratio v of steel was taken as equal to 0.3. The stress-strain relationship is shown in Figure 4, where f_y is the yield stress, f_u is the ultimate tensile strength, ε_y is the strain at the yield stress f_y, ε_h is the strain at the beginning of strain hardening branch, ε_u is the strain at the ultimate strength ε_y. The first part of the curve is linear elastic up to yielding and the second part between the elastic limit (ε_y) and the beginning of strain hardening (ε_h) is perfectly plastic. The last part of the curve represents the strain-hardening branch and it was calculated according to the constitutive law used by Gattesco [34], given in Equation (2), where E_h is the strain hardening modulus of steel

$$\sigma = f_y + E_h(\varepsilon - \varepsilon_h)\left[1 - \left[E_h(\varepsilon - \varepsilon_h)/4(f_u - f_y)\right]\right] \tag{2}$$

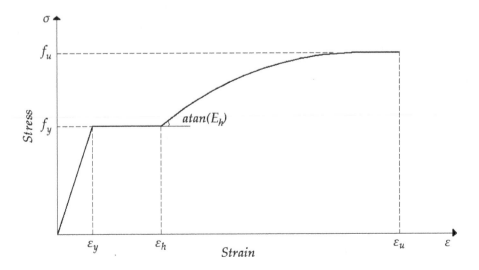

Figure 4. The steel stress-strain model.

Under load reversals, the load-bearing capacity of a steel member generally decreases as the number of load cycles increases [34]. A large literature for steel constitutive models [35–39] has been studied to end up with the adopted cyclic response of steel shown in Figure 5. To account for progressive hardening and softening effects [40], steel was assumed to have a multilinear kinematic hardening behaviour as described above. Additionally, some isotropic effects have also been considered so as to account for the Bauschinger effect. This effect, upon load reversal in the direction of plastic deformation, shows a reduction in the yield stress.

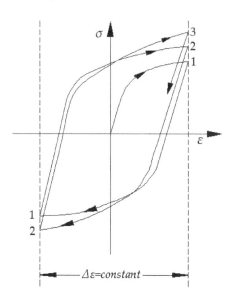

Figure 5. Cyclic behaviour of steel.

2.2.3. Steel Endplates

As it has been discussed before, modelling of endplates was necessary in order to transfer the axial compressive loading to the composite section and obtain smooth strain contour results. Two alternatives have been studied, regarding the selection of the appropriate element type. At first, endplates were modelled using the same element with steel faceplates (SHELL181). As a result, concrete elements located near the contact surface of the endplate and the concrete infill deformed locally. As this behaviour did not come up during the experiment, it was concluded that SHELL181 does not properly model endplate behaviour. This fact can be justified since endplates used in experiments are relatively thicker than side plates so as to safely impose the compressive loads and they cannot be properly modelled using a shell element. Finally, a solid element (SOLID185) in the form of a homogenous structural solid has been used for modelling the endplates.

SOLID185 is defined by eight nodes having three degrees of freedom at each node: translations in the nodal x, y, and z directions [28]. Further, the element has plasticity, hyperelasticity, stress stiffening, creep, large deflection, and large strain capabilities. The Von Mises yield criterion with isotropic hardening rule was also used for the modelling of steel endplates.

2.2.4. Shear Connectors

There are many alternatives considering modelling of shear connectors. In this research headed studs have been used to guarantee composite action between steel and concrete. The case of overlapping shear connectors has been considered and it has been concluded that in the case of overlapping headed shear studs there is an interaction resulting in an augmented pull-out resistance. The beneficial effect of this interaction was neglected in this research and will be investigated in a future study.

In order to make the most efficient choice in terms of analysis time and modelling behaviour, the slenderness of a typical composite double-steel plate shear wall should be considered. Slenderness is defined as the ratio of the overall thickness of the wall to the height of each shear connector after the welding procedure. This ratio is calculated for every case considered in this research. It was concluded that the slenderness ratio is high enough to assume that each shear connector is exclusively defined by axial internal forces. As a result, nonlinear springs (COMBIN39) were used to represent the headed studs.

The element COMBIN39 has no mass and it is defined by two (preferably coincident) node points and a generalised force-deflection curve [28]. The need for coincident nodes demands the use of a common meshing for steel and concrete. Moreover, it has a longitudinal or torsional capability. The adopted longitudinal option is a uniaxial tension-compression element with, at each node, up to three degrees of freedom (translations).

Many researchers have selected nonlinear springs to model the shear connection between steel and concrete in composite beams [41,42]. Queiroz et al. [43] proposed a three-dimensional model, in which each shear connector has been modelled using a nonlinear spring (COMBIN39) parallel to the direction of the relative movement between the composite slab and the steel beam. On the vertical to the relative movement direction, nodes have been coupled. However, this assumption is not valid for double-steel plate concrete walls, since if the nodes are coupled, pry-out failure of headed studs will not be included as a possible failure mode of the specimen and as a consequence, the entire model will assume a full shear connection between faceplates and the infill concrete. In general, shear connectors used in composite walls not only offer shear but also tensile resistance.

In this paper, a simplified modelling approach for the shear connection behaviour in composite walls is proposed. Further, in previous studies, each shear connector has been modelled using one spring. In this research, every shear connector has been modelled using two springs: one parallel and one normal to the direction of the relative movement between faceplates and the infill concrete so as to simulate their shear and tension capacity. The inclusion of these springs requires as input data a load-slip curve. Either empirical formulations or curves obtained directly from available push-out tests [40] can be utilised. In this study, as there were no push-out test results available, the majority of the empirical formulations available in the literature have been studied in order to end up to a load-slip curve that fits better to the experimental behaviour of each specimen. Finally, the following load (Q)-slip (δ) model proposed by Ollgaard et al. [44] has been adopted, Equation (3), where Q_u is the ultimate load capacity of a steel shear stud and the units are kilo-pound (kip) for load and inch (in.) for slip

$$Q = Q_u\left(1 - e^{-18\delta}\right)^{2/5} \tag{3}$$

The ultimate shear capacity Q_u of a shear stud is an indispensable parameter in load-slip models. The failure mode of the steel-concrete interface is quite complicated. Failure may occur in the concrete or in the shear connector. Typical concrete failures are breakout, pry out or localised crushing. On the other hand, the stud shank may fail in shear or the weld may fracture as well. Sometimes the failure can be mixed, including two or more of the failure modes mentioned above. Therefore, researchers proposed relations to calculate the load bearing capacity considering both concrete and steel properties. In this study, the following EC4 [40] provisions have been adopted.

The design shear resistance of a headed stud automatically welded should be determined from the minimum value derived from Equations (4) and (5), where γ_v is the partial factor (the recommended value is 1.25 for design, but in this study it is taken equal to 1 for comparison purposes), d and h_{sc} are the shank diameter and the overall nominal height of the stud respectively, f_u is the specified ultimate tensile strength of the material of the stud (its value cannot be greater than 500 MPa), f_{ck} is the characteristic cylinder compressive strength of the concrete (its density should not be less than 1750 kg/m^3) and α is a parameter calculated from Figure 6

$$P_{Rd} = 0.8f_u\pi d^2/4\gamma_v \tag{4}$$

$$P_{Rd} = 0.29ad^2\sqrt{f_{ck}E_{cm}}/\gamma_v \qquad (5)$$

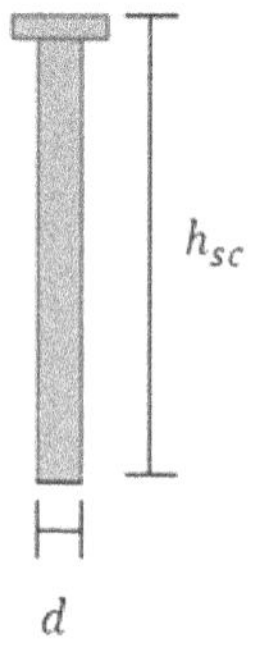

For $\frac{h_{sc}}{d} = [3,4] \rightarrow a = 0.2\left[\frac{h_{sc}}{d} + 1\right]$

For $\frac{h_{sc}}{d} > 4 \rightarrow a = 1$

Figure 6. Calculation of the parameter a.

The procedure listed above results to a multilinear load-slip curve for the first spring, which was placed parallel to the relative motion of steel plates and infill concrete. The second spring is characterised by the tensile strength of each headed stud, which is known either from preliminary tensile tests or the specifications of the manufacturer. In this study, the tensile capacity of headed studs has been calculated based on relations existing in the literature [45,46] and finally a multilinear load(Q)-slip(δ) curve has been used to model the behaviour of the second spring. The representation of the proposed model for shear connectors and details about their connection with steel and concrete at the interface are shown in Figure 7.

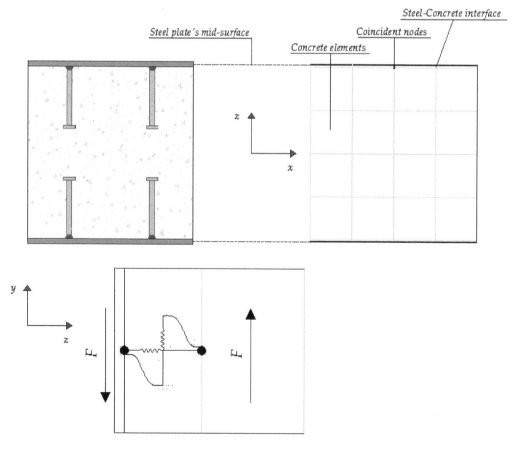

Figure 7. Finite element modelling of shear connectors.

2.2.5. Contact Elements

The specimens used in this study achieve the mechanical interlock and the shear bond between steel and concrete with the use of shear studs. Friction forces are also developed at the interface. Regarding boundary contact conditions, contact and non-contact regions are not a priori known. This contact problem is called a unilateral problem with friction. This highly nonlinear problem has to be modelled in order to simulate the actual behaviour of a double-steel plate composite shear wall.

ANSYS software program [24] uses the Coulomb friction model for the formulation of this kind of contact problems as shown in Equation (6), where μ is the coefficient of friction, τ is the equivalent Coulomb friction shear stress and P is the contact pressure at the steel-concrete interface. As soon as the shear stress τ at the steel-concrete interface exceeds the term μP, relative slip between steel plates and concrete occurs

$$\tau = \mu P \tag{6}$$

Three-dimensional nonlinear surface-surface "contact pair" elements (CONTA173 & TARGE170) [28] have been used to model the nonlinear behaviour of the interfacial surface between infill concrete and steel plates in order to achieve composite action. The concrete and steel surfaces were assumed to be deformable. Contact elements overlay the elements used for modelling steel plates and infill concrete. Each contact pair has been constructed by using area to area contact element types. During the analysis, contact is detected at the Gauss points. However, due to the fact that contact boundary conditions differ across the model, different contact surface properties should be considered.

Concrete Infill—Steel Plates

Elements generated for this contact were able to simulate the existence or absence of pressure when there is contact or separation between them respectively. Regarding the friction coefficient, Rabbat et al. [47] concluded that the average coefficient of static friction should be taken between 0.57 and 0.7. In the present work it was not deemed negligible; instead, trials have been done using three different friction coefficients: 0.3, 0.5 and 0.7. It has been concluded that in the case of in-plane lateral loading, interfacial friction can be neglected since the variation of the friction coefficient did not affect the load-displacement curve of the analysed specimens. As a result, the comparison between friction coefficients has been conducted for compression loading.

Concrete Infill—Endplates

For this contact interaction, the same contact elements have been used. However, this contact is considered as continuously bonded. During the experimental procedure, this behaviour is ensured by welding the endplates to the faceplates and the possible side plates and by welding strong shear connectors to transfer gradually the applied load to the concrete infill.

2.2.6. Foundation

Experimental results reported by Epackachi et al. [22] indicated that the initial stiffness of composite walls constructed with a baseplate connected to a RC foundation may be substantially affected by the flexibility of the connection with a potentially significant impact on the dynamic response of the supported structure. In order to address this issue two different numerical models, namely detailed and simplified, as shown in Figure 8, have been developed to identify the importance of modelling the foundation for the seismic performance of the composite walls. The detailed models explicitly accounted for every construction detail of the foundation. However, foundations may differ in practice based on soil properties. Therefore, simplified models were also developed, where the base of the wall was assumed fixed using rigid zones on the base nodes of steel faceplates and concrete respectively. Beam elements were used to represent transverse tie bars. Specifically, the main objective of the comparison between detailed and simplified numerical models was to investigate the efficiency of simplified models to predict the in-plane shear strength of double-steel plate concrete walls with the understanding that ignoring the flexibility of the foundation may lead to an overestimation of the stiffness.

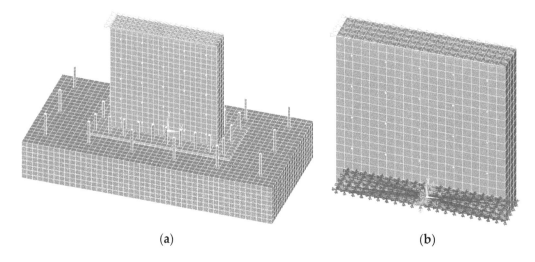

(a)   (b)

Figure 8. Computational model finite element grid, loading and support conditions (**a**) Detailed model; (**b**) Simplified model.

2.3. Meshing

ANSYS software [24] includes two different methods for mesh generation, the solid modelling method and the direct generation method. The solid modelling method requires from the user to describe the size, shape and boundaries of the whole object and to induce controls on the element types and mesh sizes. Then the software generates the elements, meshes and nodes automatically. On the other hand, in the direct generation method all the geometries, elements, meshes and nodes are to be defined by the user. Although the latter method is more time consuming, it has been adopted for this study since, regarding the multi-material problem (double-steel plate composite shear walls) which has to be solved, it was more beneficial and powerful in terms of control over the model and geometries.

Moreover, meshing the relatively thin steel plates is a quite challenging procedure. ANSYS [24] requires the size of an element to be within standard ratios in order to derive its three-dimensional stress distributions. If the dimension size ratio of an element is equal or less than 1/20, the program will generate shape ratio warnings. As a result, this stage demands a great attention and control of the shape warnings, which is granted by using the direct generation method.

A mesh refinement analysis has been conducted in order to obtain the best results regarding the analysis time (number of elements) and the realistic simulation of a composite wall. Three different mesh densities A, B and C have been examined as shown in Figure 9. The calculated discrepancies were 5.3%, 1.4% and 7.2% for Mesh A, Mesh B and Mesh C, respectively. Although all three simulations predicted similar results, it was noted that excellent results were obtained when the medium coarse Mesh B has been used. This may be attributed to the fact that several damage processes result in concrete damage and headed stud steel anchors deformation. As a result, Mesh B has been adopted for the finite element analysis. Finally, it should be noted that the results of the mesh refinement analysis were in complete agreement with the basic concepts of the finite element method. In the finite element modelling, as the number of elements increases, the stiffness of the system decreases since it gains higher indeterminacy and extra degrees of freedom. In other words, a higher number of elements provide the system with the ability to deform in a less rigid shape. As a result, a classic finite element composite wall model should demonstrate higher deformation as the number of element increases and this was the key parameter for choosing the appropriate mesh.

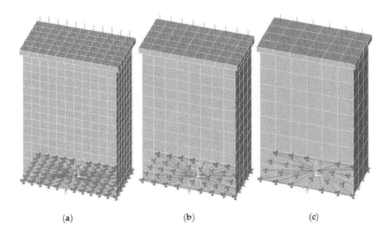

(a)   (b)   (c)

Figure 9. Computational model finite element grid, loading and support conditions (**a**) Mesh A (**b**) Mesh B (**c**) Mesh C.

2.4. Loading

Compression loading has been applied at the top side of the endplate with the form of pressure as it is shown in Figure 9, whereas in-plane monotonic and cyclic lateral loading has been applied by imposing displacements at the top concrete and steel nodes as shown in Figure 8. As a result, shear has been applied in the form of uniform displacements. Displacement values were not divided, every steel and concrete node at the top side of the specimen had the same displacement.

Two load steps have been defined to distinguish the elastic and the plastic stage for each specimen. The first load-step was defined to go from the zero stress state up to the approximate yielding point of the wall. The second point can be determined from the experimental results, but it is better to choose this point conservatively. This load-step was given through a small number of sub-steps, as the software did converge easily because of the linear behaviour of the wall during this stage. After running the model, the exact yield point was determined and in the case that the actual yielding point was smaller than the assumed one, a small part of the nonlinear behaviour was already derived with less accuracy than the one required for the nonlinear part. Therefore, the model has been adjusted and run again. The second load step was assumed to go from yielding to failure. It is crucial as it indicates the nonlinear behaviour and ductility of the composite wall. In this study, the applied load was chosen to be 110% of the expected ultimate load. In this way, the model would continue to deform after failure and exactly record the failure mode and its initiation. As a result, the failure mode of each specimen has been accurately defined.

2.5. Nonlinear Solution and Convergence Criteria

The analysis performed accounted for geometrical and contact nonlinearities, stress stiffening and large deflections. The adopted Newton-Raphson [48] solution method implied incremental loading and solved the model for unknown displacements. According to this method, the incremental loading has been applied to the system and then a nonlinear system of equations was solved to derive the incremental displacements. The tangential stiffness matrix was updated after each iteration. The convergence procedure was force-based and thus considered absolute.

More specifically, this method solved a series of successive linear approximations. The finite element discretisation procedure resulted in three main matrices of coefficients, unknowns (degree of freedom displacements-DOFs) and loads. The problem is generally considered as nonlinear when the coefficient matrix itself is a function of unknown DOFs. Equations (7–10) exhibit the Newton-Raphson adopted procedure, where $[K]$ is the coefficient matrix, $\{u\}$ is the vector of unknown DOF values, $\{F^a\}$ is the vector of applied loads, $[K_i^T]$ is the Jacobian matrix of coefficients (tangent matrix), $\{F_i^{nr}\}$ is the vector of restoring loads corresponding to the element internal loads, $\{\Delta u_i\}$ is the incremental displacements in the current iteration, i is the subscript representing the current iteration and $\{R\}$ is the residual load vector. Specifically, Equation (7) is the original form and Equation (8) is the modified form proposed by Bathe et al. [49]

$$[K]\{u\} = \{F^{\alpha}\} \tag{7}$$

$$\left[K_i^T\right]\{\Delta u_i\} = \{F^{\alpha}\} - \{F_i^{nr}\} \tag{8}$$

$$u_{i+1} = \{u_i\} - \{\Delta u_i\} \tag{9}$$

$$\{R\} = \{F^{\alpha}\} - \{F^{nr}\} \tag{10}$$

The solution of the problem derives from the following numerical procedure:

(a)   The first load step is considered as the load target that the model has to converge on $\{F^a\}$.

(b)   The first incremental load vector is applied $\{F_i^{nr}\}$. It is a vector of restoring loads that corresponds to the internal loads of elements.

(c)   DOF values are assumed from the restoring displacements $\{u_i\}$, which derive from the result of the previously convergence attempt or they are equal to zero at the first substep.

(d)   The software computes the Jacobean of the coefficient matrix based on the assumed DOFs $[K_i^T]$.

(e)   Having obtained the incremental loads $\{F_i^{nr}\}$, the incremental displacement can now be calculated using Equation (8).

(f)   The incremental displacements will be added to the assumed values of displacements and form the second iteration shown in Equation (9). This creates a new vector of restoring loads based on the assumed values of displacements.

This iterative process ends when both the incremental displacement and the residual load vector $\{R\}$ lie in the convergence criteria. Then, the new target will be set on the next substep. In this study, 200 iterations are considered in each sub-step to achieve convergence. For example, a single iteration is depicted graphically in Figure 10a. Figure 10b shows the next iteration of this example.

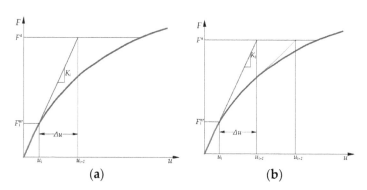

(a)   (b)

Figure 10. Example of Newton-Raphson Solution (**a**) First Iteration (**b**) Next Iteration.

3. Validation Results

3.1. In-Plane Shear Loading

3.1.1. Validation with First Set of Specimens

The accuracy of the developed finite element models was first verified using the experimental results reported by Epackachi et al. [22] because they comprehensively describe foundation detailing making the comparison of detailed and simplified models feasible. They tested four double-steel plate concrete walls under displacement-controlled cyclic loading. The dimensions and material properties of the specimens are summarised in Table 1, where H is the height of the wall, L is the length of the wall, t is the thickness of the wall, t_p is the thickness of steel plates, s is the spacing of the headed studs, b is the spacing of tie bars, f_y is the measured yield stress of steel plates and f_c is the concrete compressive strength. In specimens with headed studs and tie bars, the slenderness ratio of the faceplates is equal to the minimum value of s/t_p and b/t_p. The design variables considered in the testing program included spacing of the connectors and a reinforcement ratio equal to $2t_p/t$ for the tested specimens, which included only two steel faceplates. Two of the specimens had only headed studs, whereas the rest had also transverse tie bars, which have been modelled using beam elements.

Table 1. Experimental Database—Details of tested specimens.

Loading	Specimen	H mm	L mm	t mm	t_p mm	s_x mm	s_y mm	b mm	Slenderness	f_y MPa	f_c MPa
	NS50	960	960	246.4	3.2	160.0	160.0	-	50.0	299.1	23.5
	NS75	960	960	246.4	3.2	240.0	240.0	-	75.0	299.1	23.5
	NS100	1280	960	246.4	3.2	320.0	320.0	-	100.0	299.1	23.5
	NS20	640	640	200.0	3.2	65.0	65.0	-	20.0	287.0	31.2
	NS30	640	640	200.0	3.2	97.0	97.0	-	30.0	287.0	31.2
	NS40	640	640	200.0	3.2	130.0	130.0	-	40.0	287.0	31.2
	NS50	640	640	200.0	3.2	162.0	162.0	-	50.0	287.0	31.2
	C24/490-T6	380	280	250.0	6.0	90.0	120.0	-	20.0	428.5	24.0
	C24/490-T6	500	370	250.0	6.0	135.0	180.0	-	30.0	428.5	24.0
	C24/490-T6	620	460	250.0	6.0	180.0	240.0	-	40.0	428.5	24.0
Axial	H16/490-T6	380	280	250.0	6.0	90.0	120.0	-	20.0	428.5	16.0
Compression	H16/490-T6	500	370	250.0	6.0	135.0	180.0	-	30.0	428.5	16.0
	H16/490-T6	620	460	250.0	6.0	180.0	240.0	-	40.0	428.5	16.0
	TS1-0.6	490	280	139.7	4.7	70.0	70.0	-	15.0	275.0	16.0
	TS1-0.8	552	276	137.2	4.7	92.0	92.0	-	19.7	275.0	16.0
	TS1-1.2	560	280	152.4	4.7	140.0	140.0	-	30.0	275.0	16.0
	TS1-1.4	486	324	146.1	4.7	162.0	162.0	-	34.7	275.0	16.0
	TS1-1.6	552	368	146.1	4.7	184.0	184.0	-	39.4	275.0	16.0
	TS2-0.6	495	330	174.9	4.9	82.6	82.6	-	16.9	259.2	30.3
	TS2-0.8	495	330	174.9	4.9	111.1	111.1	-	22.7	259.2	30.3
	TS2-1.0	495	330	174.9	4.9	136.5	136.5	-	27.9	259.2	32.2
	TS2-1.2	495	330	174.9	4.9	165.1	165.1	-	33.7	259.2	32.2
Shear&	S2-15-NN	1200	1200	200.0	2.3	70.0	70.0	-	30.4	340.0	41.6
Axial	S2-30-NN	1200	1200	200.0	2.3	70.0	70.0	-	30.4	340.0	42.0
	S3-15-NN	1200	1200	200.0	3.2	100.0	100.0	-	31.3	351.0	41.6
	S3-30-NN	1200	1200	200.0	3.2	100.0	100.0	-	31.3	351.0	40.1
	S2-00-NN	1200	1200	200.0	2.3	70.0	70.0	-	30.4	340.0	42.2
	S3-00-NN	1200	1200	200.0	3.2	100.0	100.0	-	31.3	351.0	41.9
In-plane	S4-00-NN	1200	1200	200.0	4.5	135.0	135.0	-	30.0	346.0	42.8
Shear	SC1	1524	1524	305.0	4.8	102.0	102.0	305.0	21.3	262.0	30.3
	SC2	1524	1524	305.0	4.8	-	-	152.0	31.7	262.0	30.3
	SC3	1524	1524	229.0	4.8	114.0	114.0	229.0	23.8	262.0	36.5
	SC4	1524	1524	229.0	4.8	-	-	114.0	23.8	262.0	36.5

The validation procedure has been conducted for all the specimens, but since the general trend is the same, for brevity, only the load-displacement curves obtained from the FEM analysis of two specimens are plotted with respect to the test results, in Figures 11 and 12. These figures include comparisons of the lateral force-lateral displacement curves predicted by the simplified and detailed numerical models with the corresponding experimental curves for specimens SC1 and SC4, respectively. As shown, the detailed models accounted for the foundation flexibility and successfully predicted the experimentally measured stiffness of the test specimens. On the other hand, the simplified models overestimated the stiffness but predicted the shear capacity and failure mechanism of the specimens with acceptable accuracy as shown in Figure 13. However, the simulation of a foundation is not always feasible since it depends on the overall design of the composite wall and the soil properties. For this reason, the simplified models with a fixed base could be used to preliminarily estimate their lateral load capacity using finite element analysis and as soon as detailing information is provided; the detailed models can be used for the calculation of the composite wall stiffness.

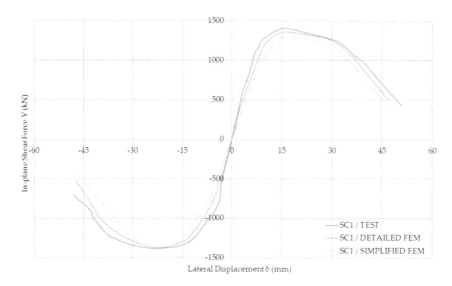

Figure 11. In-plane shear force—Lateral displacement Curves of SC1.

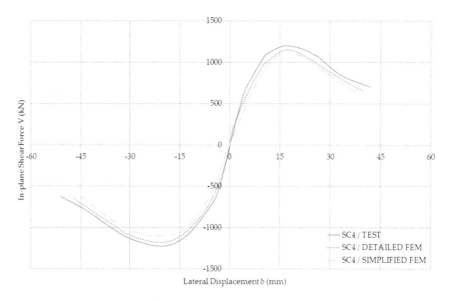

Figure 12. In-plane shear force—Lateral displacement Curves of SC4.

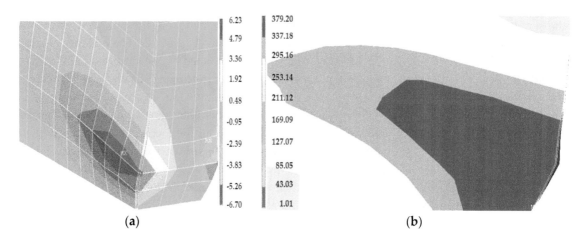

(a)   (b)

Figure 13. (a) Out-of-plane displacement (mm) of the analysed specimen SC4; (b) Failure mode of analysed specimen SC4—Distribution of Von Mises stresses (MPa) at the right toe of the wall.

3.1.2. Validation with Second Set of Specimens

Ozaki et al. [11] tested nine double-steel plate concrete panels under cyclic in-plane shear, but two of them had additional stiffeners such as partitioning webs. As a result, only seven test specimens have been used for the validation studies listed in Table 1. There were three groups of specimens S2, S3 and S4 with reinforcement ratios of 2.3%, 3.4% and 4.5%, respectively. Specimens S2-00-NN, S3-00-NN and S2-00-NN were subjected to pure in-plane shear with no axial compression. They are included in Table 1 for comparison with specimens S2-15-NN and S3-15-NN that were subjected to 353 kN of axial compression producing an average compressive stress of 1.47 MPa and specimens S2-30-NN and S3-30-NN that were subjected to 706 kN of axial compression producing an average compressive stress of 2.94 MPa.

The in-plane shear force and shear strain response results from the finite element analysis have been compared with the experimental results as shown in Figures 14–17. As shown, there is an excellent agreement between experimental and numerical results. Therefore, it has been concluded that the simplified finite element model can predict the behaviour of all the composite walls with or without axial forces with reasonable accuracy.

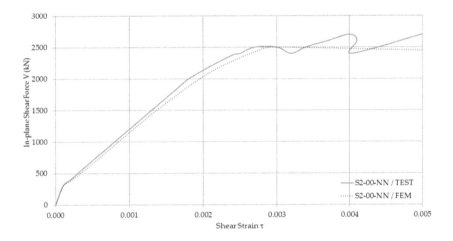

Figure 14. In-plane shear force—Shear strain Curves of S2-00-NN.

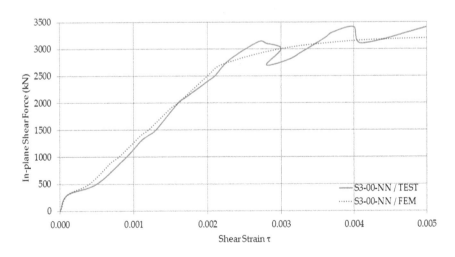

Figure 15. In-plane shear force—Shear strain Curves of S3-00-NN.

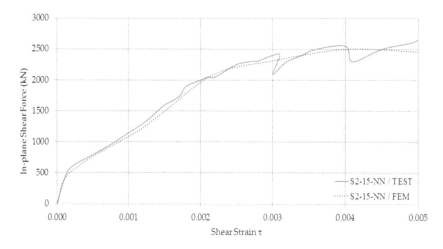

Figure 16. In-plane shear force—Shear strain Curves of S2-15-NN.

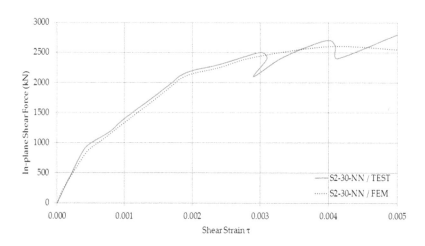

Figure 17. In-plane shear force—Shear strain Curves of S2-30-NN.

Finally, it was concluded that since the numerical results showed good agreement with experimental data [11,22]; the modelling approach reasonably predicts the in-plane shear (seismic performance) of composite walls.

3.2. Compression Loading

The finite element models were validated using the experimental results reported by Akiyama et al. [25], Usami et al. [9], Choi et al. [26] and Zhang [27]. The dimensions and material properties of the specimens are summarised in Table 1. The comparison of experimental and numerical results including yield and ultimate strength and critical displacements are summarised in Table 2 for the first seven specimens listed in Table 1. Additionally, experimental and numerical load-deflection curves are compared in Figures 18–23 for the remaining specimens. More specifically, the comparison between the three different mesh densities is presented in Figures 18–23 and the comparison between the three different friction coefficients is presented in Figures 24–27.

Table 2. Experimental versus numerical modelling results.

Specimen	Results	P_y (kN)	P_u (kN)	δ_y (mm)	δ_u (mm)	Failure Mode
NS50	Test	5884.0	7256.9	1.88	4.25	
	ANSYS	**5852.2**	**7132.1**	**1.85**	**4.08**	
	Error%	0.54	1.72	1.60	4.00	
NS75	Test	5001.4	7011.8	1.5	3.5	(a) buckling of surface plates (b) yielding of side plates
	ANSYS	**4976.5**	**6915.3**	**1.48**	**3.43**	(c) ultimate strength (d) rapid loss of load carrying capacity
	Error%	0.50	1.38	1.33	2.00	
NS100	Test	5393.7	7364.8	2.38	4.63	
	ANSYS	**5371.2**	**7245.1**	**2.35**	**4.59**	
	Error%	0.42	1.63	1.26	0.86	
NS20	Test	3210.0	5730.2	0.7	2.58	
	ANSYS	**3189.3**	**5620.1**	**0.66**	**2.41**	
	Error%	0.64	1.92	5.71	6.59	
NS30	Test	4710.0	5470.0	2.17	3.28	
	ANSYS	**4683.3**	**5392.1**	**2.14**	**3.16**	
	Error%	0.57	1.42	1.38	3.66	
NS40	Test	4940.0	4999.8	3.3	3.65	extensive local buckling & concrete crushing
	ANSYS	**4916.3**	**4879.9**	**3.26**	**3.58**	
	Error%	0.48	2.40	1.21	1.92	
NS50	Test	4120.0	5050.0	3.2	4.18	
	ANSYS	**4101.1**	**4945.9**	**3.19**	**4.11**	
	Error%	0.46	2.06	0.31	1.67	

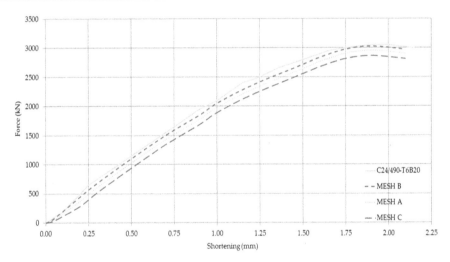

Figure 18. Axial force—Shortening Curves of C24/490-T6B20 (Comparison of mesh densities).

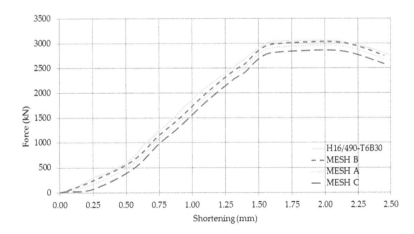

Figure 19. Axial force—Shortening Curves of H16/490-T6B30 (Comparison of mesh densities).

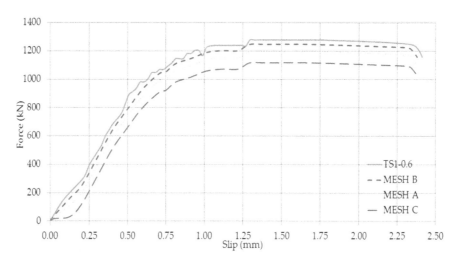

Figure 20. Axial force—Slip Curves of TS1-0.6 (Comparison of mesh densities).

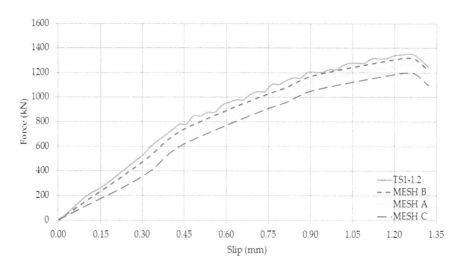

Figure 21. Axial force—Slip Curves of TS1-1.2 (Comparison of mesh densities).

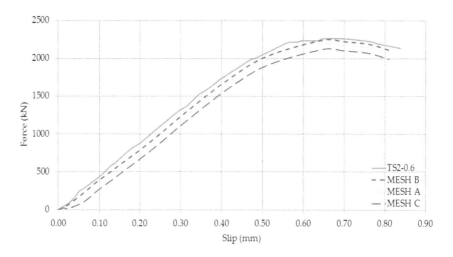

Figure 22. Axial force—Slip Curves of TS2-0.6 (Comparison of mesh densities).

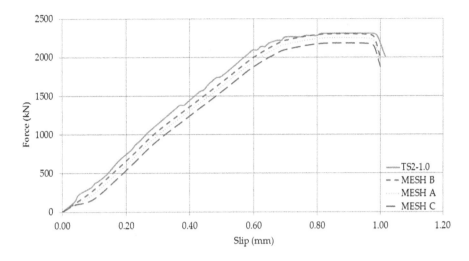

Figure 23. Axial force—Slip Curves of TS2-1.0 (Comparison of mesh densities).

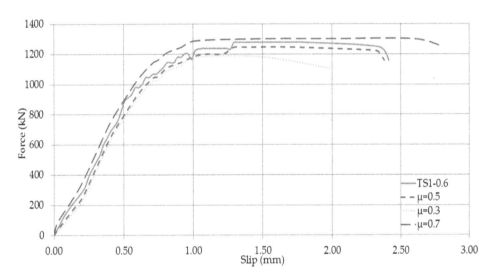

Figure 24. Axial force—Slip Curves of TS1-0.6 (Comparison of friction coefficients).

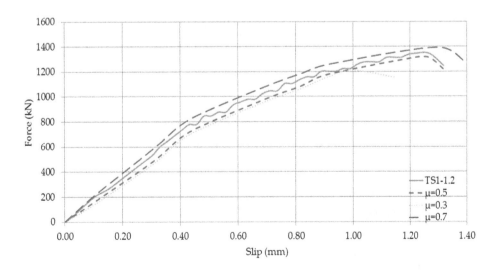

Figure 25. Axial force—Slip Curves of TS1-1.2 (Comparison of friction coefficients).

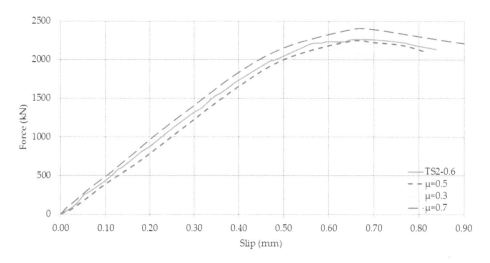

Figure 26. Axial force—Slip Curves of TS2-0.6 (Comparison of friction coefficients).

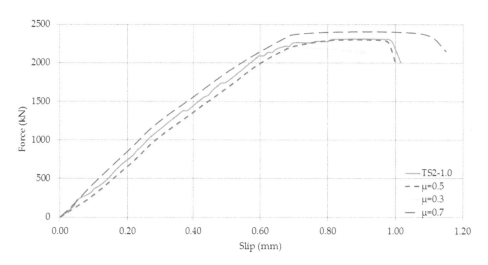

Figure 27. Axial force—Slip Curves of TS2-1.0 (Comparison of friction coefficients).

The validation of the numerical model has been conducted using all the developed meshing configurations A, B and C as shown in Figures 18–23. All three simulations predicted almost identical results. Noticeable differences have been observed in the ultimate loads and slips, which are within the margin of error expected for a numerical simulation. Nevertheless, it was noted that excellent results were obtained when the medium coarse Mesh B has been used. This may be attributed to the fact that several damage processes result in concrete damage and deformation of headed stud steel anchors. As a result, Mesh B has been adopted for the finite element analysis.

The comparison between the three different friction coefficients is presented in Figures 24–27. It is evident that the differences in the elastic range are negligible. Considering the post-elastic stage of the specimens, it is evident that a friction coefficient equal to 0.3 resulted in less capacity and ductility than the experimental one. In contrast, the capacity and the corresponding displacement declined as the friction coefficient augmented. Finally, a constant friction coefficient of 0.5 was considered as ideal for the simulation of the steel-concrete interface.

The results from these comparisons clearly prove that the numerical model perfectly predicts the elastic response of each specimen. However, after yielding the numerical results show a slightly different behaviour in the nonlinear part. It is observable that after yielding, the experimental load-deflection behaviour is slightly stiffer than the numerical results. This behaviour is attributed to the simplified strain hardening behaviour of steel that was considered in the finite element modelling.

Furthermore, the numerical results of this research have been compared with analysis results reported by Vazouras and Avdelas [23] in order to identify the importance of modelling the slenderness of the wall with the use of shear connectors and the unilateral contact between the steel plates and concrete with the use of contact elements on the seismic performance of double-steel plate concrete walls. In general, the assumption of a perfect bond between the steel plates and the infill concrete did not significantly affect the pre-peak strength response of the composite walls in the range of steel plate slenderness studied in this research [23]. However, the numerical post-peak resistance was less than the experimental value when a perfect bond was assumed. This fact is mainly attributed to premature fracture of the faceplates caused by the assumption of a perfect bond.

4. Parametric Analysis

4.1. Design Procedure

The objective of the parametric analysis was to investigate the influence of important parameters on the seismic behaviour of composite walls. This section summarises the results of a parametric study on the monotonic and cyclic lateral response of sixteen composite walls used to investigate the effects of the aspect ratio H/L, reinforcement ratio ρ, the yield strength of the faceplates f_y and the uniaxial compressive strength of concrete f_c on the in-plane response of SC walls. The geometric reinforcement ratio ρ is defined as the steel area A_s to the concrete area A_c.

The dimensions and material properties of specimens in the parametric analysis are described analytically in Table 3. Two aspect ratios 0.75 and 2.0 have been considered to study the behaviour of low and high aspect ratio walls by setting the length L of the specimens equal to 2000 mm and varying the height H. Steel plates of S235 ($f_y = 235$ MPa) and S355 ($f_y = 355$ MPa) were selected to represent low and high values of yield strength, respectively. The ultimate steel tensile strength was calculated based on EC3 provisions [50] as 360 MPa and 510 MPa. The elastic modulus of steel was taken as equal to 210,000 MPa. The uniaxial concrete compressive strength was considered equal to 30 MPa and 40 MPa to represent low and high strength concrete, respectively.

Table 3. Dimensions and material properties of specimens in the parametric study.

Specimen	Variables						
	H (mm)	t (mm)	t_p (mm)	f_y (MPa)	f_c (MPa)	Aspect Ratio (H/L)	Reinf. Ratio (%)
AE1	1500	200	4	235	30	0.75	4.6
AE2	1500	200	4	235	40	0.75	4.6
AE3	1500	200	4	355	30	0.75	4.6
AE4	1500	200	4	355	40	0.75	4.6
AE5	1500	200	8	235	30	0.75	9.6
AE6	1500	200	8	235	40	0.75	9.6
AE7	1500	200	8	355	30	0.75	9.6
AE8	1500	200	8	355	40	0.75	9.6
AE9	4000	200	4	235	30	2.0	4.6
AE10	4000	200	4	235	40	2.0	4.6
AE11	4000	200	4	355	30	2.0	4.6
AE12	4000	200	4	355	40	2.0	4.6
AE13	4000	200	8	235	30	2.0	9.6
AE14	4000	200	8	235	40	2.0	9.6
AE15	4000	200	8	355	30	2.0	9.6
AE16	4000	200	8	355	40	2.0	9.6

In order to generate the cyclic behaviour of the composite shear wall, loading was simulated by applying the displacement control scheme rather than direct loading. A displacement-controlled, reversed cyclic loading protocol was used according to the recommendations of ACI 374.1-05 [51]. This loading protocol is based on imposing displacements proportional to the yield displacement of each specimen. For this reason, a monotonic analysis was conducted first up to the failure of each specimen and then the specimens were subjected to a cyclic alternating lateral force. Two additional loading steps at displacements equal to 10% and 75% of the reference displacement were added to the proposed deformation history to capture the wall response before and after cracking of the infill concrete. Additionally, the loading procedure was extended for each specimen by two more load steps after the failure load. Figure 28 presents the loading protocol used to test the first specimen. The loading protocol consisted of nineteen load steps with two cycles in each step. In each loading cycle, a push was imposed first, followed by a pull, where "push" was defined as the loading in the positive direction and "pull" was defined as the loading in the negative direction.

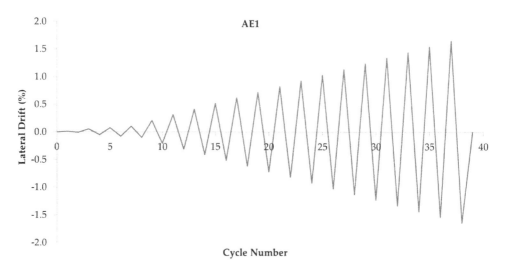

Figure 28. Cyclic loading protocol of specimen AE1.

Key analysis results, in terms of monotonic and cyclic loading, are summarised in Tables 4 and 5, respectively. The total shear force of the wall at yield V_y, the maximum shear force V_u and the failure lateral load V_f are included in the analysis results. Additionally, the yield displacement δ_y, the displacement at the ultimate shear force δ_u, the displacement at failure δ_f and the corresponding drift ratios are listed in Tables 4 and 5. The criteria used for the definition of the ultimate state and failure mode of each specimen were based on the degradation of the in-plane shear capacity. Specifically, failure was defined at 80% of the peak load [52], since it provided an excellent indication of the excessive deformation, mainly out-of-plane, at the bottom of the wall and excessive concrete cracking (especially during cyclic loading) and crushing.

Table 4. Monotonic analysis results of the parametric study.

Specimen	Yielding Point			Ultimate Point			Failure Point		
	V_y (kN)	δ_y (mm)	d_y (%)	V_u (kN)	δ_u (mm)	d_u (%)	V_{uf} (kN)	δ_f (mm)	d_f (%)
AE1	1192.1	1.54	0.103	2286.4	4.68	0.31	1829.1	21.60	1.44
AE2	1659.2	1.02	0.068	2851.3	5.04	0.34	2281.0	21.90	1.46
AE3	2197.4	2.24	0.149	3305.0	6.30	0.42	2644.0	20.55	1.37
AE4	2717.9	2.05	0.136	4261.4	6.66	0.44	3409.1	21.15	1.41
AE5	2023.9	1.03	0.069	4225.8	4.91	0.33	3380.6	20.40	1.36
AE6	2571.1	1.38	0.092	5386.8	6.35	0.42	4309.4	20.70	1.38
AE7	3345.0	2.70	0.180	7219.4	7.86	0.52	5775.5	19.35	1.29
AE8	3727.6	2.40	0.160	8233.6	7.77	0.52	6586.9	19.95	1.33
AE9	306.9	3.07	0.077	507.1	35.17	0.88	405.7	73.20	1.83
AE10	385.8	2.99	0.075	564.9	39.99	1.00	451.9	76.80	1.92
AE11	431.5	9.13	0.228	965.3	51.19	1.28	772.2	70.40	1.76
AE12	507.1	7.12	0.178	1045.3	52.06	1.30	836.3	75.20	1.88
AE13	533.8	6.00	0.150	1174.3	40.86	1.02	939.5	70.00	1.75
AE14	649.4	5.74	0.143	1290.0	49.00	1.22	1032.0	73.60	1.84
AE15	840.7	11.62	0.290	2157.4	71.65	1.79	1725.9	67.20	1.68
AE16	916.3	10.54	0.264	2410.9	71.38	1.78	1928.7	72.00	1.80

Table 5. Cyclic analysis results of the parametric study.

Specimen	Yielding Point			Ultimate Point				Failure Point			
	V_y (kN)		δ_y (mm)	V_u (kN)		δ_u (mm)		V_{uf} (kN)		δ_f (mm)	
	+	-		+	-	+	-	+	-	+	-
AE1	1222.3	1185.6	1.54	2289.6	2175.1	4.62	4.62	1831.7	1740.1	21.56	21.56
AE2	1692.9	1642.5	1.02	2854.4	2739.4	5.10	5.10	2283.5	2191.6	21.42	21.42
AE3	2255.2	2188.2	2.24	3309.7	3144.2	6.50	6.50	2647.8	2515.4	20.10	20.10
AE4	2775.7	2693.2	2.05	4266.3	4095.7	6.88	6.88	3413.1	3276.6	20.66	20.66
AE5	2054.9	1993.8	1.03	4231.7	4062.4	5.03	5.01	3385.4	3250.0	20.07	20.07
AE6	2597.5	2520.3	1.38	5394.3	5178.5	6.53	6.52	4315.4	4142.8	20.34	20.34
AE7	3399.6	3298.5	2.70	7229.5	6940.4	8.07	8.06	5783.6	5552.3	19.04	19.04
AE8	3769.7	3657.6	2.40	8245.1	7915.3	7.98	7.98	6596.1	6332.3	19.60	19.60
AE9	290.0	303.8	3.07	489.9	470.3	33.77	37.15	392.9	376.2	70.61	77.67
AE10	365.7	379.9	2.99	547.4	525.5	38.87	42.76	440.6	420.4	74.75	78.5
AE11	407.2	426.2	9.13	934.9	897.5	50.06	55.07	748.9	718.0	68.43	70.5
AE12	481.1	498.9	7.12	1012.8	972.2	50.86	55.94	818.3	777.8	73.32	77.7
AE13	511.6	529.4	6.00	1149.2	1103.2	39.97	43.97	922.0	882.6	67.20	69.2
AE14	622.8	643.0	5.74	1253.3	1203.2	47.91	52.71	1005.9	962.6	70.58	76.2
AE15	805.7	832.2	11.62	2100.6	2016.6	70.07	77.07	1699.6	1613.3	64.38	66.3
AE16	876.9	906.2	10.54	2343.2	2249.5	69.74	76.71	1890.9	1799.6	69.12	74.6

4.2. Analysis Results

The first parameter evaluated was the effect of the aspect ratio on composite walls. It has been concluded that as the aspect ratio increased, the lateral load capacity and stiffness of double-steel plate concrete walls declined. Additionally, analysis results listed in Tables 4 and 5 indicate that as the aspect ratio increased, the displacement corresponding to the peak shear force and the ductility augmented. Furthermore, buckling of the steel plates in high aspect ratio walls was not detrimental to performance and had a minimal effect on the ultimate shear strength and overall performance of the specimens. Similar results were obtained for the other values of concrete strength investigated in this research.

Additionally, the effect of reinforcement ratio on the in-plane response of the double-steel plate concrete walls has been investigated. Although the reinforcement ratio had a negligible effect on the initial stiffness and ductility, it significantly affected the lateral strength, namely lower reinforcement ratios led to less lateral capacity. Furthermore, it can be seen that an increase in the aspect ratio substantially reduced the effect of other design variables on the response of SC walls. However, the displacement at the peak shear force was not substantially affected by the reinforcement ratio.

Furthermore, the effects of concrete compressive strength and steel yield strength on the in-plane response of the composite walls have been evaluated. As refers to the first parameter, the yield and ultimate strength augmented as the concrete strength increased. In fact, the aspect ratio played a critical role, since the influence of the concrete compressive strength on the peak lateral load increased as the aspect ratio decreased. Considering the second parameter, the shear load capacity soared with the increase of steel yield strength. It can be noticed that the increase of steel yield strength had a more pronounced impact on specimens with aspect ratios lower than 2.0.

Finally, the comparison of cyclic and monotonic analysis results presented in Tables 4 and 5 indicated that the difference between the capacities predicted through monotonic and cyclic analysis was negligible. This fact is mainly attributed to the exceptional post-elastic behaviour of steel. Specifically, its high tensile strength and ductility prevented the abrupt deterioration of the composite wall capacity due to the brittle behaviour of the concrete material characterised by crushing at the toes of the wall. In general, it can be concluded that a monotonic analysis can provide a good estimation of the general behaviour of composite walls. However, this conclusion should be further investigated with extensive parametric analysis.

5. Conclusions

The objective of this study was to develop a reliable three-dimensional finite element model for the nonlinear analysis of double-steel composite shear walls, focusing on the shear connection behaviour.

For this purpose, the commercial finite element software ANSYS 15.0 [24] was used. Validation studies have been undertaken using the results of four axial compression and two in-plane shear experimental programs. Measured global and local responses have been used to validate the proposed model. Additionally, the importance of including foundation flexibility in the numerical model has been addressed. Furthermore, it has been shown that the introduction of interface contact friction elements between the infill concrete and the steel plates leads to a significant changing of the results especially for the post-peak range of response.

As a result, the nonlinear behaviour of a double-steel plate concrete wall can be predicted using:

- A multilinear stress-strain curve for concrete, using user-specified material properties. In the absence of experimental data, the curve can be estimated from relations proposed by EC2 [31]. In the case of partially confined concrete, the best way for indicating the concrete crushing failure mode is by evaluating the concrete strain contour results. Considering fully confined infill concrete, the William-Warnke criterion [29] can be used as failure criterion due to multiaxial stress state.

- A multilinear stress-strain curve for steel based on the von Mises yield criterion with isotropic hardening rule. The strain-hardening branch can be efficiently calculated using the constitutive law proposed by Gattesco [34]. The shortfall in the load-bearing capacity of steel due to cyclic loading should also be accounted for.

- Two load-slip curves for modelling the behaviour of the two nonlinear springs used to model the behaviour of a single shear connector.

- Shell and solid elements to model steel faceplates, infill concrete and steel endplates, respectively.

- Contact elements to simulate the behaviour of the steel-concrete interface.

As a conclusion, using the assumptions listed above, a robust finite element model can be constructed, which has been proved to be effective in terms of predicting yield, ultimate loads, displacements and final failure modes. Finally, the developed numerical model has been used to perform a parametric analysis. The objective of the parametric analysis was to investigate the influence of important parameters on the seismic behaviour of composite walls. It has been concluded that the shear strength and lateral stiffness of double-steel composite shear walls were governed by the aspect ratio and the reinforcement ratio. Specifically, the shear strength of an SC wall augmented, as the aspect ratio decreased or as the reinforcement ratio increased.

Author Contributions: Michaela Elmatzoglou and Aris Avdelasanalysed the data; Michaela Elmatzoglou and Aris Avdelasanalysed wrote the paper.

References

1. Bruhl, J.C.; Varma, A.H.; Johnson, W.H. Design of composite SC walls to prevent perforation from missile impact. *Int. J. Impact Eng.* **2014**, *75*, 75–87. [CrossRef]

2. Sener, K.C.; Varma, A.H. Steel-plate composite walls: Experimental database and design for out-of-plane shear. *J. Constr. Steel Res.* **2014**, *100*, 197–210. [CrossRef]

3. Varma, A.H.; Zhang, K.; Chi, H.; Booth, P.N.; Baker, T. In-plane shear behaviour of SC composite walls: theory vs. experiment. In Proceedings of the 21th International Conference on Structural Mechanics in Reactor Technology (SMiRT21), International Association for Structural Mechanics in Reactor Technology (IASMiRT), New Delhi, India, 6–11 November 2011.

4. Varma, A.H.; Malushte, S.R.; Sener, K.C.; Lai, Z. Steel-plate composite (SC) walls for safety related nuclear facilities: Design for in-plane forces and out-of-plane moments. *Nucl. Eng. Des.* **2014**, *269*, 240–249. [CrossRef]

5. American Institute of Steel Construction. Specification for safety-related steel structures for nuclear facilities/Supplement No. 1; AISC N690-12s1. Available online: https://www.aisc.org/globalassets/aisc/

publications/standards/specification-for-safety-related-steel-structures-for-nuclear-facilities-in-cluding-supplement-no.-1-ansiaisc-n690-12-anisaisc-n690s1015.pdf (accessed on 21 February 2017).

6. American Institute of Steel Construction. Seismic provisions for structural steel buildings, Public ballot No. 2; AISC 341-16. Available online: http://www.alacero.org/sites/default/files/u16/bc_11-15_3.2_aisc_341-16_draft_1_marzo_2015.pdf (accessed on 21 February 2017).

7. Vecchio, F.J.; McQuade, I. Towards improved modeling of steel-concrete composite wall elements. *Nucl. Eng. Des.* **2011**, *241*, 2629–2642. [CrossRef]

8. Wong, P.S.; Vecchio, F.J.; Trommels, H. *VecTor2 and Formworks User's Manual*, 2nd ed.; University of Toronto: Toronto, ON, Canada, 2013.

9. Usami, S.; Akiyama, H.; Narikawa, M.; Hara, K.; Takeuchi, M.; Sasaki, N. Study on a concrete filled structure for nuclear power plants (Part 2): Compressive loading tests on wall members. In Proceedings of the 13th International Conference on Structural Mechanics in Reactor Technology (SMiRT13), International Association for Structural Mechanics in Reactor Technology (IASMiRT), Porto Alegre, Brazil, 13–18 August 1995.

10. Sasaki, N.; Akiyama, H.; Narikawa, M.; Hara, K.; Takeuchi, M.; Usami, S. Study on a concrete filled steel structure for nuclear power plants (Part 2): Shear and bending loading tests on wall member. In Proceedings of the 13th International Conference on Structural Mechanics in Reactor Technology (SMiRT13), International Association for Structural Mechanics in Reactor Technology (IASMiRT), Porto Alegre, Brazil, 13–18 August 1995.

11. Ozaki, M.; Akita, S.; Niwa, N.; Matsuo, I.; Usami, S. Study on steel-plate reinforced concrete bearing wall for nuclear power plants part 1: shear and bending loading tests of SC walls. In Proceedings of the 16th International Conference on Structural Mechanics in Reactor Technology (SMiRT16), International Association for Structural Mechanics in Reactor Technology (IASMiRT), Washington, DC, USA, 12 August 2001.

12. Zhou, J.; Mo, Y.L.; Sun, X.; Li, J. Seismic performance of composite steel plate reinforced concrete shear wall. In Proceedings of the 12th International Conference on Engineering, Science, Construction, and Operations in Challenging Environments-Earth and Space, Honolulu, Hawaii, USA, 14–17 March 2010.

13. Mansour, M.; Hsu, T. Behaviour of Reinforced Concrete Elements under Cyclic Shear I: Experiments. *J. Struct. Eng.* **2005**, *131*, 44–53. [CrossRef]

14. Mansour, M.; Hsu, T. Behaviour of Reinforced Concrete Elements under Cyclic Shear II: Theoretical Model. *J. Struct. Eng.* **2005**, *131*, 54–65. [CrossRef]

15. Zhong, J.X. *Model-Based Simulation of Reinforced Concrete Plane Stress Structures*; University of Houston: Houston, TX, USA, 2005.

16. Ma, X.; Nie, J.; Tao, M. Nonlinear finite-element analysis of double-skin steel-concrete composite shear wall structures. *IACSIT J. Eng. Technol.* **2013**, *5*, 648–652.

17. Rafiei, S.; Hossain, K.M.A.; Lachemi, M.; Behdinan, K. Profiled sandwich composite wall with high performance concrete subjected to monotonic shear. *J. Constr. Steel Res.* **2015**, *107*, 124–136. [CrossRef]

18. SIMULIA. *ABAQUS Analysis User's Manual*; Version 6.12; Dassault Systèmes Simulia Corp.: Providence, RI, USA, 2012.

19. Ali, A.; Kim, D.; Cho, S.G. Modeling of nonlinear cyclic load behaviour of I-shaped composite steel-concrete shear walls of nuclear power plants. *Nucl. Eng. Technol.* **2013**, *45*, 89–98. [CrossRef]

20. Kurt, E.G.; Varma, A.H.; Booth, P.; Whittaker, A.S. SC wall piers and basemat connections: Numerical investigation of behaviour and design. In Proceedings of the 22nd International Conference on Structural Mechanics in Reactor Technology (SMiRT22), International Association for Structural Mechanics in Reactor Technology (IASMiRT), San Francisco, CA, USA, 18–23 August 2013.

21. Livermore Software Technology Corporation (LSTC). LS-DYNA. *Keyword User's Manual*, Version 971 R6.0.0; Available online: http://lstc.com/pdf/ls-dyna_971_manual_k.pdf (accessed on 21 February 2017).

22. Epackachi, S.; Nguyen, N.H.; Kurt, E.G.; Whittaker, A.S.; Varma, A.H. In-Plane Seismic Behaviour of Rectangular Steel-Plate Composite Wall Piers. *J. Struct. Eng.* **2014**, *1*, 1–9.

23. Vazouras, K.; Avdelas, A. Behaviour of composite steel walls-Numerical Analysis & Preliminary Findings. In Proceedings of the 7th European Conference on Steel and Composite Structures (EUROSTEEL), Naples, Italy, 10–12 September 2014.

24. ANSYS Inc. *ANSYS Mechanical User's Guide*; Version 15.0; ANSYS Inc, Southpointe: Canonsburg, PA, USA, 2013.

25. Akiyama, H.; Sekimoto, H.; Fukihara, M.; Nakanishi, K.; Hara, K. A Compression and Shear Loading Tests of Concrete Filled Steel Bearing Wall. In Proceedings of the Transactions of the 11th International Conference on Structural Mechanics in Reactor Technology (SMiRT-11), Tokyo, Japan, 18–23 August 1991.

26. Choi, B.J.; Kang, C.K.; Park, H.Y. Strength and behaviour of steel plate–concrete wall structures using ordinary and eco-oriented cement concrete under axial compression. *Thin-Walled Struct.* **2014**, *84*, 313–324. [CrossRef]

27. Zhang, K. Axial Compression Behaviour and Partial Composite Action of SC Walls in Safety-Related Nuclear Facilities. Ph.D. Dissertation, Purdue University, West Lafayette, IN, USA, 2014.

28. ANSYS Inc. *ANSYS Mechanical APDL Element Reference*, Version 15.0; ANSYS Inc, Southpointe: Canonsburg, PA, USA, 2013.

29. William, K.J.; Warnke, E.D. Constitutive model for the triaxial behaviour of concrete. In Proceedings of the International Association for Bridge and Structural Engineering, ISMES-Bergamo, Italy, 17–19 May 1974.

30. Barbosa, A.F.; Ribeiro, G.O. Analysis of Reinforced Concrete Structures Using Ansys Nonlinear Concrete Model. *Comput. Mech. New Trends Appl.* **1998**, *1998*, 1–7.

31. European Committee for Standardization. *Eurocode 2—Design of Concrete Structures, Part 1-1: General Rules and Rules for Buildings*; European Committee for Standardization (CEN): Brussels, Belgium, 2004.

32. Ellobody, E.; Young, B.; Lam, D. Behaviour of normal and high strength concrete-filled compact steel tube circular stub columns. *J. Constr. Steel Res.* **2006**, *62*, 706–715. [CrossRef]

33. Lee, P.S.; Noh, H.C. Inelastic buckling behaviour of steel members under reversed cyclic loading. *Eng. Struct.* **2010**, *32*, 2579–2595. [CrossRef]

34. Gattesco, N. Analytical modeling of nonlinear behaviour of composite beams with deformable connection. *J. Constr. Steel Res.* **1999**, *52*, 195–218. [CrossRef]

35. Tsavdaridis, K.D. Seismic Analysis of Steel-Concrete Composite Buildings: Numerical Modeling. *Encycl. Earthq. Eng.* **2014**. [CrossRef]

36. Wan, S.; Loh, C.H.; Peng, S.Y. Experimental and theoretical study on softening and pinching effects of bridge columns. *Soil Dyn. Earthq. Eng.* **2001**, *21*, 75–81. [CrossRef]

37. White, C.S.; Bronkhorst, C.A.; Anand, L. An improved isotropic-kinematic hardening model for moderate deformation metal plasticity. *Mech. Mater.* **1990**, *10*, 127–147. [CrossRef]

38. Kojic, M.; Bathe, K.J. *Inelastic Analysis of Solids and Structures*; Springer: New York, NY, USA, 2005.

39. Ucak, A.; Tsopelas, P. Constitutive model for cyclic response of structural steels with yield plateau. *J. Struct. Eng.* **2011**, *137*, 195–206. [CrossRef]

40. European Committee for Standardization. *Eurocode 4—Design of Composite Steel and Concrete Structures, Part 1-1: General Rules and Rules for Buildings*; European Committee for Standardization (CEN): Brussels, Belgium, 2004.

41. Mistakidis, E.S.; Thomopoulos, K.; Avdelas, A.; Panagiotopoulos, P.D. Shear connectors in composite beams: A new accurate algorithm. *Thin-Walled Struct.* **1994**, *18*, 191–207. [CrossRef]

42. Panagiotopoulos, P.D.; Avdelas, A.V. A Hemivariational Inequality Approach to the Unilateral Contact Problem and Substationarity Principles. *Ing. Arch.* **1984**, *54*, 401–412. [CrossRef]

43. Queiroz, F.D.; Vellasco, P.C.G.S.; Nethercot, D.A. Finite element modelling of composite beams with full and partial shear connection. *J. Constr. Steel Res.* **2007**, *63*, 505–521. [CrossRef]

44. Ollgaard, J.G.; Slutter, R.G.; Fisher, J.W. Shear Strength of Stud Connectors in Lightweight and Normal-Weight Concrete. *AISC Eng. J.* **1971**, *10*, 55–64.

45. American Concrete Institute Committee 318 (ACI). *Building Code Requirements for Structural Concrete (ACI 318-08) and Commentary (ACI 318R-08)*; American Concrete: Farmington Hills, MI, USA, 2008.

46. Precast/Prestressed Concrete Institute (PCI). *PCI Design Handbook: Precast and Prestressed Concrete*, 7th ed.; Precast/Prestressed Concrete Institute: Chicago, IL, USA, 2010.

47. Rabbat, B.G.; Russell, H.G. Friction Coefficient of Steel on Concrete or Grout. *J. Struct. Eng.* **1985**, *111*, 505–515. [CrossRef]

48. Tsavdaridis, K.D.; Mello, C.D. Vierendeel bending study of perforated steel beams with various novel web opening shapes through nonlinear finite-element analyses. *J. Struct. Eng.* **2012**, *138*, 1214–1230. [CrossRef]

49. Bathe, K.J. *Finite Element Procedures*; Prentice-Hall: Englewood Cliffs, NJ, USA, 1996.

50. European Committee for Standardization. *Eurocode 3—Design of Steel Structures, Part 1-1: General Rules and Rules for Buildings*; European Committee for Standardization (CEN): Brussels, Belgium, 2005.

51. ACI 374 Committee. *Acceptance Criteria for Moment Frames Based on Structural Testing and Commentary*; American Concrete Institute: Farmington Hills, MI, USA, 2005.

52. Park, R. Ductility evaluation from laboratory and analytical testing. In Proceedings of the 9th World Conference on Earthquake Engineering, Tokyo-Kyoto, Japan, 2–9 August 1998.

Aerodynamic Performance of a NREL S809 Airfoil in an Air-Sand Particle Two-Phase Flow

Dimitra C. Douvi *, Dionissios P. Margaris * and Aristeidis E. Davaris

Fluid Mechanics Laboratory (FML), Mechanical Engineering and Aeronautics Department, University of Patras, GR-26500 Patras, Greece; c1.davar@gmail.com
* Correspondence: dimdouvi@gmail.com (D.C.D.); margaris@mech.upatras.gr (D.P.M.)

Academic Editor: Demos T. Tsahalis

Abstract: This paper opens up a new perspective on the aerodynamic performance of a wind turbine airfoil. More specifically, the paper deals with a steady, incompressible two-phase flow, consisting of air and two different concentrations of sand particles, over an airfoil from the National Renewable Energy Laboratory, NREL S809. The numerical simulations were performed on turbulence models for aerodynamic operations using commercial computational fluid dynamics (CFD) code. The computational results obtained for the aerodynamic performance of an S809 airfoil at various angles of attack operating at Reynolds numbers of $Re = 1 \times 10^6$ and $Re = 2 \times 10^6$ in a dry, dusty environment were compared with existing experimental data on air flow over an S809 airfoil from reliable sources. Notably, a structured mesh consisting of 80,000 cells had already been identified as the most appropriate for numerical simulations. Finally, it was concluded that sand concentration significantly affected the aerodynamic performance of the airfoil; there was an increase in the values of the predicted drag coefficients, as well as a decrease in the values of the predicted lift coefficients caused by increasing concentrations of sand particles. The region around the airfoil was studied by using contours of static pressure and discrete phase model (DPM) concentration.

Keywords: aerodynamic performance; S809; airfoil; two-phase flow; sand particles; CFD code

1. Introduction

In the last few years, renewable sources of energy have been used extensively in many applications, such as power generation. Renewable sources of energy are significantly superior to fossil energy, due to the fact that they are free and abundant and have a low impact on the environment. Specifically, wind energy is becoming more important every year and, therefore, wind power generators have attracted a great deal of attention from research teams in pursuing optimal aerodynamic performance.

The aerodynamic performance of wind turbine blades can be affected by many conditions, such as sand concentration in dry, dusty environments. Although much research has been conducted on the detrimental effects of certain meteorological phenomena, to the authors' best knowledge, very few publications are available in the literature that discuss the issue of aerodynamic influences due to sand particles in the air.

Nowadays, computational fluid dynamics can solve complex flow problems, such as an air–sand particle two-phase flow problem. Additional transport equations for the secondary phase are solved using the CFD code and the interaction terms by which the mass, momentum, and energy exchanges between the phases can be handled.

For several years, great effort has been devoted to the study of the aerodynamic performance of wind turbine airfoils in air flow. One of the first examples of CFD calculations of the aerodynamic characteristics of an S809 airfoil was presented by Wolfe and Ochs [1]. In particular, Wolfe and Ochs [1] studied a steady-state laminar flow over an S809 airfoil using the commercial code CFD-ACE [2].

By comparing the computed pressure and aerodynamic coefficients with wind tunnel data from Delft University, it was revealed that the transition point from laminar to turbulent flow should be correctly modeled to ensure that the simulations for attached flow are accurate, and that the standard k–ε turbulence model is not suitable at angles of attack with flow separation.

In 2006, Gupta and Gordon Leishman [3] modified the Leishman–Beddoes dynamic stall model in order to represent the unsteady aerodynamic behavior of the S809 airfoil for wind turbine applications, and they found that there was a good agreement between the predictions and experimental data for various angle of attack time histories. The results obtained suggest that the Leishman–Beddoes model coupled with a lifting-line model is able to predict the unsteady behavior of airfoil sections in attached flow, light stall, and deep dynamic stall, with knowledge of the static stall characteristics.

Qu et al. [4] have demonstrated that the Reynolds number has a direct impact on the aerodynamic performance of a wind turbine airfoil. More specifically, numerical simulations and experiments were used to predict the two-dimensional flow over an NREL S809 airfoil, and it was observed that, at Reynolds numbers varying from 1.5×10^4 to 2×10^5, both drag and lift coefficients experience great changes, while at Reynolds numbers from 2×10^5 to 5×10^6 the changes are smoother and very small.

Later, a numerical simulation of transition effect on the aerodynamic performance of an S809 airfoil was conducted by Zhong et al. [5]. First, they observed the lift and drag characteristics in multiple turbulence models, paying no attention to transition, and then they simulated the aerodynamic performance of an S809 airfoil in order to investigate the laminar-to-turbulence transition effect on the airfoil's aerodynamic characteristics and the flow separation near the trailing edge. It was observed that transition significantly influences the lift and drag characteristics, as well as the flow separation near the trailing edge.

In a recent paper Douvi and Margaris [6] presented a comparison between the aerodynamic performance of NACA 0012 and NREL S809 wind turbine airfoils at various angles of attack and operating at different Reynolds numbers using CFD code. After validating the obtained computational results by comparing them with experimental data, they concluded that the realizable k–ω turbulence model was the most appropriate to describe the aerodynamic performance of both airfoils. It was also found that the S809 airfoil was more advantageous compared to the NACA 0012 airfoil.

Several publications have also appeared in recent years documenting the impact of a two-phase flow over the aerodynamic behavior of airfoils. In 2010, Wan and Pan [7] investigated the degradation on aerodynamic performance of an airfoil due to heavy rain, using a discrete phase model in order to simulate the two-phase flow. Wan and Chou [8] reinvestigated the influence of heavy rain on the aerodynamic performance of a high lift airfoil by simulating the rain conditions with a discrete phase model combined with high lift devices' surface roughness effects. The results obtained by Wan and Pan [7] as well as by Wan and Chou [8] suggest that the degradation rate increases with the rain rate.

Next, Douvi and Margaris [9] utilized a discrete phase model on a CFD code in order to predict not only the aerodynamic characteristics of a NACA 0012 wind turbine airfoil under raining conditions, but also the flow field over the airfoil. The results emerged were compared with reliable experimental data, and after a comparison between simulations in both dry and wet conditions was conducted, it was possible to conclude that rain causes a decrease of the lift coefficient and an increase of the drag.

Another solution is described by Wu and Cao [10], who numerically simulated the flow over a NACA 0012 airfoil in heavy rain via a two-way coupled Eulerian–Lagrangian development. The predicted aerodynamic force coefficients agree well with the experimental results, and it was found that there was, approximately, a 3° rain-induced increase in stall angle of attack. Wu and Cao [10] also found that the airfoil aerodynamic efficiency degradation in a heavy rain environment was due to an uneven water film caused by the loss of boundary momentum by raindrop splashback and the effective roughening of the airfoil surface.

In 2014, Ren et al. [11] published a paper in which they described a numerical study about the influence of rime ice conditions on a NREL S809 airfoil under various temperatures and liquid water contents, operating at a Reynolds number of $Re = 1 \times 10^6$. The numerical calculations accomplished on the transition shear-stress transport (SST) turbulent model using Fluent and Lewice software under the same icing conditions. However, the researchers have arrived at the conclusion that there was not good agreement between the numerical results obtained with Lewice and the experiments.

Recently, Olivieri et al. [12] studied the behavior of small particles affected by the Basset history term force in an isotropic and homogeneous turbulent flow, utilizing an Eulerian-Lagrangian approach. It was shown that the small-scale clustering of inertial particles is reduced by the Basset history term, as well as that by consideration of the Basset history at a low Reynolds numbers there are significant changes on the balance of forces, which determine the instantaneous acceleration of the particles.

In a paper by Sardina et al. [13], a stochastic model was proposed, and direct numerical simulation and large eddy simulations (LES) were used, in order to study the constant growth of cloud droplets because of their condensation in turbulent clouds in a homogeneous isotropic turbulent flow. It was concluded that the size of the droplet distribution increases with time and also that, given enough time, every warm cloud would precipitate.

Next, the focus of De Marchis et al. [14] has been on the effect of the wall roughness on dilute wall-bounded turbulent flows, because of the interaction between inertial particles that influence the macroscopic behavior of such two-phase systems, and coherent turbulent structures characteristic of the wall region. They used DNS at friction Reynolds number $Re_\tau = 180$ combined with Lagrangian heavy particle tracking in a turbulent channel flow in order to characterize the effect of inertia on particle preferential accumulation.

However, to the authors' best knowledge, very few publications are available in the literature that discuss the issue of the impact of an air-sand particle two-phase flow on the aerodynamic performance of an airfoil. An interesting approach to this issue has been proposed by Khakpour et al. [15] in 2007, who studied the effect of sand particles on the flow over a S819 wind turbine airfoil and found that a greater particles mass flow rate results in a decrease of the pressure coefficient.

In 2009 Knopp et al. [16] presented an extension for $k-\omega$ turbulence models, based on the equivalent sand grain approach, to account for wall roughness. Briefly, the grid requirements are the same for simulation of flows over both rough surfaces and smooth walls, the skin friction for transitional roughness Reynolds numbers prediction is improved and there is no need to modify the SST $k-\omega$ model. Knopp et al. [16] indicate that this new method can be utilized to predict the aerodynamic effects of surface roughness on the flow past an airfoil in high lift conditions.

Salem et al. [17] have proposed a computational fluid dynamics (CFD) model coupled with a deposition model using the full two-dimensional Navier–Stokes equations and the SST $k-\omega$ turbulence model in order to assess the performance degradation of wind turbine NACA 63-215 airfoil operating in dusty regions. The developed model predictions were validated by being compared with existing experimental data and the flow separation was identified by the numerical results.

However, studies on the aerodynamic performance of a NREL S809 wind turbine airfoil in an air-sand particle two-phase flow are still lacking. Therefore, the aim of the present paper is to investigate the air-sand particle steady incompressible two-phase flow over a NREL S809 wind turbine airfoil at various angles of attack and operating at Reynolds numbers of $Re = 1 \times 10^6$ and $Re = 2 \times 10^6$, using CFD code. The computational results are compared with reliable existing experimental data on air flow over an S809 airfoil, in order to find the impact of sand particles on lift and drag coefficients and, consequently, the aerodynamic performance of the airfoil.

2. Discrete Two-Phase Flow over an Airfoil

Air-sand particle two-phase flow can be characterized as a discrete phase flow, which can be investigated computationally by the help of the Euler-Lagrange approach. The continuum air phase interacts with the dispersed phase, which consists of sand particles, and mass, energy, and momentum of the dispersed phase are exchanged with the air phase. Especially for air-sand particle two-phase flow, there is only momentum transfer from the air to the particles.

Regarding the discrete air-sand particle two-phase flow over an airfoil, sand particles influence plenty of characteristics, such as the shear stress factor, the pressure gradient, and the boundary layer and, as a result, the aerodynamic performance of the airfoil. More specifically, the lift force, in other words the component of the net affecting force on the airfoil acting normal to the incoming flow stream decreases, while the drag force, which is the component of the net force acting parallel to the incoming flow stream, increases due to the change in momentum caused by the reflected particles, as they impact the airfoil.

3. Computational Method

3.1. Computational Mesh

First of all, before the numerical study, the NREL S809 wind turbine airfoil profile was imported to the geometry system. Notably, the S809 is a 21% thick, laminar-flow airfoil, designed specifically for HAWT applications by Somers [18]. In 1980, the S809 profile was developed using the Eppler design code by Eppler and Somers [19,20].

Second, the meshes, as well as the boundary conditions, were created in the mesh component system, where two-dimensional and three-dimensional models can be produced using structured or unstructured meshes consisting of a variety of quadrilateral, triangular, or tetrahedral elements. The mesh is denser in regions where greater computational accuracy is needed, namely in the region close to the airfoil. These applications can be accessed from ANSYS Workbench, which combines access to ANSYS applications with utilities that manage the product workflow.

Next, it was necessary to choose the most appropriate structured mesh; in other words, to conduct a grid independence study. In general, as more nodes are used, the more accurate the numerical solution becomes. However, utilizing additional nodes results in an increase of the required computer memory, as well as an increase of the computational time. Increasing the number of nodes until the mesh is sufficiently fine, so that further refinement does not change the results, can determine the appropriate number of nodes needed.

After the conduction of the grid independence study, a C-type grid topology consisted of 80,000 quadrilateral cells was shown to be the most appropriate for a grid independent solution for an S809 airfoil; the domain height was set to 25 chord lengths, while the height of the first cell adjacent to the surface was set to 10^{-5}, corresponding to a maximum y^+ of approximately 0.2, a sufficient size to properly resolve the inner parts of the boundary layer. The C-type grid and the detail of the mesh close to the S809 airfoil are presented in Figure 1.

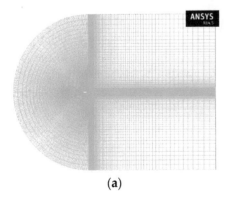 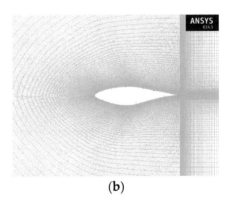

(a)   (b)

Figure 1. (a) C-type grid with 80,000 quadrilateral cells; and (b) detail of the mesh close to the S809 airfoil.

3.2. Turbulence Models

The utilized segregated, implicit solver, ANSYS Fluent 14.5 [21], solves conservation equations for mass and momentum for all flows, as well as additional transport equations if the flow is turbulent. In the current study, the simulation of the air-sand particle steady incompressible two-phase flow over the airfoil is accomplished via an Euler-Lagrange approach in ANSYS Fluent, the Lagrangian discrete phase model (DPM). The continuum air phase is solved by the Navier–Stokes equations, while the dispersed phase, consisted of a large number of spherical sand particles, is solved by tracking them through the calculated flow field.

Given the viscosity of the fluid, μ, the drag coefficient, C_D, the relative Reynolds number, Re, the density of the particle, ρ_p, the diameter of the particle, d_p, the velocity of the particle, u_p, the velocity of the fluid, u, the mass flow rate of the particles, $\dot{m}_p$, the time step, Δt, and other interaction forces, F_{other}, the change in momentum of a sand particle through each control volume can be calculated by the following equation:

$$F = \sum \left(\frac{18\mu C_D Re}{\rho_p d_p^2 24} (u_p - u) + F_{other} \right) \dot{m}_p \Delta t \tag{1}$$

The integration of the force balance on the particle predicts the trajectory of a discrete phase particle. The force balance is written in a Lagrangian reference frame. The forces acting on the particle are equal to the particle inertia and, particularly in the x direction, this equality can be expressed as:

$$\frac{du_p}{dt} = F_D \left(\vec{u} - \vec{u}_p \right) + \frac{\vec{g}}{\rho_p} (\rho_p - \rho) + \vec{F} \tag{2}$$

where:

$$F_D = \frac{18\mu}{\rho_p d_p^2} \frac{C_D Re}{24} \tag{3}$$

where $F_D \left(\vec{u} - \vec{u}_p \right)$ is the drag force per unit particle mass and $\vec{F}$ is an additional acceleration term, also the force per unit particle mass.

In the above equations $\vec{u}_p$ is the particle velocity, $\vec{u}$ is the fluid phase velocity, ρ_p is the density of the particle, ρ is the fluid density, μ is the molecular viscosity of the fluid, d_p is the particle diameter and Re is the relative Reynolds number, which is defined as:

$$Re \equiv \frac{\rho d_p \left| \vec{u}_p - \vec{u} \right|}{\mu} \tag{4}$$

The flow behavior is turbulent; therefore, the numerical simulations were accomplished on realizable k–ε and SST k–ω turbulence models, which are appropriate for aerodynamic applications. This section outlines these two turbulence models. In the two-phase flow, because of particles damping and production of turbulence eddies, two-way turbulence coupling is enabled in order to consider the effect of particles' existence in turbulent quantities.

The realizable k–ε model proposed by Shih et al. [22] is one of the simplest turbulence complete models that consists of two equations. In the realizable k–ε model, two separate transport equations are solved and the turbulent velocity and length scales can be determined independently. The term "realizable" implies that certain mathematical restrictions on the Reynolds stresses, which are consistent with the physics of turbulent flows, are satisfied. Notably, the realizable k–ε model contains a new eddy-viscosity formula involving a variable c_μ originally proposed by Reynolds [23] and a new model equation for dissipation (ε) based on the dynamic equation of the mean–square vorticity fluctuation.

Next, Menter [24] developed the shear-stress transport (SST) k–ω model in order to combine effectively the robust and exact formulation of the k–ω model in the near-wall region with the free-stream independence of the k–ε model in the far field, by converting the k–ε model into a k–ω formulation. The SST k–ω model includes some refinements, which make it more accurate and reliable for a wider class of flows, such as adverse pressure gradient flows, airfoils, and transonic shock waves, than the standard k–ω model.

The numerical simulations were accomplished using ANSYS Fluent 14.5 [21] and calculations were made for angles of attack ranging from $-9°$ to $16°$ for two different concentrations of sand particles in the air flow, more specifically 1% and 10%, while the diameter of sand particles was chosen to be 0.5 mm and the density 2196.06 kg/m^3. Regarding the Reynolds numbers for the simulation, they were chosen to be Re = 1×10^6 and Re = 2×10^6, in order to be validated in the present simulations by being compared to reliable experimental data regarding the air flow over the airfoil. Moreover, the flow can be described as incompressible, an assumption close to reality, so it is not necessary to solve the energy equation. The free stream temperature was chosen to be same as the environmental temperature, in other words, equal to 300 K. Subsequently, the density of the air is $\rho = 1.225$ kg/m^3 and the viscosity is $\mu = 1.7894 \times 10^{-5}$ kg/ms.

Notably, the sand particles are tracked at the minimum distance upstream of the airfoil where the flow is undisturbed as to simplify the solution and to reduce the computational time. Figure 2 illustrates the distance upstream of the airfoil where the particles are tracked. The horizontal axis velocity is chosen to be equal to air velocity, while the vertical axis velocity is calculated by the approach method and depends on the diameter of the sand particles.

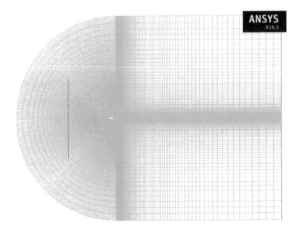

Figure 2. The minimum distance upstream of the airfoil where the particles are tracked.

4. Results and Discussion

Numerical simulations were conducted at various angles of attack and at Reynolds numbers of Re = 1×10^6 and Re = 2×10^6. The component of the net affecting force on the airfoil acting normal to the incoming flow stream is known as the lift force, while the component of the net force acting parallel to the incoming flow stream is known as the drag force. The lift and drag coefficients were possible to be predicted by means of the realizable k–ε and SST k–ω turbulence models, and then to be examined and compared with reliable experimental data regarding the one-phase air flow over the S809 airfoil by Somers [18].

Figures 3 and 4 illustrate the simulation results of the lift coefficient for the S809 airfoil versus the angle of attack at Reynolds numbers of Re = 1×10^6 and Re = 2×10^6, respectively, for one-phase flow and two-phase flows of two different concentrations of sand particles in the air. Regarding the numerical results for the one phase air flow, it is obvious that the lift coefficient increases linearly with the angle of attack in the range of $-9°$ to $9°$. The turbulence models are shown to have the same behavior and good agreement with the experimental data. Nevertheless, for angles of attack higher than $12°$, there is a disagreement between the experimental data and the computational results. Furthermore, it can be observed that sand concentration affects the lift coefficients. More specifically, there is a downward translation of the lift coefficient curve as the concentrations of sand particles increase, which has, as a result, a degradation of the aerodynamic performance. This degradation increases as the angle of attack and the concentration of sand particles increase.

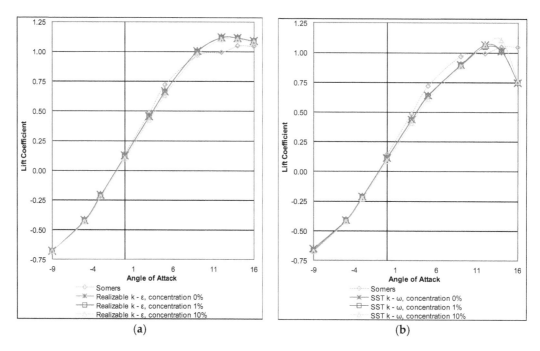

Figure 3. Comparison between reliable experimental data and simulation results of the lift coefficient curve for an S809 airfoil for (**a**) realizable k–ε; and (**b**) SST k–ω turbulence models at Re = 1 × 10⁶ for one-phase and two-phase flows consisting of two different concentrations of sand particles in the air.

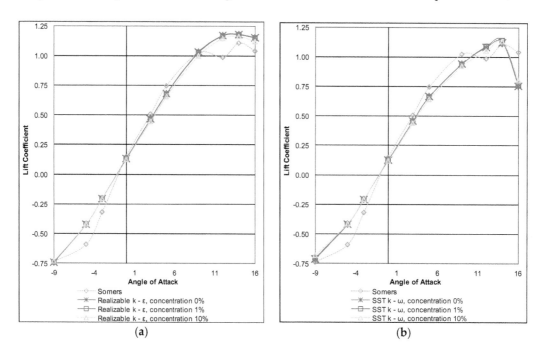

Figure 4. Comparison between reliable experimental data and simulation results of the lift coefficient curve for an S809 airfoil for (**a**) realizable k–ε; and (**b**) SST k–ω turbulence models at Re = 2 × 10⁶ for one-phase and two-phase flows consisting of two different concentrations of sand particles in the air.

Figures 5 and 6 depict the simulation results of the drag coefficient for the S809 airfoil versus the angle of attack at Re = 1 × 10⁶ and Re = 2 × 10⁶, respectively. For both Reynolds numbers the predicted drag coefficient increases as the angle of attack and the concentrations of sand particles in the air increase. This increase is much more obvious for 10% concentration of sand particles in the air flow. The larger total drag is caused by the mixture of air and sand particles, which results in larger skin frictional drag. Despite that there is a significant difference between experimental data and numerical results.

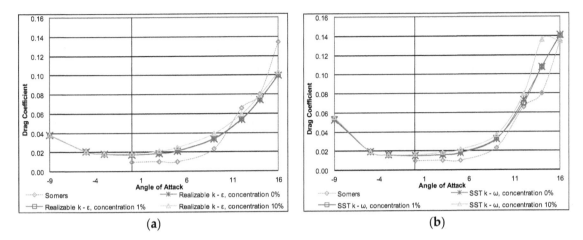

Figure 5. Comparison between reliable experimental data and simulation results of the drag coefficient curve for an S809 airfoil for (**a**) realizable k–ε; and (**b**) SST k–ω turbulence models at Re = 1 × 10⁶ for one-phase and two-phase flows consisting of two different concentrations of sand particles in the air.

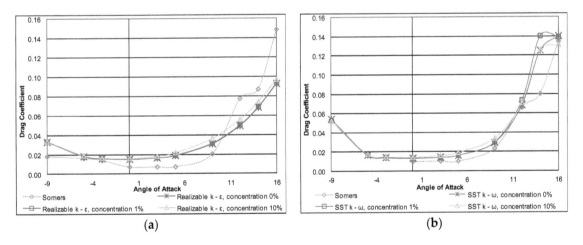

Figure 6. Comparison between reliable experimental data and simulation results of the drag coefficient curve for an S809 airfoil for (**a**) realizable k–ε; and (**b**) SST k–ω turbulence models at Re = 2 × 10⁶ for one-phase and two-phase flows consisting of two different concentrations of sand particles in the air.

As follows from the figures shown above, it can be concluded that the realizable k–ε turbulence model seems to be more appropriate than SST k–ω model to describe the two-phase flow over the S809 airfoil since the effect of sand concentration on the aerodynamic performance of the airfoil is more obvious for a wider range of angles of attack.

Next, Figures 7–12 present the region around the S809 airfoil using contours of static pressure at angles of attack equal to −3°, 0°, 3°, and 9°, and at Reynolds numbers of Re = 1 × 10⁶ and Re = 2 × 10⁶ with the realizable k–ε model for air flow and air-sand particle two-phase flow consisting of 1% and 10% concentration of sand particles in the air.

To begin with, Figure 7 shows the contours of static pressure at various angles of attack and at Re = 1 × 10⁶ for an S809 airfoil for air flow. Notably, the stagnation points, in other words the points in a flow where the fluid velocity is zero and, thus, the static pressure is equal to the total, are obvious. As can be seen, the pressure on the lower surface of the airfoil is greater than the pressure of the incoming flow stream. As a result, the airfoil is effectively "pushed" upward, normal to the incoming flow stream. Moreover, it can be seen that as the angle of attack increases, the trailing edge stagnation point moves forward on the airfoil.

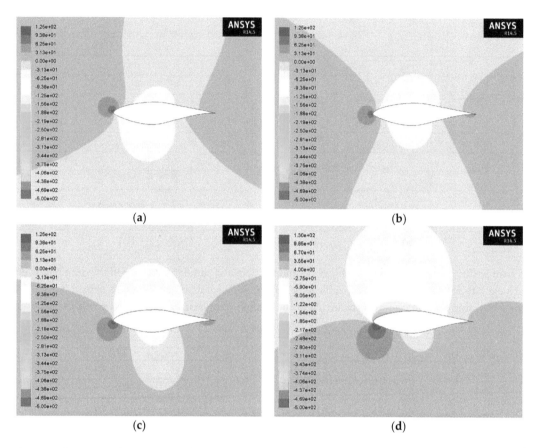

Figure 7. Contours of static pressure at (**a**) $-3°$; (**b**) $0°$; (**c**) $3°$; and (**d**) $9°$ angles of attack at Re = 1×10^6 with the realizable k–ε turbulence model for an S809 airfoil for air flow.

Regarding the effect of sand particles on the aerodynamic performance, the contours shown in Figure 8 in the case of 1% concentration of sand particles in the air seem to be almost the same with the respective static pressure contours for the air flow.

In Figure 9 are shown the contours of static pressure in the case of 10% concentration of sand particles in the air. In comparison with the contours for the air flow a very small difference can be observed. More specifically, the pressure seems to achieve lower values on the lower surface and higher values on the upper surface as the concentration increases.

The contours of static pressure at various angles of attack and at Re = 2×10^6 for air flow and air-sand particle two-phase flow for 1% and 10% concentration of sand particles in the air are given in Figures 10–12 and they seem to have similar behavior with the contours of static pressure at Re = 1×10^6. However, as the Reynolds number increases, the upper surface pressure achieves lower values for each angle of attack.

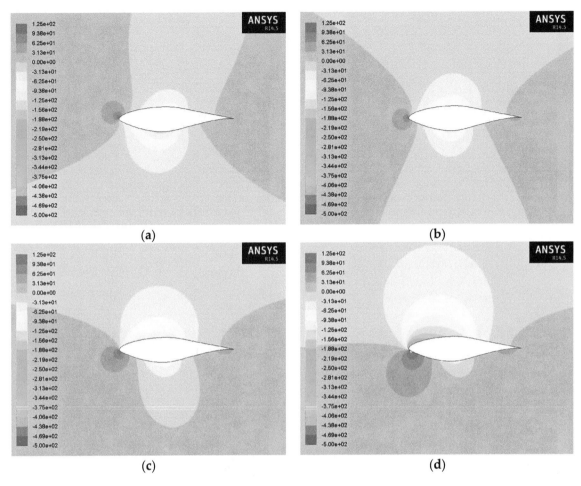

Figure 8. Contours of static pressure at (**a**) −3°; (**b**) 0°; (**c**) 3°; and (**d**) 9° angles of attack at Re = 1 × 10⁶ with the realizable k–ε turbulence model for an S809 airfoil for air-sand particle two-phase flow and 1% concentration of sand particles in the air.

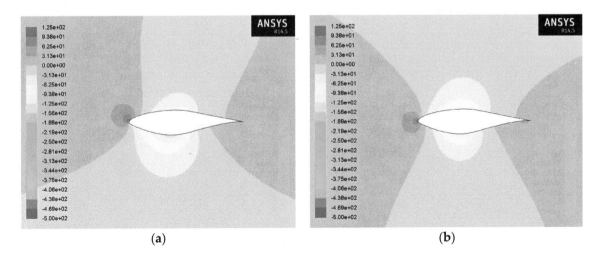

Figure 9. *Cont.*

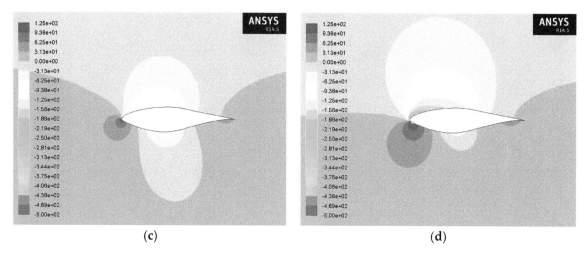

Figure 9. Contours of static pressure at (**a**) −3°; (**b**) 0°; (**c**) 3°; and (**d**) 9° angles of attack at Re = 1 × 10⁶ with the realizable k–ε turbulence model for and S809 airfoil for air-sand particle two-phase flow and 10% concentration of sand particles in the air.

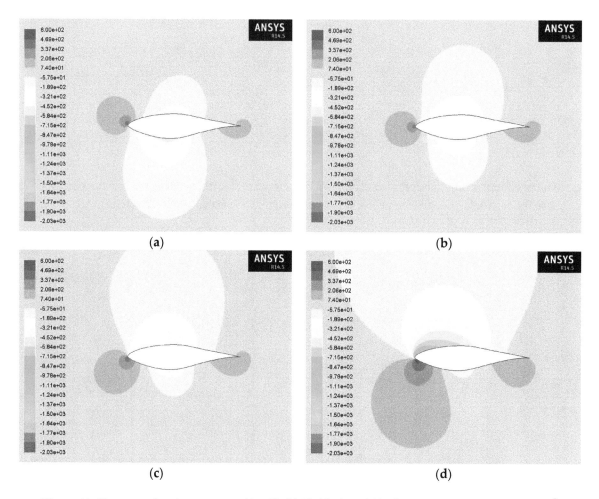

Figure 10. Contours of static pressure at (**a**) −3°; (**b**) 0°; (**c**) 3°; and (**d**) 9° angles of attack at Re = 2 × 10⁶ with the realizable k–ε turbulence model for an S809 airfoil for air flow.

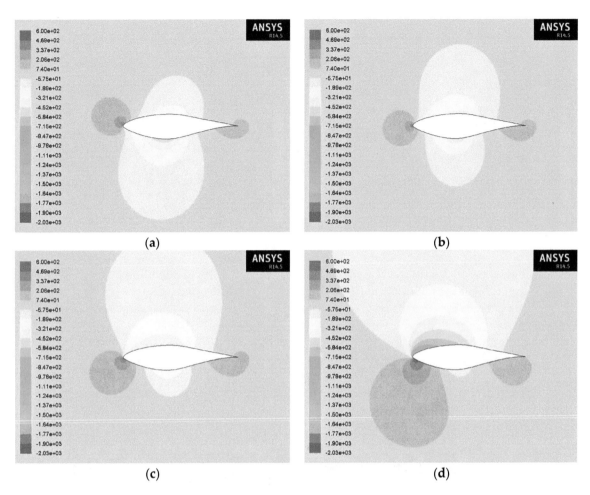

Figure 11. Contours of static pressure at (**a**) −3°; (**b**) 0°; (**c**) 3°; and (**d**) 9° angles of attack at Re = 2 × 10⁶ with the realizable k–ε turbulence model for an S809 airfoil for air-sand particle two-phase flow and 1% concentration of sand particles in the air.

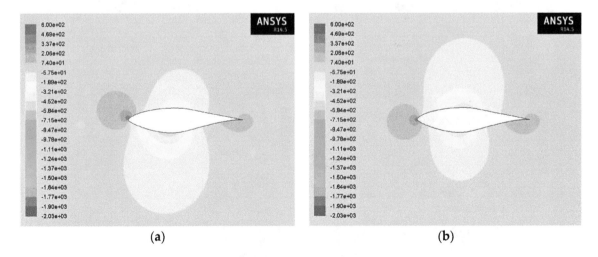

Figure 12. *Cont.*

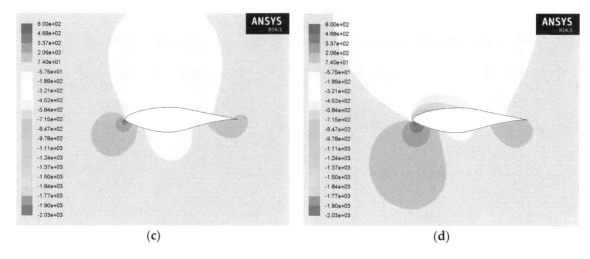

Figure 12. Contours of static pressure at (**a**) −3°; (**b**) 0°; (**c**) 3°; and (**d**) 9° angles of attack at Re = 2 × 10⁶ with the realizable k–ε turbulence model for an S809 airfoil for air-sand particle two-phase flow and 10% concentration of sand particles in the air.

Subsequently, Figures 13 and 14 provide the contours of sand particle concentration over the S809 airfoil at various angles of attack and at Re = 1 × 10⁶ for 1% and 10% concentration of sand particles in the air, respectively, with the realizable k–ε turbulence model. As can be seen, the sand particles tend to concentrate mainly in the region of the trailing edge to the middle of the airfoil, and as the concentration of them in the air increases, the airfoil is surrounded by more particles.

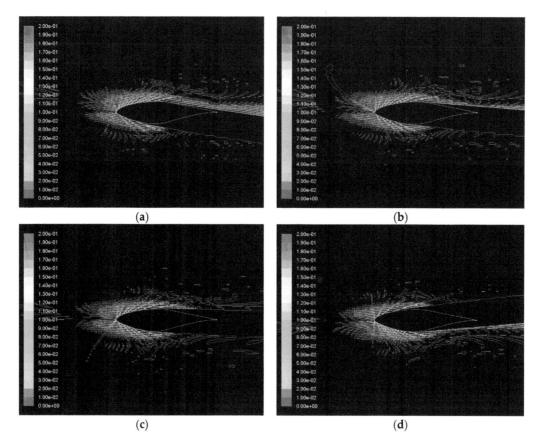

Figure 13. Contours of DPM concentration at (**a**) −3°; (**b**) 0°; (**c**) 3°; and (**d**) 9° angles of attack at Re = 1 × 10⁶ with the realizable k–ε turbulence model for an S809 airfoil for air-sand particle two-phase flow and 1% concentration of sand particles in the air.

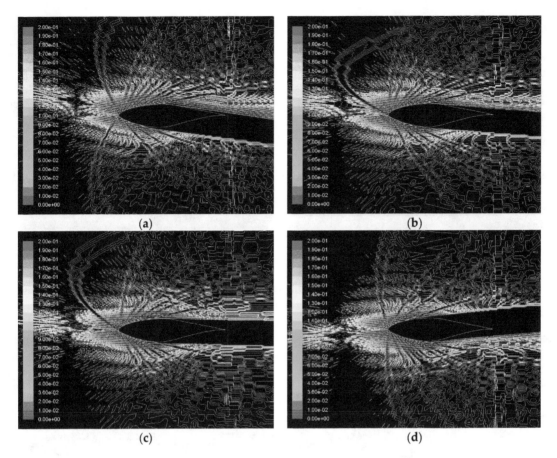

Figure 14. Contours of DPM concentration at (**a**) $-3°$; (**b**) $0°$; (**c**) $3°$; and (**d**) $9°$ angles of attack at $Re = 1 \times 10^6$ with the realizable k–ε turbulence model for an S809 airfoil for air-sand particle two-phase flow and 10% concentration of sand particles in the air.

Similarly, regarding the contours of sand particles concentration over the S809 airfoil at a Reynolds number of $Re = 2 \times 10^6$ with the realizable k–ε turbulence model for 1% concentration of sand particles in the air as shown in Figure 15, and 10% concentration of sand particles in the air as illustrated in Figure 16, the sand particles seem to have the same behavior as the concentration of them in the air increases, as for the case of $Re = 1 \times 10^6$. Furthermore, it can be observed that, as the Reynolds number increases, the sand particles drift towards the trailing edge of the airfoil.

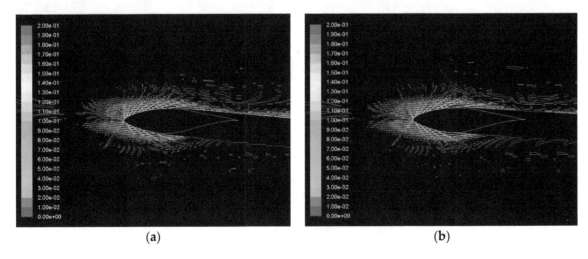

Figure 15. *Cont.*

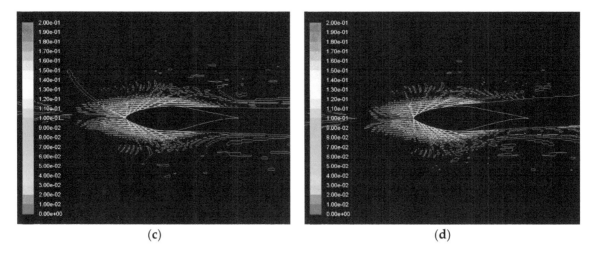

(c)   (d)

Figure 15. Contours of DPM concentration at (**a**) $-3°$; (**b**) $0°$; (**c**) $3°$; and (**d**) $9°$ angles of attack at Re $= 2 \times 10^6$ with the realizable k–ε turbulence model for an S809 airfoil for air-sand particle two-phase flow and 1% concentration of sand particles in the air.

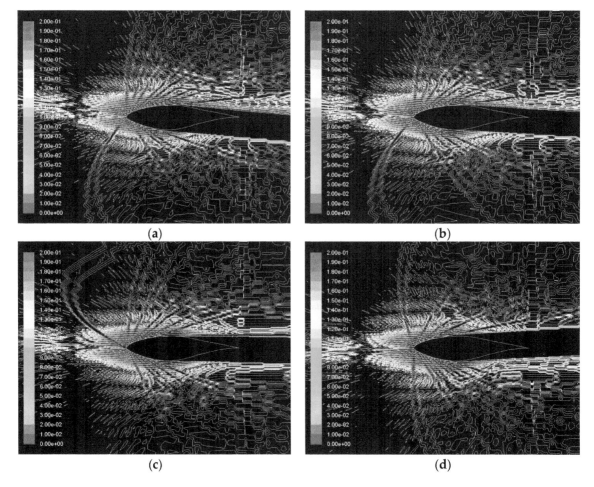

(a)   (b)

(c)   (d)

Figure 16. Contours of DPM concentration at (**a**) $-3°$; (**b**) $0°$; (**c**) $3°$; and (**d**) $9°$ angles of attack at Re $= 2 \times 10^6$ with the realizable k–ε turbulence model for an S809 airfoil for air-sand particle two-phase flow and 10% concentration of sand particles in the air.

5. Conclusions

The present study set out to determine the effect of air-sand particle two-phase flow, consisting of two different concentrations of sand particles in the air, on the aerodynamic performance of an S809 airfoil at Reynolds numbers of Re = 1×10^6 and Re = 2×10^6.

Summing up the results, it can be concluded that the aerodynamic performance of the S809 airfoil degrades in the two-phase flow; in other words, the lift coefficient decreases and, simultaneously, the drag coefficient increases. In general, the degradation increases as the angle of attack and the concentration of sand particles increase for both Reynolds numbers. The mixture of air and sand particles change the skin friction to greater values and, thus, the total drag is larger.

From the outcome of the current investigation it is also possible to conclude that the realizable k–ε model seems to be the most appropriate turbulence model to predict the degradation of the aerodynamic performance of a S809 airfoil due to the concentration of sand particles in the air flow at a wide range of angles of attack.

Moreover, based on the illustration of the flow field around the S809 airfoil, our understanding of the effects of sand concentration in air can be enhanced. It has been shown that the static pressure in the case of a 1% concentration of sand is almost the same with the pressure in the air flow, while in the case of a 10% concentration, a very small difference can be observed. It is apparent that the lower surface of the airfoil seems to have lower values, and the upper surface higher values, of static pressure as the sand concentration increases for both Reynolds numbers.

Finally, the contours of sand particle concentration over the S809 airfoil suggests that, in general, the sand particles tend to concentrate mainly in the region of the trailing edge to the middle of the airfoil, and as the concentration of them in the air increases, the airfoil is surrounded by more particles. Additionally, the particles drift towards the trailing edge of the airfoil by increasing the Reynolds number.

Author Contributions: Dimitra C. Douvi performed the simulations for Reynolds number of Re = 2×10^6 and wrote the paper; Dimitra C. Douvi and Dionissios P. Margaris analyzed the data; Aristeidis E. Davaris performed the simulations for Reynolds number of Re = 1×10^6.

References

1. Wolfe, W.P.; Ochs, S.S. CFD Calculations of S809 Aerodynamic Characteristics. In Proceedings of the 35th Aerospace Sciences Meeting and Exhibit, AIAA, Reno, NV, USA, 6–9 January 1997.
2. CFD Research Corporation. *CFD-ACE, Theory Manual*; Version 1.0; CFD Research Corporation: Huntsville, AL, USA, 1993.
3. Gupta, S.; Leishman, J.G. Dynamic Stall Modeling of the S809 Airfoil and Comparison with Experiments. In Proceedings of the Collection of Technical Papers—44th AIAA Aerospace Sciences Meeting, Reno, NV, USA, 9–12 January 2006.
4. Qu, H.; Hu, J.; Gao, X. The Impact of Reynolds Number on Two-Dimensional Aerodynamic Airfoil Flow. In Proceedings of the 2009 World Non-Grid-Connected Wind Power and Energy Conference, WNWEC 2009, Nanjing, China, 24–26 September 2009.
5. Zhong, W.; Wang, T.; Wang, Q. Numerical Simulation of Transition Effect on Aerodynamic Performance of Aerofoil S809. *Taiyangneng Xuebao/Acta Energiae Sol. Sin.* **2011**, *32*, 1523–1527. (In Chinese)
6. Douvi, D.C.; Margaris, D.P. Comparison Between New and Existing Turbulence Models for Numerical Simulation of the Flow Over NACA 0012 and S809 Airfoils for Two Reynolds Numbers. In Proceedings of the 6th International Conference on "Experiments/Process/System Modelling/Simulation/Optimization", Athens, Greece, 8–11 July 2015.
7. Wan, T.; Pan, S.-P. Aerodynamic efficiency study under the influence of heavy rain via Two-Phase Flow Approach. In Proceedings of the 27th Congress of the International Council of the Aeronautical Sciences 2010, ICAS 2010, Cancun, Mexico, 7–13 March 2010.

8.   Wan, T.; Chou, C.-J. Reinvestigation of High Lift Airfoil under the Influence of Heavy Rain Effects. In Proceedings of the 50th AIAA Aerospace Sciences Meeting Including the New Horizons Forum and Aerospace Exposition, Nashville, Tennessee, 9–12 January 2012.

9.   Douvi, E.C.; Margaris, D.P. Aerodynamic performance investigation under the influence of heavy rain of a NACA 0012 airfoil for wind turbine applications. *Int. Rev. Mech. Eng.* **2012**, *6*, 1228–1235.

10. Wu, Z.; Cao, Y. Numerical Simulation of Flow over an Airfoil in Heavy Rain via a Two-Way Coupled Eulerian-Lagrangian Approach. *Int. J. Multiph. Flow* **2015**, *69*, 81–92. [CrossRef]

11. Ren, P.-F.; Xu, Y.; Song, J.-J.; Xu, J.-Z. Numerical Study about the Influence of Rime Ice Conditions on Airfoil. *Kung Cheng Je Wu Li Hsueh Pao/J. Eng. Thermophys.* **2014**, *35*, 663–668.

12. Olivieri, S.; Picano, F.; Sardina, G.; Iudicone, D.; Brandt, L. The effect of the Basset history force on particle clustering in homogeneous and isotropic turbulence. *Phys. Fluids* **2014**, *26*, 041704. [CrossRef]

13. Sardina, G.; Picano, F.; Brandt, L.; Caballero, R. Continuous Growth of Droplet Size Variance due to Condensation in Turbulent Clouds. *Phys. Rev. Lett.* **2015**, *115*, 184501. [CrossRef] [PubMed]

14. De Marchis, M.; Milici, B.; Sardina, G.; Napoli, E. Interaction between turbulent structures and particles in roughened channel. *Int. J. Multiph. Flow* **2016**, *78*, 117–131. [CrossRef]

15. Khakpour, Y.; Bardakji, S.; Nair, S. Aerodynamic Performance of Wind Turbine Blades in Dusty Environments. In Proceedings of the ASME 2007 International Mechanical Engineering Congress and Exposition, IMECE2008, Seattle, WA, USA, 11–15 November 2007.

16. Knopp, T.; Eisfeld, B.; Calvo, J.B. A New Extension for k–ω Turbulence Models to Account for Wall Roughness. *Int. J. Heat Fluid Flow* **2009**, *30*, 54–65. [CrossRef]

17. Salem, H.; Diab, A.; Ghoneim, Z. CFD Simulation and Analysis of Performance Degradation of Wind Turbine Blades in Dusty Environments. In Proceedings of the 2013 International Conference on Renewable Energy Research and Applications, ICRERA 2013, Madrid, Spain, 20–23 October 2013.

18. Somers, D.M. *Design and Experimental Results for the S809 Airfoil*; National Renewable Energy Laboratory: Golden, CO, USA, 1997.

19. Eppler, R.; Somers, D.M. *A Computer Program for the Design and Analysis of Low-Speed Airfoils*; NASA: Hampton, VA, USA, 1980.

20. Eppler, R.; Somers, D.M. *Supplement to: A Computer Program for the Design and Analysis of Low-Speed Airfoils*; NASA: Hampton, VA, USA, 1980.

21. ANSYS® Academic Research, Release 14.5. Available online: http://www.ansys.com/ (accessed on 21 February 2017).

22. Shih, T.-H.; Liou, W.W.; Shabbir, A.; Yang, Z.; Zhu, J. A New k–ε Eddy-Viscosity Model for High Reynolds Number Turbulent Flows—Model Development and Validation. *Comput. Fluids* **1995**, *24*, 227–238. [CrossRef]

23. Reynolds, W.C. Fundamentals of Turbulence for Turbulence Modeling and Simulation. Available online: http://www.dtic.mil/cgi-bin/GetTRDoc?Location=U2&doc=GetTRDoc.pdf&AD=ADP005793 (accessed on 28 February 2017).

24. Menter, F.R. Two-Equation Eddy-Viscosity Turbulence Models for Engineering Applications. *AIAA J.* **1994**, *32*, 1598–1605. [CrossRef]

5

A Hybrid Computation Model to Describe the Progression of Multiple Myeloma and Its Intra-Clonal Heterogeneity

Anass Bouchnita [1,2,3,*]**, Fatima-Ezzahra Belmaati** [3]**, Rajae Aboulaich** [3]**, Mark J. Koury** [4]
and Vitaly Volpert [1,5,6]

[1]   Institut Camille Jordan, UMR 5208 CNRS, University Lyon 1, Villeurbanne 69622, France;
      volpert@math.univ-lyon1.fr
[2]   Laboratoire de Biométrie et Biologie Evolutive, UMR 5558 CNRS, University Lyon 1,
      Villeurbanne 69622, France
[3]   Mohammadia School of Engineering, Université Mohamed V, Rabat 10080, Morocco;
      fati.belmaati@gmail.com (F.-E.B.); aboulaich@emi.ac.ma (R.A.)
[4]   Vanderbilt University Medical Center, Nashville, TN 37232-6307, USA; mark.koury@vanderbilt.edu
[5]   Institute of Numerical Mathematics, Russian Academy of Sciences, Moscow 119333, Russia
[6]   INRIA Team Dracula, INRIA Lyon La Doua, Villeurbanne 60603, France
[*]   Correspondence: anass.bouchnita@univ-lyon1.fr

Academic Editor: Rainer Breitling

Abstract: Multiple myeloma (MM) is a genetically complex hematological cancer that is characterized by proliferation of malignant plasma cells in the bone marrow. MM evolves from the clonal premalignant disorder monoclonal gammopathy of unknown significance (MGUS) by sequential genetic changes involving many different genes, resulting in dysregulated growth of multiple clones of plasma cells. The migration, survival, and proliferation of these clones require the direct and indirect interactions with the non-hematopoietic cells of the bone marrow. We develop a hybrid discrete-continuous model of MM development from the MGUS stage. The discrete aspect of the model is observed at the cellular level: cells are represented as individual objects which move, interact, divide, and die by apoptosis. Each of these actions is regulated by intracellular and extracellular processes as described by continuous models. The hybrid model consists of the following submodels that have been simplified from the much more complex state of evolving MM: cell motion due to chemotaxis, intracellular regulation of plasma cells, extracellular regulation in the bone marrow, and acquisition of mutations upon cell division. By extending a previous, simpler model in which the extracellular matrix was considered to be uniformly distributed, the new hybrid model provides a more accurate description in which cytokines are produced by the marrow microenvironment and consumed by the myeloma cells. The complex multiple genetic changes in MM cells and the numerous cell-cell and cytokine-mediated interactions between myeloma cells and their marrow microenviroment are simplified in the model such that four related but evolving MM clones can be studied as they compete for dominance in the setting of intraclonal heterogeneity.

Keywords: multiple myeloma; intra-clonal heterogeneity; hybrid model

1. Introduction

Multiple myeloma (MM) is initiated through the acquisition of genetic changes that transform the plasma cells from normal to malignant. These changes often result in the development of selective advantage, leading to the excessive proliferation of myeloma cells. The development of MM leads to several harmful clinical conditions including anemia, renal failure, recurrent infections, hypercalcemia, and osteoporosis with bone fractures. These pathological conditions can frequently result in the death of the patient.

The evolution of myeloma from the clonal premalignant plasma cell condition termed monoclonal gammopathy of unknown significance (MGUS) through the intermediate stage of smoldering myeloma to the malignant MM stage is mediated by multiple sequential genetic changes, including chromosomal translocations, hyperdiploidy, and mutations, which permit independent growth and spread of MM in the bone marrow [1,2]. A wide variety of genetic changes involving many different genes have been documented in MM cases. In addition to these sequential genetic changes, MM cells require specific interactions with the non-hematopoietic cells of the bone marrow including the stromal cells (BMSCs), osteoblasts, osteoclasts, and cells associated with vascular supply of the marrow [1,2]. These marrow microenvironment interactions with the MM cells include direct binding of cell surface adhesion proteins and their binding partners on the other cell types as well as diffusible, soluble molecules that are secreted by one cell type and are bound and internalized by another cell type. These soluble molecules are often chemokines and cytokines produced by other marrow cells, and their receptors are expressed on the MM cells. However, specific molecules produced by MM cells indirectly affect growth of the malignancy by inducing localized resorption of bone, death of hematopoietic cells, and expansion of vessels supplying blood to the MM. The combined effects of sequential genetic changes within the evolving myeloma cells and interactions of the MM cells with the marrow microenvironment affect the migration, proliferation, and survival of the MM cells.

There are three types of mathematical models of tumor growth and intra-clonal heterogeneity. The first type is the continuous model in which partial and ordinary differential equations are used to describe the density of premalignant and malignant cells [3–5]. Some continuous models study the effects of nutrients and inhibitors on tumor growth that may or may not be accompanied by necrosis [6,7], while others focus on the nonlinear three-dimensional spatial aspects of tumors [8]. The question of clonal competition within tumors has been studied by other continuous models [9,10], and the role of clonal heterogeneity in drug resistance has been previously explored [11]. While these continuous models sustain mathematical analysis and provide key insights in the development of tumors, they do not describe the cell-cell interactions and intracellular regulation of single cells. The second type of mathematical models describing tumor growth is the discrete model which usually represents cells as individual objects that interact with each other. These interactions determine the fate of each cell [12–17]. Cellular automatons provide a simple yet powerful tool to understand the mechanisms of tumor growth [18,19]. The discrete models usually describe cells in on-lattice or off-lattice grids. They focus on the interactions between cells and how they lead to the development of tumors, but discrete models do not link the different processes taking place at different scales. The third type of tumor growth model, which is known as a hybrid model, combines the features of both continuous and discrete models, thereby benefiting from the advantages of both of them [20–22]. In hybrid models, the concentrations of intracellular and extracellular proteins are described by partial and ordinary differential equations while the cells are introduced as individual objects. The heterogeneous nature of tumors has been studied by some of these models [23–26]. The models describing MM development usually study the impact of MM on different biological systems such as bone remodeling [27] and erythropoiesis [28].

In this work, we develop a hybrid model describing the development and intra-clonal heterogeneity in MM as described in Walker et al. [29]. In this model, malignant cells are represented by elastic spheres that can move, grow, interact, divide and die by apoptosis. Their fate is determined by intracellular and extracellular regulation networks. The growth of the cellular radii between cell divisions and the formation of two daughter cells with each division lead to the expansion of the tumor. To investigate the role of the bone marrow (BM) microenvironment in the growth of myeloma tumors, we specifically consider another population of cells, the bone marrow stromal cells (BMSCs). These cells secrete cytokines such as stromal cell-derived factor 1 (SDF-1), insulin-like growth factor 1

(IGF-1),and interleukin 6 (IL-6) which are necessary to the survival, homing and growth of malignant plasma cells. The concentration of each of these cytokines is modelled by a reaction–diffusion equation. The intracellular regulation of malignant cells is represented by a system of ordinary differential equations which depends on the concentration of extracellular cytokines. We characterize each cell by a specific genotype, and we consider that after its division, daughter cells will either inherit the same genotype or acquire a slightly different one due to random mutations. As the result, aggressive clones emerge during tumor progression in a parallel pattern. Although experiments show the possibility of clones emerging in both linear and branching evolutionary patterns, we restrict this study to the parallel evolutionary case. The MM cells consume cytokines, leading to competition between clones for the available resources. We study the dynamics of clonal competition and its role in the progression of MM.

2. Hybrid Model of MM Development

We developed a hybrid discrete-continuous model of MGUS progression to MM. The discrete aspect of the model is observed at the cellular level: cells are represented as individual objects which move, interact, divide, and die by apoptosis. Each of these actions is regulated by intracellular and extracellular processes described by continuous models. The hybrid model consists of the following submodels: cell motion due to chemotaxis, intracellular regulation of plasma cells, extracellular regulation in the bone marrow, and acquisition of mutations upon cell division. It is an extension of a previously developed simpler model [30]. While the previous model considers the cytokines in the extracellular matrix to be uniformly distributed, the present study provides a more accurate description by considering that these cytokines are produced by the BMSCs and consumed by the myeloma cells. Furthermore, a more detailed description of the intracellular pathways regulating the fate of plasma cells is provided in the present model.

The model is based on the direct effects of sequential genetic changes and marrow microenvironmental chemokine and cytokine activity that influence the chemotaxis, proliferation and survival of MM, but does not include the MM effects on bone resorption, hematopoietic cell loss, or development of specialized vasculature. The complex multiple genetic changes in MM cells and the numerous cell-cell and cytokine-mediated interactions between myeloma cells and their marrow microenviroment are simplified in the model so that four related but evolving clones develop in a process termed intra-clonal heterogeneity [31,32] (See Figure 1). Competition among these four MM clones is based on differences in cellular growth and survival rates and interactions with the marrow microenvironment. This competition results in predominance of the more fit clones and decline and ultimate extinction of the less fit ones. An early event in the MM model (Figure 1a) is a standard-risk genetic change, a t(11;14) translocation that involves the immunoglobulin heavy chain switch region on chromosome 14, inducing overexpression of the gene encoding cyclin D1, a regulator of cell cycle progression located on chromosome 11 [33]. This t(11;14) clone has deregulated cell cycle progression due to the translocation, and it undergoes two separate secondary genetic events: mutations involving the oncogenes *N-RAS* and *K-RAS*, which are common secondary events in the development of multiple myeloma [2]. The resultant clone with t(11;14)/mutant *N-RAS* has significantly enhanced proliferation compared to the parent t(11;14) clone, while the t(11;14)/ mutant *K-RAS* clone has much less of an increase in proliferation relative to the t(11;14) parental clone. Thus, the two descendant clones have differing degrees of increased *RAS* activity, resulting in a proliferative advantage for the t(11;14)/mutant *N-RAS* clone compared to both the t(11;14) parental clone and t(11;14)/ mutant *K-RAS* clone. A subsequent genetic event in the t(11;14)/*K-RAS* clone is, however, a mutation in the gene encoding interferon regulatory factor 4 (IRF4). Mutant IRF4 is a protein that can enhance survival and proliferation of MM cells. *IRF4* mutation has been associated with mutations of *N-RAS* or *K-RAS* [32], and it allows the t(11;14)/*K-RAS* mutant/*IRF4* mutant clone in the model to compete more successfully with the t(11;14)/*N-RAS* clone than either the parent t(11;14) clone or the t(11;14)/*K-RAS* mutant clone.

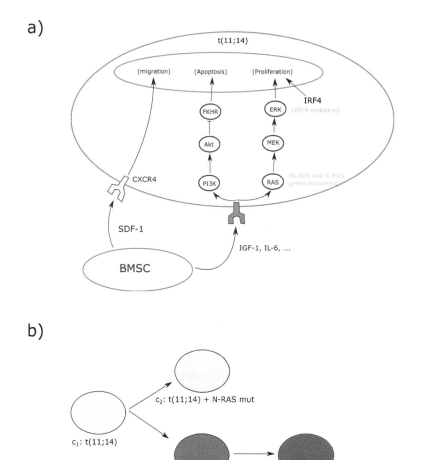

Figure 1. (**a**) The intracellular regulation of myeloma cells as described in the model. Bone marrow stromal cells (BMSCs) secrete the cytokines insulin-like growth factor 1 (IGF-1), interleukin-6 (IL-6), and chemokine stromal cell-derived factor 1 (SDF-1) which are necessary to the survival, homing and proliferation of myeloma cells. Via their respective receptors, IGF-1 and IL-6 activate the RAS/ERK pathway which promotes the cell proliferation. They inhibit apoptosis through the phosphatidylinositol-3 kinase/protein kinase B/Forkhead in rabdomyosarcoma (Akt/FKHR) pathway. The cell migrates and homes to BMSCs through the SDF-1/CXCR4 axis. The IRF4 mutation, which has been associated with concomitant RAS mutations, promotes survival and proliferation. BMSCs, which are much larger cells than the myeloma cells, are shown in reduced in size in this figure as well as the receptors of both IGF-1 and IL-6; (**b**) The parallel evolution pattern of multiple myeloma clones resulting in intra-clonal heterogeneity. More aggressive clones result from a more aggressive *N-RAS* mutation in clone 2 or the acquisition of IRF4 mutation in addition to the less aggressive *K-RAS* in clone 4. Each clone is shown by its corresponding color in the model.

Among the many possible microenvironmental factors that may influence the growth of MM in the marrow, the simplified model includes the chemokine stromal cell-derived factor 1 (SDF-1). It is produced by multiple cell types but mainly by BMSCs. Other extracellular cytokines included in the model are interleukin 6 (IL-6) and insulin-like growth factor 1 (IGF-1), which are produced by other types of non-hematopoietic cells in the marrow as well as BMSCs. The marrow stromal cells are considered as sources of SDF-1, IL-6, and IGF-1 in the model (Figure 1a). SDF-1, through its receptor CXCR4, mediates the homing of circulating myeloma cells to the marrow and their migration within the marrow space [34,35]. IL-6 and IGF-1 induce multiple effects after binding to their respective specific surface receptors on the MM cells, but in the model we restrict our study to their effects on the RAS/Extracellular signal-regulated kinases (RAS/ERK) pathway that promotes proliferation and the phosphatidylinositol-3 kinase/protein kinase B/Forkhead in rabdomyosarcoma (Akt/FKHR) pathway that regulates apoptosis [2] (Figure 1a).

2.1. Cell Motion

We represent each cell as an elastic sphere. It contains two parts: an incompressible part and a compressible one. As the cell grows, its radius increases and hence it pushes the neighboring cells. The motion of each cell is determined by Newton's second law. Let us denote the cell number by i. Then we have the following equation for the coordinate x_i of the center of the $i - th$ cell:

$$m\ddot{x}_i + m\mu\dot{x}_i - \sum_{j\neq i} f_{ij} - f_{ch} = 0, \tag{1}$$

where m is the mass of cell, μ is the friction coefficient, f_{ij} is the interaction force between the cells i and j, f_{ch} is the chemotactic force which depends on the concentration of SDF-1. We consider f_{ij} in the following form:

$$f_{ij} = \begin{cases} K\dfrac{h_0 - hij}{h_{ij} - (h_0 - h_1)}, & h_0 - h_i < h_{ij} < h_0 \\ 0, & h_{ij} \geq h_0 \end{cases} \tag{2}$$

Here h_{ij} is the distance between the center of the cells i and j, h_0 is the sum of their radii, K is a positive parameter and h_1 represents the incompressible part of each cell. The numerical implementaton of Newton's equation is presented in Appendix A.1. The chemotactic force represents the motion of the cell in response to SDF-1 stimulus. Let us denote the concentration of SDF-1 by S. Then the expression of f_{ch} is given by:

$$f_{ch} = \kappa\nabla S,$$

where κ is a positive constant and ∇S denotes the SDF-1 gradient.

2.2. Extracellular Regulation

We consider a square two-dimensional computational domain with the side equal to 1000 microns. The hybrid model contains two types of cells: myeloma cells and BMSCs. The former have a diameter of 10 microns while the latter are considered to have six-fold larger radii as observed in experimental data. Furthermore, they secrete cytokines that are necessary for the survival and proliferation of myeloma cells such as SDF-1, IL-6, and IGF-1. Let us denote the total concentration of the last two cytokines by I and the concentration of SDF-1 by S. Assuming that these cytokines have the same diffusion coefficient, production rate, consumption rate, and degradation rate, we describe their concentrations in the extracellular matrix by:

$$\frac{\partial I}{\partial t} = D\Delta I + W - \sum_i \lambda I - \sigma I, \tag{3}$$

$$\frac{\partial S}{\partial t} = D\Delta S + W - \sum_i \lambda S - \sigma S, \tag{4}$$

where D is the diffusion coefficient, W the production factor, λ the consumption rate by each myeloma cell, and σ the degradation rate. We set the Dirichlet boundary condition $I = 0$ and $S = 0$ at all boundaries. We have prescribed zero Dirichlet boundary condition to represent the local dynamics of tumor growth in a bone marrow site surrounded by adipose tissue. The finite difference method was used to implement the reaction-diffusion equations. The used numerical methods and implementation algorithm are presented in Appendix A.2.

2.3. Intracellular Regulation

Although myeloma cells are genetically complex [2], we will restrict the intracellular regulation to two pathways (Figure 1a). These pathways are the RAS/ERK pathway which is responsible for cell proliferation and the Akt/FKHR pathway which regulates its survival. Other pathways such as the janus kinase/signal transducer and activator of transcription (JAK/STAT) pathway are not considered in the model. We have chosen these two pathways in order to study the role of aquired RAS mutations in the progression of MM and how it is affected by the extracellular matrix. Let us denote the concentrations of ERK, Akt, and FKHR as e, a, and f, respectively. We describe these concentrations inside each cell as follows:

$$\frac{de}{dt} = \alpha_1(z)(\kappa I) - \beta_1 e, \quad \frac{da}{dt} = \alpha_2(\kappa I) - \beta_2 a, \quad \frac{df}{dt} = \alpha_3 - \beta_3 af - \gamma_3 f. \tag{5}$$

where α_i and β_i, $i = 1, 2, 3$ and γ_3 are positive constants. The coefficient $\alpha_1(z)$ depends on the genotype z, and this coefficient varies depending on the effect of RAS mutations. The cell will die by apoptosis if $f > f^*$ during its lifetime cycle. If the myeloma cell survives, then it will self-renew, if $e > e^*$ by the end of its life cycle. Otherwise, the cell will die by apoptosis. We consider that the proliferation threshold e^* depends on the *IRF4* gene expression. The values of both intracellular and extracellular regulation parameters are provided in Appendix B.

Myeloma Cells Division and Mutations

In the present study, we investigate the progression of MGUS into MM through RAS mutations [29]. We characterize each cell by an aggressiveness phenotype which represents the cumulative effects of acquired RAS mutations. We introduce an aggressiveness phenotype function $f(z)$ resulting from the RAS genotype for each cell. After its division, the daughter myeloma cell will keep the genome of the mother cell with a probability of one-third. Otherwise, it will acquire a mutation and either increases or diminishes its aggressiveness by a positive value ϵ. We represent the genotype and resultant RAS activation that determine aggressiveness as due to describing the frequency and effects of RAS mutations in the resulting clones in Figure 2a. Furthermore, we assume that the ERK threshold for cell division is reduced upon the mutation of the *IRF4* gene as shown in Figure 2b. We consider four clones of MM denoted by c_1, c_2, c_3, and, c_4 (Figure 1b). The clone c_1 is the initial clone which does not harbour any RAS mutations. The clone c_2 is more aggressive than clone c_1. It consists of MM cells that acquired the *N-RAS* gene mutation. The clones c_3 and c_4 belong to a lineage that is independent from the clone c_2. They emerge when the cells of c_1 acquire the *K-RAS* gene mutation for clone c_3 and an additional *IRF4* gene mutation for clone c_4. The latter clone is therefore more aggressive than the former. We show the relationships between these different clones in Figure 1b.

a)   b)

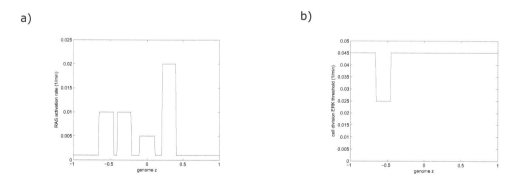

Figure 2. (a) The activation rate of RAS protein as a function of the genotype function z; (b) The ERK threshold for division as a function of the genotype function z, it decreases due to the *IRF4* mutation found in the clone c_4.

3. Results

Initially, there are 47 myeloma cells in a bone marrow site containing a single BMSC, although the initial number of these cells is not essential for the results of the simulations. All of these malignant cells are considered to be tumor-initiating cells because they belong to the same initial clone. The motion of the malignant cells depends on their distance from the BMSC. Closer cells move faster than farther ones due to the increase in SDF-1 gradient near the BMSC. During their motion, myeloma cells consume the cytokines necessary for their survival such as IL-6 and IGF-1. These cytokines promote survival by activating the RAS/ERK pathway, and dowregulating the Akt/FKHR pathway. Depending upon its initial distance from the BMSC, the myeloma cell will either survive and get closer to the BMSC or it will die by apoptosis. The surviving myeloma cells will surround the BMSC and form the tumor niche. Initially, this niche consists of cells belonging to the same clone. After some time, other subclones will emerge in the course of tumor growth. We have shown the different steps of myeloma cells homing to a BMSC in Figure 3. The initial condition for the simulation is shown in Figure 3a. Due to the low number of myeloma cells in the beginning of the simulation, the BMSC secretes a high concentration of the chemokine SDF-1 which attracts the myeloma cells located close to it (Figure 3b). The surviving myeloma cells adhere to the BMSC and surround it while other cells divide and remain farther away (Figure 3c). During this process, cells whose aggressiveness phenotype belongs to the intermediate state between the clones $c_1 - c_2$ and $c_1 - c_3$ emerge (Figure 3d) and the global concentration of SDF-1 starts to reach stability due to its consumption by myeloma cells (Figure 4a).

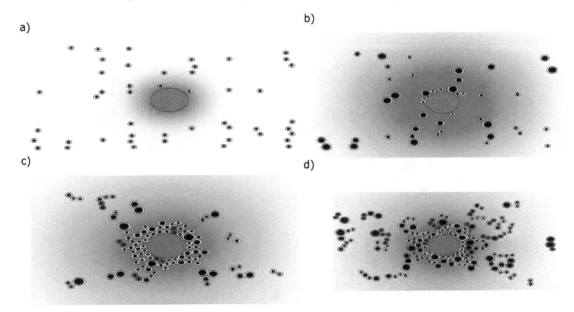

Figure 3. The sequential steps of myeloma cells homing to a BMSC. Myeloma cells are represented by the cells with the smaller radii and the BMSC is the large cell in the middle. Each clone of multiple myeloma (MM) cells is denoted by a specific color. The red color gradient represents the summed concentrations of the cytokines SDF-1, IL-6, and IGF-1 shown with white (0) to red (1). (**a**) After their infiltration, the myeloma cells move towards the BMSC; (**b**) The surviving cells surround the BMSC; (**c**) The myeloma cells divide and form the tumor niche; (**d**) The tumor expands and more aggressive subclones start emerging.

MGUS progresses to aggressive MM through the acquisition of random mutations by myeloma cells. In this respect, more aggressive subclones emerge in the course of MGUS progression due to the acquisition of RAS-associated mutations. The aggressive subclones need lower concentrations of IL-6 and IGF-1 to survive, resulting in the expansion and the persistence of the tumor (Figure 4b). Because of their rapid proliferation, they crowd out other clones and consume most of the available resources. Ultimately, these less aggressive subclones remain relatively stable in growth pattern. Still, a few of them manage to survive in proximity to the BMSC where there is a higher concentration of the IL-6 and IGF-1 cytokines, while the more aggressive subclones occupy the outer region of the tumor. The different steps of tumor development and intraclonal competition are shown in Figure 5. As the tumor progresses, the concentrations of IL-6 and IGF-1 become stable due to their consumption by the growing number of myeloma cells. As a result, the aggressive subclones expand to the detriment of the less aggressive ones. By the end of the simulation, we see that the tumor size is stable but the competition between clones is still in progress (Figure 5c vs. Figure 5d).

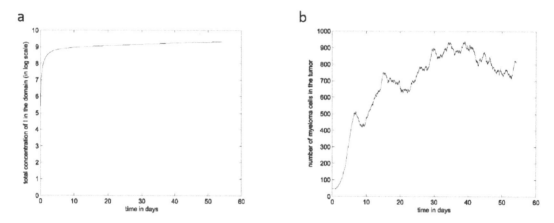

Figure 4. (**a**) The total concentration of the IL-6 and IGF-1 cytokines over time in log scale; (**b**) The total number of malignant cells over time.

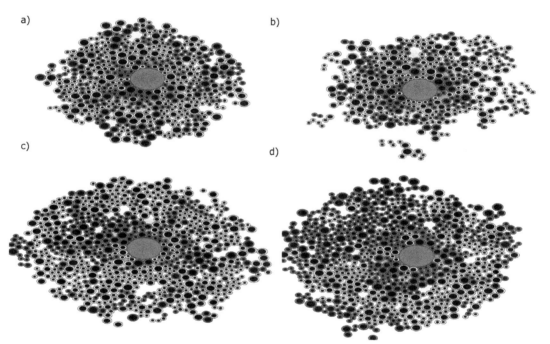

Figure 5. Snapshots of a simulation showing the competition between clones. (**a**) The tumor consists mainly of the clone c_1 (shown in yellow) with few cells in the intermediate state (in purple) between clones and the emergence of the clone c_2 (in cyan) in the sides. The size of the tumor remains limited because clone c_1 cells need relatively high concentration of I to survive; (**b**) Compared to the clone c_1, the clone c_2 cells expand and survive in areas with lower concentration of cytokines; (**c**) The clone c_2 cells surround the tumor and crowd out the cells of the clone c_1 leading to the reduction of their population. The clones c_3 (in blue) and c_4 (in magneta); (**d**) The subclone c_4 is as aggressive as the subclone c_2 due to the additional *IRF4* mutation and it manages to coexist with it in the remote areas with fewer cytokines.

The emergence of more aggressive clones not only reduces the populations of the less aggressive ones but also increases the total number of malignant cells. These clones survive in areas farther from the BMSC, making the tumor expand. We show the total number of malignant cells over time in Figure 4b. The proportions of each clone in the total population show that in the end of the simulation, the clone c_1 only represents $\approx 5\%$ of the total population. The subclone c_2 is predominant, with $\approx 60\%$ of cells (Figure 6). Overall, the global population of malignant cells increases with the emergence of more resistant subclones. The emergence of the subclone c_2 leads to an increase in the number of malignant cells because the cells belonging to this subclone can survive far from the BMSCs. The subclone c_3 emerges few hours after c_2 but barely manage to survive because of limited resources. It gives rise to the subclone c_4, which is as aggressive as the subclone c_2 due to the additional *IRF4* mutation. As the tumor progresses, these two subclones c_2 and c_4 become predominant because they are better adapted to survive in sites with limited resources. By the end of the simulation, the number of malignant cells oscillates around a stable value as well as the total concentration of cytokines in the domain (Figure 4). We show the percent of the malignant cell population occupied by each clone over time in Figure 6.

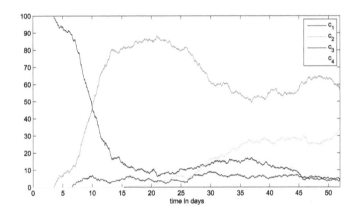

Figure 6. The proportion of each clone in the total population over time.

4. Discussion

Bone marrow stromal cells play an important role in the pathogenesis of MM. After extravasation into the bone marrow, MGUS and myeloma cells migrate and home to the areas surrounding BMSCs. This homing process is mediated by the chemokine SDF-1. It promotes the chemotaxis and homing of myeloma cells upon the interaction with its receptor CXCR4 [36]. However, it is crucial for myeloma cells to be sufficiently close to BMSCs to be attracted by the secreted SDF-1. Otherwise, they will die if they are left without enough resources to survive and divide. The progression of MGUS to MM with t(11;14) translocation is marked by the emergence of new aggressive subclones which is crucial for the expansion of the tumor because it allows its adaptation to limited resources. As the tumor progresses, the aggressive subclones become predominant because lower concentrations of IL-6 and IGF-1 allow them to survive.

To study the development of MM tumors and its intraclonal heterogeneity, we developed a specific hybrid discrete-continuous model. The model was able to reproduce the experimental results presented in [29]. We have used it to investigate the central role of the BMSCs in myeloma cell homing and the progression of MGUS to MM. BMSCs participate in the homing of myeloma cells and provide them with the necessary cytokines for their survival and proliferation. Numerical simulation results suggest that the initial distance between the BMSC and infiltrating myeloma cells is of paramount importance for the survival of the latter. After their homing, new, more aggressive myeloma subclones emerge due to the acquisition of RAS mutations. Other gene mutations such as the one acquired by the *IRF4* gene further increase the aggressiveness of some of these subclones. They compete with each other for the available cytokines, resulting in the predominance of the more fit subclones. To better quantify the heterogeneity of clones during MM progression, we show the kernel density plots at different stages of MGUS to MM progression in Figure 7. The x-axis shows the aggressiveness phenotype function scaled from 0 to 1. These results show the predominating subclones at the different stages of tumor progression. Our findings suggest that the total number of malignant cells oscillates around a stable value after a few weeks of MM development in agreement with the in vivo experiments conducted in [37]. However, we speculate that MM tumors can further expand due to other mechanisms such as stimulation of IL-6 and IGF-1 production by BMSC, the migration to other BMSCs [38], or the emegence of more resistant clones due to other mutations.

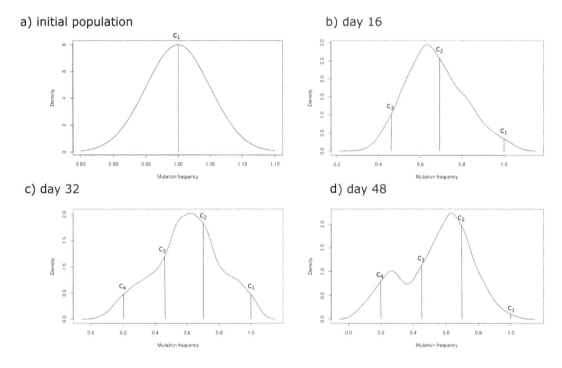

Figure 7. Gaussian kernel density plots indicating the frequency of cells acquiring each specific mutation at the different stages of the simuation. (**a**) The initial population composed of cells belonging to the subclone c_1; (**b**) c_2 is the most predominant subclone after 16 hours of the beginning of the simulation; (**c**) The *K-RAS* subclones c_3 and c_4 emerge and start expanding; (**d**) The clones c_2 and c_4 represent the majority of the population because they are equally aggressive.

The multi-scale model follows a systems biology approach [39] by integrating different interfering biological processes in one model. To understand complex phenomena such as MGUS progression to MM, it is important to properly use available data in describing events at the single cell level where processes such as gene expression and mutations take place as well as the larger tissue level where each cell interacts with its environment. Systems biology approaches focus on the whole system rather than the sum of its components. Similarly, this study is more focused on the behavior of the global model of MM homing and tumor growth than the various individual processes which regulate it.

Although the model presented here was able to reproduce the experiments describing MM intra-clonal heterogeneity, it has several limitations. Firstly, the intracellular regulation network was limited to two pathways while in reality MM is more biochemically complex [2]. Furthermore, the number of considered mutations is also reduced compared to those found in MM cases. Interactions of the myeloma cells and BMSCs with other components of the bone marrow such as the osteoblasts and osteoclasts were not included in the present model. Other mechanisms affecting myeloma cell proliferation were introduced implicitly as a random perturbation of the cell cycle in the myeloma cells. The simplification of the myeloma cell transduction pathways and mutations included was due to limitations of computational power and the difficulty of studying complex models. We have limited the model to two pathways of intracellular regulation because we wanted to study the effect of cytokines IL-6 and IGF-1 on the fate of the myeloma cells and how that fate is affected by RAS mutations and the IRF4 mutation that is associated with mutant RAS genes. Also, we assumed that IL-6 and IGF-1 play the same role in the activation of the ERK/RAS and Akt/FKHR pathways. This hypothesis was made because it is difficult to distinguish the interfering actions of the different cytokines in the cell culture experiments. Finally, the study was restricted to a site of the bone marrow containing a single BMSC. Other configurations with more BMSCs and other marrow cell types can be considered as well. In future works, we will introduce the action of treatment and study the role of the intraclonal heterogeneity in MM drug resistance.

Acknowledgments: The last author was partially supported by the Russian Science Foundation (Grant No. 15-11-00029).

Author Contributions: All authors of the paper have contributed to the study design. A.B., M.J.K and V.V. conceived and developed the hybrid model. A.B., F.-E.B. and R.A. performed the numerical simulations. A.B., F.-E.B., R.A., M.J.K and V.V. wrote the paper and analyzed the results. All authors read and approved the final manuscript.

Appendix A. Numerical Implementation

Appendix A.1. Equations for Cell Motion and Intracellular Regulation

We solve the following problem which describes the motion of each cell:

$$m\ddot{x}_i + m\mu\dot{x}_i - \sum_{j \neq i} f_{ij} - f_{ch} = 0, \tag{A1}$$

First, we write the late equation as a system of displacement x_i and velocity v_i:

$$\begin{cases} m\dot{v}_i + m\mu v_i - \sum_{j \neq i} f_{ij} - f_{ch} = 0, \\ \dot{x}_i = v_i \end{cases}$$

We first determine the velocity using the first equation of the system, then we compute the displacement of the cell using the second equation. The forces term were introduced implicitly at each timestep. The equations for intracellular regulation are solved using the Euler explicit scheme.

Appendix A.2. Reaction-Diffusion Equations for Extracellular Cytokines Concentration

We consider a rectangular two-dimensional domain Ω and we denote its boundaries by Γ. We use the alternating direction implicit method to solve the following problem:

$$(P): \begin{cases} \frac{\partial S}{dt} = D\Delta S + W - \sigma I, & in\ \Omega \\ S(x,y,0) = \phi(x,y), & in\ \Omega \\ S = 0 & on\ \Gamma, \end{cases}$$

where D is the diffusion coefficient, W and σ are the production and degradation rates respectively, and $\phi(x,y)$ represents the initial condition condition for I. We consider the two-dimensional grid $(x_i, y_j, t_n) = (ih, jh, n\delta t)$, where h and δt are the space and time steps respectively and we discretize it: $i = 1, 2, ..., N_x$ and $j = 1, 2, ..., N_y$. We first rewrite the problem (P) in the following form:

$$(P_1): \begin{cases} \frac{\partial S}{dt} = \frac{D}{2}\left(\frac{\partial^2 S}{\partial x^2} + \frac{\partial^2 S}{\partial y^2}\right) + \frac{D}{2}\left(\frac{\partial^2 S}{\partial x^2} + \frac{\partial^2 S}{\partial y^2}\right) + W - \sigma S, & in\ \Omega \\ S(x,y,0) = \phi(x,y), & in\ \Omega \\ S = 0 & on\ \Gamma, \end{cases}$$

We split the first equation of the problem (P_1) into two sub-steps as follows:

$$\begin{cases} \frac{S_{i,j}^{n+1/2}-S_{i,j}^n}{\delta t/2} = D\frac{S_{i-1,j}^{n+1/2}-2S_{i,j}^{n+1/2}+S_{i+1,j}^{n+1/2}}{h^2} + D\frac{S_{i,j-1}^n-2S_{i,j}^n+S_{i,j+1}^n}{h^2} + W - \sigma S_{i,j}^{n+1/2}, \\ \frac{S_{i,j}^{n+1}-S_{i+1/2,j}^n}{\delta t/2} = D\frac{S_{i-1,j}^{n+1}-2S_{i,j}^{n/2}+S_{i+1,j}^{n+1}}{h^2} + D\frac{S_{i,j-1}^{n+1/2}-2S_{i,j}^{n+1/2}+S_{i,j+1}^{n+1/2}}{h^2} + W - \sigma S_{i,j}^{n+1}. \end{cases} \quad \text{(A2)}$$

We solve the first equation for each fixed j to obtain $S^{n+1/2}$. Next, we solve the second to obtain S^n. Let us consider the first equation:

$$\frac{S_{i,j}^{n+1/2} - S_{i,j}^n}{\delta t/2} = D\frac{S_{i-1,j}^{n+1/2} - 2S_{i,j}^{n+1/2} + S_{i+1,j}^{n+1/2}}{h^2} + D\frac{S_{i,j-1}^n - 2S_{i,j}^n + S_{i,j+1}^n}{h^2} + W - \sigma S_{i,j}^{n+1/2}.$$

Rearranging the terms we obtain:

$$\underbrace{\frac{D}{h^2}}_{a_{i,j}} S_{i-1,j}^{n+1/2} + \underbrace{\left(-\frac{2D}{h^2} - \frac{1}{\delta t/2} - \sigma\right)}_{b_{i,j}} S_{i,j}^{n+1/2} + \underbrace{\frac{D}{h^2}}_{c_{i,j}} S_{i+1,j}^{n+1/2} =$$

$$\underbrace{-\frac{S_{i,j}^n}{\delta t/2} - D\frac{S_{i,j-1}^n - 2S_{i,j}^n + S_{i,j+1}^n}{h^2} - W}_{f_{i,j}}.$$

Therefore, we can write the first equation of the system (A2) in the form:

$$a_{i,j}S_{i-1,j}^{n+1/2} + b_{i,j}S_{i,j}^{n+1/2} + c_{i,j}S_{i+1,j}^{n+1/2} = f_{i,j},$$

For each fixed $j, j = 1, 2, ..., N_y - 1$, we solve numerically:

$$a_i S_{i-1}^{n+1/2} + b_i S_i^{n+1/2} + c_i S_{i+1}^{n+1/2} = f_i, \quad \forall i = 1, 2, ..., N_x - 1 \quad \text{(A3)}$$

with the boundary conditions $S_{i=0}^n = 0$, $S_{i=Nx}^n = 0$. We solve the Equation (A3) using Thomas algorithm. For that, we write the left boundary condition $S_{i=0} = 0$ as follows:

$$0 = L_{1/2}S_1 + K_{1/2},$$

where $L_{1/2} = 0$ and $K_{1/2} = 0$. Then, from the Equation (A3) for $i = 1$:

$$a_1 S_0^{n+1/2} + b_1 S_1^{n+1/2} + c_1 S_2^{n+1/2} = f_1,$$

we obtain $S_1^{n+1/2}$:

$$S_1^{n+1/2} = L_{3/2}S_{1,j} + K_{3/2},$$

where we denote $L_{3/2} = \frac{-c_1}{b_1}$, $K_{3/2} = \frac{a_1 S_{1,0} - f_1}{-b_1}$. We continue for $i = 2, 3, ..., N_x - 1$:

$$S_i = L_{i+1/2}S_{i+1} + K_{i+1/2}, \quad \text{(A4)}$$

where $L_{i+1/2} = \frac{-c_i}{b_i + a_i L_{i-1/2}}$, $K_{i+1/2} = \frac{f_i + a_i K_{i-1/2}}{b_i + a_i L_{i-1/2}}$. We first obtain the coefficients $L_{i+1/2}, K_{i+1/2}$ using the Equation (A3). Next, we find the solution $S^{n+1/2}$ for the sub-step $n + 1/2$ by backward sweep using the Equation (A4). We apply the same procedure on the second equation of the system (A2) to compute the next step solution S^n.

Appendix B. Parameter Values

Because of the simplifications made to the regulation network of myeloma cells, the parameters were fitted to reproduce the experimental results. The average cell cycle of the cancerous cells was considered to be stochastic. Both the extracellular and intracellular proteins concentrations are considered to be nondimensional.

Table A1. Values of intracellular regulation parameters for myeloma cells. δ is an arbitrary length unit.

Parameter	Value	Unit
Myeloma cell cycle length	26	h
Cell cycle variation	13	h
space variable and step	1	δ
time variable	1	min
time step	0.01	min
β_1	0.001	min^{-1}
α_2	0.03	min^{-1}
β_2	0.002	min^{-1}
α_3	0.001	min^{-1}
β_3	0.01	min^{-1}
γ_3	0.00083	min^{-1}

Table A2. Values of extracellular regulation parameters. δ is an arbitrary length unit.

Parameter	Value	Unit
D	0.5×10^{-5}	$\delta^2 \cdot min^{-1}$
W	0.0003	$molecules \cdot \delta^{-2} \cdot min^{-1}$
λ	0.1	NU
σ	1×10^{-7}	min^{-1}

References

1. Palumbo, A.; Anderson, K. Multiple myeloma. *N. Engl. J. Med.* **2011**, *364*, 1046–1060.
2. Morgan, G.J.; Walker, B.A.; Davies, F.E. The genetic architecture of multiple myeloma. *Nat. Rev. Cancer* **2012**, *12*, 335–348.
3. Adam, J.A. A simplified mathematical model of tumor growth. *Math. Biosci.* **1986**, *81*, 229–244.
4. Glass, L. Instability and mitotic patterns in tissue growth. *J. Dyn. Syst. Meas. Control* **1973**, *95*, 324–327.
5. McElwain, D.L.S.; Morris, L.E. Apoptosis as a volume loss mechanism in mathematical models of solid tumor growth. *Math. Biosci.* **1978**, *39*, 147–157.
6. Byrne, H.M.; Chaplain, M.A.J. Growth of non-necrotic tumours in the presence and absence of inhibitors. *Math. Biosci.* **1995**, *130*, 151–181.
7. Byrne, H.M.; Chaplain, M.A.J. Growth of Necrotic Tumours in the Presence and Absence of Inhibitors. *Math. Biosci.* **1996**, *135*, 187–216.
8. Wise, S.M.; Lowengrub, J.S.; Frieboes, H.B.; Cristini, V. Three-dimensional multispecies nonlinear tumor growth—I: Model and numerical method. *J. Theor. Biol.* **2008**, *253*, 524–543.
9. Stiehl, T.; Baran, N.; Ho, A.D.; Marciniak-Czohra, A. Clonal selection and therapy resistance in acute leukaemias: Mathematical modelling explains different proliferation patterns at diagnosis and relapse. *J. R. Soc. Interface* **2014**, *11*, 20140079.
10. Walenda, T.; Stiehl, T.; Braun, H.; Fröbel. J.; Ho, A.D.; Schroeder, T.; Goecke, T.W.; Rath, B.; Germing, U.; Marciniak-Czohra, A.; et al. Feedback Signals in Myelodysplastic Syndromes: Increased Self-Renewal of the Malignant Clone Suppresses Normal Hematopoiesis. *PLoS Comp. Biol.* **2014**, *10*, e1003599.
11. Panetta, J.C. A mathematical model of drug resistance: Heterogeneous tumors. *Math. Biosci.* **1998**, *147*, 42–61.

12. Basanta, D.; Haralambos, H.; Deutsch, A. Studying the emergence of invasiveness in tumours using game theory. *Eur. Phys. J. B* **2008**, *63*, 393–397.

13. Enderling, H.; Hlatky, L.; Hahnfeldt, P. Migration rules: Tumours are conglomerates of self-metastases. *Br. J. Cancer* **2009**, *100*, 1917–1925.

14. Piotrowska, M.J.; Angus, S.D. A quantitative cellular automaton model of in vitro multicellular spheroid tumour growth. *J. Theor. Biol.* **2009**, *258*, 165–178.

15. Drasdo, D.; Hoehme, S. A single-cell-based model of tumor growth in vitro: Monolayers and spheroids. *Phys. Biol.* **2005**, *2*, 133.

16. Shirinifard, A.; Gens, J.S.; Zaitlen, B.L.; Poplawski, N.J.; Swat, M.; Glazier, J.A. 3D Multi-Cell Simulation of Tumor Growth and Angiogenesis. *PLoS ONE* **2009**, *4*, e7190.

17. Swat, M.H.; Thomas, G.L.; Shirinifard, A.; Clandenon, S.G.; Glazier, J.A. Emergent Stratification in Solid Tumors Selects for Reduced Cohesion of Tumor Cells: A Multi-Cell, Virtual-Tissue Model of Tumor Evolution Using CompuCell3D. *PLoS ONE* **2015**, *10*, e0127972.

18. Hatzikirou, H.; Brusch, L.; Schaller, C.; Simon, M.; Deutsch, A. Prediction of traveling front behavior in a lattice-gas cellular automaton model for tumor invasion. *Comput. Math. Appl.* **2010**, *59*, 2326–2339.

19. Aubert, M.; Badoual, M.; Fereol, S.; Christov, C.; Grammaticos, B. A cellular automaton model for the migration of glioma cells. *Phys. Biol.* **2006**, *3*, 93–100.

20. Ramis-Conde, I.; Drasdo, D.; Chaplain, M.A.J.; Anderson, A.R.A. Modeling the influence of the E-cadherin-β-catenin pathway in cancer cell invasion: A multiscale approach. *Biophys. J.* **2008**, *95*, 155–165.

21. Ramis-Conde, I.; Chaplain, M.A.J.; Anderson, A.R.A.; Drasdo, D. Multi-scale modelling of cancer cell intravasation: The role of cadherins in metastasis. *Phys. Biol.* **2009**, *6*, 016008.

22. Zhang, L.; Wang, Z.; Sagotsky, J.A.; Deisboeck, T.S. Multiscale agent-based cancer modeling. *J. Math. Biol.* **2009**, *58*, 545–559.

23. Anderson, A.R.A. A hybrid mathematical model of solid tumour invasion: the importance of cell adhesion. *Math. Med. Biol.* **2005**, *22*, 163–186.

24. Fang, J.S.; Gillies, R.D.; Gatenby, R.A. Adaptation to hypoxia and acidosis in carcinogenesis and tumor progression. *Semin. Cancer Biol.* **2008**, *18*, 330–337.

25. Vincent, T.L.; Gatenby, R.A. An evolutionary model for initiation, promotion, and progression in carcinogenesis. *Int. J. Oncol.* **2008**, *32*, 729–737.

26. Chisholm, R.H.; Lorenzi, T.; Lorz, A.; Larsen, A.K.; de Almeida, L.N.; Escargueil, A.; Clairambault, J. Emergence of drug tolerance in cancer cell populations: An evolutionary outcome of selection, nongenetic instability, and stress-induced adaptation. *Cancer Res.* **2015**, *75*, 930–939.

27. Ayati, B.P.; Edwards, C.M.; Webb, G.F.; Wikswo, J.P. A mathematical model of bone remodeling dynamics for normal bone cell populations and myeloma bone disease. *Biol. Direct* **2010**, *5*, 28.

28. Bouchnita, A.; Eymard, N.; Moyo, T.K.; Koury, M.J.; Volpert, V. Bone marrow infiltration by multiple myeloma causes anemia by reversible disruption of erythropoiesis. *Am. J. Hematol.* **2016**, *91*, 371–378.

29. Walker, B.A.; Wardell, C.P.; Melchor, L.; Hulkki, S.; Potter, N.E.; Johnson, D.C.; Fenwick, K.; Kozarewa, I.; Gonzalez, D.; Lord, C.J.; et al. Intraclonal heterogeneity and distinct molecular mechanisms characterize the development of t(4;14) and t(11;14) myeloma. *Blood* **2012**, *120*, 1077–1086.

30. Bouchnita, A.; Belmaati, F.E.; Aboulaich, R.; Ellaia, R.; Volpert, V. Mathematical modelling of intra-clonal heterogeneity in multiple myeloma. In Proceedings of the CARI 2016, Hammamet, Tunisia, 11–14 October 2016.

31. Brioli, A.; Melchor, L.; Cavo, M.; Morgan, G.J. The impact of intra-clonal heterogeneity on the treatment of multiple myeloma. *Br. J. Haematol.* **2014**, *165*, 441–454.

32. Melchor, L.; Brioli, A.; Wardell, C.P.; Murison, A.; Potter, N.E.; Kaiser, M.F.; Fryer, R.A.; Johnson, D.C.; Begum, D.B.; Wilson, S.H.; et al. Single-cell genetic analysis reveals the composition of initiating clones and phylogenetic patterns of branching and parallel evolution in myeloma. *Leukemia* **2014**, *28*, 1705–1715.

33. Chesi, M.; Bergsagel, P.L.; Brents, L.A.; Smith, C.M.; Gerhard, D.S.; Kuehl, W.M. Dysregulation of cyclin D1 by translocation into an IgH gamma switch region in two multiple myeloma cell lines. *Blood* **1996**, *88*, 674–681.

34. Bouyssou, J.M.C.; Ghobrial, I.M.; Roccaro, A.M. Targeting SDF-1 in multiple myeloma tumor microenvironment. *Cancer Lett.* **2015**, *380*, 315–318.

35. Vanderkerken, K.; van Camp, B.; de Greef, C.; Broek, I.V.; Asosingh, K.; van Riet, I. Homing of the myeloma cell clone. *Acta Oncol.* **2000**, *39*, 771–776.

36. Hideshima, T.; Mitsiades, C.; Tonon, G.; Richardson, P.G.; Anderson, K.C. Understanding multiple myeloma pathogenesis in the bone marrow to identify new therapeutic targets. *Nat. Rev. Cancer* **2007**, *7*, 585–598.

37. Rozemuller, H.; van der Spek, E.; Bogers-Boer, L.H.; Zwart, M.C.; Verweij, V.; Emmelot, M.; Groen, R.W.; Spaapen, R.; Bloem, A.C.; Lokhorst, H.M.; et al. A bioluminescence imaging based in vivo model for preclinical testing of novel cellular immunotherapy strategies to improve the graft-versus-myeloma effect. *Haematologica* **2008**, *93*, 1049–1057.

38. Manier, S.; Sacco, A.; Leleu, X.; Ghobrial, I.M.; Roccaro, A.M. Bone marrow microenvironment in multiple myeloma progression. *BioMed Res. Int.* **2012**, *2012*, 157496.

39. Kitano, H. Systems Biology: A brief overview. *Science* **2002**, *295*, 1662–1664.

6

An Accurate Computational Tool for Performance Estimation of FSO Communication Links over Weak to Strong Atmospheric Turbulent Channels

Theodore D. Katsilieris, George P. Latsas, Hector E. Nistazakis * and George S. Tombras

Department of Electronics, Computers, Telecommunications and Control, Faculty of Physics, National and Kapodistrian University of Athens, Athens 15784, Greece; tkatsil@phys.uoa.gr (T.D.K.); glatsas@phys.uoa.gr (G.P.L.); gtombras@phys.uoa.gr (G.S.T.)
* Correspondence: enistaz@phys.uoa.gr

Academic Editors: Ali Cemal Benim and Demos T. Tsahalis

Abstract: The terrestrial optical wireless communication links have attracted significant research and commercial worldwide interest over the last few years due to the fact that they offer very high and secure data rate transmission with relatively low installation and operational costs, and without need of licensing. However, since the propagation path of the information signal, i.e., the laser beam, is the atmosphere, their effectivity affects the atmospheric conditions strongly in the specific area. Thus, system performance depends significantly on the rain, the fog, the hail, the atmospheric turbulence, etc. Due to the influence of these effects, it is necessary to study, theoretically and numerically, very carefully before the installation of such a communication system. In this work, we present exactly and accurately approximate mathematical expressions for the estimation of the average capacity and the outage probability performance metrics, as functions of the link's parameters, the transmitted power, the attenuation due to the fog, the ambient noise and the atmospheric turbulence phenomenon. The latter causes the scintillation effect, which results in random and fast fluctuations of the irradiance at the receiver's end. These fluctuations can be studied accurately with statistical methods. Thus, in this work, we use either the lognormal or the gamma–gamma distribution for weak or moderate to strong turbulence conditions, respectively. Moreover, using the derived mathematical expressions, we design, accomplish and present a computational tool for the estimation of these systems' performances, while also taking into account the parameter of the link and the atmospheric conditions. Furthermore, in order to increase the accuracy of the presented tool, for the cases where the obtained analytical mathematical expressions are complex, the performance results are verified with the numerical estimation of the appropriate integrals. Finally, using the derived mathematical expression and the presented computational tool, we present the corresponding numerical results, using common parameter values for realistic terrestrial free space optical communication systems.

Keywords: free space optics; turbulence strength; outage probability; average capacity; lognormal distribution; gamma–gamma distribution

1. Introduction

The optical wireless—or free space optical (FSO)—communication systems offer high bandwidth and secure access along with low installation and maintenance cost without needing any operational license. Thus, this technology attracts very significant research of experimental and commercial interest, especially in the last few years [1–8]. However, the performance and the availability of terrestrial FSO links depends strongly on the atmospheric conditions in the area where the link is installed. More specifically, the fog, the rain, the hail, etc. affect significantly their effectivity, while another very significant phenomenon for the availability and performance decreasing is the atmospheric turbulence which causes the scintillation effect that induces rapid fluctuations of the optical signal on the receiver's side. Thus, the FSO channels have randomly time-varying characteristics due to the scintillation effect [9–12]. In order to study these signal's fluctuations, many statistical models have been proposed and tested experimentally for various atmospheric turbulence conditions. More specifically, for the case of strong to very strong turbulence conditions, the K-distribution model is usually used, for saturated turbulence, the negative exponential statistical distribution, and, for weak turbulence, the lognormal, the gamma, the Malaga and the Rayleigh distributions can be used, while, for moderate to strong cases, the gamma–gamma, the Malaga and the I-K models are used [12–32]. In this work, we use either the lognormal distribution model, which is accurate enough for the cases of weak turbulence conditions, or the gamma–gamma which is the suitable statistical distribution to model the irradiance fluctuations at the receiver for the cases of moderate to strong turbulence [13,14,17,18,27–32].

In this work, taking into account the fog and atmospheric turbulence, the performance and the availability of the FSO links are estimated by means of the average capacity and outage probability metrics [13,27–29]. Thus, we derive either closed form mathematical expressions or accurate approximate ones, for the evaluation of these metrics as functions of the transmitted power, the attenuation due to the fog, the atmospheric turbulence and the link's parameters. The obtained expression are using either the lognormal distribution, for the cases where the turbulence strength can be assumed as weak, or the gamma–gamma for moderate to strong turbulence.

Next, using the derived mathematical expressions, we design, implement and present a new mathematical tool that evaluates accurately these two abovementioned performance quantities, using as input realistic parameters for the link, the fog attenuation, the transmitted power and the strength of the atmospheric turbulence effect. The computational tool, through the proposed algorithm, estimates the system's performance and availability by means of the derived expression for the average capacity and the outage probability, respectively. Furthermore, due to the complexity of the derived mathematical expressions that are using the gamma–gamma distribution model, the algorithm re-evaluates the metric value without using the derived analytical expression but with the computational estimation of the corresponding integrals, in order to verify the results and the validity of the analytical predictions [33]. Moreover, it should be mentioned that, in the future, the influences of other effect, e.g., rain, hail, etc., can be added. However, due to the operational wavelength of the FSO links, the fog and the turbulence effects play very significant roles in their performance, and, for this reason, we study them theoretically and computationally in this work [33].

The work presented in this manuscript is organized as follows: in Section 2, we introduce the FSO system, the channel model, the link parameters, the fog attenuation, the atmospheric turbulence effect, the lognormal and the gamma distributions. Next, in Section 3, we present the performance metrics for the FSO communication link and we derive the mathematical expressions for the estimation of the outage probability and the average capacity. In Section 4, we present the algorithm structure for the computational tool, while, in Section 5, we present the numerical results for common realistic FSO configurations. In Section 6, the final conclusions are presented and the Appendix A with the pseudo-code algorithm follows.

2. Channel Model

We consider a point-to-point terrestrial FSO link, with additive white Gaussian noise (AWGN), in which the information signal, i.e., the laser beam, propagates along a horizontal path. The channel can be assumed that is stationary and ergodic and the statistical channel model is given as [29]:

$$y = \eta\, I\, x + n, \tag{1}$$

where y is the received signal, x is the modulated signal, i.e., takes the values "0" or "1", η is the detector's responsivity, n is the AWGN with zero mean value and variance $N_0/2$, whereas I is the normalized instantaneous irradiance on the receiver's side [20].

As mentioned above, the atmospheric turbulence effect affects significantly the performance of an FSO link due to the scintillation effect, which results in fast and large irradiance fluctuations on the receiver's end. Taking into account the atmospheric turbulence strength, the operational wavelength of the communication system and the link's length, the Rytov variance can be estimated, which is a parameter that measures the severity of intensity scintillation caused by the distributed atmospheric turbulence, i.e., the strength of the turbulence effect [34]. More specifically, the Rytov variance, σ_I^2, is given as [29,35]:

$$\sigma_I^2 = 1.23 C_n^2 k^{7/6} L^{11/6}, \tag{2}$$

where $k = 2\pi/\lambda$ is the wave number, λ is the wavelength, L stands for the link length and C_n^2 represents the refractive index structure parameter, and it is proportional to the atmospheric turbulence strength [36]. The Rytov variance represents the normalized irradiance variance or the scintillation index and characterizes the turbulence strength as follows [3,37]:

$$
\begin{array}{ll}
\sigma_I^2 \leq 0.3 & \text{(weak fluctuations)} \\
0.3 < \sigma_I^2 < 5 & \text{(moderate to strong fluctuations)} \\
\sigma_I^2 \gg 1 & \text{(saturation fluctuations)}
\end{array}
\tag{3}
$$

Taking into account that the irradiance fluctuations at the receiver of the FSO link, due to the scintillation effect, are studied with statistical models, and the main criterion for their choice is the atmospheric turbulence strength, the regions that appear in Equation (3) can be used. Thus, in this work, for the case of weak turbulence conditions, i.e., $\sigma_I^2 \leq 0.3$, the lognormal distribution model is used, while for values larger than 0.3 and up to 5, the turbulence strength can be assumed as moderate to strong and the gamma–gamma distribution is suitable.

The irradiance fluctuations at the receiver results in fluctuations in the dependent quantities. More specifically, the instantaneous electrical signal-to-noise ratio (SNR) at the receiver, γ, behaves as a random variable and is given as [36]:

$$\gamma = \frac{(\eta \, I \, P_r)^2}{N_0}, \tag{4}$$

while the expected electrical SNR on the receiver's side, μ, is given as [29,31]:

$$\mu = \frac{(\eta \, E \, [\, I \,] P_r)^2}{N_0}, \tag{5}$$

where P_r is the expected signal power at the receiver while N_0 is given as [32,38,39]:

$$N_0 = \frac{4 K_B T_{abs} B F_n}{R_L} + 2 q_e B \left(I_{ph} + I_D \right) + (RIN) I_{ph}^2, \tag{6}$$

with K_B being the Boltzmann constant, T_{abs} being the absolute system temperature, F_n is the photodiode noise figure, R_L the load resistor [36], I_D, is the dark current on photodetector [40], RIN the relative intensity noise process and a typical value is -130 dB/Hz, and q_e is the electron charge, whereas $I_{ph} = P_r \eta$ is the average receiver photocurrent [31].

Furthermore, it should be mentioned here that another significant performance mitigation factor of the FSO link, is the background, or the ambient noise, and is caused by the background radiation, which is collected by the lens of the receiver of the optical system in addition to the information signal [4,41–45]. In order to decrease its influence, optical filters of bandwidth B_f, before the receiver's lens are usually used [45]. Thus, assuming that the background noise is Gaussian with spectral density N_b, the total power of the ambient noise, which arrives at the receiver's input, is $B_f N_b$. The influence of the ambient noise at the total system's noise is given through [45] and Equation (6) and has the mathematical form:

$$N_0 = \frac{4K_B T_{abs} B F_n}{R_L} + 2q_e B \left(I_{ph} + I_D \right) + 2B\eta^2 N_b^2 B_f / r + (RIN) I_{ph}^2, \tag{7}$$

where $r = \omega_{FOV}/\omega_D$, ω_{FOV} represents the receiver's field of view while ω_D stands for the solid angle subtended by the background source at the receiver [45].

For the estimation of the expected signal at the receiver's side, P_r, taking into account the visibility at the area of the FSO link and losses due to the scintillation effect, using [2,33,46,47], we make a conclusion of the following expression:

$$P_r = P_T \, G_T G_R \left(\frac{\lambda}{4\pi L} \right)^2 \left(\frac{D_R}{D_T + \theta L} \right)^2 10^{-(La_{tot} + L_m)/10}, \tag{8}$$

where P_T is the transmitted power, G_T, G_R are the gains of transmitter and receiver, respectively, which are computed from initial parameters [33], D_R and D_T are the transmitter's and receiver's aperture, θ stands for the beam's divergence, a_{tot}, represents the atmospheric attenuation that includes the fog phenomenon, a_f, the rain, a_r, the snow a_{sn}, and the scintillation effect, a_s, which affect significantly the performance of the FSO links while L_m, stands for the miscellaneous losses of the system, as it is presented in [2,4,33,46,47]. More specifically, the attenuation parameter due to the fog is given through the Kim or the Kruse model depending on the effect's strength, and the atmospheric visibility V with sky droplets are set to $\tau_{TH} = 5\%$ [47]. Furthermore, the scintillation losses parameter in dB is given as: $a_s = \sqrt{92.68 \cdot (2\pi 10^9/\lambda)^{7/6} C_n^2 L^{11/6}}$ [47].

All of the above parameters are taken into account by our tool and some common values are presented in Table 1. Thus, for the specific case, for negligible ambient noise using the suitable infrared filters [48], from Equations (5)–(8), the average electrical SNR at the receiver, as a function of the transmitted power, is given as:

$$\mu = \frac{\left(\eta P_T \, G_T G_R \left(\frac{\lambda}{4\pi L} \right)^2 \left(\frac{D_R}{D_T + \theta \cdot L} \right)^2 10^{-(L \cdot a_{tot} + L_m)/10} \right)^2}{(4K_B T_{abs} B F_n / R_L) + 2q_e B \left(I_{ph} + I_D \right) + (RIN) I_{ph}^2}, \tag{9}$$

while, for the case where the ambient noise cannot be assumed as negligible, from Equations (5), (6) and (8), the average electrical SNR is given as:

$$\mu = \frac{\left(\eta P_T \, G_T G_R \left(\frac{\lambda}{4\pi L} \right)^2 \left(\frac{D_R}{D_T + \theta \cdot L} \right)^2 10^{-(L \cdot a_{tot} + L_m)/10} \right)^2}{(4K_B T_{abs} B F_n / R_L) + 2q_e B \left(I_{ph} + I_D \right) + 2B\eta^2 N_b^2 B_f / r + (RIN) I_{ph}^2}. \tag{10}$$

It should be mentioned here that, although the ambient noise represents a major interference source, especially in daytime hours, its influence can be minimized using specific infrared filters in front of the receiver's lens for common realistic FSO links [48]. Thus, for the computational tool that we present below, the influence of the ambient noise is considered negligible.

2.1. Lognormal Turbulence Model

The lognormal distribution is a suitable distribution model in order to emulate the irradiance fluctuations at the receiver's side due to the scintillation effect for the cases of weak turbulence conditions. The corresponding PDF for γ is given as [9,29]:

$$f_\gamma(\gamma) = \left[\frac{1}{2\gamma\sigma\sqrt{2\pi}} exp\left(-\frac{(\ln(\gamma/\mu)+\sigma^2)^2}{8\sigma^2} \right) \right], \tag{11}$$

where σ^2 is the variance for planar wave of the lognormal distribution that depends on the channel's characteristics and is given as [3,27,29]:

$$\sigma^2 = exp\left[\frac{0.49\sigma_l^2}{\left(1+0.65d^2+1.11\sigma_l^{12/5}\right)^{7/6}} + \frac{0.51\sigma_n^2\left(1+0.69\sigma_l^{12/5}\right)^{-5/6}}{\left(1+0.9d^2+0.62d^2\sigma_l^{12/5}\right)^{5/6}} \right] - 1, \tag{12}$$

where $d = 0.5D_R\sqrt{k/L}$ [29].

2.2. Gamma–Gamma Turbulence Model

Another very significant statistical distribution model, for the research area of the FSO link is the gamma–gamma, which has been proven to be very accurate at describing the irradiance fluctuations due to the scintillation effect for the cases of moderate to strong turbulence channels [14,17,31,35]. Its PDF, as a function of γ is given as [17,36]:

$$f_\gamma(\gamma) = \frac{(ab)^{(a+b)/2}}{\Gamma(a)\Gamma(b)} \frac{\gamma^{(a+b)/4-1}}{\mu^{(a+b)/4}} K_{a-b}\left(2\sqrt{ab\sqrt{\frac{\gamma}{\mu}}} \right), \tag{13}$$

where $\Gamma(.)$ represents the gamma function, K_v is the modified Bessel function of the second kind of order v, and a, b are parameters which can be defined from the link's parameters and given through the expressions [35,39]:

$$
\begin{aligned}
a &= \left[exp\left(\frac{0.49\sigma_l^2}{\left(1+0.65d^2+1.11\sigma_l^{12/5}\right)^{7/6}} \right) - 1 \right]^{-1}, \\
b &= \left[exp\left(\frac{0.51\sigma_l^2\left(1+0.69\sigma_l^{12/5}\right)^{-5/6}}{\left(1+0.9d^2+0.62d^2\sigma_l^{12/5}\right)^{5/6}} \right) - 1 \right]^{-1}.
\end{aligned} \tag{14}
$$

3. Performance of the FSO System

3.1. Outage Probability of the System

A very significant metric for the estimation of the availability of the optical communication system is the outage probability, P_{out}. More specifically, this quantity represents the probability of the instantaneous SNR to fall below a critical threshold, γ_{th}, which is set by the receiver's sensitivity limit [9,27,29,30]:

$$P_{out} = P_r(\gamma \le \gamma_{th}) = \int_0^{\gamma_{th}} f_\gamma(\gamma)d\gamma. \tag{15}$$

From Equation (15) and using the expressions (10)–(12), we reach a conclusion of the following closed form mathematical expression for the estimation of the outage probability of the FSO link through the lognormal distribution model, as a function of the transmitted power and the attenuation parameters due to the fog and the scintillation effect:

$$P_{out} = \tfrac{1}{2}erfc\left(\frac{1}{2\sqrt{2}\sigma}\left[\ln\left(\frac{\left(\eta P_T\, G_T G_R\left(\frac{\lambda}{4\pi L}\right)^2\left(\frac{D_R}{D_T+\theta L}\right)^2 10^{-(L\cdot a_{tot}+L_m)/10} \right)^2}{\gamma_{th}\left[(4K_B T_{abs}BF_n/R_L)+2q_eB(I_{ph}+I_D)+2B\eta^2N_b^2B_f/r+(RIN)I_{ph}^2\right]} \right) - \sigma^2 \right] \right). \tag{16}$$

Similarly as above, from Equation (15) and using the expressions (10), (13) and (14), the following closed mathematical expression is derived for the outage probability estimation of the FSO link, as a function of the transmitted power and the attenuation parameters due to the fog and the scintillation effect using the gamma-gamma distribution model:

$$
\begin{aligned}
&P_{out} \\
&= \frac{\left(a^2 b^2 \gamma_{thhh}\right)^{\frac{(a+b)}{4}}}{\Gamma(a)\Gamma(b)} \left(\frac{\left(4K_B T_{abs} BF_n / R_L\right) + 2q_e B\left(I_{ph}+I_D\right) + 2B\eta^2 N_b^2 B_f / r + (RIN)I_{ph}{}^2}{\left(\eta P_T \ G_T G_R \left(\frac{\lambda}{4\pi L}\right)^2 \left(\frac{D_R}{D_T+\theta L}\right)^2 10^{-\frac{L a_{tot}+L_m}{10}}\right)^2} \right)^{\frac{(a+b)}{4}} \\
&\times G_{1,3}^{2,1}\left(ab \sqrt{ \frac{\gamma_{th}\cdot\left(\left(\frac{4K_B T_{abs} BF_n}{R_L}\right) + 2q_e B\left(I_{ph}+I_D\right) + 2B\eta^2 N_b^2 B_f / r + (RIN)I_{ph}{}^2\right)}{\left(\eta P_T \ G_T G_R \left(\frac{\lambda}{4\pi L}\right)^2 \left(\frac{D_R}{D_T+\theta L}\right)^2 10^{-\frac{L a_{tot}+L_m}{10}}\right)^2}} \ \Bigg| \ \begin{matrix} 1-\frac{a+b}{2} \\ \frac{a-b}{2}, \frac{b-a}{2}, -\frac{a+b}{2} \end{matrix} \right),
\end{aligned}
\tag{17}
$$

where $G_{p,q}^{m,n}[.]$ stands for the Meijer G-function [49].

In order to design and realize the scope of this work's computational tool, we implement the outage probability, especially for the gamma–gamma model case, with both, numerical and analytical ways (see Appendix A) for accuracy reasons due to the complexity of the Meijer Function [49].

3.2. Average Channel Capacity

Another significant quantity that can be used for FSO's performance estimation is the average capacity of the optical channel. In practice, this metric represents the practical capacity, i.e., the maximum data rate, which can be supported by the optical channel under the specific circumstances. The average capacity $\langle C \rangle$ is given as [13,36]:

$$
\langle C \rangle = B \int_0^\infty \log_2\left(1 + \frac{(\eta I P_r)^2}{N_0}\right) f_I(I) dI,
\tag{18}
$$

where B stands for the system's bandwidth.

From the average channel capacity mathematical expression [13,28,29], and using Equation (11), we obtain the following accurate approximate expression, as a function of the transmitted power, the attenuation parameters, the fog and the scintillation effect:

$$
\begin{aligned}
&\langle \widetilde{C} \rangle = C_0 \left\{ \sum_k \frac{a_k}{k} \left[erfcx\left(\sqrt{2}\sigma k + \frac{A}{2\sqrt{2}\sigma}\right) + erfcx\left(\sqrt{2}\sigma k - \frac{A}{2\sqrt{2}\sigma}\right) \right] + \frac{4\sigma}{\sqrt{2\pi}} + A exp\left(\frac{A^2}{8\sigma^2}\right) erfcx\left(-\frac{A}{2\sqrt{2}\sigma}\right) \right\} \\
&A = ln\left(\frac{\left(\eta P_T \ G_T G_R \left(\frac{\lambda}{4\pi L}\right)^2 \left(\frac{D_R}{D_T+\theta\cdot L}\right)^2 10^{-(L\cdot a_{tot}+L_m)/10}\right)^2}{\left(4K_B T_{abs} B\cdot F_n / R_L\right) + 2q_e B\left(I_{ph}+I_D\right) + 2B\eta^2 N_b^2 B_f / r + (RIN)I_{ph}{}^2} \right) - \sigma^2,
\end{aligned}
\tag{19}
$$

where $\langle \widetilde{C} \rangle = \langle C \rangle / B$ and $C_0 = \left(exp(-A^2/8\sigma^2)\right)/(2\ln(2))$, while the eight a_k parameters that are taken into account are given in [13,29].

Similarly to the previous case for weak turbulence conditions, for the case of moderate to strong turbulence, the average capacity is estimated through expression (18), but, in this case, with the gamma–gamma statistical distribution model. Thus, from [3,14,36], and using the expression (10), we reach a conclusion of the following closed form mathematical expression for the FSO's average capacity, as a function of the transmitted power and the the attenuation parameters due to the fog and the scintillation effect:

$$
\begin{aligned}
&\langle \widetilde{C} \rangle \\
&= \left(\frac{\left[(ab)^2\left(4K_B T_{abs} BF_n / R_L + 2q_e B\left(I_{ph}+I_D\right) + 2B\eta^2 N_b^2 B_f / r + (RIN)I_{ph}{}^2\right)\right]^{(a+b)/4}}{4\pi \ln(2)\Gamma(a)\Gamma(b)\left(\eta P_T \ G_T G_R \left(\frac{\lambda}{4\pi L}\right)^2 \left(\frac{D_R}{D_T+\theta\cdot L}\right)^2 10^{-(L a_{tot}+L_m)/10}\right)^{\frac{a+b}{2}}} \right) \\
&\times G_{2,3}^{6,1}\left(\frac{(ab)^2\left(\frac{4K_B T_{abs} BF_n}{R_L} + 2q_e B\left(I_{ph}+I_D\right) + \frac{2B\eta^2 N_b^2 B_f}{r} + (RIN)I_{ph}{}^2\right)}{\left(4\eta P_T \ G_T G_R \left(\frac{\lambda}{4\pi L}\right)^2 \left(\frac{D_R}{D_T+\theta\cdot L}\right)^2 10^{-(L a_{tot}+L_m)/10}\right)^2} \ \Bigg| \ \begin{matrix} -\frac{a+b}{4}, -\frac{a+b}{4}+1 \\ \frac{a-b}{4}, \frac{a-b+2}{4}, \frac{b-a}{4}, \frac{b-a+2}{4}, -\frac{a+b}{4}, -\frac{a+b}{4} \end{matrix} \right)
\end{aligned}
\tag{20}
$$

4. Algorithm Structure for the Computational Tool

Here, we present the algorithm structure of the computational tool, which is the main scope of this work and evaluates the performance of an FSO link, as a function of the link parameters, the transmitted power and the attenuation due to the fog and scintillation effect, by means of the estimation of the outage probability and average capacity metrics. Moreover, here, we assume that the ambient noise, although, in general, is a significant mitigation factor for the system's performance, can have its influence be suppressed significantly using the suitable infrared filters. Thus, for the specific computational tool that we present below, we use the above derived Equations (16) and (17) for the outage probability estimation and Labels (19) and (20) for the average capacity, for weak or moderate to strong turbulence conditions, respectively, assuming that the ambient noise can be considered neglected [48].

The entire tool has been designed on a Graphical User Interface (GUI) that is quite easy and user-friendly. Figure 1 presents a schematic diagram of the algorithm and the numerical tool and fully describes its operation while, in Figure 2, the GUI is shown. The user must insert values for all of the initial parameters and then the calculations can be performed.

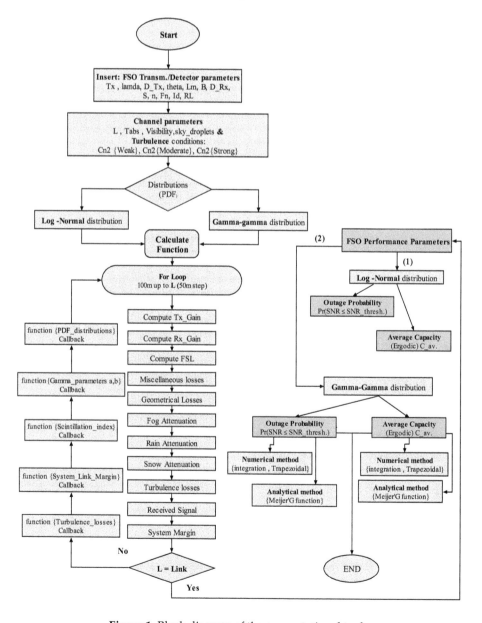

Figure 1. Block diagram of the computational tool.

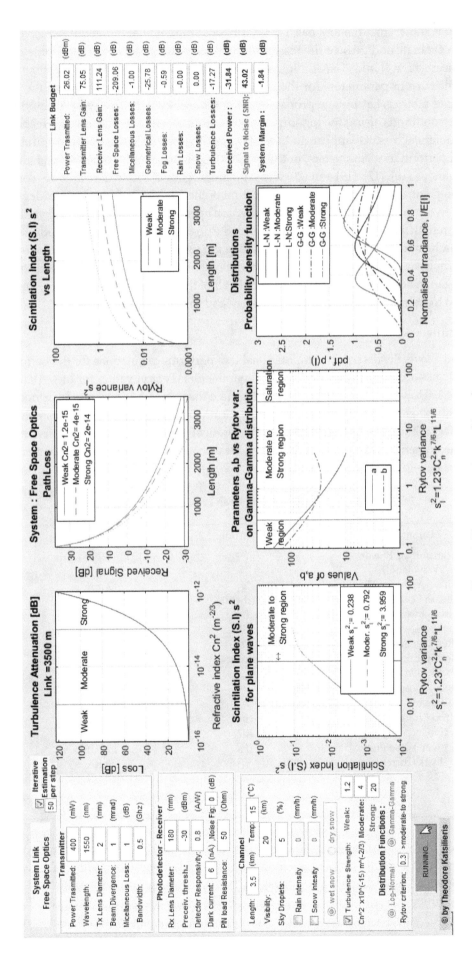

Figure 2. The computation tool interface.

In Figure 1, it is shown that the tool has a main function, the calculate function, which controls other functions to evaluate and present the results both numerically and graphically inside the loop until achieving the case L = "Link", i.e., "Link" representing the total link length, and estimating the SNR values for the current parameters for these conditions. Then, the code estimates the specific system performance metrics, i.e., outage probability and average capacity, for weak or moderate to strong turbulence conditions, using the lognormal or the gamma–gamma distribution, respectively. The obtained numerical results appear in new pop-up figures. To compute accurately the above-mentioned performance parameters, in the specific tool, we use both numerical and analytical methods (see Equations (16), (17), (19) and (20) and Appendix A), and obtained results are compared.

The transition point, which represents the upper limit of the weak turbulence regime, depends on the value of the Rytov parameter. More specifically, for σ_l^2 smaller than the critical value "0.3", the turbulence strength is assumed to be weak and the lognormal distribution model and the corresponding mathematical expressions derived above are used. On the other hand, for σ_l^2 larger than "0.3", the turbulence strength is assumed to be moderate or strong and the expressions obtained with the gamma–gamma distribution model are used. In all of the above-mentioned cases, the user of the computational tool should insert the link parameters and the attenuation strength.

5. Numerical Results

As mentioned above, the described computational tool performs calculations for the performance estimation of FSO links according to their operational parameters. Typical values for these parameters are given in Table 1. However, it is worth mentioning here that any other parameter values can be used, in order to investigate the performance of each optical wireless communication system. Taking into account the fact that this tool not only uses the theoretical mathematical expressions presented above, but also the numerical estimation methods, it is clear that the specific performance metrics can be estimated accurately for almost any practical case.

Table 1. The common parameter values of an FSO communication link.

Parameter	Symbol	Value
Transmitted Power	P_T	400 mW (26 dBm)
Wavelength	λ	1550 nm
Transmitted Aperture Diameter	D_T	2 mm
Beam Divergence	θ (theta)	1 mrad
Miscellaneous Losses	L_m	1 dB
Bandwidth	B	0.5 Ghz
Receiver Aperture	D_R	180 mm
Receiver Sensitivity	S (threshold)	-30 or -40 dBm
Sky Droplets	τ_{TH}	5%
Detector Responsitivity	η	0.8 A/W
Boltzmann Constant	K_B	1.38×10^{-23}
Electron Charge Constant	q_e	1.602×10^{-19} Cb
Relative Intensity Noise	RIN	-130 dB/Hz
Receiver Noise Figure	F_n	1 (0 dB)
Dark Current	I_D	6 nA
Load Resistor	R_L	50 Ω
Temperature	$Tabs$	288 K
Visibility	V	20 km

In Table 1, we present some common values that have been inserted in the proposed computational tool. These values have been used as initial conditions as can be seen in Figure 2. The way that the results are obtained is described analytically in the block diagram of the code in Figure 1. More specifically, three values of the parameter C_n^2 have been used, i.e., 7.8×10^{-16} m$^{-2/3}$, 6.0×10^{-15} m$^{-2/3}$, $C_n^2 = 20.0 \times 10^{-15}$ m$^{-2/3}$, for weak, moderate and strong turbulence conditions, respectively [36], for link lengths up to 5 km. For these parameter values and contiguous to these, by using the specific computational tool, the following figures for the presented above performance metrics are obtained.

Thus, in Figure 3a, the outage probability curves are presented for weak to strong turbulence strength and for the −30 dBm receiver's threshold. It is clear that for weak turbulence the optical system can work reliably even for link distances up to 3.5 km. In Figure 3b, we use a −40 dBm receiver threshold for similar C_n^2 parameters for links up to 5 km. From the above figures, it is obvious that decreasing the receiver's threshold increases the availability of the system. In addition, for stronger atmospheric turbulence effects, the total effective link length falls below 1700 m. However, as mentioned above, the link parameters, such as visibility, attenuation, receiver's threshold, absolute temperature, detector responsivity, miscellaneous losses, etc., which appear in Table 1, have been used in our computational tool and produce the specific results, are changed depending on the specific optical wireless link that is investigated. Thus, if both the link and environment parameters have been studied, the proposed computational tool can be easily and accurately used for the outage performance of the link and thus for the estimation of its reliability and availability.

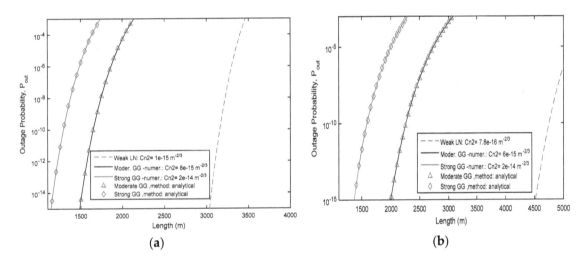

Figure 3. Outage probability estimation, with the proposed computational tool for weak to strong turbulence conditions, (**a**) for links up to 4 km with receiver threshold set as −30 dBm; (**b**) for total link length up to 5 km with receiver threshold set as −40 dBm. These results use the lognormal or the gamma–gamma distribution as mentioned in the plot legend.

In Figure 4, following the same procedure as in the case with the outage probability, it is clear that the capacity performance of the channel decreases significantly when turbulence strength is getting stronger. In addition to outage probability, this performance parameter has no change from decreasing the receiver's threshold, and thus has no dependence on this. However, it can been seen that the channel's capacity, due to the extremely large bandwidth of the optical channel, is high enough to support high fidelity communications, even for large attenuation values, strong atmospheric turbulence effect and long link lengths. Similarly as above, the curves of Figure 4 are only results that have been obtained with the proposed computational tool and, obviously, will change if the link and atmospheric parameters are altered.

Another very significant conclusion from Figures 3 and 4 is that the analytical and the numerical results for both performance quantities, i.e., outage probability and average capacity, are very close to each other. This remark confirms that the approximate or the exact mathematical Equations (16), (17), (19) and (20), which have been presented above, are accurate enough to present in an FSO link in detail. Thus, the computational tool that we present here potentially could be used as an effective and accurate tool for design and implementation of FSO links and networks.

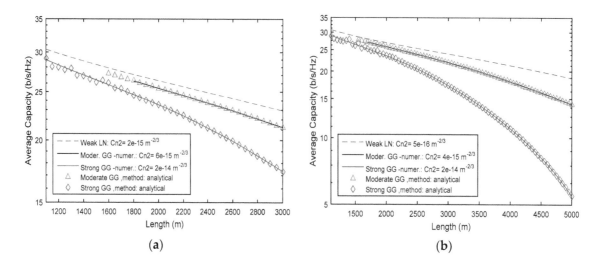

Figure 4. Average capacity performance metric for weak to strong atmospheric turbulence conditions (**a**) for links up to 3 km with receiver threshold set as −40 dBm; (**b**) for links up to 5 km with receiver threshold set as −30 dBm. These results use the suitable distribution model, i.e., lognormal or gamma–gamma depending on the value of the Rytov parameter, as presented in Equation (3).

From the computational tool and Figures 3 and 4, we also obtain accurate numerical results, which are included in Tables 2 and 3.

Table 2. Outage probability for an FSO link with the parameters of Table 1.

Threshold	Length	C_n^2 (m$^{-2/3}$)	Rytov Variance [1], σ_l^2	Outage Probability		SNR, μ (dB)
				Pr ($<10^{-3}$)	Drop System	
−30 dB	4 km	1.0×10^{-15}	0.253	0.00065	3450 m	62.08
		8.0×10^{-15}	2.023	0.00046	2100 m	47.88
		2.0×10^{-14}	5.057	0.00044	1700 m	33.87
−40 dBm	5 km	7.8×10^{-16}	0.297	5.4×10^{-7}		54.52
		6×10^{-15}	2.284	0.00070	3050	38.53
		2.0×10^{-14}	7.613	0.00057	2250	17.00

[1] $\sigma_l^2 \leq 0.3$ denotes weak turbulence, whereas $0.3 < \sigma_l^2 < 5$ denotes moderate to strong (3).

Table 3. Average channel capacity for an FSO link with the parameters of Table 1.

Theshold	Length	C_n^2 (m$^{-2/3}$)	Rytov Variance [1], σ_l^2	Average Capacity (b/s/Hz)		SNR, μ (dB)
				Capacity	Distribution	
−40 dBm	3 km	2×10^{-15}	0.298	22.91	LN	69.11
		6×10^{-15}	0.895	21.22	GG	64.14
		2.0×10^{-14}	2.984	17.32	GG	52.60
−30 dBm	5 km	5.0×10^{-16}	0.190	18.63	LN	56.21
		4×10^{-15}	1.523	14.18	GG	43.24
		2.0×10^{-14}	7.613	5.46	GG	17.00

[1] $\sigma_l^2 \leq 0.3$ denotes weak turbulence, whereas $0.3 < \sigma_l^2 < 5$ denotes moderate to strong (3).

Tables 2 and 3 present the performance results for an FSO link with parameters shown in Table 1. From the above results, we use the lognormal distribution that is used to simulate weak turbulence strength, i.e., Rytov variance smaller than 0.3. Under these conditions, the obtained results show maximum effective link value of about 3.45 km with availability above 99.9%, i.e., $P_{out} \cong 6.5 \times 10^{-4}$. In addition, the normalized average capacity also has the maximum efficiency of 18.63 (b/s/Hz) for weak turbulence conditions at 5 km. For longer link lengths, the scintillation effect strongly affects the system's operation, and, thus, the lognormal distribution cannot give accurate results. For this reason, for moderate to strong turbulence conditions, i.e., $\sigma_l^2 > 0.3$, we use the gamma–gamma distribution [1,3,21,30]. Thus, from Figures 3 and 4 and Tables 2 and 3, it is clear that when the turbulence strength increases, the system's performance decreases significantly.

Due to complexity of the above derived mathematical expressions, for the case of gamma–gamma distribution (see Appendix A), the estimation of the average capacity and outage probability metric is attained from our tool with two methods. First, we evaluate the results from Equations (17) and (20) and by numerically integrating Equations (13) and (18), respectively. This procedure is followed in order to verify our results before the presentation of the final results. The worst turbulence case that we simulate was at 5 km with $\sigma_l^2 = 7.613$ and the system's average capacity was 5.46 b/s/Hz with signal level SNR at 17.00 dB.

6. Conclusions

In this work, we studied an FSO link and we present approximate and exact mathematical expressions for the estimation of its performance by means of the evaluation of its average capacity and outage probability as functions of the transmitted power, the ambient noise and the attenuation parameters due to the propagation of the optical beam through the atmosphere. The obtained mathematical expressions have been derived for weak up to strong turbulence conditions, using the suitable statistical distribution models, i.e., the lognormal or the gamma, respectively, in order to describe accurately the resulting irradiance fluctuations. Based on the obtained mathematical expressions, we design and present in detail an accurate computational tool for the estimation of the performance of the FSO links, taking into account realistic values for its parameters, depending on the specific atmospheric conditions in the place where the FSO link will be installed. Moreover, this computational tool has been designed to estimate the performance results using both the theoretical expressions and the numerical evaluation. This way, the obtained performance results are estimated with two methods and the extracted computational results are verified. Thus, this computational application can be used for the performance estimation of an FSO link or even a more complex network architecture, with the necessary modifications. Finally, using the presented tool, we present numerical results for the average capacity and the outage probability of common FSO links, and we discuss their behavior for common parameter values for practical FSO links.

Author Contributions: The authors of this work have been cooperated in all the issues of the manuscript in order to obtain the above final form.

Appendix A

The specific integral which is evaluated numerically, using the trapezoidal method, for the estimation of the outage probability for moderate to strong turbulence conditions, i.e., using the gamma–gamma distribution, is given as [27]:

$$P_{out} = \int_0^{\gamma_{th}} \frac{(ab)^{(a+b)/2}}{\Gamma(a)\Gamma(b)} \frac{\gamma^{(a+b-4)/4} \left(4K_B T_{abs} BF_n/R_L + 2q_e B\left(I_{ph}+I_D\right) + 2B\eta^2 N_b^2 B_f + (RIN)I_{ph}^2\right)^{(a+b)/4}}{\left(\eta P_T\ G_T G_R\left(\frac{\lambda}{4\pi L}\right)^2 \left(\frac{D_R}{D_T+\theta\cdot L}\right)^2 10^{-(La_{tot}-Lm)/10}\right)^{\frac{a+b}{2}}} \times$$

$$K_{a-b}\left(2\sqrt{ab\sqrt{\left(\frac{\gamma\left(4K_B T_{abs} BF_n/R_L + 2q_e B\left(I_{ph}+I_D\right) + 2B\eta^2 N_b^2 B_f + (RIN)I_{ph}^2\right)}{\left(\eta P_T\ G_T G_R\left(\frac{\lambda}{4\pi L}\right)^2 \left(\frac{D_R}{D_T+\theta L}\right)^2 10^{-(La_{tot}+Lm)/10}\right)^2}\right)}}\right) d\gamma. \tag{A1}$$

Below, we present the pseudo code for this part of our algorithm for the case of negligible ambient noise. For brevity, only the key steps are detailed.

Algorithm A1. Outage Probability on Gamma—Gamma Distribution

Require: Received signal Equation (6) P_r; parameters **a**, **b** from Equation (13); the receiver sensitivity **thresh** as clear value not in dBm; the number of lengths **N** that we simulate until achieving the final path;

fgg=@(x,aa,bb,xm) *%implement the Equation (14) as a function of x, aa, bb ,xm parameters*

for i1=1 to 3 do *% i1 the number of 3 conditions that we study like weak, moderate, strong*

  for i=1 to N do *%Loop until achieve the final path*

    X=logspace(−10,10,10000) *%create the regions for numerical method trapezoidal*

    Ftrapez = fgg(X,**a(i,i1)**,**b(i,i1)**,**Pr(i,i1)**) *% the trapez function*

    Pout_trapez(i,i1)=trapz(X,ftrapez) *%the Outage probability with numerical method of trapezoidal*

    Pout_integ(i,i1)=integral(@(x)fgg(x,**a,b,Pr(i,i1)**),0,**thresh**) *%the integration method of outage probability with regions from 0 to thresh*

  end

find first element >=10^{-20} of Pout_integ that is j to avoid any chances of getting stuck in the Meijer implementation below and update i with j

  for i to **N** do *%Loop until achieve the final path*

  A=**a**(i1)+**b**(i1)/2, B= **a**(i1)+**b**(i1)/2,C=**b**(i)-**a**(i)

  K=((**a***b**)^A)/(gamma(**a**)*gamma(**b**))

  K1(i)=(**thresh** / **Pr(i,i1)**)^A/2 , z= **a**(i1)* **b**(i1) *($\sqrt{}$ **thresh** / **Pr(i,i1)**))

  Gmeijer(i)= meijerG((2,1,[1-A],[B,C,-A],**a***b**),z) *%the analytical method by meijer function in eq(18)*

  Pout_mejer(i,i1)= K1(i)*K*Gmeijer(i) *% Outage probability by analytical method*

  end

end

Output: Pout_trapez, Pout_int,Pout_mejer .

References

1. Ghassemlooy, Z.; Popoola, W.O. Terrestrial Free-Space Optical Communications. In *Mobile and Wireless Communications: Network Layer and Circuit Level Design*, 1st ed.; Fares, S.A., Adachi, F., Eds.; InTech: Rijeka, Coatia, 2010.

2. Henniger, H.; Wilfert, O. An Introduction to Free-Space Optical Communications. *Radioengineering* **2010**, *19*, 203–212.

3. Majumdar, A.K. *Advanced Free Space Optics (FSO): A System Approach*, 1st ed.; Springer Series in Optical Sciences: New York, NY, USA, 2015; Volume 186. [CrossRef]

4. Khalighi, M.A.; Uysal, M. Survey on Free Space Optical Communication: A Communication Theory Perspective. *IEEE Commun. Surv. Tutor.* **2014**, *16*, 2231–2258. [CrossRef]

5. Michael, S.; Parenti, R.R.; Walther, F.G.; Volpicelli, A.M.; Moores, J.D.; Wilcox, W.J.; Murphy, R. Comparison of scintillation measurements from 5 km communications link to standard statistical models. In *SPIE Atmospheric Propagation VI*; Thomas, L.M.W., Gilbreath, G.C., Eds.; SPIE: Orlando, FL, USA, 2009; Volume 7324, ISBN: 9780819475909.

6. Libich, J.; Zvanovec, S. Measurements Statistics of three joint wireless optical links. In Proceedings of the International Workshop on Optical Wireless Communications (IWOW), Pisa, Italy, 22 October 2012.

7. Perez, J.; Zvanovec, S.; Ghassemlooy, Z.; Popoola, W.O. Experimental characterization and mitigation of turbulence induced signal fades within an ad hoc FSO network. *Opt. Soc. Am.* **2014**, *22*. [CrossRef] [PubMed]

8. Mazin, A.A.A. Performance Analysis of the Fog Effect on Free Space Optical Communication System. *IOSR J. Appl. Phys. (IOSR-JAP)* **2015**, *7*, 16–24.

9. Popoola, W.O.; Ghassemlooy, Z.; Leitgeb, E. BER and Outage Probability of DPSK Subcarrier Intensity Modulated Free Space Optics in Fully Developed Speckle. *J. Commun.* **2009**, *4*, 546–554. [CrossRef]

10. Sandalidis, H.G.; Tsiftsis, T.A.; Karagiannidis, G.K. Optical wireless communications with heterodyne detection over turbulence channels with pointing errors. *J. Lightwave Technol.* **2009**, *27*, 4440–4445. [CrossRef]

11. Gappmair, W. Novel results on pulse-position modulation performance for terrestrial free-space optical links impaired by turbulent atmosphere and pointing errors. *IET Commun.* **2012**, *6*, 1300–1305. [CrossRef]

12. Gappmair, W.; Hranilovic, S.; Leitgeb, E. Performance of PPM on Terrestrial FSO Links with Turbulence and Pointing Errors. *IEEE Commun. Lett.* **2010**, *14*, 468–470. [CrossRef]

13. Laourine, A.; Stephenne, A.; Affes, S. Estimating the Ergodic Capacity of Log Normal Channels. *IEEE Commun. Lett.* **2007**, *11*, 568–570.

14. Epple, B. Simplified channel model for simulation of free-space optical communications. *IEEE/OSA J. Opt. Commun. Netw.* **2010**, *2*, 293–304. [CrossRef]

15. Peppas, K.P.; Stassinakis, A.N.; Topalis, G.K.; Nistazakis, H.E.; Tombras, G.S. Average Capacity of Optical Wireless Communication Systems Over I-K Atmospheric Turbulence Channels. *IEEE/OSA J. Opt. Commun. Netw.* **2012**, *4*, 1026–1032. [CrossRef]

16. Andrews, L.C.; Phillips, R.L. I-K distribution as a universal propagation model of laser beams in atmospheric turbulence. *J. Opt. Soc. Am. A* **1985**, *2*, 160–163. [CrossRef]

17. Al-Habash, M.A.; Andrews, L.C.; Phillips, R.L. Mathematical model for the irradiance probability density function of a laser beam propagating through turbulent media. *Opt. Eng.* **2001**, *40*, 1554–1562. [CrossRef]

18. Kamalakis, T.; Sphicopoulos, T.; Muhammad, S.S.; Leitgeb, E. Estimation of the power scintillation probability density function in free-space optical links by use of multicanonical Monte Carlo sampling. *Opt. Lett.* **2006**, *31*, 3077–3079. [CrossRef] [PubMed]

19. Garrido, J.M.; Balsells, A.; Jurado-Navas, J.; Paris, F.; Castillo-Vasquez, M.; Puerta-Notario, A. On the capacity of M-distributed atmospheric optical channels. *Opt. Lett.* **2013**, *38*, 3984–3987. [CrossRef] [PubMed]

20. Varotsos, G.K.; Nistazakis, H.E.; Volos, C.K.; Tombras, G.S. FSO Links with Diversity Pointing Errors and Temporal Broadening of the Pulses Over Weak to Strong Atmospheric Turbulence Channels. *Opt. Int. J. Light Electron Opt.* **2016**, *127*, 3402–3409. [CrossRef]

21. Vetelino, F.S.; Young, C.; Andrews, L. Fade statistics and aperture averaging for Gaussian beam waves in moderate-to-strong turbulence. *Opt. Soc. Am. Appl. Opt.* **2007**, *46*, 3780–3789. [CrossRef]

22. Djordjevic, G.T.; Petkovic, M.I. Average BER performance of FSO SIM-QAM systems in the presence of atmospheric turbulence and pointing errors. *J. Mod. Opt.* **2016**, *63*, 715–723. [CrossRef]

23. Wilson, S.G.; Braudt-Pearce, M.; Cao, Q.; Leveque, J.H. Free-Space Optical MIMO Transmission with Q-ary PPM. *IEEE Trans. Commun.* **2005**, *53*, 1402–1412. [CrossRef]

24. Prabu, K.; Bose, S.; Kumar, D.S. BPSK based subcarrier intensity modulated free space optical system in combined strong atmospheric turbulence. *Opt. Commun.* **2013**, *305*, 185–189. [CrossRef]

25. Nistazakis, H.E.; Assimakopoulos, V.D.; Tombras, G.S. Performance estimation of free space optical links over negative exponential atmospheric turbulence channels. *Opt. Int. J. Light Electron Opt.* **2011**, *122*, 2191–2194. [CrossRef]

26. Zvanovec, S.; Perez, J.; Ghassemlooy, Z.; Rajbhandari, S.; Libich, J. Route diversity analyses for free-space optical wireless links within turbulent scenarios. *Opt. Express* **2013**, *21*, 7641–7650. [CrossRef] [PubMed]

27. Nistazakis, H.E.; Katsis, A.; Tombras, G.S. On the reliability and performance of fso and hybrid fso communication systems over turbulent channels. In *Turbulence: Theory, Types and Simulations*; Nova Science Publishers: Hauppauge, NY, USA, 2011.

28. Laourine, A.; Stephenne, A.; Affes, S. Capacity of Log Normal Fading Channels. In Proceedings of the International Conference on Wireless Communications and Mobile Computing 2007 (IWCMC2007), Honolulu, HI, USA, 12–17 August 2007; pp. 13–17.

29. Nistazakis, H.E.; Tsiftis, T.A.; Tombras, G.S. Performance analysis of the free space optical communications systems over atmospheric turbulence channel. *IET Commun.* **2009**, *3*, 1402–1409. [CrossRef]

30. Vetelino, F.S.; Young, C.; Andrews, L.; Recolons, J. Aperture averaging effects on the probability density of irradiance fluctuations in moderate to strong turbulence. *Opt. Soc. Am. Appl. Opt.* **2007**, *46*. [CrossRef]

31. Bekkali, A.; Naila, C.B.; Kazaura, K.; Wakamori, K.; Matsumoto, M. Transmission Analysis of OFDM-Based Wireless Services Over Turbulent Radio-on-FSO links Modeled by Gamma-Gamma Distribution. *IEEE Photonics J.* **2010**, *2*, 510–520. [CrossRef]

32. Stassinakis, A.N.; Nistazakis, H.E.; Tombras, G.S. Comparative Performance Study of One or Multiple Receivers Schemes for FSO Links Over Gamma Gamma Turbulence Channels. *J. Mod. Opt.* **2012**, *59*, 1023–1031. [CrossRef]

33. Katsilieris, T.D.; Latsas, G.P.; Nistazakis, H.E.; Tombras, G.S. A computational tool which has been designed for performance estimations of wireless hybrid FSO/MMW communication links. In Proceedings of the 7th International Conference from Scientific Computing to Computational Engineering (IC-SCCE), Athens, Greece, 6–9 July 2016.

34. Higgs, C.; Barclay, H.T.; Murphy, D.V.; Primmerman, C.A. Atmospheric Compensation and Tracking Using Active Illumination. *Linc. Lab. J.* **1998**, *11*, 5–26.

35. Uysal, M.; Li, J.T.; Yu, M. Error rate performance analysis of coded free-space optical links over gamma–gamma atmospheric turbulence channels. *IEEE Trans. Commun.* **2006**, *5*, 1229–1233. [CrossRef]

36. Nistazakis, H.E.; Tombras, G.S.; Tsigopoulos, A.D.; Karagianni, E.A.; Fafalios, M.E. Capacity estimation of optical wireless communication systems over moderate to strong turbulence channels. *J. Commun. Netw.* **2009**, *11*, 387–392. [CrossRef]

37. Kiasaleh, K. Channel estimation for FSO channels subject to gamma–gamma turbulence. In Proceedings of the International Conference on Space Optical Systems and Applications (ICSOS2012), Corsica, France, 9–12 October 2012.

38. Kharraz, O.; Forsyth, D. PIN and APD photodetector efficiencies in the longer wavelength range 1300–1550 nm. *Opt. Int. J. Light Electron Opt.* **2013**, *124*, 2574–2576. [CrossRef]

39. Nistazakis, H.E.; Stassinakis, A.N.; Muhammad, S.S.; Tombras, G.S. BER Estimation for Multi Hop RoFSO QAM or PSK OFDM Communication Systems Over Gamma Gamma or Exponentially Modeled Turbulence Channels. *Opt. Laser Technol.* **2014**, *64*, 106–112. [CrossRef]

40. Avago Technologies. Note 922. Available online: https://docs.broadcom.com/docs/5965-8666E (accessed on 13 November 2016).

41. Gagliardi, R.M.; Karp, S. *Optical Communications*, 2nd ed.; John Wiley & Sons: Hoboken, NJ, USA, 1995.

42. Khalighi, M.A.; Xu, F.; Jaafar, Y.; Bourennane, S. Double-laser differential signaling for reducing the effect of background radiation in free-space optical systems. *IEEE/OSA J. Opt. Commun. Netw.* **2011**, *3*, 145–154. [CrossRef]

43. Rollins, D.; Baars, J.; Bajorins, D.; Cornish, C.; Fischer, K.; Wiltsey, T. Background light environment for free-space optical terrestrial communications links. In *Proceedings of SPIE, Optical Wireless Communications V*; Korevaar, E.J., Ed.; SPIE: Redmond, DC, USA, 2002; Volume 4873, pp. 99–110.

44. Mendoza, B.R.; Rodríguez, S.; Pérez-Jiménez, R.; Ayala, A.; González, O. Comparison of Three Non-Imaging Angle-Diversity Receivers as Input Sensors of Nodes for Indoor Infrared Wireless Sensor Networks: Theory and Simulation. *Sensors* **2016**, *16*, 1086. [CrossRef] [PubMed]

45. Leeb, W.R. Degradation of signal to noise ratio in optical free space data links due to background illumination. *Appl. Opt.* **1989**, *28*, 3443–3449. [CrossRef] [PubMed]

46. ITU-R Recommendation P.1814-1. *Prediction Methods Required for the Design of Terrestrial Free-Space Optical Links*; International Telecommunication Union: Geneva, Switzerland, 2007.

47. Muhammad, S.S.; Köhldorfer, P.; Leitgeb, E. Channel Modeling for Terrestrial Free Optical Links. In Proceedings of the 7th International Conference on Transparent Optical Networks (ICTON), Barcelona, Spain, 3–7 July 2005; pp. 407–410.

48. Tsiftsis, T.A.; Sandalidis, H.G.; Karagiannidis, G.K.; Uysal, M. FSO Links with Spatial Diversity Over Strong Atmospheric Turbulence Channels. In Proceedings of the IEEE International Conference on Communications (ICC), Beijing, China, 19–23 May 2008.

49. Adamchik, V.S.; Marichev, O.I. The Algorithm for Calculating Integrals of Hypergeometric Type Function and its Realization in Reduce System. In Proceedings of the International Conference on Symbolic and Algebraic Computation, Tokyo, Japan, 20–24 August 1990; pp. 212–224.

7

Esoteric Twist: An Efficient in-Place Streaming Algorithmus for the Lattice Boltzmann Method on Massively Parallel Hardware

Martin Geier * and Martin Schönherr *

Institute for Computational Modeling in Civil Engineering, TU Braunschweig, 38106 Braunschweig, Germany
* Correspondence: geier@irmb.tu-bs.de (M.G.); schoen@irmb.tu-bs.de (M.S.)

Academic Editor: Christian F. Janßen

Abstract: We present and analyze the Esoteric Twist algorithm for the Lattice Boltzmann Method. Esoteric Twist is a thread safe in-place streaming method that combines streaming and collision and requires only a single data set. Compared to other in-place streaming techniques, Esoteric Twist minimizes the memory footprint and the memory traffic when indirect addressing is used. Esoteric Twist is particularly suitable for the implementation of the Lattice Boltzmann Method on Graphic Processing Units.

Keywords: lattice Boltzmann; EsoTwist; in place streaming; indirect addressing; GPGPUs

1. Introduction

The lattice Boltzmann method (LBM) is a simple algorithm used in computational fluid dynamics for solving the Navier–Stokes equations. The efficient implementation of the lattice Boltzmann method has received considerable attention from the computer scientist community [1–3]. The LBM has several properties that make it interesting from a performance oriented algorithmic point of view. The ratio of floating point operations to memory access is relatively low so that the performance of the method is usually bandwidth limited. The LBM uses more variables than mathematically necessary for solving the Navier–Stokes equation, which adds to the relatively large data traffic. Still, the LBM is often considered to be efficient if implemented correctly. The algorithm is perfectly suitable for massively parallel implementation [4]. The time integration is second order accurate even though it depends only on the previous time step [5]. A particular feature of the LBM in distinction to finite difference schemes is that the number of input variables of the local (i.e., node-wise) time integration scheme equals the number of output variables. This is important as it implies that each input datum is required only once. In a finite difference scheme, functional values usually have to be gathered in a finite neighborhood of a grid node and the same datum is required to update several grid nodes. Most algorithmic and hardware optimizations of recent years focused on the reuse of data. Spatial blocking and scan-line algorithms are prominent examples developed for accelerating finite differences methods [6]. Caching is a generic hardware optimization meant to improve performance for repeatedly used data. It is interesting to note that the LBM does not benefit from such optimizations because it does not reuse data in a single time step. The LBM benefits from hardware cache only indirectly or when the cache is so large that it can hold the state variables until they are reused in the next time step. This zero-data-redundancy is not necessarily a disadvantage of the LBM. For example, it has been argued by Asinari et al. [7] that the LBM was inefficient due to the utilization of the distribution functions which increase the memory requirements and should intuitively increase traffic between the CPU and the main memory. Asinari et al. [8] proposed replacing the distribution functions with macroscopic variables, which reduced the memory footprint but counter-intuitively increased the memory traffic since data had to be read repeatedly for the computation of finite differences [7]. In addition, the savings in memory turned out to be smaller than naively assumed: the LBM can overwrite each input datum with the output datum while the finite difference method requires a source and a destination array to avoid the overwriting of data that is still required for neighboring grid nodes. In addition to these purely algorithmic differences, there are differences in accuracy between finite difference and LBM implementations. Depending on the details of the model and the validation example, either the finite difference method [9] or the LBM [10] excels over the other. In the current paper, we will not discuss the numerical modeling underlying the LBM. Instead, we focus entirely on its efficient implementation. By doing so, we exploit the features of the method and arrive at a result that is very different from what one should do to implement a finite difference method efficiently.

2. Lattice Boltzmann Method

In this section, we describe the LBM from a purely algorithmic point of view without considering the details of the modeling. We direct the reader to various text books for an introduction to the method [11–14].

The LBM is a computational method to solve the lattice Boltzmann equation which can be written in three dimensions as:

$$f_{ijk(x+i)(y+j)(z+k)(t+1)} = f_{ijkxyzt} + \Omega_{ijkxyzt}. \tag{1}$$

Here, the indexes i, j and k are integer values indicating the direction in which the distribution $f_{ijkxyzt}$ moves on a Cartesian lattice with the nodes being located at positions x, y and z. The time step is indicated by t. The so-called collision operator $\Omega_{ijkxyzt}$ is a function of all local distributions $f_{ijkxyzt}$ but neither depends on the state of any other lattice node nor on the state of the same node at any time other than t. It is hence seen that communication between lattice nodes happen only on the left-hand side of (1), the so-called streaming. The right-hand side, the so-called collision, is entirely local. It is also seen that the lattice Boltzmann equation is a local mapping from $Q \to Q$ variables. Each datum is used only once.

The LBM can be implemented for different velocity sets where the indexes i, j and k take different values. Without loss of generality, we restrict us here to the technically most relevant case with 27 velocities and $i, j, k \in \{-1, 0, 1\}$.

3. Implementation of the Lattice Boltzmann Method

The LBM has a superficial algorithmic similarity to a finite difference time domain technique and it is admissible to implement it in a likewise fashion. A naive approach would utilize two data arrays $f_{ijkxyzt}$ and $f^*_{ijkxyzt}$ and rewrite (1) as:

$$f^*_{ijk(x+i)(y+j)(z+k)t} = f_{ijkxyzt} + \Omega_{ijkxyzt}. \tag{2}$$

After completing one time step, the post-collision distributions might be redefined as the new pre-collision distributions:

$$f_{ijkxyz(t+1)} = f^*_{ijkxyzt}. \tag{3}$$

This updated algorithm is denoted as AB-pattern [15,16]. In a finite difference time domain method, such an update was necessary in order to avoid the overwriting of data at the neighboring node. In the LBM, this is not necessary because the collision maps a set of inputs to the same number of outputs. It is hence admissible to overwrite the input directly by the output and a secondary array is never required. A naive implementation of this concept would require moving the distributions in a separate step:

$$f^*_{ijkxyzt} = f_{ijkxyzt} + \Omega_{ijkxyzt}, \tag{4}$$

$$f_{ijk(x+i)(y+j)(z+k)(t+1)} = f^*_{ijkxyzt}. \tag{5}$$

It is desired to implement the LBM in such a way that only one array is required while both streaming and collision are combined in a single step, i.e., we are looking for an algorithm that requires only a single array to hold the distributions and reads and writes each datum only once in each time step. Such a technique is called in-place streaming and several methods have been proposed in literature. An early example of an in-place streaming algorithm is the swap algorithm of Mattila et al. [17] and Latt [18]. The swap algorithm combines the streaming and the collision in a single step, but it does not overwrite the input of the local collision by the output. As a result, the swap algorithm requires a certain order in which the lattice nodes have to be processed. This is a severe disadvantage, as it limits the application of the algorithm to serial computations with a clear order of the instructions. The method is not applicable to massively parallel computations.

An alternative approach to in-place streaming is the compressed grid that approximately saves half the memory [19]. The idea behind the compressed grid is to extend a rectangular simulation domain by one line of nodes in all directions and keep a certain order in the processing of the grid nodes, which, after the update of the first line of nodes, are written to spare line of nodes. Once the nodes in the first line are processed, they are no longer required and the second line of nodes can be written to the first line of nodes and so on until all lines have been processed. The compressed grid method works only for a rectangular domain and requires a fixed order of updating the nodes.

Bailey [16] studied the implementation of the LBM on Graphics Cards where lattice nodes are updated in random order by thousands of threads in parallel. He proposed an algorithm called AA-pattern that overwrites the input with the output by distinguishing between odd and even time steps (see Figure 1). In the odd time step, the distributions are not streamed and the local distribution are directly overwritten. In the even time step, the distributions are fetched from the neighboring nodes and written back to the neighboring nodes in an opposite direction after collision. In such a way, the distributions move two lattice spacings every second time step. The AA-pattern requires the code to be implemented twice, once for the even and once for the odd time steps.

The AA-pattern solves the concurrency problem of the swap algorithm, but it was designed to run on a full matrix implementation. Real world applications of computational fluid dynamics usually require a higher geometrical flexibility and local grid-refinement. For this purpose, it is usually desired to implement the LBM as a sparse matrix method. The AA-pattern permits an implementation on sparse matrices, but it requires pointers to all neighboring nodes, which implies a relatively large memory footprint. In the reminder of this paper, we present and discuss the properties of the Esoteric Twist data structure that solves the concurrency problem similar to the AA-pattern but leads to substantial savings in memory when indirect addressing is used.

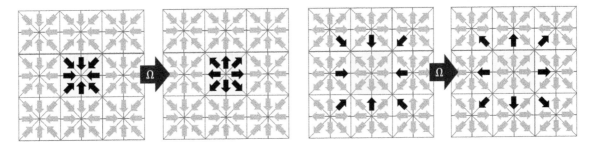

Figure 1. AA-pattern in 2D. (**left**) Odd time step; (**right**) Even time step.

4. Esoteric Twist

The Esoteric Twist, or short EsoTwist, algorithm combines the following desired features:

- Streaming and collision are combined in one step.
- Each datum is read once and written once in each time step.
- The method is thread safe; all nodes can be processed in arbitrary order or entirely in parallel.
- The method is well suitable for indirect addressing, i.e., has a small memory footprint.

The swap algorithm fulfills all but the last two features, and the AA-pattern fulfills all but the last feature. The AA-pattern has to access all neighboring nodes in every second time step, which implies that it first has to read the pointer to all neighbors from an index array if indirect addressing is used. We show below that the EsoTwist method is more economical in terms of memory footprint and memory reads for indirect addressing. In this section, we first introduce the EsoTwist method for the general case.

The name Esoteric Twist originates from the unintuitive (esoteric) observation that the streaming step can be eliminated if the distributions are written back in opposite (twisted) order compared to the reading before collision. As in the case of the AA-pattern, the key to a thread safe in-place streaming is that the collision operator writes only to the memory from which it draws its inputs. We assume that modern computers have access to a slow but vast memory that holds all the distributions of all nodes and a fast but small memory in which all operations associated with a collision at a single node can be executed. We will call the former the main memory and the latter the registers. We assume, as in the AA-pattern, that the distributions belonging to one node are transferred from the main memory to the registers before collision and written back to the main memory after collision. We assume that the transfer between main memory and registers is expensive and should be minimized. Since the distributions ought to move, they either need to be drawn from the neighboring nodes (pull-scheme) before collision or they have to be sent to the neighboring nodes after collision (push-scheme). In the EsoTwist approach, all distributions that move in negative direction with $i, j, k < 0$ are pulled while all distributions moving in positive directions with $i, j, k > 0$ are pushed. The procedure is depicted in Figure 2 for the two-dimensional case. The yellow node in Figure 2 is the one for which we consider one update step. The collision on the node depends on all Q incoming distributions and it returns Q outgoing distributions. Only the incoming distributions moving in positive x- and y-directions are read from the yellow node itself. The distributions moving in negative directions are read from the respective neighbors in the positive directions as depicted in the figure. After collision, the distributions are written back to the places where the distributions moving in the opposite direction were read from. As is the case in the AA-pattern, each distribution swaps places with the distribution moving in the opposite direction after collision. For the movement of the distribution to happen, the method has to distinguish between odd and even time steps, as depicted in Figure 2. This can be realized in different ways. Unlike in the case of the AA-pattern, EsoTwist does not necessarily require two implementations of the method for odd and even time steps. A much simpler realization of the method is obtained by storing the distributions in a structure of arrays, i.e., by grouping the distributions in arrays according to the direction in which they are moving. After one time step is completed, all pointers to the arrays are swapped with the pointers to the arrays moving in the opposite direction. Then, the next time step is executed as before. However, a structure of arrays is not necessarily desired. The EsoTwist method can also be implemented like the AA-pattern by explicitly distinguishing between odd and even time steps. Algorithm 1 shows the concept of the EsoTwist algorithm in one dimension. The complete algorithm in three dimensions is shown in the Appendix A.

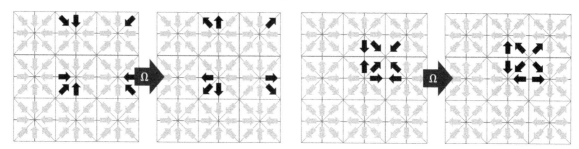

Figure 2. The EsoTwist algorithm in 2D. (**left**) Odd time step; (**right**) Even time step.

It is of note here that an algorithm almost identical to EsoTwist was presented in [20]. However, the authors apparently missed the fact that they could simply combine collision and swapping the directions into a single step. Instead, they swapped the distributions in a separate step, which unnecessarily doubles the data traffic.

Algorithm 1: The basic EsoTwist Algorithm for a one-dimensional LBM with three speeds in a structure of arrays format. The asterisk marks the post-collision distribution. The capital F denotes a register to which the distribution is read from the distributions in main memory f for the collision. The distribution f_1 moving in a positive direction and the stationary distribution f_0 are read at the index n while the distribution f_{-1} moving in a negative direction is read from the neighbor in a positive direction. After collision, the distribution moving in positive direction F_1^* is written to the neighbor in a positive direction at the slot where the distribution going to the opposite direction was originally read. The distribution going in negative direction F_{-1}^* is now written to location n. In that way, both the distribution going in a negative direction and the distribution going in a positive direction moved a distance of one node during the time step. After all nodes have been collided, it is sufficient to swap the pointers to the arrays f_{-1} and f_1 to execute the streaming of all nodes.

> **for** *all time steps* **do**
>> **for** *all nodes n* **do**
>>> $n_x \leftarrow neighborX(n);$
>>> $F_{-1} \leftarrow f_{-1}(n_x);$
>>> $F_0 \leftarrow f_0(n);$
>>> $F_1 \leftarrow f_1(n);$
>>> $F^* \leftarrow collision(F);$
>>> $f_{-1}(n_x) \leftarrow F_1^*;$
>>> $f_0(n) \leftarrow F_0^*;$
>>> $f_1(n) \leftarrow F_{-1}^*;$
>> **end**
>> $swapPointer(f_{-1}, f_1);$
> **end**

4.1. Indirect Addressing

In almost all real-world applications of computational fluid dynamics, it would be unpractical to discretize the computational domain with a rectangular Cartesian grid. To discretize domains of arbitrary shape, sparse matrices are the most flexible choice. In a sparse matrix implementation, each node has to access its neighbors via a pointer, or equivalently via an index which has to be stored in an additional array. For example, if a three-dimensional LBM with 27 velocities is implemented on a sparse matrix using the AA-pattern, each node has to find the 26 neighbors of the node in the even time step. The AA-pattern is efficient in the sense that it has to find the neighbors only every other time step. Still, it has to store the pointer to these neighbors. A pointer usually occupies the same amount of memory as a scalar datum such that 26 pointers basically occupy almost as much memory as the distributions themselves. This memory can be substantially reduced by applying pointer chasing. For example, using the AA-pattern, it would be sufficient to store pointers in the six axial directions and access the diagonal neighbors by querying, for example, the neighbor in the positive x-direction for its neighbor in the negative y-direction. Applying this technique reduces the number of pointers per node from 26 to 6. This number can be reduced further to four if the nodes are aligned in one of the cardinal directions along the array. However, each of these optimizations reduce the flexibility of the method. The alignment of the grid along one of the cardinal axes in connection with indirect addressing usually means that the grid cannot be modified after its generation, which is an obstacle for adaptive simulations. That is to say, the feature that nodes on a sparse matrix gird can be inserted and deleted ad libitum is lost once the nodes are aligned along one dimension in order to eliminate the pointers in this direction. We will hence not consider the alignment of the data along one of the cardinal directions in our analysis for sparse matrix grids.

Using pointer chasing, the AA-pattern has to store links to six neighbors at each node ($6 \times N$ data values for N nodes). The total memory requirement without further meta data for an LBM with 27 discrete speeds is $33 \times N$ data values. Since the AA-pattern streams data only every other time step, it requires $(27 + 26/2) \times N = 40 \times N$ reads and $27 \times N$ writes from and to the main memory in every time step with $27 \times N$ reads in the odd and $53 \times N$ reads in the even time steps. It is interesting to note that, while pointer chasing reduces the memory footprint, it does not reduce the number of reads. All 26 pointers to all neighbors have to be read every other time step.

In comparison to the AA-pattern, EsoTwist reduces both the memory footprint and the number of reads. This is due to EsoTwist being asymmetric in space. Only neighbors in positive directions in either dimension have to be accessed. In three dimensions, using 27 speeds, all distributions accessed by a node are stored at the indexes of the node and the seven neighbors in the upper octant of the surrounding cube. Thus, by applying pointer chasing, $3 \times N$ links have to be stored and each time step requires $(27 + 7) \times N = 34 \times N$ reads and $27 \times N$ writes. The total memory requirement is hence $30 \times N$ (9% less then for the AA-pattern). The data reads are even 25% less than for the AA-pattern and the data writes are the same. In their analysis, Wittmann et al. [3] conclude that the AA-pattern and EsoTwist have the lowest data traffic for the known streaming algorithm, but their analysis ignores that EsoTwist requires fewer pointers and fewer reads than the AA-pattern.

In addition to those direct savings in memory, there is also an indirect savings compared to the AA-pattern due to the fact that the fewer ghost nodes are required when indirect addressing is used (see Figure 3). Both EsoTwist and the AA-pattern store part of the distributions associated with each node at some neighboring nodes. The memory for these nodes has to be allocated even if the node itself is not part of the simulation domain. In the AA-pattern, all 26 neighbors of an existing node have to be allocated while, in EsoTwist, only the seven neighbors in the upper octant of the surrounding cube have to be allocated. Depending on the complexity of the geometry, this can result in considerable savings through a smaller number of ghost nodes.

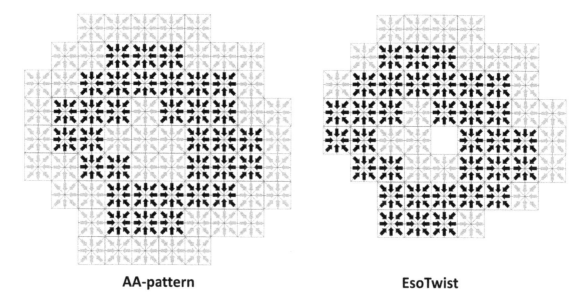

AA-pattern   **EsoTwist**

Figure 3. Ghost nodes in the AA-pattern and EsoTwist when indirect addressing is used. Since both methods store part of the distributions at neighboring nodes the memory for these ghost nodes (in gray) have to be allocated even though they are not part of the simulation domain. EsoTwist has an advantage over the AA-pattern in that it requires these neighbors only in positive directions. Thus, fewer ghost nodes are required for EsoTwist than for the AA-pattern.

It should be noted that the above analysis ignores the effect of caching for the number of reads and writes such that no general conclusion on performance can be drawn at this stage. Modern CPUs usually read complete cache lines at once and this enhances performance when data is aligned. However, since, in the current subsection, we consider sparse matrix grids, we have no general guarantee that our nodes are arranged in any favorable ordering and that we would benefit from caching. The above analysis is valid for the worst case scenario of completely unaligned data.

4.2. Variants

Even though pointers are an indispensable element of all software on the machine level, several popular programming languages (e.g., Fortran) do not support pointers explicitly. This is very unfortunate since a simple operation that is efficiently executed by the hardware in nano-seconds has to be mimicked by more complicated and certainly less efficient operations. Still, it is possible to implement EsoTwist without pointers. One possibility is to combine the arrays for distributions moving in opposite directions into one array of twice the length. Staying with our example of the D3Q27 velocity set, we would have one array of length N for the distributions f_{000} and thirteen arrays of length $2N$ for the other distributions. For example, let $g_{1-10}[n]$ be the array for the distributions f_{1-10} and f_{-110}. Now, let $odd = 1$ and $even = 0$ for odd time steps and $odd = 0$ and $even = 1$ for even time steps. It is possible to access the distributions without pointer exchange trough:

$$f_{1-10}[n] = g_{1-10}[n + odd * N], \qquad (6)$$
$$f_{-110}[n] = g_{1-10}[n + even * N]. \qquad (7)$$

Thus, it is also possible to implement EsoTwist in a programming language that does not support pointers.

Another consideration concerns the structure of arrays data type. On massively parallel hardware like GPGPUs that apply single instruction multiple data operations, it is beneficial to store the data in different arrays according to the directions. However, this is not the optimal data layout for serial computing since all 27 distributions are stored in different locations of the main memory and none of them would share a single cache line. On those machines, storing all data belonging to a node together would be optimal. Geller [21] proposed a compromise that enhanced the performance of EsoTwist on serial computers. He suggested to use two containers, one for the local distributions and one for the distributions at neighboring nodes. In this way, half the data required for the collision could always be accessed together. Only the static distribution was stored separately.

EsoTwist has also been implemented successfully for block structured grids [22,23]. Block structuring can be used to increase locality of the data and is useful for load balancing parallel codes. Inside a block, no pointers to neighboring nodes are required. In connection with EsoTwist, each block needs only to access its seven neighboring blocks in the upper octant of the surrounding cube for data exchange. Hence, each block would require only three links to neighboring blocks if pointer chasing is used. Block structured grids might increase performance through high data locality, and they largely simplify the parallelization of the method, but they also have some disadvantages compared to the application of EsoTwist on sparse matrix grids. The data transfer at the interfaces between the blocks does not happen automatically and requires an explicit step of data exchange. Usually, also at least one additional layer of nodes is required to facilitate the exchange of data. In terms of memory occupation for a cubic block in three dimensions with $N \times N \times N$ nodes, $(N+1)^3 - N^3$ ghost nodes are usually required. Using pointer chasing, only three links to neighboring blocks are required per block. In contrast, sparse matrices require three links per node and ghost cells only on the domain boundaries. Assuming that each datum (distributions and pointers) occupies the same size in memory, we can determine the breakeven point in memory consumption when block structured grids occupy less memory than a sparse matrix representation. For a method with 27 speeds, we have to equate the three pointers with the average amount of additional data required for the block structured grids:

$$3 = \frac{27((N+1)^3 - N^3) + 3}{N^3}. \tag{8}$$

This solves to $N \approx 27.98$. We hence see that a block size of at least $28 \times 28 \times 28$ nodes is required to occupy less memory on a block structured grid compared to a sparse matrix. This analysis does not take into account that block structured grids usually contain nodes which do not belong to the domain. In principle, a block has to be allocated completely whenever at least one node in the block is located in the fluid domain. It is hence seen that memory economy is usually a poor motivation for the use of block structured grids, at least when combined with EsoTwist.

The EsoTwist data structure has also been implemented in a variant that secures memory alignment of all distributions [24]. This was historically important for the implementation of the lattice Boltzmann method on Nvidia GPUs of older generations [25] where data was always read in form of sixteen adjacent four byte values. The trick in this EsoStripe called variant is that the distributions of adjacent points are stored in a distance of sixteen, such that whenever sixteen nodes are processed simultaneously by the vector processor, the data access is completely aligned. While this leads to more than a 25% performance increase on GeForce GTX 465, no performance gain was observed on newer hardware when compared to non-aligned reads and writes [24]. In that case, data alignment was found to not be essential for newer hardware.

4.3. Implicit Bounce Back

EsoTwist has an interesting feature concerning lattice nodes which are excluded from the computation. If a lattice node is not touched, i.e., if no distributions are read and no distributions are written, the direction in which the populations on this node move is reversed through the pointer exchange. In the LBM, a reversal of the directions of the distributions is used to model solid walls in the so-called simple bounce back scheme. Using EsoTwist bounce back is implicitly applied to all nodes skipped during the update, and these nodes will thus behave like solid walls. Applying simple bounce back in EsoTwist is entirely for free since the respective nodes do not even need to be touched. This way of imposing bounce back by omission of the node is called implicit bounce back. This property is shared by other swap methods like the one proposed by Mattila et al. [17] and Latt [18] and by the AA-pattern [16].

5. Results

The EsoTwist data structure has been successfully implemented both on parallel CPU systems [22,23] and on GPUs [26–28]. Here, we focus on the implementation for GPUs in connection with indirect addressing.

5.1. Performance Model

Our performance model is based on the observation that the LBM is typically a memory bandwidth limited algorithm [3,29–32]. The EsoTwist method for a 27 speed lattice requires 27 distributions that have to be read and written in every time step. Even though only three pointers to neighbors are stored with every node, we still need to read seven such pointers per node and time step through pointer chasing. One additional number is used to indicate the type of the node. Since this indicator is also used as a pointer to an array of boundary conditions (each node can have its individual boundary condition), this number must also have at least four bytes. In total, our method requires $27 + 7 + 1 = 35$ reads and 27 writes per node and time step which sums to

$\#Bytes = 62 \times 4$ Bytes $= 248$ Bytes. The performance of our code is measured in Million Node Updates Per Second (MNUPS). The bandwidth occupancy P is calculated by:

$$P = \frac{\#MNUPS \times \#Bytes}{bandwidth} \times 100\%. \tag{9}$$

When comparing results of EsoTwist to results from a full matrix code, we have to take into account that the full matrix code does not require any pointers such that it has only 28 reads and 27 writes in every time step per node.

5.2. Comparison to Full Matrix Implementation

Here, we compare the performance of EsoTwist on sparse matrices with a full matrix implementation. In order to make the setup comparable, we chose a cubic domain with $128 \times 128 \times 128$ nodes. In the first example, we simulate duct flow with implicit bounce back boundary condition and use the Bhatnagar Gross Krook collision model [33]. This example is run on an old Nvidia Tesla C1060 GPU with a bandwidth of 102 GBytes/s. The full matrix implementation obtains 205 MNUPS (41.2% bandwidth) and the sparse matrix implementation obtains 191 MNUPS (43.2% bandwidth).

In our second example, we compare the performance of a simulation with the same grid size but with a cascaded collision kernel [34] on a GeForce GTX Titan X (Maxwell GM200), which is a much more recent GPU than the Tesla C1060. The theoretical peak bandwidth of the GeForce GTX Titan X is 336.6 GBytes/s. The full matrix version of the code uses the AB-pattern [15,16]. Despite the fact that the cascaded kernel is computationally more intensive, we obtain much better performance figures on this newer hardware. The full matrix version runs with 999.425 MNUPS (60.8% bandwidth), and the sparse matrix version runs with 993.514 MNUPS (68.2% bandwidth).

It is observed in both cases that, while the performance on the full matrix is higher in terms of lattice updates, the sparse matrix version makes better use of the bandwidth. The differences in execution speed are marginal. The sparse matrix version obtains 93.2% of the execution speed of the full matrix version on the outdated Tesla C1060 and 99.4% on the more recent GeForce GTX Titan X. This result is a further confirmation of the observation by Linxweiler [24] that progress in hardware reduces the advantage of highly optimized full matrix codes over more flexible codes.

5.3. Isotropy

We probe the isotropy of the EsoTwist method by comparing the execution speed of a simulation of the same geometry under three different orientations. This is done because the nodes on this grid are filled along one of the cardinal directions first, depending on whether the orientation of the geometry neighboring nodes are either close together or far apart. The problem hence probes how the method reacts to different levels of data locality. The geometry is shown in Figure 4. It is composed of three rectangular pipes with different cross sections. Each pipe is 128 grid nodes long. The cross-sections of the pipes are 5×5, 10×10 and 20×20 grid nodes, respectively. Simulations are executed on a Nvidia GeForce GTX Titan GPU running with device driver version 331.82 and the CUDA (Compute Unified Device Architecture) toolkit version 6.0. The theoretical bandwidth of this GPU is 288.4 GBytes/s [35]. The computational model used was the BGK collision kernel in single precision. We observe similar performance regardless of the orientation of the domain in space. For the larger pipe oriented along the x-axis, we obtain 738.5 MNUPS (59.1% peak bandwidth); for the larger pipe oriented along the y-axis, we obtain 729.8 MNUPS (58.4% peak bandwidth) and, for the z direction, we obtain 727.3 MNUPS (58.2% peak bandwidth). Our performance figures compare to between 407 and 684 MNUPS reported for the GeForce GTX Titan by Tomczak and Szafran [36] using a lattice Boltzmann method with nineteen speeds (D3Q19 lattice) in double precision in a tiling layout (similar to block structuring) and two data sets (AB-pattern), which corresponds to between 48% and 72.6% bandwidth (the numbers are taken directly from [36] as our performance model does not apply directly to their code). The relatively wide range in the performance of [36] is due to differences in the data locality in the different test cases.

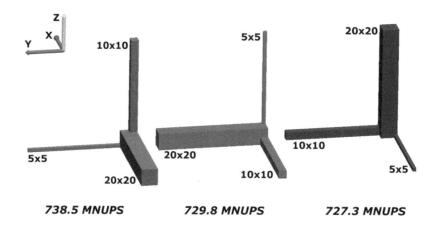

738.5 MNUPS   729.8 MNUPS   727.3 MNUPS

Figure 4. Different orientations of the same test geometry to probe the isotropy of EsoTwist with indirect addressing. The performance in terms of Million Node Updates Per Second is seen to depend only weakly on the orientation. Picture reproduced from [37].

5.4. Porous Material

Our implementation of the LBM using EsoTwist with indirect addressing on GPUs participated in a comparative study between different Computational Fluid Dynamics (CFD) methods. Simulation results were presented in [27]. Our method was found to be the most efficient when compared to the competing methods to solve the Navier–Stokes equations in porous media. Here, we present only performance values.

We discretize a random packing of 6864 mono-disperse spheres (beads) with radius 0.5 mm as depicted in Figure 5. The bead pack is discretized with Cartesian grids using two different resolutions: 40 μm (Figure 6) and 20 μm (Figure 7). The full matrix representation of the grids would contain 1.74×10^7 and 1.39×10^8 grid nodes for the 40 μm and the 20 μm case, respectively. By the use of indirect addressing, the number of nodes is reduced to 9.05×10^6 (52%) and 6.465×10^7 (46.5%), respectively. We hence see that indirect addressing eliminates about half of the grid nodes in this case. It is interesting to note that, in the case of the AA-pattern without pointer chasing, there would hardly be any advantage of the sparse data structure over the full matrix in this case since the number of pointers required for indirect addressing is almost as large as the memory required to store the distributions. In the case of EsoTwist combined with pointer chasing, only three pointers have to be stored with each grid node. The 20 μm case was simulated for 72 s in real time, which translates to 1,600,000 time steps. Other than in the previous simulation, the current test case applied second order accurate boundary conditions to capture the curvature of the beads and the simulation domain was decomposed and distributed over several GPUs. On two Nvidia K40c GPUs, we obtained a performance of 525.2 MNUPS and on six Tesla C1060 we obtained 448.6 MNUPS. The 40 μm test case was simulated on a single K40c GPU and run for 400.000 time steps. It obtained a performance of 233.3 MNUPS. However, these performance figures do not include the fact that the simulation of a porous medium is boundary dominated and that the application of the second order accurate interpolation boundary condition [26] is done in a separate step. In addition, it must be taken into account that the complex cumulant collision kernel [26] was used. The application of the second order boundary conditions produce about the same data traffic as one collision. In the case of the 40 μm simulation, we had about 4.26×10^6 boundary nodes such that the bandwidth occupancy including the application of the boundary conditions is calculated as 27.5%. These performance figures hence show that, even though the optimal performance is never obtained in real-world applications with complex boundary conditions, the performance remains comparable to the optimal case.

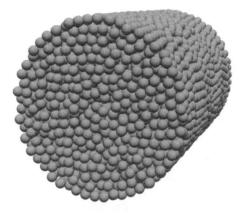

Figure 5. The random packing of 6864 spheres is discretized with a sparse matrix. Picture reproduced from [37].

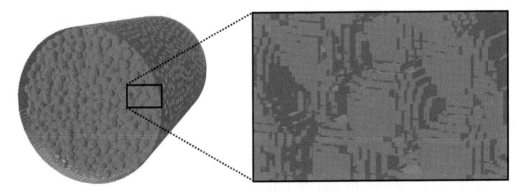

Figure 6. The discretization of the random packing of spheres with a lattice spacing of 40 μm. Picture reproduced from [37].

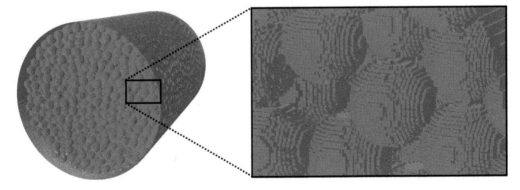

Figure 7. The discretization of the random packing of spheres with a lattice spacing of 20 μm. Picture reproduced from [37].

6. Conclusions

We presented the Esoteric Twist data structure for efficient thread safe execution of the LBM on massively parallel hardware. EsoTwist requires only a single read and write operation for each datum in each time step and only a single place in main memory. When combined with indirect addressing, EsoTwist requires the smallest number of pointers to neighboring nodes of any LBM algorithm using sparse matrices known to us. To our knowledge, EsoTwist has the smallest memory footprint of any sparse matrix LBM implementations, and it requires the smallest number of reads of any known LBM algorithm using sparse matrices. These claims are also confirmed by comparing to a recent analysis of Wittmann et al. [3]. Ignoring that EsoTwist requires, in fact, less pointers and reads than the AA-pattern, Wittmann et al. concluded that the AA-pattern and EsoTwist have the lowest data traffic of the known streaming algorithms. While being efficient, EsoTwist is also very flexible and is easily applied to real-world applications with complex boundaries. It also combines very favorably with local grid refinement techniques as shown in several publications [22,23,26,28].

Our results show comparable performance in terms of memory bandwidth (up to $\sim 68.2\%$ peak bandwidth) to a block structured code with two distributions on recent Nvidia GPUs [36] and to full matrix codes. In terms of execution time, the sparse matrix EsoTwist method was found to obtain 99.4% of the performance of the AB-pattern on a recent GPU. It is of note that the ratio on older hardware was found to be inferior (93.2% for a Tesla C1060). It is hence seen that progress in hardware allows for more flexibility of the code without severe performance penalty.

Acknowledgments: This work was funded by the TU-Braunschweig.

Author Contributions: M.G. conceived the Esoteric Twist algorithm. M.S. implemented the GPU version and conducted the presented simulations.

Appendix A. EsoTwist in 3D

Here, we present some pseudocode of the EsoTwist algorithm. We present separately the routine for read (Algorithm A1) and write (Algorithm A2) that are used in the EsoTwist algorithm in three dimensions (Algorithm A3).

Algorithm A1: Reading the data from the main memory to the registers. An efficient implementation of the method writes out all for-loops explicitly.

Function $readNode(n, n_x, n_y, n_z, n_{xy}, n_{xz}, n_{yz}, n_{xyz})$

  for $\{i, j, k\} \in \{\{0,0,0\}, \{0,0,1\}, \{0,1,0\}, \{0,1,1\}, \{1,0,0\}, \{1,0,1\}, \{1,1,0\}, \{1,1,1\}\}$ **do**
    | $F_{ijk} \leftarrow f_{ijk}[n]$;
  end

  for $\{i, j, k\} \in \{\{-1,0,0\}, \{-1,0,1\}, \{-1,1,0\}, \{-1,1,1\}\}$ **do**
    | $F_{ijk} \leftarrow f_{ijk}[n_x]$;
  end

  for $\{i, j, k\} \in \{\{0\bar{1},0\}, \{0,\bar{1},1\}, \{1,\bar{1},0\}, \{1,\bar{1},1\}\}$ **do**
    | $F_{ijk} \leftarrow f_{ijk}[n_y]$;
  end

  for $\{i, j, k\} \in \{\{0,0,-1\}, \{0,1,-1\}, \{1,0,-1\}, \{1,1,-1\}\}$ **do**
    | $F_{ijk} \leftarrow f_{ijk}[n_z]$;
  end

  for $\{i, j, k\} \in \{\{-1,-1,0\}, \{-1,-1,1\}\}$ **do**
    | $F_{ijk} \leftarrow f_{ijk}[n_{xy}]$;
  end

  for $\{i, j, k\} \in \{\{-1,0,-1\}, \{-1,1,-1\}\}$ **do**
    | $F_{ijk} \leftarrow f_{ijk}[n_{xz}]$;
  end

  for $\{i, j, k\} \in \{\{0,-1,-1\}, \{1,-1,-1\}\}$ **do**
    | $F_{ijk} \leftarrow f_{ijk}[n_{yz}]$;
  end

  | $F_{-1-1-1} \leftarrow f_{-1-1-1}[n_{xyz}]$;

Algorithm A2: Writing data back to main memory. An efficient implementation of the method writes out all for-loops explicitly. Note that the direction of the distributions has been swapped compared to the Algorithm A1.

Function $writeNode(n, n_x, n_y, n_z, n_{xy}, n_{xz}, n_{yz}, n_{xyz})$

   for $\{i, j, k\} \in \{\{0,0,0\}, \{0,0,1\}, \{0,1,0\}, \{0,1,1\}, \{1,0,0\}, \{1,0,1\}, \{1,1,0\}, \{1,1,1\}\}$ **do**
      | $f_{ijk}[n] \leftarrow F^*_{-i-j-k}$;
   end
   for $\{i, j, k\} \in \{\{-1,0,0\}, \{-1,0,1\}, \{-1,1,0\}, \{-1,1,1\}\}$ **do**
      | $f_{ijk}[n_x] \leftarrow F^*_{-i-j-k}$;
   end
   for $\{i, j, k\} \in \{\{0,-1,0\}, \{0,-1,1\}, \{1,-1,0\}, \{1,-1,1\}\}$ **do**
      | $f_{ijk}[n_y] \leftarrow F^*_{-i-j-k}$;
   end
   for $\{i, j, k\} \in \{\{0,0,-1\}, \{0,1,-1\}, \{1,0,-1\}, \{1,1,-1\}\}$ **do**
      | $f_{ijk}[n_z] \leftarrow F^*_{-i-j-k}$;
   end
   for $\{i, j, k\} \in \{\{-1,-1,0\}, \{-1,-1,1\}\}$ **do**
      | $f_{ijk}[n_{xy}] \leftarrow F^*_{-i-j-k}$;
   end
   for $\{i, j, k\} \in \{\{-1,0,-1\}, \{-1,1,-1\}\}$ **do**
      | $f_{ijk}[n_{xz}] \leftarrow F^*_{-i-j-k}$;
   end
   for $\{i, j, k\} \in \{\{0,-1,-1\}, \{1,-1,-1\}\}$ **do**
      | $f_{ijk}[n_{yz}] \leftarrow F^*_{-i-j-k}$;
   end
   $f_{-1-1-1}[n_{xyz}] \leftarrow F^*_{111}$;

Algorithm A3: EsoTwist in 3D: the algorithm requires three arrays $neighborX$, $neighborY$ and $neighborZ$ with links to the neighboring node of n. The functions $readNode()$ (Algorithm A1) and $writeNode()$ (Algorithm A2) transfer the distributions f_{ijk} to the registers F_{ijk} and back.

---

for *all time steps* **do**
   for *all nodes n* **do**
      | $n_x \leftarrow neighborX[n]$;
      | $n_y \leftarrow neighborY[n]$;
      | $n_z \leftarrow neighborZ[n]$;
      | $n_{xy} \leftarrow neighborY[n_x]$;
      | $n_{xz} \leftarrow neighborZ[n_x]$;
      | $n_{yz} \leftarrow neighborZ[n_y]$;
      | $n_{xyz} \leftarrow neighborZ[n_{xy}]$;
      | $readNode(n, n_x, n_y, n_z, n_{xy}, n_{xz}, n_{yz}, n_{xyz})$;
      | $F^* \leftarrow collideNode(F)$;
      | $writeNode(n, n_x, n_y, n_z, n_{xy}, n_{xz}, n_{yz}, n_{xyz})$;
   end
   for $i \in -1\ldots1$; $j, k \in 0\ldots1$; $j + k \neq 0$ **do**
      | $swapPointer(f_{ijk}, f_{-i-j-k})$;
   end
   $swapPointer(f_{100}, f_{-100})$;
   $swapPointer(f_{10-1}, f_{-101})$;
   $swapPointer(f_{1-10}, f_{-110})$;
   $swapPointer(f_{0-11}, f_{01-1})$;
end

References

1. Axner, L.; Bernsdorf, J.; Zeiser, T.; Lammers, P.; Linxweiler, J.; Hoekstra, A. Performance evaluation of a parallel sparse lattice Boltzmann solver. *J. Comput. Phys.* **2008**, *227*, 4895–4911.

2. Wittmann, M.; Zeiser, T.; Hager, G.; Wellein, G. Comparison of different propagation steps for lattice Boltzmann methods. *Comput. Math. Appl.* **2013**, *65*, 924–935.

3. Wittmann, M.; Zeiser, T.; Hager, G.; Wellein, G. Modeling and analyzing performance for highly optimized propagation steps of the lattice Boltzmann method on sparse lattices. *arXiv* **2014**, arXiv:1410.0412.

4. Schönherr, M.; Kucher, K.; Geier, M.; Stiebler, M.; Freudiger, S.; Krafczyk, M. Multi-thread implementations of the lattice Boltzmann method on non-uniform grids for CPUs and GPUs. *Comput. Math. Appl.* **2011**, *61*, 3730–3743.

5. Dellar, P.J. An interpretation and derivation of the lattice Boltzmann method using Strang splitting. *Comput. Math. Appl.* **2013**, *65*, 129–141.

6. Hager, G.; Wellein, G.; Wittmann, M.; Zeiser, T.; Fehske, H. Efficient Temporal Blocking for Stencil Computations by Multicore-Aware Wavefront Parallelization. In Proceedings of the 2009 33rd Annual IEEE International Computer Software and Applications Conference (COMPSAC 2009), Seattle, WA, USA, 20–24 July 2009; Volume 1, pp. 579–586.

7. Obrecht, C.; Asinari, P.; Kuznik, F.; Roux, J.J. Thermal link-wise artificial compressibility method: GPU implementation and validation of a double-population model. *Comput. Math. Appl.* **2016**, *72*, 375–385.

8. Asinari, P.; Ohwada, T.; Chiavazzo, E.; Rienzo, A.F.D. Link-wise artificial compressibility method. *J. Comput. Phys.* **2012**, *231*, 5109–5143.

9. Ohwada, T.; Asinari, P. Artificial compressibility method revisited: Asymptotic numerical method for incompressible Navier-Stokes equations. *J. Comput. Phys.* **2010**, *229*, 1698–1723.

10. Dubois, F.; Lallemand, P.; Obrecht, C.; Tekitek, M.M. Lattice Boltzmann model approximated with finite difference expressions. *Comput. Fluids* **2016**, doi:10.1016/j.compfluid.2016.04.013.

11. Thorne, D.T.; Michael, C. *Lattice Boltzmann Modeling: An Introduction for Geoscientists and Engineers*, 2nd. ed.; Springer: Berlin/Heidelberg, Germany, 2006.

12. Mohamad, A.A. *Lattice Boltzmann Method: Fundamentals and Engineering Applications with Computer Codes*; Springer Science & Business Media: Berlin, Germany, 2011.

13. Guo, Z.; Shu, C. *Lattice Boltzmann Method and Its Applications in Engineering*; World Scientific: Singapore, 2013; Volume 3.

14. Krüger, T.; Kusumaatmaja, H.; Kuzmin, A.; Shardt, O.; Silva, G.; Viggen, E.M. *The Lattice Boltzmann Method: Principles and Practice*; Springer: Cham, Switzerland, 2016.

15. Wellein, G.; Zeiser, T.; Hager, G.; Donath, S. On the single processor performance of simple lattice Boltzmann kernels. *Comput. Fluids* **2006**, *35*, 910–919.

16. Bailey, P.; Myre, J.; Walsh, S.; Lija, D.J.; Saar, M.O. Accelerating lattice Boltzmann fluid flow simulations using graphics processors. In Proceedings of the 2009 International Conference on Parallel Processing, Vienna, Austria, 22–25 September 2009; pp. 550–557.

17. Mattila, K.; Hyväluoma, J.; Rossi, T.; Aspnäs, M.; Westerholm, J. An efficient swap algorithm for the lattice Boltzmann method. *Comput. Phys. Commun.* **2007**, *176*, 200–210.

18. Latt, J. *How to Implement Your DdQq Dynamics with Only q Variables Per Node (Instead of 2q)*; Technical Report; Tufts University; Medford, MA, USA, 2007.

19. Pohl, T.; Kowarschik, M.; Wilke, J.; Iglberger, K.; Rüde, U. Optimization and profiling of the cache performance of parallel lattice Boltzmann codes. *Parallel Process. Lett.* **2003**, *13*, 549–560.

20. Neumann, P.; Bungartz, H.J.; Mehl, M.; Neckel, T.; Weinzierl, T. A Coupled Approach for Fluid Dynamic Problems Using the PDE Framework Peano. *Commun. Comput. Phys.* **2012**, *12*, 65.

21. Geller, S. ICON Technology & Process Consulting Ltd., Braunschweig, Germany. Personal communication, 2016.

22. Far, E.K.; Geier, M.; Kutscher, K.; Krafczyk, M. Simulation of micro aggregate breakage in turbulent flows by the cumulant lattice Boltzmann method. *Comput. Fluids* **2016**, *140*, 222–231.

23. Far, E.K.; Geier, M.; Kutscher, K.; Krafczyk, M. Distributed cumulant lattice Boltzmann simulation of the dispersion process of ceramic agglomerates. *J. Comput. Methods Sci. Eng.* **2016**, *16*, 231–252.

24. Linxweiler, J.   Ein Integrierter Softwareansatz zur Interaktiven Exploration und Steuerung von Strömungssimulationen auf Many-Core-Architekturen. Ph.D. Thesis, TU Braunschweig, Braunschweig, Germany, June 2011. (In German)

25. Tölke, J.; Krafczyk, M. TeraFLOP computing on a desktop PC with GPUs for 3D CFD. *Int. J. Comput. Fluid Dyn.* **2008**, *22*, 443–456.

26. Geier, M.; Schönherr, M.; Pasquali, A.; Krafczyk, M. The cumulant lattice Boltzmann equation in three dimensions: Theory and validation. *Comput. Math. Appl.* **2015**, *70*, 507–547.

27. Yang, X.; Mehmani, Y.; Perkins, W.A.; Pasquali, A.; Schönherr, M.; Kim, K.; Perego, M.; Parks, M.L.; Trask, N.; Balhoff, M.T.; et al.   Intercomparison of 3D pore-scale flow and solute transport simulation methods. *Adv. Water Resour.* **2016**, *95*, 176–189.

28. Pasquali, A.; Schönherr, M.; Geier, M.; Krafczyk, M. Simulation of external aerodynamics of the DrivAer model with the LBM on GPGPUs. In Proceedings of the ParCo2015, Edinburgh, UK, 1–4 September 2015.

29. Zeiser, T.; Wellein, G.; Hager, G.; Donath, S.; Deserno, F.; Lammers, P.; Wierse, M. *Optimized Lattice Boltzmann Kernels as Testbeds for Processor Performance*; Regional Computing Center of Erlangen (RRZE): Erlangen, Germany, 2004; Volume 1.

30. Welleina, G.; Lammersb, P.; Hagera, G.; Donatha, S.; Zeisera, T. Towards optimal performance for lattice Boltzmann applications on terascale computers. In Proceedings of the Parallel CFD Conference, Busan, Korea, 15–18 May 2006; Elsevier: Amsterdam, The Netherlands, 2006; pp. 31–40.

31. Williams, S.; Oliker, L.; Carter, J.; Shalf, J. Extracting ultra-scale lattice Boltzmann performance via hierarchical and distributed auto-tuning. In Proceedings of the 2011 International Conference for High Performance Computing, Networking, Storage and Analysis (SC), Seattle, WA, USA, 12–18 November 2011; pp. 1–12.

32. Feichtinger, C.; Habich, J.; Köstler, H.; Rüde, U.; Aoki, T.   Performance modeling and analysis of heterogeneous lattice boltzmann simulations on cpu–gpu clusters. *Parallel Comput.* **2015**, *46*, 1–13.

33. Qian, Y.H.; d'Humières, D.; Lallemand, P. Lattice BGK Models for Navier-Stokes Equation. *EPL (Europhys. Lett.)* **1992**, *17*, 479.

34. Geier, M.; Greiner, A.; Korvink, J.G. A factorized central moment lattice Boltzmann method. *Eur. Phys. J. Spec. Top.* **2009**, *171*, 55–61.

35. Jeong, H.; Lee, W.; Pak, J.; Choi, K.J.; Park, S.H.; Yoo, J.S.; Kim, J.H.; Lee, J.; Lee, Y.W. Performance of Kepler GTX Titan GPUs and Xeon Phi System. *arXiv* **2013**, arXiv:1311.0590.

36. Tomczak, T.; Szafran, R.G. Memory layout in GPU implementation of lattice Boltzmann method for sparse 3D geometries. *arXiv* **2016**, arXiv:1611.02445.

37. Schönherr, M. Towards Reliable LES-CFD Computations Based on Advanced LBM Models Utilizing (Multi-) GPGPU Hardware. Ph.D. Thesis, TU Braunschweig, Braunschweig, Germany, July 2015.

8

Detecting Perturbed Subpathways towards Mouse Lung Regeneration Following H1N1 Influenza Infection

Aristidis G. Vrahatis [1,*], **Konstantina Dimitrakopoulou** [2], **Andreas Kanavos** [1], **Spyros Sioutas** [3] **and Athanasios Tsakalidis** [1]

[1] Department of Computer Engineering and Informatics, University of Patras, Patras 26500, Greece; kanavos@ceid.upatras.gr (A.K.); tsak@ceid.upatras.gr (A.T.)

[2] Centre for Cancer Biomarkers CCBIO and Computational Biology Unit, Department of Informatics, University of Bergen, Bergen 5020, Norway; Konstantina.Dimitrakopoulou@uib.no

[3] Department of Informatics, Ionian University Corfu, Corfu 49100, Greece; sioutas@ionio.gr

* Correspondence: agvrahatis@upatras.gr

Academic Editor: Demos T. Tsahalis

Abstract: It has already been established by the systems-level approaches that the future of predictive disease biomarkers will not be sketched by plain lists of genes or proteins or other biological entities but rather integrated entities that consider all underlying component relationships. Towards this orientation, early pathway-based approaches coupled expression data with whole pathway interaction topologies but it was the recent approaches that zoomed into subpathways (local areas of the entire biological pathway) that provided more targeted and context-specific candidate disease biomarkers. Here, we explore the application potential of PerSubs, a graph-based algorithm which identifies differentially activated disease-specific subpathways. PerSubs is applicable both for microarray and RNA-Seq data and utilizes the Kyoto Encyclopedia of Genes and Genomes (KEGG) database as reference for biological pathways. PerSubs operates in two stages: first, identifies differentially expressed genes (or uses any list of disease-related genes) and in second stage, treating each gene of the list as start point, it scans the pathway topology around to build meaningful subpathway topologies. Here, we apply PerSubs to investigate which pathways are perturbed towards mouse lung regeneration following H1N1 influenza infection.

Keywords: lung regeneration; systems biology; computation on networks and graphs

1. Introduction

We are going through the "Network Medicine" era, an emerging research field which has the potential to capture more realistically the molecular complexity of human diseases and provide computational methodologies that can discern more efficiently how such complexity controls disease manifestations, prognosis, and therapy. It integrates "Systems Medicine" and "Network Science" fields to formulate unbiased large-scale network-based analyses in order to uncover this complexity. However, the current high-throughput molecular technologies produce an unprecedented amount of biological data, posing a growing need for new "Network Medicine" tools to manage the complexity of "Big Data" and "Big Graphs" that are generated [1].

There is growing consensus that the advances in analysis methods fall behind relative to the massive amounts of omics data produced nowadays. In recent years, there was a paradigm shift that successfully moved the research focus from coupling diseases with single genes or single-nucleotide polymorphism (SNPs) to disease signatures or gene sets [2]. More recently, more sophisticated systems-level approaches gained ground and pushed forward the transition from gene-to-gene analysis to signaling pathways and complex interaction networks, thereby gaining a more realistic and holistic insight into disease mechanisms [3].

Towards this orientation, pathway-based analysis has been proved to be efficient for comprehending biological mechanisms and disease etiology [4,5]. The main concept is a simplified analysis that groups single genes into sets of functionally related and interacting proteins. In this way, the complexity is reduced to a numerically feasible number at the magnitude of hundreds and, moreover, identifying "differential" pathways between two conditions has more explanatory power than gene lists. The first works in this field ignored the pathway interacting topology and used over-representation to compare the number of interesting genes that hit a given pathway with the number of genes expected to hit the given pathway by chance [4]. Later studies used Functional class scoring (FCS) to identify coordinated changes in the expression of genes in the same pathway [6]. Other approaches focused on the effect of the upstream genes relative to the downstream genes and coupled classical enrichment analysis along with the perturbation of a specific pathway to quantify the impact of upstream genes [7,8].

More recently, pathway analysis evolved to subpathway analysis, which searches for sub-areas on the topology to interpret the related biological phenomena and provides more targeted and context-specific molecular candidate signatures for disease etiology [9–16]. Subpathways are local subnetworks in the pathway topology which can be associated with small scale biological functions, within the boundaries of the pathway, and whose deregulation can give rise to a disease. Subpathway-based analysis has dealt with various challenges and signifies rightfully the next generation in pathway analysis [12]. Examining the entire pathway topology as one unit, hinders the detection of the small scale perturbations which might reflect a pathophysiological state or response to treatment [9]. Also, different pathway subnetworks may perform the same function in the same pathway and different pathways due the high overlap may use the same subnetworks in similar roles [9]. Subpathway-based tools, with their capacity to scan the entire pathway network and zoom into the specific subareas that are deregulated, can explore deeper the biological significance of disease-associated mutations identified by genome-wide association studies and full-genome sequencing. Hence, in the recent years several tools have been published under this perspective, offering new horizons in the Network Medicine field [9–16].

In previous work [17], we developed Perturbed Subpathways (PerSubs) tool to extract perturbed disease-specific subpathways from pathway networks. An important feature of the algorithm is that it identifies perturbed subpathways from KEGG pathway maps by using as starting point, prior to scanning pathway topology, a set of interesting gene-nodes (i.e., differentially expressed genes, disease-specific genes etc.). PerSubs utilizes a measure based on two multivariate logistic functions to set the co-expression status between the members of an interacting pair as highly positive or negative. We applied PerSubs on a microarray experiment that included colony samples from control and H1N1 influenza treated lungs (12 days post infection) to study mechanisms towards lung regeneration following catastrophic damage [18]. Our results show that PerSubs can provide subpathways that reflect well processes related to tissue repair and development.

2. Materials and Methods

PerSubs algorithm [17] extracts perturbed subpathways from pathways taking into account graph topology and differential expression of the corresponding gene-nodes (Algorithm 1). Differential expression is used based on gene expressions from transcriptomics data. PerSubs extracts subpatways perturbed by a condition (disease or biological process) under study. Subpathways are extracted in the form of densely connected subgraphs around nodes of interest based on topological criteria. For this, we follow a "seed growing" approach similarly to [19], where we start from an initial Node of Interest (NoI) and we identify the perturbation caused by this node in the entire pathway network. Users can provide a list of genes of interest, but here we selected as nodes of interest the significantly differentially expressed genes.

Node (gene/protein) differential expression intensity is calculated based on a geometrical multivariate effective approach, called the Characteristic Direction (chdir) [20]. It uses a linear classification scheme, which defines a separating hyper-plane, the orientation of which can be interpreted to identify differentially expressed genes (DEG). More specifically, it incorporates a regularization scheme to deal with the problem of dimensionality, and also provides an intuitive geometrical picture of differential expression in terms of a single direction. This geometrical picture reliably characterizes the differential expression and also leads to some natural extensions of the approach such as improved gene-set enrichment analysis.

In the computation of the characteristic direction, in order to identify differentially expressed genes, initially the steps below are followed:

1. Gene expression data have N samples, in which the expression of p genes is measured.
2. Each sample's expression profile forms a row of the matrix X ($N \times p$) (each of sample's expression comes from one of K classes (e.g., disease or normal state) belonging to the set G).
3. Bayes rule provides an expression for the class posteriors $P(G|X)$,

$$P(G = k|X = x) = \frac{f_k(x)\pi_k}{\sum_{i=1}^{K} f_i(x)\pi_i},$$

   where $f_k(x)$ is the class-conditional density of X, x is a particular instance of the values in a gene expression profile, π_k is the prior probability of class k.
4. The class-conditional density can be modeled as a multivariate Gaussian:

$$f_k(x) = \frac{1}{2\pi^{\frac{p}{2}}|\Sigma_\kappa|^{\frac{1}{2}}} e^{-\frac{1}{2}(x-\mu_\kappa)^{-1}\Sigma_\kappa^{-1}(x-\mu_\kappa)},$$

   where μ_κ and Σ_κ is mean and covariance respectively.
5. Then, linear discriminant analysis (LDA) is applied based on the assumption that the covariance matrix is the same for each class ($\Sigma_\kappa = \Sigma \forall k$). The log-ratio of class posteriors $P(G|X)$, provides a measure of the relative likelihood of classifying to those classes. Hence, the log ratio of classifying to classes κ and l is formulated as:

$$log\frac{Pr(G = k|X = x)}{Pr(G = l|X = x)} = log\frac{\pi_k}{\pi_l} - \frac{1}{2}\gamma^T\Sigma^{-1}\gamma + x^T\Sigma^{-1}\gamma,$$

   where, γ is $(\mu_k - \mu_l)\,\pi_k$, is the class mean, andit is assumed that both classes have the same covariance matrix, Σ ($\Sigma_\kappa = \Sigma \forall k$), $\mu_k = \sum_{g_i=k}\frac{x_i}{N_k}$, $\Sigma = \Sigma_{k=1}^{k}\Sigma_{gi=k}(x_i - \mu_k)^T/(N - K)$, where x_i is a row from the data matrix X.
6. Finally, the orientation of the separating hyper-plane (between classes k and l) is defined by the normal p-vector, in the third term on the right hand side, that we label b,

$$b = \Sigma^{-1}(\mu_k - \mu_l)$$

The Characteristic Direction method is significantly more sensitive than existing methods for identifying DEGs. In our methodology, the chdir value is used as weight for the corresponding node and the final pathway graph is weighted with respect to edges with the mean chdir value of the corresponding gene values. This weight promotes the interconnecting nodes with high differential expression.

Subsequently, in order to extract perturbed subpathways from pathways, we use some graph theoretical properties to determine the densely connected neighborhood of a node. Let $G = (V, E)$ a weighted directed graph, where V is the node set and E the edge set, with w_{vu} denoting the edge weight from node v to node u. With $N(v)$ we represent the neighbors of node v. For a subgraph $S \subseteq G$, the internal degree $N_{INT}(v, S)$ of a node $v \in S$ is defined as the number of edges connecting v with nodes within S and the external degree as the number of edges connecting v with nodes not belonging to S. The weighted internal degree is defined as the sum of weights of internal edges divided by internal degree:

$$NW_{INT}(v, S) = \frac{1}{N_{INT}(v, s)} \sum_{u \in N(v) \cap S} w_{vu}$$

Similarly, we define external weighted degree. The density of a graph is defined as the number of edges divided by the number of all possible edges. The weighted density of a (sub)graph is defined as the sum of all edge weights over the number of all possible edges:

$$DW(G) = \frac{1}{|V|(|V| - 1)} \sum_{(v,u) \in E} w_{vu}$$

The algorithm operates on two phases, firstly the node set is expanded by selecting some of the external neighbors and secondly the selected node set is pruned. Initially, we start with a set S including only the NoI node s. Then, for each NoI's neighbor $v \in N(s)$, we compute the internal and external unweighted and weighted degree. In order to select a highly connected subset, a node v is included in the set S, if it satisfies the following two criteria:

$$\text{Criterion 1} : \frac{N_{INT}(v, S)}{N_{INT}(v, S) + N_{EXT}(v, S)} > a$$

$$\text{Criterion 2} : NW_{INT}(v, S) > NW_{EXT}(v, S)$$

where α is a parameter set for direct neighbors of NoI and for other nodes. After a fine tuning with repetitive trials, the optimal parameter value of α was set to 0.55 and 0.85 respectively.

In the second phase we aim to obtain a more compact set by maximizing the weighted density. For this, we remove one by one nodes until we reach to a maximum value. The order of nodes is determined by the magnitude of the first criterion, with the less significant nodes examined first for removal. The algorithm is iterated in terms of the external neighbors of the selected nodes, until no more nodes can be added to the set S.

Algorithm 1. Pseudocode of PerSubs Algorithm

Input: NoI, G, $\alpha 1$, $\alpha 2$
Output: final subpathway S
I. S = {NoI} // initialize
II. For each v in S // inclusion step
    a. Find neighbors $N(v)$
    b. Keep not included neighbors: $N(v) = N(v) - S$
    c. For every u in $N(v)$
        i. Calculate N_{INT}, N_{EXT}, NW_{INT}, NW_{EXT}
        ii. If $u \in N(NoI)$
            1. Evaluate if Criterion1 > $\alpha 1$
        iii. Else
            1. Evaluate if Criterion1 > $\alpha 2$
        iv. Evaluate Criterion2
        v. if Criterion1 = true AND Criterion2 = true
            1. Include u: $S = S \cup u$
III. For each v in S ordered by increasing Criterion1   // pruning step
    a. if $DW(S - v) > DW(S)$
        i. Remove v: $S = S - v$
IV. Repeat steps II and III until no new nodes added

The output of PerSubs is a list of subpathways that can serve as potential network biomarkers for the case under study. Further, we evaluate statistically the resulted subpathways in order to keep the most reliable ones based on a permutation strategy. The gene labels in the RNA-Seq dataset are randomly shuffled 1000 times and each time PerSubs is re-applied. The subpathways starting from the same gene are compared based on their average weight. For each subpathway, the p-value is the percentage of cases where the average weight is lower than the respective value in the real condition (p-value < 0.05).

3. Results

We applied PerSubs on mouse microarray data [18] that explore the extent of lung regeneration following catastrophic damage after infection with H1N1virus. In particular, the experiment contains samples from 3 colonies from control and H1N1 influenza treated lungs (12 days post infection). The complete dataset is deposited in NCBI's Gene Expression Omnibus (GEO, http://www.ncbi.nlm.nih.gov/geo/) and is accessible through the accession number GSE32600. By applying PerSubs, we detected subpathways (Figure 1) which contain both differentially expressed and co-expressed associated genes, as to their expression change between control and infection state. All non-metabolic pathway maps of *Mus musculus* (mmu) were downloaded from KEGG [21] and were converted to gene-gene networks based on the CHRONOS R Bioconductor package [11].

Influenza infection in the lungs causes severe inflammatory damage to the lung through a respiratory outbreak of the innate immune response and the resulting lung injury can lead to other complications or chronic damage if not treated [22]. Zooming into H1N1 influenza A strain, it has been shown to induce acute respiratory distress syndrome (ARDS), pneumonia, alveolar damage, hypoxemia, and massive increase in inflammatory cytokines [18]. Influenza is a very common respiratory pathogen and as such it has been extensively studied to reveal its infection kinetics and pathogenicity [18]. Comprehending the influenza infection phases and especially repair stage will be an enabling step towards preventing these complications by assisting the lung to recover properly [22].

In this work we explore the (sub)pathways perturbed after H1N1 viral infection of mouse lungs at a specific time point (12 days post infection (dpi)). In the original work of [18], the tissue damage based on immune cell infiltration displayed peak at 11 dpi, declined at 21 dpi and mostly cleared in the lung at 60 dpi. Also, in the interval 10–12 dpi the weight loss of animals reached a peak and recovered at 20 dpi. In this work we first identified a set of differentially expressed genes (DEGs) between control and infected samples and then applied PerSubs with each DEG as starting point to detect the perturbed sub-topologies. In Table 1, we present some representative identified KEGG pathway terms. The pathway "ECM-receptor interaction" was found significantly enriched in two Influenza A related studies [23,24]. It has been reported that cellular processes such as adhesion, dynamic behaviors and apoptosis, regulated by ECM-receptor interaction, influence the entry or replication of influenza viruses [23]. Regarding "TGF-b signaling", it has been shown that respiratory viral infections offset secretion of TGF-β which in turn is implicated in decreasing pulmonary inflammation and extending host survival [25,26]. Also, TGF-β is involved in tissue repair and respiratory tract re-modeling of by stimulating matrix protein production, epithelial proliferation and differentiation. Moving forward, "Cytokine-cytokine receptor interaction" pathway has been shown to participate into activating the immune and inflammatory response to prevent from virus infections [24]. Moreover, "PPAR signaling" and "complement and coagulation" cascades have been suggested to repair excessive tissue damage by exhibiting anti-inflammatory functions [27]. Finally, with respect to "leukocyte transedothelial migration", it has been suggested that circulating blood leukocytes migrate to tissue injury and infection site to terminate the primary inflammatory trigger and thus assist tissue repair [28,29].

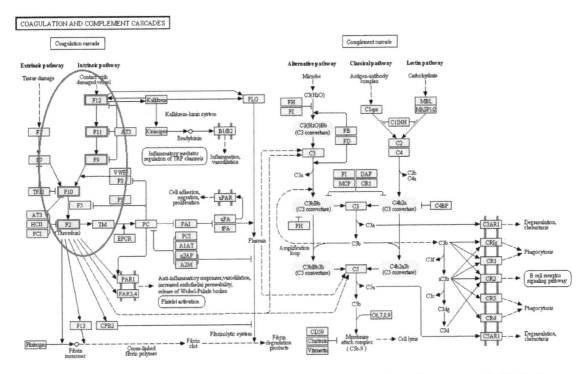

Figure 1. Snapshot of KEGG pathway map (04610) "Coagulation and complement cascades" with the detected by PerSubs subpathway highlighted in red.

In total, our results show that PerSubs extracted a repertoire of diverse subpathways that go in line with the findings of the original study and can serve as novel candidates for investigating further the host response and repair mechanisms.

Table 1. Pathway terms detected by PerSubs along with the detected subpathway members.

Pathway Names	Subpathway Members	References
ECM-receptor interaction	*Gp1ba, Gp5, Itga2b, Itgav, Itgb3, Gp9, Vwf*	[23,24]
TGF-beta signaling	*Acvr2a, Acvr2b, Inhba, Nodal*	[25,26]
Cytokine-cytokine receptor interaction	*Tgfbr1, Tgfbr2, Tgfb2*	[24]
PPAR signaling	*Cpt-1, Cpt-2, Mcad, Aco, Ucp-1, Pparα*	[24,27]
Leukocyte transendothelial migration	*Itgal, Itgb2, Icam1, Rhoa*	[28,29]
Coagulation and complement cascades	*F12, F11, F9, F10, F2*	[24]

Author Contributions: A.G.V. conceived of the study, designed the methodological framework, implemented the experimental analysis and drafted the manuscript. K.D. contributed in the interpretation of the results. A.K. contributed in the implementation of the methodological framework. All the above actions were supervised by S.S. and A.T. All authors read and approved the final manuscript.

References

1. Barabási, A.L.; Gulbahce, N.; Loscalzo, J. Network medicine: A network-based approach to human disease. *Nat. Rev. Genet.* **2011**, *12*, 56–68. [CrossRef] [PubMed]

2. Wang, L.; Jia, P.; Wolfinger, R.D.; Chen, X.; Zhao, Z. Gene set analysis of genome-wide association studies: methodological issues and perspectives. *Genomics* **2011**, *98*, 1–8.

3. Khatri, P.; Sirota, M.; Butte, A.J. Ten years of pathway analysis: Current approaches and outstanding challenges. *PLoS Comput. Biol.* **2012**, *8*, e1002375. [CrossRef] [PubMed]

4. Jin, L.; Zuo, X.-Y.; Su, W.-Y.; Zhao, X.-L.; Yuan, M-Q.; Han, L.-Z.; Zhao, X.; Chen, Y.-D.; Rao, S.-Q. Pathway-based analysis tools for complex diseases: A review. *Genom. Proteom. Bioinform.* **2014**, *12*, 210–220. [CrossRef] [PubMed]

5. Wang, K.; Li, M.; Bucan, M. Pathway-based approaches for analysis of genomewide association studies. *Am. J. Hum. Genet.* **2007**, *81*, 1278–1283. [CrossRef] [PubMed]

6. Shi, J.; Walker, M.G. Gene set enrichment analysis (GSEA) for interpreting gene expression profiles. *Curr. Bioinform.* **2007**, *2*, 133–137. [CrossRef]

7. Tarca, A.L.; Draghici, S.; Khatri, P.; Hassan, S.S.; Mittal, P.; Kim, J.S.; Kim, C.J.; Kusanovic, J.P.; Romero, R. A novel signaling pathway impact analysis. *Bioinformatics* **2009**, *25*, 75–82. [CrossRef] [PubMed]

8. Rahnenfuhrer, J.; Domingues, F.S.; Maydt, J.; Lengauer, T. Calculating the statistical significance of changes in pathway activity from gene expression data. *Stat. Appl. Genet. Mol. Biol.* **2004**, *3*, 1055. [CrossRef] [PubMed]

9. Chen, X.; Xu, J.; Huang, B.; Li, J.; Wu, X.; Ma, L.; Jia, X.; Bian, X.; Tan, F.; Liu, L.; et al. A sub-pathway-based approach for identifying drug response principal network. *Bioinformatics* **2011**, *27*, 649–654. [CrossRef] [PubMed]

10. Judeh, T.; Johnson, C.; Kumar, A.; Zhu, D. TEAK: Topology enrichment analysis framework for detecting activated biological subpathways. *Nucleic Acids Res.* **2013**, *41*, 1425–1437. [CrossRef] [PubMed]

11. Vrahatis, A.G.; Dimitrakopoulou, K.; Balomenos, P.; Tsakalidis, A.K.; Bezerianos, A. CHRONOS: A time-varying method for microRNA-mediated sub-pathway enrichment analysis. *Bioinformatics* **2016**, *32*, 884–892. [CrossRef] [PubMed]

12. Vrahatis, A.G.; Balomenos, P.; Tsakalidis, A.K.; Bezerianos, A. DEsubs: An R package for flexible identification of differentially expressed subpathways using RNA-seq experiments. *Bioinformatics* **2016**, *32*, 3844–3846. [CrossRef] [PubMed]

13. Dimitrakopoulos, G.N.; Balomenos, P.; Vrahatis, A.G.; Sgarbas, K.; Bezerianos, A. Identifying disease network perturbations through regression on gene expression and pathway topology analysis. In Proceedings of the 2016 IEEE 38th Annual International Conference of the Engineering in Medicine and Biology Society (EMBC), Lake Buena Vista (Orlando), FL, USA, 17–20 August 2016; pp. 5969–5972.

14. Vrahatis, A.G.; Dimitrakopoulos, G.N.; Tsakalidis, A.K.; Bezerianos, A. Identifying miRNA-mediated signaling subpathways by integrating paired miRNA/mRNA expression data with pathway topology. In Proceedings of the 2015 37th Annual International Conference of the IEEE Engineering in Medicine and Biology Society (EMBC), Milan, Italy, 25–29 August 2015; pp. 3997–4000.

15. Nam, S.; Chang, H.R.; Kim, K.T.; Kook, M.C.; Hong, D.; Kwon, C.H.; Jung, H.R.; Park, H.S.; Powis, G.; Liang, H.; et al. PATHOME: An algorithm for accurately detecting differentially expressed subpathways. *Oncogene* **2014**, *33*, 4941–4951. [CrossRef] [PubMed]

16. Li, C.; Li, X.; Miao, Y.; Wang, Q.; Jiang, W.; Xu, C.; Li, J.; Han, J.; Zhang, F.; Gong, B.; Xu, L. SubpathwayMiner: A software package for flexible identification of pathways. *Nucleic Acids Res.* **2009**, *37*, e131. [CrossRef] [PubMed]

17. Vrahatis, A.G.; Rapti, A.; Sioutas, S.; Tsakalidis, A.K. PerSubs: A graph-based algorithm for the identification of perturbed subpathways caused by complex diseases. In Proceedings of the Genetics, Geriatrics and Neurodegenerative Diseases Research, Sparta, Greece, 20–23 October 2016.

18. Kumar, P.A.; Hu, Y.; Yamamoto, Y.; Hoe, N.B.; Wei, T.S.; Mu, D.; Sun, Y.; Joo, L.S.; Dagher, R.; Zielonka, E.M.; et al. Distal airway stem cells yield alveoli in vitro and during lung regeneration following H1N1 influenza infection. *Cell* **2011**, *147*, 525–538. [CrossRef] [PubMed]

19. Maraziotis, I.A.; Dimitrakopoulou, K.; Bezerianos, A. Growing functional modules from a seed protein via integration of protein interaction and gene expression data. *BMC Bioinform.* **2007**, *8*, 408. [CrossRef] [PubMed]

20. Clark, N.R.; Hu, K.S.; Feldmann, A.S.; Kou, Y.; Chen, E.Y.; Duan, Q.; Ma'ayan, A. The characteristic direction: A geometrical approach to identify differentially expressed genes. *BMC Bioinform.* **2014**, *15*, 79. [CrossRef] [PubMed]

21. Kanehisa, M.; Goto, S. KEGG: Kyoto encyclopedia of genes and genomes. *Nucleic Acids Res.* **2000**, *28*, 27–30. [CrossRef] [PubMed]

22. Tan, K.S.; Choi, H.; Jiang, X.; Yin, L.; Seet, J.E.; Patzel, V.; Engelward, B.P.; Chow, V.T. Micro-RNAs in regenerating lungs: An integrative systems biology analysis of murine influenza pneumonia. *BMC Genom.* **2014**, *15*, 587. [CrossRef] [PubMed]

23. Chen, Y.; Zhou, J.; Cheng, Z.; Yang, S.; Chu, H.; Fan, Y.; Li, C.; Wong, B.H.; Zheng, S.; Zhu, Y.; et al. Functional variants regulating LGALS1 (Galectin 1) expression affect human susceptibility to influenza A (H7N9). *Sci. Rep.* **2015**, *5*, 8517. [CrossRef] [PubMed]

24. Li, Y.; Zhou, H.; Wen, Z.; Wu, S.; Huang, C.; Jia, G.; Chen, H.; Jin, M. Transcription analysis on response of swine lung to H1N1 swine influenza virus. *BMC Genom.* **2011**, *12*, 398. [CrossRef] [PubMed]

25. Furuya, Y.; Furuya, A.K.; Roberts, S.; Sanfilippo, A.M.; Salmon, S.L.; Metzger, D.W. Prevention of Influenza Virus-Induced Immunopathology by TGF-β Produced during Allergic Asthma. *PLoS Pathog.* **2015**, *11*, e1005180. [CrossRef] [PubMed]

26. Carlson, C.M.; Turpin, E.A.; Moser, L.A.; O'Brien, K.B.; Cline, T.D.; Jones, J.C.; Tumpey, T.M.; Katz, J.M.; Kelley, L.A.; Gauldie, J.; et al. Transforming growth factor-β: Activation by neuraminidase and role in highly pathogenic H5N1 influenza pathogenesis. *PLoS Pathog.* **2010**, *6*, e1001136. [CrossRef] [PubMed]

27. Croasdell, A.; Duffney, P.F.; Kim, N.; Lacy, S.H.; Sime, P.J.; Phipps, R.P. PPARγ and the Innate Immune System Mediate the Resolution of Inflammation. *PPAR Res.* **2015**, *2015*, 549691. [CrossRef] [PubMed]

28. Pociask, D.A.; Scheller, E.V.; Mandalapu, S.; McHugh, K.J.; Enelow, R.I.; Fattman, C.L.; Kolls, J.K.; Alcorn, J.F. IL-22 is essential for lung epithelial repair following influenza infection. *Am. J. Pathol.* **2013**, *182*, 1286–1296. [CrossRef] [PubMed]

29. Nourshargh, S.; Alon, R. Leukocyte migration into inflamed tissues. *Immunity* **2014**, *41*, 694–707. [CrossRef] [PubMed]

9

Scatter Search Applied to the Inference of a Development Gene Network

Amir Masoud Abdol [1], Damjan Cicin-Sain [2,3], Jaap A. Kaandorp [1] and Anton Crombach [2,3,4,*]

[1] Computational Science Lab, University of Amsterdam, Science Park 904, 1098XH Amsterdam, The Netherlands; A.M.Abdol@uva.nl (A.M.A.); J.A.Kaandorp@uva.nl (J.A.K.)

[2] EMBL/CRG Systems Biology Research Unit, Centre for Genomic Regulation (CRG), The Barcelona Institute of Science and Technology, 08003 Barcelona, Spain; cicinsain@gmail.com

[3] Universitat Pompeu Fabra (UPF), 08003 Barcelona, Spain

[4] Centre for Interdisciplinary Research in Biology, College de France, CNRS, INSERM, PSL Research University, 75231 Paris, France

* Correspondence: anton.crombach@college-de-france.fr

Academic Editors: Gennady Bocharov, Olga Solovyova and Vitaly Volpert

Abstract: Efficient network inference is one of the challenges of current-day biology. Its application to the study of development has seen noteworthy success, yet a multicellular context, tissue growth, and cellular rearrangements impose additional computational costs and prohibit a wide application of current methods. Therefore, reducing computational cost and providing quick feedback at intermediate stages are desirable features for network inference. Here we propose a hybrid approach composed of two stages: exploration with scatter search and exploitation of intermediate solutions with low temperature simulated annealing. We test the approach on the well-understood process of early body plan development in flies, focusing on the gap gene network. We compare the hybrid approach to simulated annealing, a method of network inference with a proven track record. We find that scatter search performs well at exploring parameter space and that low temperature simulated annealing refines the intermediate results into excellent model fits. From this we conclude that for poorly-studied developmental systems, scatter search is a valuable tool for exploration and accelerates the elucidation of gene regulatory networks.

Keywords: network inference; scatter search; parallel simulated annealing; gap gene network; *D. melanogaster*

1. Introduction

One of the big challenges in current-day biology is efficient network inference (also known as reverse engineering) [1]. It is the so-called inverse problem of deducing which genes interact and how strong each interaction is on the basis of the network's observed output, its expression dynamics. By tackling this challenge successfully, we gain insight in the internal dynamics of a regulatory network. In turn, this understanding aides the explanation of existing experimental results and helps us formulate hypotheses and new experiments to further probe the biological system under study. While on the experimental side obtaining the required data is often laborious and difficult, here we take the data as a given and focus on the computational side of network inference.

With the currently available computational power of a single workstation, network inference in a unicellular context is a successful endeavour, such as for yeast genetic and metabolic networks [2,3], and for the optimization of specific bio-molecules in bacteria [4] and in mammalian cell lines [5–7]. Moreover, the study of such systems is supported by software tools [8], formal languages for model description that enhance sharing and re-use [9,10], and crowd-sourcing efforts (e.g., DREAM Challenges [11]).

In developmental biology, network inference is used to compare and better understand how organisms create spatial and temporal patterns to grow and shape themselves. Networks of interacting genes are key players in these dynamical processes. Well-known examples are body plan formation in insects [12–16] and sea-anemones [17], limb development [18,19], and vulva cell differentiation [20]. The multicellular context, however, means an additional computational challenge. In the tissue that is being patterned, each cell has a gene network and (in general) communicates with other cells, thus creating a large system of coupled gene networks. This means that as we move from describing a single cell to a multicellular setting, the number of variables of the system increases dramatically (though the number of parameters remains rather similar to the single cell case). As a result, to do a rigorous, automated, fitting of model parameters, increased system size makes calculations computationally demanding. In fact, one is often restricted to high-performance computing (HPC) facilities.

Regardless of whether one studies single cells or patterning tissues, when one is deriving a network from data, swift feedback from the inference algorithm is highly desirable. The effort of building a model usually requires several iterations of inferring the regulatory network to arrive at a satisfactory solution. Hence a fast algorithm is not only convenient, it also allows for a better study of the network through alternative scenarios and systematic assessment of the influence of parameters on the system. Each iteration of inference provides information that may be used to adjust the algorithm and to analyse the solutions that have been produced. It follows that an important feature is the computational cost of an algorithm used for network inference.

Here, we address the issue of computational cost and swift feedback in the context of a developmental regulatory network—the gap gene system, introduced below—responsible for early body plan formation in insects. We introduce a hybrid, two-stage optimization approach to infer the network. The idea behind the two-stage approach is to first explore parameter space with scatter search. Scatter search is a population-based approach, that has been building a solid reputation for solving combinatorial and nonlinear optimization problems [21,22]. Indeed, a solver based on scatter search was found to be the best stochastic solver tackling 1000 global optimization problems and outperformed other methods in black-box challenges [23]. In the last decade, scatter search has been adapted for nonlinear dynamic biological systems (and continues to be further developed, see Discussion) [21,22]. Its biggest advantage is that it is a computationally light method and thus provides rapid feedback on the structure of the network.

Once after several rounds of exploration a set of promising solutions is established, in a second stage low temperature simulated annealing is used to refine them. We evaluate the strengths and weaknesses of the hybrid approach against 'normal' simulated annealing. We use a parallel implementation of simulated annealing, pLSA, that over the last two decades has been our algorithm of choice as it finds excellent solutions that faithfully reproduce expression data and spatial patterns [12,14,24]. While we restrict ourselves here to a comparison of scatter search with simulated annealing, we note that also evolutionary optimization algorithms have been used to tackle the challenge of insect body plan formation [25–27].

As a benchmark system, we use the gap gene network of the fruit fly *Drosophila melanogaster* (Figure 1a). It is the regulatory network that lays down the initial body plan of the fly during the blastoderm stage of early development, before the onset of gastrulation (Figure 1b). It consists of three maternal gradients, namely Bicoid (Bcd), Caudal (Cad), and Hunchback (Hb), that are interpreted by four trunk gap genes, *hb*, *Krüppel* (*Kr*), *giant* (*gt*), and *knirps* (*kni*)). As a result, the trunk gap genes form a series of broad stripes along the antero-posterior (A–P) axis. At the posterior end, the terminal gap genes *tailless* (*tll*) and *huckebein* (*hkb*) regulate the trunk gap genes. The gap gene system is one of the best understood developmental networks from both an experimental and modelling point of view, and thus a good benchmark case [28].

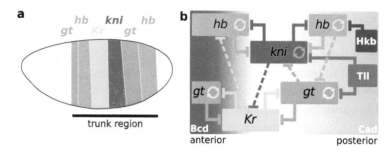

Figure 1. Body plan patterning in *D. melanogaster*. In both panels, the trunk gap genes are *hunchback* (*hb*), *Krüppel* (*Kr*), *giant* (*gt*), and *knirps* (*kni*)). External inputs to these four genes are the maternal factors Bicoid (Bcd), Caudal (Cad), and the terminal gap proteins Tailless (Tll), and Huckebein (Hkb). (**a**) Schematic depiction of a *Drosophila* embryo with the anterior (head) oriented to the left and its dorsal side to the top. Gap gene expression domains are shown as vertical bands along the trunk region. Expression in the head and terminal area is omitted; (**b**) The gap gene network mapped onto the expression domains of the trunk region. Background gradients of Bcd (purple) and Cad (cyan) activate the gap genes. Each rectangle is an expression domain. Circular arrows indicate self-activation, interactions with T-bars represent inhibition. Dashed interactions signal a net effect.

In comparison to other developmental systems, the *Drosophila* embryo has some key advantages. The early embryo is a syncytium (multi-nucleated cell), so we may ignore intercellular signalling. There is no tissue growth or rearrangement during the blastoderm stage. Moreover, patterning by gap genes in the trunk region occurs only along the A–P axis, and is decoupled from other patterning processes, such as those along the dorsal-ventral axis. These properties allow us to simplify the system to a one-dimensional array of (dividing) nuclei along the A–P axis. Indeed, due to its modelling-friendly properties, the gap gene system has been studied with a variety of models and methods [29–35].

We employ the gene circuit approach to model the *Drosophila* embryo [12–14,24,36–38]. A gene circuit is a dynamical hybrid model of coupled ordinary differential equations (ODEs). An embryo is represented as a row of nuclei that divide over time, where each nucleus has an identical instance of the gap gene regulatory network. The ODEs encode the network through regulated synthesis of gene products (mRNA or protein), Fickian gene product diffusion between neighbouring nuclei, and linear decay of the gene product. For *D. melanogaster*, the system has 41 parameters and fitting these may be classified as an optimization task of medium size. Originally, gene circuits were developed to fit quantitative protein expression data [12,13,38]. The acquisition and processing of such data are a laborious and time-consuming effort, and are not easily applied to nonmodel organisms. Recent studies, however, have shown the wider applicability of the gene circuit approach by developing protocols based on mRNA expression data, not only in *D. melanogaster* [14], but also in nonmodel organisms [15,16]. Moreover, gene circuits allow for simultaneous inference of which interactions are present, whether they are activating/inhibiting, and the strength of these interactions. It sets the gene circuit approach apart from other modelling efforts, where the topology is predefined and the task is to establish which interaction strengths fit the data best (known as parameter estimation). Together, these properties make fitting gene circuits an ideal test case for scatter search. It is a challenging task, it has an immediate practical relevance in systems biology, and has been shown to be successful for the inference of unknown gene regulatory networks.

We show that a hybrid, two-stage approach to network inference problems in developmental biology delivers equally good results as simulated annealing, our current default method. We find that scatter search efficiently and effectively explores the parameter space, and that low temperature simulated annealing turns good solutions into excellent ones. These results suggest that it is a promising method for inferring unknown networks, such as the one laying down the body plan of the sea anemone *Nematostella vectensis* [17,39,40], where multiple rounds of exploration are likely necessary. Moreover, given the additional computational costs for simulating systems in which morphogenetic processes play an important role (e.g., 2D and 3D models including cell migration, tissue rearrangements, growth, cell death) a light explorative method will be a prerequisite for success.

2. Materials and Methods

2.1. Scatter Search Method

Scatter search is a global optimization algorithm related to the family of evolutionary algorithms [41]. As do evolutionary algorithms, the method maintains a population of solutions and combines these solutions to obtain new ones. However, the underlying search strategy is different (see [21,22] for an in depth discussion). We implemented a sequential version of scatter search, closely following a set of guidelines developed for applications in biology [21,22].

The algorithm operates as follows (Figure 2). In an initial phase, (1) scatter search generates a large set of diverse solutions, named the *Scatter Set*. The goal is to have an initial set of solutions that reasonably covers the parameter search space. To this end, the diversity of solutions is maximised by subdividing parameter space into bins and uniformly sampling parameter values across these bins. Then (2) the algorithm creates the main population of solutions named the *Reference Set*. A set of solutions is selected from the *Scatter Set* on the basis of their quality and diversity: half of the reference set contains the best solutions, i.e., elite solutions, and the other half consists of diverse solutions (in terms of parameter values). This dual use of the *Reference Set* is maintained during the optimization phase.

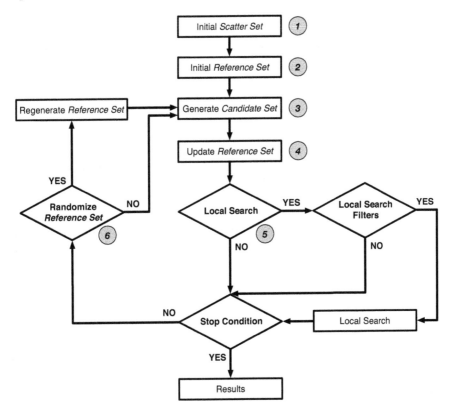

Figure 2. Scatter search algorithm design as presented in [21]. See main text for details.

After initialization, scatter search iterates the following steps until a stop condition is satisfied. In our case, the algorithm performs a fixed number of iterations. In every iteration, (3) the algorithm produces a set of candidate solutions, *Candidate Set*, by creating linear combinations of every pair of solutions in *Reference Set*. Next, (4) the worst solutions in *Reference Set* are replaced by better candidates, taking into account quality and diversity of the candidates. Before starting the next iteration,

(5) the algorithm may apply a local search on the members of *Reference Set* to accelerate convergence. By default the Nelder-Mead simplex algorithm is used, additionally we used Stochastic Hill climbing. In our implementation, the user decides beforehand if local search is enabled, and under which conditions it is applied (*Local Search Filters* in Figure 2) . These filters help to avoid time-consuming evaluations of solutions. We provide one, *filter_different_enough*, that checks if a solution has sufficiently distinct parameters from other members of *Reference Set*. This avoids regions of search space that are already being explored. The second filter, *filter_good_enough*, only allows good individuals, as local search is most effective if the starting solution is good [42,43]. Finally, (6) occasionally no candidates replace the current members of *Reference Set*. In such a case, we consider the algorithm to be stuck in a specific region of parameter space. Scatter search overcomes such an impasse by randomizing a part of *Reference Set* using a newly generated *Scatter Set*.

Scatter search is implemented in C and requires two third-party libraries: SUNDIALS (http://computation.llnl.gov/projects/sundials) and GSL (https://www.gnu.org/software/gsl) [44]. Source code is available on GitHub at https://github.com/amirmasoudabdol/flyOpt. We compiled the code with GCC 4.7.2 (https://gcc.gnu.org)) using the -O2 optimization flag. We have run scatter search simulations on the Lisa system of SURFsara (https://userinfo.surfsara.nl/systems/lisa) using search parameters as listed in Table 1. We saturated single nodes (Intel Xeon CPUs at 2.6 GHz, 16 cores) with the maximum of 16 runs to suppress hardware parallelism. We note that these tests were run on a HPC facility simply for convenience. The software does not use any parallel computation features and the hardware of current-day workstations is often comparable to that of the Lisa system.

Table 1. Parameter settings for sequential scatter search.

Name	Value	Description
iterations	10,000	Maximum number of iterations
reference set size	22	Number of individuals in set
scatter set size	1000	Number of individuals in set
local search frequency	25	Do search every n iterations
local search score	2.0×10^5	Cost must be lower than x
regenerate reference set	50	Refresh set every n iterations
stop criterion		Maximum number of iterations is reached

2.2. Parallel Simulated Annealing

Simulated annealing (SA) is a probabilistic global optimization algorithm, originally formulated in the 1980s [45]. It operates in analogy to metallurgic annealing, the process of slowly cooling metal in order to reach a low-energy equilibrium state. In simulated annealing the energy level is the cost of a solution, and the notion of cooling is implemented as slowly reducing the probability of accepting a new candidate with a worse cost.

The basic structure of SA has three components. First of all, it requires a so-called 'move' function that creates from the current solution a neighbouring 'mutant' solution. Second, there is a policy to accept or reject the new solution. The cost of the old and new candidates and the current temperature are taken into account to make the decision. Third, an annealing schedule determines how to lower the temperature as the algorithms progresses. The key parameter is the temperature. It determines the acceptance rate of new solutions with worse cost than the current one: the lower the temperature, the lower the probability of acceptance. Thus, starting with a high temperature, SA initially samples across the entire parameter space. As the algorithm moves from one solution to another, the annealing schedule lowers the temperature and over many 'moves' the algorithm biases progressively towards better solutions. The (occasional) acceptance of worse solutions ensures that it escapes local optima.

The strength of SA is that it works very well for a wide variety of (biological) optimization problems. Moreover, given certain requirements, it is mathematically proven to find the global minimum. However, its weakness is a large computational footprint. Therefore, we use parallel

Lam Simulated Annealing (pLSA), developed by [46]. It is a parallel implementation of SA with the adaptive annealing schedule of [47,48]. The approach is based on the observation that the acceptance policy maintains a Boltzmann distribution of energies. By combining statistics from all processing nodes, and a mixing of node states at given intervals, such a Boltzmann distribution is ensured also in the parallel case.

pLSA is implemented in C and uses MPI, SUNDIALS, and GSL. pLSA is run (with settings given in Table 2) at the Barcelona Supercomputing Center, using Mare Nostrum 3 computing facilities. It is compiled with the Intel compiler v13.0.1 using the -O3 optimization flag and Intel MPI library. A single pLSA run is executed on 64 cores. Nodes have Intel Sandybridge CPUs (8 cores) at 2.6 GHz, with at least 2 GB of working memory per core.

Table 2. Parameter settings for parallel simulated annealing.

Name	Value	Description
initial moves	96,000	Initial moves to establish unbiased Boltzmann distribution
processing nodes	64	Number of CPU cores used
moves per iteration	41	One move per gene circuit parameter
mixing interval	25	Synchronization every n iterations
start temperature	1.0×10^6	High starting temperature
stop criterion	0.0001	Cost change in last 5 moves less than value

2.3. Gene Circuits, Simulation, and Analysis

The gap gene regulatory network is modelled as a gene circuit [24], described in detail elsewhere [13,14]. In short, we model the trunk region of the *D. melanogaster* embryo as a linear array of nuclei. The trunk region is defined for mRNA expression data from 35% to 87% A–P position, and for protein data 35–92% (0% is the anterior pole). In each nucleus, there is continuous regulation and expression of gap genes, while over time the number of nuclei doubles through discrete mitotic division. Gene regulation and expression over time t is governed by coupled ordinary differential equations (ODEs):

$$\frac{dg_i^a}{dt} = R^a \Phi(u_i^a) + D^a(n)\left(g_{i-1}^a + g_{i+1}^a - 2g_i^a\right) - \lambda^a g_i^a \tag{1}$$

with g_i^a, gene expression product (mRNA or protein, depending on the data) at nucleus i of gap gene $a \in G$ (G is defined below). Parameters R^a, $D^a(n)$ and λ^a are production, diffusion, and decay rates. Diffusion depends on the number of previous divisions n. Eukaryotic gene regulation is phenomenologically modelled as a sigmoid response curve Φ with a summation over genetic interactions u_i^a:

$$\Phi(u_i^a) = \frac{1}{2}\left(\frac{u_i^a}{\sqrt{(u_i^a)^2 + 1}} + 1\right)$$

$$u_i^a = \sum_{b \in G} W^{ba} g_i^a + \sum_{m \in M} E^{ma} g_i^m + h^a \tag{2}$$

with trunk gap genes $G = \{hb, Kr, gt, kni\}$ and external inputs $M = \{Bcd, Cad, Tll, Hkb\}$. Parameter matrices W and E define genetic interactions between trunk gap genes and external inputs on trunk gap genes, respectively. Each parameter W^{ba} (and E^{ma}) represents the effect of regulator b (m), on gap gene a. We interpret that the regulator has an activating role if $w \in W$ ($e \in E$) is positive ($w > 0.005$); an inhibitory role if negative ($w < -0.005$); and there is no interaction if the value is near zero ($-0.005 \le w \le 0.005$). The interpretation is visualized as a network diagram (Figure 3a) or as a genetic interaction matrix (Figure 3b). Parameter h^a represents background maternal factors and is fixed at -2.5 for all trunk gap genes. In total, a gene circuit has 41 parameters.

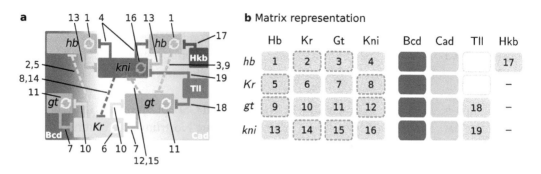

Figure 3. Gap gene network representations. (a) Diagram of the gap gene network as shown in Figure 1, with interactions between the expression domains along the A–P axis. Each number refers to an interaction in panel b; (b) Matrix representation. Column names are regulators (proteins), row names are gap genes (gene names) receiving the regulation. Gap-gap and terminal-gap interactions are numbered 1–19, and maternal gradients are coloured to match the background gradients in panel a. The gap-gap interactions with a dashed border are depicted as a net regulatory effect from one gap gene to an other in panel a (as in [14]). The regulatory effect of Tll on *hb* and *Kr* (white boxes) are ignored in panel a.

As mentioned in the Introduction, *D. melanogaster* gap genes are expressed during late blastoderm, in mitotic cycle C13 and C14A. Gene circuit equations are solved from the start of C13 (t = 0 min), when gap gene expression becomes detectable, until the onset of gastrulation at the end of C14A (t = 71.1 min). Mitosis occurs during t = 16–21 min, during which gene product synthesis is set to zero. Gene circuits have 108 ODEs in C13, and 212 ODEs in C14A. Regardless of the optimization algorithm, gene circuits are numerically integrated using two solvers. If circuits are inferred from mRNA expression data, an implicit multi-step method is used (CVODE, Sundails library) [44]. In case protein expression data are used, we employ a Runge-Kutta Cash-Karp adaptive step-size method [12].

The cost of a gene circuit is the sum of residuals when comparing the circuit output with experimental data. It is minimized by the optimization algorithms, and we formulate it as a weighted least squares [13,14]:

$$\text{cost} = \sum_{a \in G} \sum_{t \in T} \sum_{i \in N_c(n)} v_i^a(t) \left(g_i^a(t) - \text{data}_i^a(t) \right)^2 \tag{3}$$

with G the set of trunk gap genes, T the set of time points for which we have data (C13, C14A: T1–T8), $N_c(n)$ the number of nuclei after n mitotic cycles, v_i^a weights, and $\text{data}_i^a(t)$ the mRNA or protein expression level of gap gene a in nucleus i at time point t. For interpretation, we may also express the cost as a Root Mean Square (RMS), which ignores the weights v and is a normalization with respect to the total number of data points ($N_{RNA} = 1804$ and $N_{protein} = 1976$).

After optimization, the resulting solutions are judged on RMS, numerical stability, and visual inspection of model output, as described in detail elsewhere [13,14]. Analysis and plotting is performed using the previously developed SuperFIT package (https://app.assembla.com/spaces/superfit/subversion/source) [16].

3. Results

3.1. Scatter Search Efficiently Explores Parameter Space

Our first goal was to broadly characterize the performance of scatter search in the context of inferring the network of gap gene interactions in *D. melanogaster*. We generated a large set of solutions by starting 1000 scatter search simulations and taking the final best solution from each of them. We focussed on the networks derived from *D. melanogaster* mRNA expression data (Figure 4a) [14], while we obtained similar results for protein expression data (Figure 4c,d) [13]. The cost of mRNA-derived solutions, as defined in Equation (3), ranged from 1.16 to 4.04×10^5, with an average of 2.23×10^5 (and median 2.20×10^5). As scatter search only applied the local search method, if a solution's cost is below 2.0×10^5, there is a lack of solutions just below this cost (Figure 4a, 'Local search score' in Table 1). From these 1000 solutions, we sampled 200 for further study and analysis (Figure 4, blue dots).

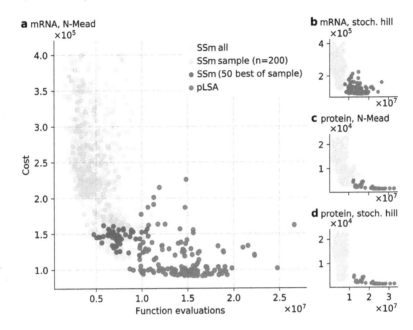

Figure 4. Performance of (sequential) scatter search method (SSm) and parallel Lam simulated annealing (pLSA). All panels plot function evaluations against cost (see Equation (3)). A function evaluation is defined as computing gene expression levels of a gene circuit from time $t = 0.0$ to 71.1 min. It is a performance measure independent of compiler settings and hardware. The cost indicates how well a gene circuit reproduces gap gene expression data (lower is better). (a) The main body of results is based on gene circuits derived from mRNA expression data, using scatter search with the Nelder-Mead algorithm as a local search method. Gene circuits from SSm are grey blue, the 200 selected circuits are blue, of which the 50 best in dark blue. Gene circuits from pLSA are red; (b–d) Gene circuit performance using mRNA and protein data expression data, and switching between Nelder-Mead and stochastic hill climbing. Circuits from scatter search are grey-blue, those from pLSA are red.

Next, we used pLSA to generate a second set of solutions by fitting 150 gene circuits to mRNA expression data. We made three noteworthy observations in the comparison of both methods (Figure 4). First, the average scatter search run executes substantially fewer function evaluations than an average pLSA run (0.5×10^7 against 1.5×10^7). Second, we defined good and excellent solutions to have, respectively, a cost $\leq 1.5 \times 10^5$ and $\leq 1.05 \times 10^5$. With this categorization, scatter search finds many good solutions, but not any excellent ones. Instead, pLSA does find excellent solutions that are suitable for in-depth biological analysis. Third, the relation between cost and function evaluations suggests there is a Pareto front, where a certain minimal number of evaluations are necessary to reach a given cost (Figure 4a). Intuitively it makes sense, as good and excellent solutions are rare and it requires computational effort to find them. We place a cautionary note, though, as we observed that the shape of the (potential) Pareto front depends on the local search method used in scatter search and the type of expression data (mRNA/protein). If we use Stochastic Hill climbing or protein data, the front changes shape and the trade-off between cost and function evaluations is less visible (Figure 4b–d).

Thus, despite the population-based approach, scatter search is a computationally light search method (also noted by [21]). Moreover, the strength of scatter search is that it efficiently surveys parameter space and identifies promising areas that can be further explored (i.e., analysing the good solutions). Its weakness, however, is that it does not find as excellent solutions as pLSA does.

3.2. Exploiting the Exploration Done by Scatter Search

Even if scatter search solutions do not reproduce expression data at the desired level of biological correctness, they provide a first view on the structure of the gene network. As argued in the Introduction, such a quick first view is a valuable source of information, especially in the case of unknown gene networks or computationally expensive models. The gap gene network of *D. melanogaster* is a good test case, as we know its structure well. We asked what biological insight is already contained in the 50 best solutions inferred by scatter search.

We created a first view of the gap gene network by categorizing the genetic interactions in the 50 best gene circuits (Figure 5a). Almost half (14/29) of the interactions show full consensus, while 10/29 show a clear trend towards activation or inhibition. In previous work, the genetic interactions were grouped in five mechanisms [12–14]. Focussing on the consensus interactions, we immediately observed the two major mechanisms: alternating cushions and maternal activation. The former is comprised of two pairs of strongly repressing gap genes, namely *hb/kni* and *gt/Kr*, while the latter requires that Bcd and Cad activate the gap genes. We see that Bcd is essential for *hb* activation, while Cad is crucial for *gt* and *kni*. *Kr* is thought to be mainly under control of Bcd [28] and we find that with two exceptions it is the case. Experiments, however, show *Kr* expression in embryos without Bcd, which may be explained by a redundant role for Cad [28]. Indeed we have consensus for activation by Cad (Figure 5a).

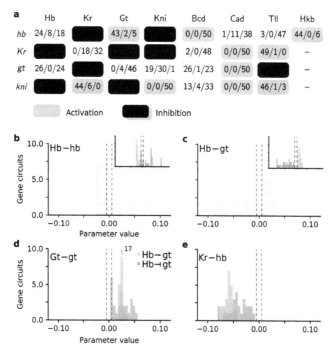

Figure 5. Exploring genetic interactions of the 50 best scatter search circuits. (**a**) Genetic interaction matrix summarizing the type of regulation found amongst the circuits (see also Figure 3). Number triplets define the number of solutions with repressive/no/activating interactions. Columns are regulators, rows target genes. The colour code indicates green for activation and red for repression. Saturated colours indicate full consensus amongst gene circuits, light colours a two-third fraction of circuits for one type of regulation; (**b**) Histogram of parameter values for *hb* self-regulation. Inset shows the same parameter values split by Hb activating (purple) and inhibiting (orange) *gt*. See also panel d; (**c**) Histogram of parameter values for Hb regulating *gt*. The distribution splits into an inhibitory and activating set of gene circuits (see inset); (**d**) Self-regulation of *gt* split along Hb–*gt* regulation. Activation (→) is purple, inhibition (⊣) is orange. The peak of the purple distribution extends to 17 gene circuits; (**e**) Regulation of *hb* by Kr split along Hb–*gt* regulation, similar to panel d.

The third mechanism is the shifting of posterior gap gene domains in an anterior direction, i.e., towards the head region. These shifts require an asymmetric regulation between neighbouring expression domains, which are only partially observed here, namely for *Kr/kni*. In *Drosophila*, the *hb/Kr* boundary is an exception as it does not display anterior shifts. Instead, the two gap genes inhibit each other strongly and establish a boundary with a fixed position along the A–P axis. Indeed, we observed a consensus for mutual inhibition. The fourth mechanism is self-activation of the gap genes, which is clear for *gt* and *kni* at this stage of network inference. Finally, we observe that Tll represses *Kr*, *gt* and *kni*, which ensures they are not expressed in the posterior terminal end.

We obtained a more detailed view by inspecting the distribution of parameters for specific interactions. We focused on the regulation of *hb* and *gt* by Hb, as scatter search predicts multiple, qualitatively different outcomes for these interactions. First, *hb* self-regulation tends towards inhibition (compare Figure 5a,b). Yet the parameter distribution gives us the insight that only a small amount of inhibition is tolerated, while neutral behaviour and especially activation are accepted for a wide range of values. Second, for the regulation of *gt* by Hb (Figure 5c), we noticed that the regulatory effect of Hb on *gt* was split along either inhibition or activation. We asked if the two alternative regulatory effects on *gt* correlate with distinct sets of gene circuits. We compared the set of gene circuits with Hb inhibiting *gt* to the circuits with Hb activating *gt*, and observed two major differences. First, and most importantly, circuits with inhibition of *gt* show a wider range of values for several interactions. Examples are *gt* self regulation (Figure 5d) and Kr regulation of *hb* (Figure 5e). Second, inhibition of *gt* by Hb correlates clearly with *hb* self-activation. Activation of *gt* by Hb, on the other hand, is accompanied by *hb* self-inhibition (Figure 5b, inset). Interestingly, the observed correlations between parameter distributions may be associated to canalizing properties of the gap gene network to position the anterior *hb* boundary at ~50% A–P position [49,50]. A dynamical systems analysis of this *hb* boundary showed a nonlinear dependence on Bcd, *gt*, and *Kr* during the late blastoderm stage [50], which may explain scatter search finding multiple regulatory solutions. Yet a complementary explanation that cannot be ruled out, is that as *hb* and *gt* expression domains appear at the edges of the modelled region, additional regulatory factors could be missing [49].

We hesitate interpreting the more subtle differences between the two sets of circuits. In this test case of the *D. melanogaster* gap gene network, it is straightforward to link our observations to our knowledge of the wildtype network structure. However, if a network is unknown, interpreting subtle cues easily leads to errors where model artefacts are taken to have a biological meaning. Nevertheless, there is a clear potential for inspecting intermediate results and drawing conclusions from them that may guide a next iteration of network inference.

3.3. Low Temperature Simulated Annealing Refines Good Solutions into Excellent Ones

After exploring the gene circuits proposed by scatter search, in the second stage we set out to refine them with the goal of obtaining solutions that are as excellent as the ones generated by simulated annealing. As the scatter search circuits perform well, we decided to take them as starting points for optimization with low temperature simulated annealing. By skipping the initial moves of simulated annealing and beginning with a relatively low temperature, we avoid the early randomizing behaviour of this search method. Instead, the algorithm is likely to make only modest changes and is likely to preserve the structure of the network. In effect, this mode of simulated annealing is focussed on a particular area of parameter space.

First we filtered the 200 solutions by removing all with a cost >2.5×10^5. We continued with 143 remaining solutions. To assess the effect of different starting temperatures, we surveyed four scenarios with a range from T = 10 to 100×10^3 (Figure 6). Moreover, for T = 50 k and 100 k, we tested how simulated annealing performed under a restriction of its search space. For each consensus interaction as inferred in the first stage (Figure 5a) the range of allowed parameter values was limited by the sign of the interaction. For instance, scatter search indicated that Kni represses *hb*, and therefore, we limited this interaction to negative values only. After fitting gene circuits, the results of non-fixed and fixed low temperature SA were compared to each other and to the standard use of pLSA by computational performance (number of function evaluations) and quality of the inferred networks.

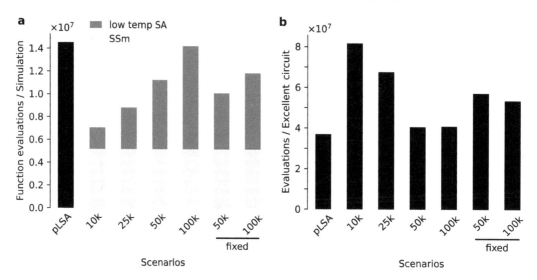

Figure 6. Performance of simulated annealing (pLSA) and the two-stage approach. (**a**) Total number of function evaluations per optimization scenario. The two-stage approaches shares the first explorative stage by scatter search (blue bars), after which different starting temperatures were used for low temperature SA; (**b**) Number of function evaluations per excellent gene circuit, defined as a circuit with an RMS < 22.0. In both panels, we replace 10^3 by the letter 'k' in scenario names. The two last columns ('50 k' and '100 k') are labelled as "fixed" to signal a constrained search space was used.

With respect to computational performance, we found that the starting temperature has a strong influence on the performance of simulated annealing. At first sight the two-stage approach appeared more efficient than pLSA (Figure 6a). With the exception of T = 100k (non-fixed), the two-stage approach required fewer function evaluations than pLSA to generate a set of excellent gene circuits. That was anticipated, as a lower starting temperature means that simulated annealing accepts worse solutions with a lower probability than is the case for a normal optimization run with pLSA. Thus convergence is more rapid. As expected, the restricted search space of fixed scenarios reduced the number of function evaluations in comparison to the corresponding non-fixed scenarios. Yet, the reduction did not lead to an increase in efficiency of finding excellent solutions (Figure 6b). We realized that restricting search space excludes many of the 143 gene circuits as valid starting points for SA, as they have one or more parameters in a forbidden area of search space. This indicates that in the non-fixed scenarios, low temperature SA still changed the topology of 'bad' networks and that this is a beneficial feature.

In general, compared to pLSA, the number of function evaluations per excellent solution is equal or higher for the hybrid, two-stage approach (Figure 6b). That would argue against our two-stage approach. However, if several iterations are needed either for the first exploratory stage or the later refining one, the hybrid approach will be less computationally costly than doing several rounds of 'full' pLSA runs. Especially, the scenario T = 50 k (non-fixed) will rival the performance of pLSA.

We continued by comparing the best solutions of both approaches. We selected the 10 circuits with lowest RMS, and generated genetic interaction matrices (Figure 7a,b) and gene expression profiles (Figure 7c,d). We found that hybrid runs from intermediate temperatures have the least number of defects (visual inspection, data not shown for T = 25 k). Most importantly, two-stage solutions are just as good as the ones generated by pLSA, both in terms of interaction matrix and expression profile.

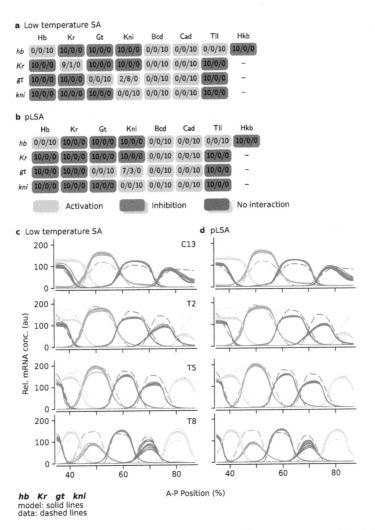

Figure 7. Comparison of the best gene circuits resulting from low temperature Simulated Annealing (SA) and parallel Lam Simulated Annealing (pLSA). Panels (**a,c**) show scenario T = 50 k, and (**b,d**) show pLSA. (**a,b**) Genetic interaction matrices. See Figure 5 and main text for details; (**c,d**) Gene expression profiles at four time points. Gene circuit expression is given by solid lines, data by dashed lines. The embryo's trunk region is shown, spanning 35–87% A–P position. Time points are mitotic cycle C13 and time classes of cycle C14A, T2/5/8.

4. Discussion

For network inference of spatiotemporal patterning, especially in flies, we traditionally used parallel Lam simulated annealing. It is a computationally costly method, but produces excellent results across different species of flies [12–16]. Here we reported on an alternative, hybrid approach consisting of two stages: first we applied scatter search to develop an initial understanding of the network, followed by low temperature SA to refine good solutions into excellent ones. The alternative approach delivered equally good results in terms of genetic interactions and gene expression profiles. However, the total cost of both stages of network inference is slightly higher than for pLSA. Thus we recommend the alternative approach if repeated rounds of exploration of parameter space and tweaking of the algorithms are necessary.

Considering only few developmental gene regulatory networks are understood in-depth, most (future) applications of network inference will involve inferring an unknown network. In such cases, a 5 to 10 iterations are usually needed to tweak the algorithm, test alternatives, and get excellent solutions. Here the advantage of an initial exploration with scatter search is clear: the intermediate information that one can extract from good solutions is valuable and can be used to guide—or reduce the number of—subsequent iterations of network inference.

We point out that interpreting intermediate solutions has to be done with caution, as some of the findings may be misleading. Our test case of the gap gene network showed that scatter search generated at least two alternative network structures. While we know that one of them is unsupported by current experimental evidence, for an unknown network this information may not be available. From a more general perspective, it shows where the optimization algorithms struggles to find a unique solution. That may not be a satisfying result at first sight, yet it indicates a lack of knowledge and suggests specific experiments to improve our understanding of the system.

For a hybrid approach, the combination of scatter search and low temperature simulated annealing is not the only viable option. As was suggested in [26], (parallel) genetic algorithms are known to be good exploratory search methods as well. Moreover, with respect to our implementation of scatter search, recently a more advanced version of scatter search has become available, called saCeSS (self-adaptive cooperative enhanced scatter search) [51]. It uses multiple instances of scatter search set at different levels of exploration and exploitation, multiple local search methods, and utilizes the small-scale parallelism of current-day workstations. One expects saCeSS to perform better than our version of scatter search. In this sense, we have presented a worst-case performance scenario in this work. Also parallel LSA is still being improved. An asynchronous version has been released and it will be interesting to check its performance in the context of network inference [52].

Summarizing, for the inference of unknown networks scatter search is a valuable exploratory tool. It has light computational demands and delivers good solutions from which relevant information can be extracted. In a two-stage setting with simulated annealing, we expect it to be particularly effective in reducing the computational cost of network inference.

Acknowledgments: We thank Johannes Jaeger for critical feedback and scientific advice. We thankfully acknowledge the computer resources, technical expertise and assistance provided by the Barcelona Supercomputing Center, which is part of the Red Española de Supercomputación. We thank SURFsara (www.surfsara.nl) for the support in using the Lisa Compute Cluster. The Centre for Genomic Regulation (CRG) acknowledges support from the Spanish Ministry of Economy and Competitiveness, 'Centro de Excelencia Severo Ochoa 2013-2017', SEV-2012-0208. AC kindly acknowledges Fondation Bettencourt Schueller.

Author Contributions: A.M.A., J.A.K., and A.C. conceived and designed the experiments; A.M.A., D.C.-S., and A.C. performed the experiments; A.M.A. and A.C. analysed the data; A.M.A., D.C.-S., and A.C. contributed software and analysis tools; A.C. and A.M.A. wrote the paper with contributions of J.A.K.

References

1. Villaverde, A.F.; Banga, J.R. Reverse engineering and identification in systems biology: Strategies, perspectives and challenges. *J. R. Soc. Interface* **2013**, *11*, 20130505.

2. Heavner, B.D.; Smallbone, K.; Price, N.D.; Walker, L.P. Version 6 of the consensus yeast metabolic network refines biochemical coverage and improves model performance. *Database* **2013**, *2013*, bat059.

3. Borodina, I.; Nielsen, J. Advances in metabolic engineering of yeast *Saccharomyces cerevisiae* for production of chemicals. *Biotechnol. J.* **2014**, *9*, 609–620.

4. Costa, R.S.; Hartmann, A.; Vinga, S. Kinetic modeling of cell metabolism for microbial production. *J. Biotechnol.* **2016**, *219*, 126–141.

5. Selvarasu, S.; Ho, Y.S.; Chong, W.P.K.; Wong, N.S.C.; Yusufi, F.N.K.; Lee, Y.Y.; Yap, M.G.S.; Lee, D.Y. Combined in silico modeling and metabolomics analysis to characterize fed-batch CHO cell culture. *Biotechnol. Bioeng.* **2012**, *109*, 1415–1429.

6. Saraiva, I.; Vande Wouwer, A.; Hantson, A.L. Parameter identification of a dynamic model of CHO cell cultures: An experimental case study. *Bioprocess Biosyst. Eng.* **2015**, *38*, 2231–2248.

7. López-Meza, J.; Araíz-Hernández, D.; Carrillo-Cocom, L.M.; López-Pacheco, F.; Rocha-Pizaña, M.D.R.; Alvarez, M.M. Using simple models to describe the kinetics of growth, glucose consumption, and monoclonal antibody formation in naive and infliximab producer CHO cells. *Cytotechnology* **2016**, *68*, 1287–1300.

8. Hoops, S.; Sahle, S.; Gauges, R.; Lee, C.; Pahle, J.; Simus, N.; Singhal, M.; Xu, L.; Mendes, P.; Kummer, U. COPASI—A COmplex PAthway SImulator. *Bioinformatics* **2006**, *22*, 3067–3074.

9. Hucka, M.; Finney, A.; Sauro, H.M.; Bolouri, H.; Doyle, J.C.; Kitano, H.; Arkin, A.P.; Bornstein, B.J.; Bray, D.; Cornish-Bowden, A.; et al. The systems biology markup language (SBML): A medium for representation and exchange of biochemical network models. *Bioinformatics* **2003**, *19*, 524–531.

10. Miller, A.K.; Marsh, J.; Reeve, A.; Garny, A.; Britten, R.; Halstead, M.; Cooper, J.; Nickerson, D.P.; Nielsen, P.F. An overview of the CellML API and its implementation. *BMC Bioinform.* **2010**, *11*, 178.

11. Karr, J.R.; Williams, A.H.; Zucker, J.D.; Raue, A.; Steiert, B.; Timmer, J.; Kreutz, C.; DREAM8 Parameter Estimation Challenge Consortium; Wilkinson, S.; Allgood, B.A.; et al. Summary of the DREAM8 parameter estimation challenge: Toward parameter identification for whole-cell models. *PLoS Comput. Biol.* **2015**, *11*, e1004096.

12. Jaeger, J.; Surkova, S.; Blagov, M.; Janssens, H.; Kosman, D.; Kozlov, K.N.; Myasnikova, E.; Vanario-Alonso, C.E.; Samsonova, M.; Sharp, D.H.; et al. Dynamic control of positional information in the early *Drosophila* embryo. *Nature* **2004**, *430*, 368–371.

13. Ashyraliyev, M.; Siggens, K.; Janssens, H.; Blom, J.; Akam, M.; Jaeger, J. Gene circuit analysis of the terminal gap gene *huckebein*. *PLoS Comput. Biol.* **2009**, *5*, e1000548.

14. Crombach, A.; Wotton, K.R.; Cicin-Sain, D.; Ashyraliyev, M.; Jaeger, J. Efficient reverse-engineering of a developmental gene regulatory network. *PLoS Comput. Biol.* **2012**, *8*, e1002589.

15. Crombach, A.; Garcia-Solache, M.A.; Jaeger, J. Evolution of early development in dipterans: Reverse-engineering the gap gene network in the moth midge *Clogmia albipunctata* (Psychodidae). *Biosystems* **2014**, *123*, 74–85.

16. Crombach, A.; Wotton, K.R.; Jimenez-Guri, E.; Jaeger, J. Gap gene regulatory dynamics evolve along a genotype network. *Mol. Biol. Evol.* **2016**, *33*, 1293–1307.

17. Leclère, L.; Rentzsch, F. RGM regulates BMP-mediated secondary axis formation in the sea anemone *Nematostella vectensis*. *Cell Rep.* **2014**, *9*, 1921–1930.

18. Sheth, R.; Marcon, L.; Bastida, M.F.; Junco, M.; Quintana, L.; Dahn, R.; Kmita, M.; Sharpe, J.; Ros, M.A. Hox genes regulate digit patterning by controlling the wavelength of a Turing-type mechanism. *Science* **2012**, *338*, 1476–1480.

19. Raspopovic, J.; Marcon, L.; Russo, L.; Sharpe, J. Modeling digits. Digit patterning is controlled by a Bmp-Sox9-Wnt Turing network modulated by morphogen gradients. *Science* **2014**, *345*, 566–570.

20. Hoyos, E.; Kim, K.; Milloz, J.; Barkoulas, M.; Pénigault, J.B.; Munro, E.; Félix, M.A. Quantitative variation in autocrine signaling and pathway crosstalk in the *Caenorhabditis* vulval network. *Curr. Biol.* **2011**, *21*, 527–538.

21. Rodriguez-Fernandez, M.; Egea, J.A.; Banga, J.R. Novel metaheuristic for parameter estimation in nonlinear dynamic biological systems. *BMC Bioinform.* **2006**, *7*, 483.

22. Egea, J.A.; Rodríguez-Fernández, M.; Banga, J.R.; Martí, R. Scatter search for chemical and bio-process optimization. *J. Glob. Optim.* **2007**, *37*, 481–503.

23. Neumaier, A.; Shcherbina, O.; Huyer, W.; Vinkó, T. A comparison of complete global optimization solvers. *Math. Program.* **2005**, *103*, 335–356.

24. Reinitz, J.; Sharp, D.H. Mechanism of *eve* stripe formation. *Mech. Dev.* **1995**, *49*, 133–158.

25. Fomekong-Nanfack, Y.; Kaandorp, J.A.; Blom, J. Efficient parameter estimation for spatio-temporal models of pattern formation: Case study of *Drosophila melanogaster*. *Bioinformatics* **2007**, *23*, 3356–3363.

26. Jostins, L.; Jaeger, J. Reverse engineering a gene network using an asynchronous parallel evolution strategy. *BMC Syst. Biol.* **2010**, *4*, 17.

27. Kozlov, K.; Samsonov, A. DEEP-differential evolution entirely parallel method for gene regulatory networks. *J. Supercomput.* **2011**, *57*, 172–178.

28. Jaeger, J. The gap gene network. *Cell. Mol. Life Sci.* **2011**, *68*, 243–274.

29. Sánchez, L.; Thieffry, D. A logical analysis of the *Drosophila* gap-gene system. *J. Theor. Biol.* **2001**, *211*, 115–141.

30. Perkins, T.J.; Jaeger, J.; Reinitz, J.; Glass, L. Reverse engineering the gap gene network of *Drosophila melanogaster*. *PLoS Comput. Biol.* **2006**, *2*, e51.

31. Perkins, T.J. The gap gene system of *Drosophila melanogaster*: Model-fitting and validation. *Ann. N. Y. Acad. Sci.* **2007**, *1115*, 116–131.

32. Wunderlich, Z.; DePace, A.H. Modeling transcriptional networks in *Drosophila* development at multiple scales. *Curr. Opin. Genet. Dev.* **2011**, *21*, 711–718.

33. Wunderlich, Z.; Bragdon, M.D.; Eckenrode, K.B.; Lydiard-Martin, T.; Pearl-Waserman, S.; DePace, A.H. Dissecting sources of quantitative gene expression pattern divergence between *Drosophila* species. *Mol. Syst. Biol.* **2012**, *8*, 604.

34. Becker, K.; Balsa-Canto, E.; Cicin-Sain, D.; Hoermann, A.; Janssens, H.; Banga, J.R.; Jaeger, J. Reverse-engineering post-transcriptional regulation of gap genes in *Drosophila melanogaster*. *PLoS Comput. Biol.* **2013**, *9*, e1003281.

35. Chertkova, A.A.; Schiffman, J.S.; Nuzhdin, S.V.; Kozlov, K.N.; Samsonova, M.G.; Gursky, V.V. In silico evolution of the *Drosophila* gap gene regulatory sequence under elevated mutational pressure. *BMC Evol. Biol.* **2017**, *17*.

36. Mjolsness, E.; Sharp, D.H.; Reinitz, J. A connectionist model of development. *J. Theor. Biol.* **1991**, *152*, 429–453.

37. Reinitz, J.; Mjolsness, E.; Sharp, D.H. Model for cooperative control of positional information in *Drosophila* by *bicoid* and maternal *hunchback*. *J. Exp. Zool.* **1995**, *271*, 47–56.

38. Jaeger, J.; Blagov, M.; Kosman, D.; Kozlov, K.N.; Myasnikova, E.; Surkova, S.; Vanario-Alonso, C.E.; Samsonova, M.; Sharp, D.H.; Reinitz, J. Dynamical analysis of regulatory interactions in the gap gene system of *Drosophila melanogaster*. *Genetics* **2004**, *167*, 1721–1737.

39. Genikhovich, G.; Fried, P.; Prünster, M.M.; Schinko, J.B.; Gilles, A.F.; Fredman, D.; Meier, K.; Iber, D.; Technau, U. Axis patterning by BMPs: Cnidarian network reveals evolutionary constraints. *Cell Rep.* **2015**, *10*, 1646–1654.

40. Botman, D.; Jansson, F.; Röttinger, E.; Martindale, M.Q.; de Jong, J. Analysis of a spatial gene expression database for sea anemone *Nematostella vectensis* during early development. *BMC Syst. Biol.* **2016**, *9*, 1–22.

41. Glover, F. A template for scatter search and path relinking. In *Artificial Evolution*; Springer: Berlin/Heidelberg, Germany, 1997; pp. 1–51.

42. Mendes, P.; Kell, D. Non-linear optimization of biochemical pathways: applications to metabolic engineering and parameter estimation. *Bioinformatics* **1998**, *14*, 869–883.

43. Aarts, E.H.; Lenstra, J.K. *Local Search in Combinatorial Optimization*; Wiley: Hoboken, NJ, USA; Princeton University Press: Princeton, NJ, USA, 2003.

44. Hindmarsh, A.C.; Brown, P.N.; Grant, K.E.; Lee, S.L.; Serban, R.; Shumaker, D.E.; Woodward, C.S. SUNDIALS: Suite of nonlinear and differential/algebraic equation solvers. *ACM Trans. Math. Softw.* **2005**, *31*, 363–396.

45. Kirkpatrick, S.; Gelatt, C.D.; Vecchi, M.P. Optimization by simulated annealing. *Science* **1983**, *220*, 671–680.

46. Chu, K.W.; Deng, Y.; Reinitz, J. Parallel simulated annealing by mixing of states. *J. Comput. Phys.* **1999**, *148*, 646–662.

47. Lam, J.; Delosme, J. *An Efficient Simulated Annealing Schedule: Derivation*; Technical Report 8816; Electrical Engineering Department, Yale: New Haven, CT, USA, 1988.

48. Lam, J.; Delosme, J. *An Efficient Simulated Annealing Schedule: Implementation and Evaluation*; Technical Report 8817; Electrical Engineering Department, Yale: New Haven, CT, USA, 1988.

49. Surkova, S.; Spirov, A.V.; Gursky, V.V.; Janssens, H.; Kim, A.R.; Radulescu, O.; Vanario-Alonso, C.E.; Sharp, D.H.; Samsonova, M.; Reinitz, J. Canalization of gene expression in the *Drosophila* blastoderm by gap gene cross regulation. *PLoS Biol.* **2009**, *7*, e1000049.

50. Gursky, V.V.; Panok, L.; Myasnikova, E.M.; Manu, M.; Samsonova, M.G.; Reinitz, J.; Samsonov, A.M. Mechanisms of gap gene expression canalization in the *Drosophila* blastoderm. *BMC Syst. Biol.* **2011**, *5*, 118, doi:10.1186/1752-0509-5-118.

51. Penas, D.R.; González, P.; Egea, J.A.; Doallo, R.; Banga, J.R. Parameter estimation in large-scale systems biology models: A parallel and self-adaptive cooperative strategy. *BMC Bioinform.* **2017**, *18*, 52.

52. Lou, Z.; Reinitz, J. Parallel simulated annealing using an adaptive resampling interval. *Parallel. Comput.* **2016**, *53*, 23–31.

10

An SVM Framework for Malignant Melanoma Detection Based on Optimized HOG Features

Samy Bakheet [1,2]

[1] Department of Mathematics and Computer Science, Faculty of Science, Sohag University, 82524 Sohag, Egypt
[2] Institute for Information Technology and Communications, Otto-von-Guericke-University Magdeburg, P.O. Box 4120, 39016 Magdeburg, Germany; sbakheet@ovgu.de

Academic Editor: Rainer Breitling

Abstract: Early detection of skin cancer through improved techniques and innovative technologies has the greatest potential for significantly reducing both morbidity and mortality associated with this disease. In this paper, an effective framework of a CAD (Computer-Aided Diagnosis) system for melanoma skin cancer is developed mainly by application of an SVM (Support Vector Machine) model on an optimized set of HOG (Histogram of Oriented Gradient) based descriptors of skin lesions. Experimental results obtained by applying the presented methodology on a large, publicly accessible dataset of dermoscopy images demonstrate that the proposed framework is a strong contender for the state-of-the-art alternatives by achieving high levels of sensitivity, specificity, and accuracy (98.21%, 96.43% and 97.32%, respectively), without sacrificing computational soundness.

Keywords: melanoma skin cancer; CAD; dermoscopy; HOG descriptors; SVM classification

1. Introduction

The National Cancer Institute (NCI) reported that melanoma is the most common form of cancer in adults ages 25 to 29. Moreover, it is estimated that there will be 76,380 new cases of melanoma and 10,130 deaths in 2016 [1]. Although melanoma, the most deadly type of skin cancer, is the fourth most common cancer and accounts for only 4% of all skin cancers, it is particularly responsible for the most deaths of all skin cancers, with nearly 9000 people dying from it each year. It has been further pointed out that approximately over 80% of all skin cancer related deaths are accounted for by melanoma. It is therefore vital that melanoma be diagnosed and treated as early as possible in order to be cured successfully. On the other hand, if the melanoma is not treated quickly and removed timely, it penetrates, and, like some other cancers, can grow deeper into the skin and spread to other parts of the body. The consequences of a late diagnosis of melanoma are very significant in terms of personal health, medical procedures and costs.

The Skin Cancer Foundation (SCF) recently reported that melanoma is the most serious form of skin cancer because it is more likely to spread to other parts of the body. Once melanoma spreads beyond the skin to other parts of the body, it becomes hard to treat. However, early detection saves lives. Research shows that when melanoma is recognized and treated in its early stages, it is nearly 100% curable. Without early treatment, the cancer can advance, spread and be fatal. Today, it is well documented that there is seemingly every reason to believe that melanoma cells originate from the presence of melanocytes in any body part. Therefore, it might seem beyond mere chance that melanocytes are the precursors of melanoma. It is a well-known fact that excessive sunlight exposure is a well-known risk factor for melanoma and generally environmental exposure of skin to ultraviolet (UV) radiation (e.g., UV-A and -B radiation) provides a strong determinant of melanoma risk, which increases substantially with prolonged exposure and more intense exposure.

Epiluminescence Microscopy (ELM), also known as dermoscopy or dermatoscopy [2], which is currently used to supplement the traditional clinical diagnosis is a noninvasive, in vivo clinical examination technique in which oil immersion and optical magnification are used to make the epidermis translucent and to allow the visual examination of sub surface structures of the skin. However, for experienced users, ELM is viewed as more accurate than clinical examination for the diagnosis of melanoma in pigmented skin lesions. Despite the detection rate of melanoma from dermoscopy being significantly higher than that achieved from unaided observation, the diagnostic accuracy of dermoscopy depends in large part on the training of the dermatologist.

Differential diagnosis of melanoma from melanocytic nevi is not straightforward and is often considered as particularly clinically challenging for skin cancer specialists, especially in the early stages. Even when using dermoscopy for diagnosis, the accuracy of melanoma diagnosis by expert dermatologists [3] is estimated to be within no more than 75%–84%, which is still considered to be rather far from satisfaction for diagnostic purposes. This greatly motivates the recent growing interest in diagnostics techniques for computer-assisted analysis of lesion images, which can instead be efficiently and effectively applied.

Despite the fundamental fact that no computer or machine has yet achieved human intelligence, relatively simple computer vision algorithms can be used to efficiently extract different types of pertinent information (such as texture features) from the image data in a robust and reliable manner, which might not be discernible by human vision. Perusal of the general clinical literature reveals that numerous algorithms and methodologies have been proposed by medical researchers and clinicians for the classification of malignant lesions using dermoscopy images. Some highly prevailing examples of these methodologies are the Pattern Analysis [4], ABCD rule [5], Menzies method [6], and 7-point checklist [7]. Most of the proposed techniques require automatic segmentation processes that turn out to be severely ill-posed and thus extremely challenging, due to the great diversity of tumor intensities, the ambiguity of boundaries between tumors and surrounding normal skin tissues, and the irregularity of the highly varying structure of the tumour cells, where dermoscopy views of histological tissues show structures mostly arranged in a variety of patterns.

A computer-vision based system, commonly called a computer aided diagnosis (CAD) system, for diagnosis or prognosis of skin cancer (e.g., melanoma) usually involves three major steps: (i) preprocessing and lesion segmentation; (ii) feature extraction and selection; and (iii) lesion classification. The only prerequisite of the first step is the acquisition of the skin lesion image. The patients can capture images of their skin lesions using smart phone cameras. The task of preprocessing relates to the noise filtering such as removal of salt-and-pepper noise and image enhancement. Afterwards, lesion segmentation is applied. During this step, the main aim is the precise separation of the skin lesion from the surrounding healthy skin in order to isolate only the region of interest (ROI).

During the step of feature extraction, a set of relevant dermoscopic features similar to those visually recognized by expert dermatologists such as asymmetry, border irregularity, color, differential structures, etc. is determined and extracted from the segmented lesion region to accurately characterize a melanoma lesion. Due to its low computational and implementation complexities, the diagnostic algorithm using the ABCD rule of dermoscopy is widely employed for efficient feature extraction in numerous computer-aided melanoma detection systems. Moreover, the ABCD rule based algorithm proved to be very much effective due to its comparative advantage in the plethora of a wide range of promising features extracted from a melanoma lesion. Finally, the features extracted from skin lesions are fed into the feature classification module in order to classify skin lesions into one of two distinct categories: cancerous or benign, by simply comparing the feature parameters with the predefined thresholds.

The remainder of the paper is structured as follows. The subsequent section presents previous work related to the paper subject. The general framework and details of the proposed approach are given in Section 3. Then, in Section 4, the experiments and evaluation results are reported and discussed. Finally, some conclusion remarks and possible future research directions are given in Section 5.

2. Related Work

In recent years, the incidence of skin cancer cases has continued to escalate rapidly and the condition now affects millions of people worldwide, mainly due to the prolonged exposure to harmful ultraviolet radiation. Over the past two decades or so, many researchers in the fields of computer vision and medical image analysis have been attracted to develop high performance automatic techniques for skin cancer detection from dermoscopic images [8,9]. Accurate skin lesion segmentation plays a crucial role in automated early skin cancer detection and diagnosis systems. For the segmentation of skin lesions presented in dermoscopic images, there are three major approaches: namely, manual, semi-automatic, and fully automatic boundary based methods. Examination of the relevant literature on medical image segmentation suggests that a combination of fundamental low-level image attributes such as color, texture, shape, etc. provides a robust set of visual features for fully automatic skin lesion segmentation.

There is an abundance of literature that details a wide range of image segmentation approaches and methodologies including, but not limited to, methods employing histogram thresholding [10,11], clustering [12,13], active contours [14,15], edge detection [16,17], graph theory [18], and probabilistic modeling [19,20]. Successful application of these methods, either individually or in combination, is expected to achieve optimum segmentation accuracy while maintaining the robustness to noise [21,22]. The features aforementioned have been extensively used in a wide variety of both very early and recent approaches for medical image segmentation [23,24].

In [10], a color space analysis and a global histogram thresholding based method for automatic border detection in dermoscopy image analysis is proposed, where a competitive performance in detecting the borders of melanoma lesions has been achieved. Also related, but in a slightly different vein, is [24]. In this work, a methodological approach to the classification of dermoscopy images is proposed, where a Euclidean distance transform based technique for the extraction of color and texture features is employed to split a given dermoscopy image into a series of clinically relevant regions. The most common approach to identifying the physical characteristics of melanoma is a rule referred to as ABCD skin cancer. As mentioned earlier, due to its effectiveness and simplicity, the ABCD rule is used by most computer-assisted diagnosis systems to classify melanomas. The findings suggest that, among all the physical characteristics of melanoma (i.e., asymmetry, border irregularity, color, and diameter), asymmetry is the most prominent for the clinical diagnosis of skin lesions [5]. In a similar vein, a number of research works have been conducted with a focus on quantifying asymmetry in skin lesions. For instance, in [25], Ng et al. use fuzzy borders as well as geometrical measurements of skin lesions (e.g., symmetric distance and circularity) to determine the asymmetry of skin lesion. Another related work is [26], where the circularity index is introduced as a measure of border irregularity in dermoscopy images to classify skin lesions. An elaborated overview of the most important implementations of advanced computer vision systems available in the literature for skin lesions characterization is provided in [23]. Moreover, as a key part of this work, the authors have presented a detailed comparison of the performance of multiple classifiers specifically developed for skin lesion diagnosis.

3. Proposed Methodology

In this section, the proposed approach for melanoma skin cancer detection is described. A brief conceptual block diagram of the approach is illustrated in Figure 1. As schematically illustrated in the figure, the general framework of our proposed approach works as follows. As an initial step, the skin lesion region that is suspected to be a melanoma lesion is first segmented from the surrounding healthy skin, by applying adaptive thresholding and morphological operations. Then, a set of low-dimensional HOG-based texture features is extracted from the skin lesion region. Thereafter, a one-dimensional vector representation is formed from the extracted features and fed into an SVM classifier for skin lesion classification. The SVM classifier is trained on a dataset comprised of both melanoma and other benign skin lesion images taken from different patients. Finally, the trained SVM model is used to classify each previously unseen skin lesion in a dermatoscopic image as a benign or malignant lesion. The details of each part of our method are described in the remainder of this section.

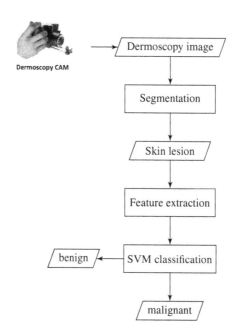

Figure 1. A general block diagram of computerized melanoma skin cancer detection.

3.1. Skin Lesion Segmentation

As stated earlier, the main purpose of the first step in computer-aided diagnosis of melanoma is the isolation of the skin lesion (i.e., lesion region of interest) from the surrounding healthy skin. Due to the limitations of capturing devices and/or improper environmental illumination conditions, acquired images are likely to suffer from poor contrast and high noise levels [27]. Therefore, it is necessary to enhance the image contrast and reduce the noise levels to increase image quality. Generally, the principal objective of image enhancement is to modify attributes of a given image so that it can be more suitable for subsequent tasks of segmentation and feature extraction. In primary image processing, images are often preprocessed by filtering techniques such as smoothing, edge enhancement, noise reduction, binarization, etc.

For the current task, due to extraneous artifacts such as skin lines, air bubbles and hair that appear in almost every image, dermoscopy images are obligatorily enhanced by filtering the noise occurring during intrusion of small hairs, scars in the human skin. This process is twofold. The first step is a simple 2D smoothing filter. This is achieved by smoothing the histogram of the input image using the band pass filtering to detect the spike regions in the histogram. The second one is connected with dark and thick hairs that need to be unpainted before the following processes of segmentation and local feature extraction. Moreover, the preprocessing involves the image resizing and contrast and brightness adjustment to compensate the non-uniform illumination in input images. To do this, histogram equalization as a contrast enhancement technique based on a histogram of the image is applied. There are various contrast enhancement techniques proposed as an extension of the traditional histogram equalization such as power constrained contrast enhancement, dynamic range compression, color model conversion, gamma correction and channel division methodologies.

For segmentation of skin lesions in the input image, our approach involves iterative automatic thresholding and masking operations, which are applied to the enhanced skin lesion images.

The procedure begins with applying the standard Otsu method [28] for automatic thresholding segmentation for each of R, G and B channel in the input image. Then, binary masks are generated for the detected structures of each color channel and a majority logic function is applied to individual color channels to produce a preliminary segmented lesion mask. It is important to emphasize that the three-channel masking procedure is used here to improve the overall segmentation quality. The application of the segmentation procedure is likely to result in a segmented image with very small blobs which are not the skin lesions, commonly called an over-segmented image. To cope with this problem, a common solution is to employ morphological area-opening [29] on the over-segmented image, which is used for choosing markers to avoid over-segmentation. Finally, the final segmented region that contains only the skin lesion can be determined by smoothing the binary image using an iterative median filter procedure with a series of gradually decreasing filter sizes (i.e., $7 \times 7, 5 \times 5$ and 3×3).

Moreover, in order to avoid detecting extremely small non skin lesions and to prevent confusing isolated artifacts with objects of interest, we take extra precautions by applying two further filters in order to guarantee that it corresponds to the skin lesion of interest. First, an adaptive morphological open-close filter is iteratively applied to the resulting binary image to erase objects that are too small from the binary image, while maintaining the shape and size of large objects. This filter is preferentially realized by a cascade of erosion and dilation operations, using locally adaptive structuring elements.

As a second filter, the so-called size filter is employed to remove objects that are less than a specified size. Once applying the size filter, almost all spurious objects with a size less than 5% of the image size are removed from the binary image. However, after filtering out all unwanted image elements and isolated artifacts, all of the contours are identified by applying a modified Canny edge detector [30] to the image to extract high contrast contours with edges having particular "preferred" orientations. Assuming that the skin lesion of interest represents the largest contour, it is easily extracted and isolated as the contour having the largest area (see Figure 2). As is obvious from the figure, the proposed approach is capable of producing very precise segmentation of the skin lesion from the surrounding healthy skin.

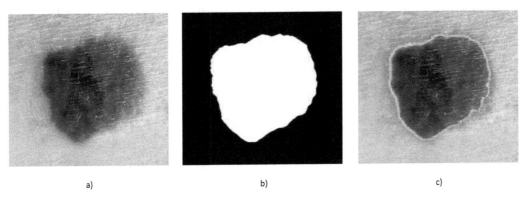

a)   b)   c)

Figure 2. Segmentation of skin lesion: (**a**) original RGB image; (**b**) binary mask; (**c**) traced skin lesion, where the lesion boundary is drawn in green overlaid on the original image.

3.2. Feature Extraction

Due to their robustness to varying illumination and local geometric transformations and simplicity in implementation, HOG [31] features have been widely adopted (and are still being adopted) by many successful object detectors such as faces, pedestrians, and vehicles. Broadly speaking, HOG are constructed typically by imitating the visual information processing in the brain, and their features have proven to be an effective way of describing local object appearances and shapes by their distribution of intensity gradients or edge directions. In this section, we explain how to extract the local HOG features from the skin lesion region. In the process of HOG feature extraction, these features are computed by taking orientation histograms of edge intensity in a local lesion region. For realizing this purpose, two computation units are locally defined, namely cell and block. Typically, the cell size is 8×8 pixels, and each block contains 2×2 cells (i.e., 16×16 pixels) for each HOG feature. Since the HOG detector depends on the window overlap principle by default, the HOG blocks typically overlap such that each cell contributes more than once to the final feature descriptor. Adjacent neighboring blocks overlap by eight pixels both horizontally and vertically.

To extract HOG features, we compute orientations of local image gradient at each pixel located at coordinate (x, y). To realize this goal, we first need to calculate the magnitude $\rho(x, y)$ and direction $\gamma(x, y)$, which are mathematically formulated as follows:

$$
\begin{aligned}
\rho(x,y) &= \sqrt{L_x(x,y)^2 + L_y(x,y)^2}, \\
\gamma(x,y) &= \arctan\left(\frac{L_y(x,y)}{L_x(x,y)}\right),
\end{aligned}
\tag{1}
$$

where L_x and L_y are the first-order Gaussian derivatives of the image patch luminance I in the x- and y-directions, respectively, which are computed for scale parameter σ as follows:

$$
L_\xi = I * \frac{\partial}{\partial \xi}\left(\frac{1}{2\pi\sigma^2} e^{-(x^2+y^2)/2\sigma^2}\right)\bigg|_{\xi=x|y'}
\tag{2}
$$

where $*$ denotes 2D discrete convolution. Then, we discretize γ into a fixed number of gradient orientation bins (e.g., nine bins). For every pixel in the orientation image, a histogram of orientations is constructed over a cell (i.e., local spatial window) such that each pixel in the cell votes for a gradient orientation bin with a vote proportional to the gradient magnitude ρ at that pixel (see Figure 3). More formally, the weight of each pixel denoted by α can be computed as follows:

$$
\alpha = b + 0.5 - \frac{\gamma(x,y)}{\pi} n,
\tag{3}
$$

where b is the bin to which γ belongs and n indicates the total number of bins. For reducing aliasing, we increment both values of two neighboring bins as

$$
\tilde{\gamma} = (1 - \alpha)\gamma(x,y), \quad \hat{\gamma} = \alpha\gamma(x,y).
\tag{4}
$$

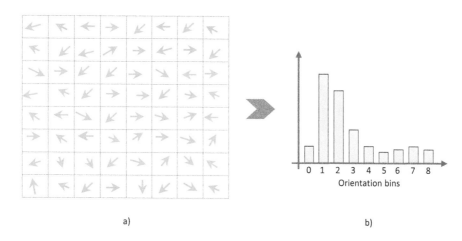

a)   b)

Figure 3. Gradient orientation voting: (**a**) cell gradient field; (**b**) a voting space of nine bins.

The weighted votes $\tilde{\gamma}$ are then accumulated into orientation bins over local spatial regions, so called cells. In this work, we use normalized histograms as feature descriptors to represent a skin lesion object or texture. In fulfillment of this purpose, we construct a normalized histogram for each block by combining all histograms belonging to that block that consists of four cells. The normalization process is formulated as follows:

$$\tilde{v}_i = \frac{v_i}{\sqrt{\|v\|_2^2 + \varepsilon^2}},$$

(5)

where i indicates the vector index running from 1 to 36 (4 cells × 9 bins), v_i is a vector corresponding to a combined histogram for a given block, 36, and ε is a small positive constant used to avoid division by zero. Figure 4 shows sample 2D plots for the HOG-based descriptor of the features extracted from three segmented skin lesions, where, from top to bottom, the first two dermoscopy images contain malignant melanoma, while the last one contains benign lesions. As suggested by the figure, the general curve behavior of HOG-based descriptors for the skin lesions containing malignant melanoma is remarkably similar in both shape and magnitude.

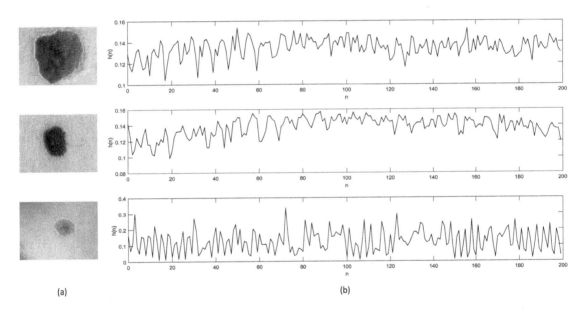

(a)   (b)

Figure 4. Sample 2D plots for the HOG based descriptor of the features extracted from three segmented skin lesion images: (**a**) original skin lesion image; (**b**) HOG-based descriptor; from top to bottom, the first two dermoscopy images contain malignant melanoma, while the last one contains benign lesions.

3.3. Skin Lesion Classification

In this section, we describe details of the feature classification module that we employed in our automatic skin lesion malignance detection system to yield the final detection results. The main purpose of the classification module is to classify a given pigmented skin lesion into one of the two classes (melanoma versus non melanoma lesions), depending on the features extracted from the given skin lesion. The classification module is primarily based on the availability of a set of previously labeled or classified skin lesions. In this case, this set of pigmented skin lesions is termed the training set and the resulting learning strategy is supervised learning.

For the automatic classification of pigmented skin lesions, there are numerous reliable classification methods [32–36] developed in literature with the aid of learning algorithms, such as Naïve Bayesian (NB), k-Nearest Neighbor (k-NN), Support Vector Machines (SVMs), Neural Networks (NNs), Conditional Random Fields (CRFs), etc. In this work, the current task of skin lesion detection is formulated as a typical binary classification problem, where there are two classes for skin lesions, and the ultimate goal is to assign an appropriate diagnostic class label (malignant melanoma or benign pigmented) to each skin lesion in dermatoscopic images.

There are numerous supervised learning algorithms [37–39] by which a skin lesion malignance detector can be trained. Due to its outstanding generalization capability and reputation of being a highly accurate paradigm, an SVM classier [40] is employed in the current detection framework. As a very effective method for universal purpose pattern recognition, SVM has been proposed by Vapnik [41,42], which is characterized by a substantial resistance to overfitting, a long-standing and inherent problem for several supervised learning algorithms (e.g., neural networks and decision trees). This great feature of SVM is principally attributable to the fact that SVM employs the structural risk minimization principle rather than the empirical risk minimization principle, which minimizes the upper bound on the generalization error.

Originally, the standard SVMs were designed for dichotomic classification problems (i.e., binary classification problems with two classes). Thus, the ultimate objective of the SVM learning is to find the optimal dichotomic hyperplane that can maximize the margin (the largest separation) of two classes. In the pursuit of this objective, on each side of this hyperplane, two parallel hyperplanes are constructed. Then, SVM attempts to find the separating hyperplane that maximizes the distance between the two parallel hyperplanes. Intuitively, a good separation is accomplished by the hyperplane having the largest distance (see Figure 5). Hence, the larger the margin, the lower the generalization error of the classifier. More formally, let $\mathcal{D} = \{(\mathbf{x}_i, y_i) \mid \mathbf{x}_i \in \mathbb{R}^d, y_i \in \{-1, +1\}\}$ be a training dataset. Coretes and Vapnik stated in their paper [43] that this problem is best addressed by allowing some examples to violate the margin constraints. These potential violations are formulated using some positive slack variables ξ_i and a penalty parameter $C \geq 0$ that penalize the margin violations. Thus, the optimal separating hyperplane is determined by solving the following Quadratic Programming (QP) problem:

$$\min_{\beta, \beta_0} \quad \frac{1}{2}\|\beta\|^2 + C\sum_i \xi_i, \tag{6}$$

subject to

$$(y_i(\langle \mathbf{x}_i, \beta \rangle + \beta_0) \geq 1 - \xi_i \quad \forall i) \wedge (\xi_i \geq 0 \quad \forall i).$$

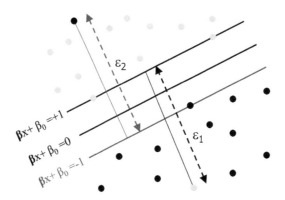

Figure 5. Generalized optimal separating hyperplane.

Geometrically, $\beta \in \mathbb{R}^d$ is a vector going through the center and is perpendicular to the separating hyperplane. The offset parameter β_0 is added to allow the margin to increase, and to not force the hyperplane to pass through the origin that restricts the solution. For computational purposes, it is more convenient to solve SVM in its dual formulation. This can be accomplished by forming the Lagrangian and then optimizing over the Lagrange multiplier α. The resulting decision function has weight vector $\beta = \sum_i \alpha_i \mathbf{x}_i y_i$, $0 \leq \alpha_i \leq C$. The instances $\mathbf{x}_i$ with $\alpha_i > 0$ are called *support vectors*, as they uniquely define the maximum margin hyperplane. In the presented approach, two classes of skin lesions are created. An SVM classifier with the radial basis function (RBF) kernel and default parameters is trained using the local features extracted from the skin lesion images in the training dataset. An advantage of using an RBF kernel over the other kernels, such as the linear kernel, is that it restricts training data to lie in specified boundaries. Another advantage is that it has fewer numerical difficulties. Finally, in the test phase, a test unseen skin lesion sample is given to the trained SVM model for classification, based on the extracted local features.

4. Simulations and Results Analysis

In this section, the simulation results are presented in order to demonstrate the performance of our proposed detector of malignant melanoma. To evaluate the performance of our detection system, several experiments have been carried out on a relatively large dataset consisting of a total of 224 digital dermoscopy images acquired from atlases of dermoscopy and collected from various medical sites (http://www2.fc.up.pt/addi and http://www.dermoscopic.blogspot.com). All of the images in the collection are provided in high resolution JPEG format and RGB color space, exhibiting a 24-bit color depth with a spatial resolution ranging from approximately 689×554 down to 352×240. The diagnosis distribution of the cases is as follows: 112 of them are benign nevus and the rest of the images are malignant melanoma cases. All samples of the cases were obtained by biopsy or excision and diagnosed by histopathology. Figure 6 presents a sample of skin lesions of melanoma from the used data.

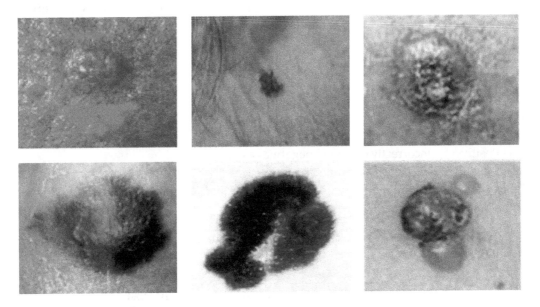

Figure 6. A sample of skin lesions of melanoma from the used data.

In terms of validation, in this work, our proposed method is evaluated using k-fold cross validation and the leave-one-patient-out technique in order to assess thoroughly the achieved performance. In fulfillment of this purpose, the image samples are randomly divided into two independent subsets, i.e., the training set and the test set. For four-fold cross-validation, as a rule, three-fourths of all the images are used for learning (or training) the SVM model and the remaining one-fourth of images are for testing purposes. The procedure is repeated several times such that each image instance is used exactly once for testing in the end. A key point worthy of mentioning here is that the leave-one-out technique has the potential to be an efficient and reliable validation procedure for small datasets.

Another important point deemed worthy of highlighting is that, for HOG features computation, the extracted region of skin lesion is converted to the grayscale image level and resized to 64×64 pixels, as it proved to perform best in our experiments. Note that the HOG features are not only invariant to changes in illuminations or shadowing, but also nearly invariant against translations and rotations if the translations or rotations are much smaller than that of the local spatial and orientation bin sizes. Hence, they have proved to be robust, fast, and applicable to numerous detection and classification tasks.

For performance evaluation, the results obtained by the proposed technique are quantitatively assessed in terms of three commonly used performance indices, namely, sensitivity (SN), specificity (SP) and accuracy (AC). The three indices are defined as follows. Sensitivity (also called true positive rate or recall) generally measures the proportion of positives that are correctly identified as such (e.g., the percentage of samples that are correctly identified as having the disease). Briefly, sensitivity refers to the ability to positively identify the case with melanoma, i.e.,

$$SN = \frac{TP}{TP + FN} \times 100 \; (\%). \tag{7}$$

Specificity (also called true negative rate) is the likelihood that a non-diseased patient has a negative test result, i.e.,

$$SP = \frac{TN}{TN + FP} \times 100 \; (\%). \tag{8}$$

In other words, the specificity of a test refers to how well a test identifies patients who do not have a disease. In general, accuracy is the probability that a randomly chosen instance (positive or negative, relevant or irrelevant) will be correct. More specifically, accuracy is the probability that the diagnostic test yields the correct determination, i.e., it is estimated as follows:

$$AC = \frac{TP + TN}{TP + TN + FP + FN} \times 100 \; (\%), \tag{9}$$

where:
TP (True Positives) = correctly classified positive cases,
TN (True Negative) = correctly classified negative cases,
FP (False Positives) = incorrectly classified negative cases,
FN (False Negative) = incorrectly classified positive cases.

Table 1 shows the results of sensitivity, specificity, and accuracy of the proposed system for melanoma detection.

Table 1. Results of sensitivity (SN), specificity (SP), and accuracy (AC) for the proposed system for melanoma detection.

TP	TN	FP	FN	SN (%)	SP (%)	AC (%)
55	54	2	1	98.21	96.43	97.32

The data reported in the above table merit the following interesting observations. The first most remarkable result is that the proposed method achieves values of 98.21%, 96.43% and 97.32% for overall sensitivity, specificity, and accuracy, respectively, which are quite encouraging and comparable with those of other recent contemporary methods. Recall that, generally, intuition suggests that high values of evaluation indices (i.e., sensitivity, specificity, and accuracy) and low computational demands lead to the feasibility of the application of the proposed approach in real time. On a closer inspection of the results in the above table, one can clearly see that the vast majority of cases of malignant melanoma are correctly diagnosed with quite a high accuracy rate, while, only in two cases, benign lesions are misdiagnosed as malignant melanoma. Moreover, it should be emphasised that it is an experimentally established fact that the extracted local HOG features not only have a great potential to promote the quantitative discrimination between normal skin and melanoma, but they also turn out to be quite robust to various types of melanoma skin cancer. In general, we conclude that the experimental results show supporting evidence that the proposed framework is useful for improving the performance of the early detection of melanoma skin cancer, without sacrificing its real-time guarantees.

In order to quantify the performance of the proposed approach, an experimental comparison of our method to several state-of-the-art baselines [44,45] is provided. A summary of this comparison is presented in Table 2. In light of this comparison, it is pointed out that the proposed method is competitive with existing state-of-the-art methods, while maintaining desired real-time performance. It is worthwhile to mention that the first method [44] has been tested for a total of only 20 samples, whereas the other method [45] has been tested for a total of 102 samples. In addition, they have used similar experimental setups. Thus, the comparison seems to be meaningful. As a final point, in this work, all of the algorithms were implemented in Microsoft Visual Studio 2013 with OpenCV Vision Library version 3.0 for the graphical processing functions. All tests and evaluations were performed on a PC with an Intel(R) Core(TM) i7 CPU - 3.07 GHz processor, 4GB RAM, running a Windows 7 Professional 64-bit operating system. As it might be expected, the testing results show that the presented detection system performs stably, achieving near real-time performance on image sizes of VGA (640×480) due to the use of optimized algorithmic implementations in OpenCV library in combination with custom C++ functions.

Table 2. Comparison of our method with other state-of-the-art baselines.

Method	SN (%)	SP (%)	AC (%)
Our method	**98.21**	**96.43**	**97.32**
Elgamal [44]	100.0	95.00	97.00
Sheha et al. [45]	92.30	91.60	92.00

5. Conclusions

In this paper, we have proposed an effective framework of a CAD system for melanoma skin cancer mainly by application of an SVM model on an optimized set of HOG-based descriptors of skin lesions. Evaluations on a large dataset of dermoscopic images have demonstrated that the proposed framework exhibits superior performance over two recent state-of-the-art alternatives in terms of performance indices of sensitivity, specificity and accuracy by achieving 98.21%, 96.43%, and 97.32%, respectively, without losing real-time compliance. Directions for future work will be two-fold. On one hand, we intend to further expand the approach to allow the SVM classifier to recognize several different types of melanoma cells. On the other hand, we will explore the potential of combining both color and texture features for melanoma classification.

Acknowledgments: This research was supported by the Transregional Collaborative Research Center SFB/TRR 62 "Companion Technology for Cognitive Technical Systems" funded by the German Research Foundation (DFG). I would also like to give special thanks to anonymous reviewers for their insightful comments and constructive suggestions to improve the quality of the paper.

References

1.   Sloot, S.; Rashid, O.; Sarnaik, A.; Zager, J. Developments in Intralesional Therapy for Metastatic Melanoma. *Cancer Control* **2016**, *23*, 12–20.

2.   Vestergaard, M.; Macaskill, P.; Holt, P.; Menzies, S. Dermoscopy compared with naked eye examination for the diagnosis of primary melanoma: A meta-analysis of studies performed in a clinical setting. *Br. J. Dermatol.* **2008**, *159*, 669–676.

3.   Argenziano, G.; Soyer, H.P.; Chimenti, S.; Talamini, R.; Corona, R.; Sera, F.; Binder, M.; Cerroni, L.; De Rosa, G.; Ferrara, G.; et al. Dermoscopy of pigmented skin lesions: Results of a consensus meeting via the Internet. *J. Acad. Dermatol.* **2003**, *48*, 679–693.

4. Pehamberger, H.; Steiner, A.; Wolff, K. In vivo epiluminescence microscopy of pigmented skin lesions. I. Pattern analysis of pigmented skin lesions. *J. Am. Acad. Dermatol.* **1987**, *17*, 571–583.

5. Stolz, W.; Riemann, A.; Cognetta, A. ABCD rule of dermatoscopy: A new practical method for early recognition of malignant melanoma. *Eur. J. Dermatol.* **1994**, *4*, 521–527.

6. Menzies, S.W. A Method for the diagnosis of primary cutaneous melanoma using surface microscopy. *Dermatol. Clin.* **2001**, *19*, 299–305.

7. Argenziano, G.; Fabbrocini, G.; Carli, P.; De Giorgi, V.; Sammarco, E.; Delfino, M. Epiluminescence microscopy for the diagnosis of doubtful melanocytic skin lesions. Comparison of the ABCD rule of dermatoscopy and a new 7-point checklist based on pattern analysis. *Arch. Dermatol.* **1998**, *134*, 1563–1570.

8. Masood, A.; Al-Jumaily, A.A. Computer aided diagnostic support system for skin cancer: A review of techniques and algorithms. *Int. J. Biomed. Imaging* **2013**, *2013*, 1–22.

9. Korotkov, K. Automatic Change Detection in Multiple Skin Lesions. Ph.D. Thesis, Universitat de Girona, Girona, Spain, 2014.

10. Garnavi, R. Computer-Aided Diagnosis of Melanoma. Ph.D Thesis, University of Melbourne, Melbourne, Australia, 2011.

11. Celebi, M.E.; Wen, Q.; Hwang, S.; Iyatomi, H.; Schaefer, G. Lesion border detection in dermoscopy images using ensembles of thresholding methods. *Skin Res. Technol.* **2013**, *19*, e252–e258.

12. Zhou, H.; Schaefer, G.; Sadka, A.H.; Celebi, M.E. Anisotropic mean shift based fuzzy c-means segmentation of dermoscopy images. *IEEE J. Sel. Top. Signal Proc.* **2009**, *3*, 26–34.

13. Schmid, P. Segmentation of digitized dermatoscopic images by two-dimensional color clustering. *IEEE Trans. Med. Imaging* **1999**, *18*, 164–171.

14. Zhou, H.; Li, X.; Schaefer, G.; Celebi, M.E.; Miller, P. Mean shift based gradient vector flow for image segmentation. *Comput. Vis. Image Underst.* **2013**, *117*, 1004–1016.

15. Erkol, B.; Moss, R.H.; Stanley, R.J.; Stoecker, W.V.; Hvatum, E. Automatic lesion boundary detection in dermoscopy images using gradient vector flow snakes. *Skin Res. Technol.* **2005**, *11*, 17–26.

16. Abbas, Q.; Celebi, M.E.; García, I.F.; Rashid, M. Lesion border detection in dermoscopy images using dynamic programming. *Skin Res. Technol.* **2011**, *17*, 91–100.

17. Rajab, M.I.; Woolfson, M.S.; Morgan, S.P. Application of region-based segmentation and neural network edge detection to skin lesions. *Comput. Med. Imaging Graph.* **2004**, *28*, 61–68.

18. Yuan, X.; Situ, N.; Zouridakis, G. A narrow band graph partitioning method for skin lesion segmentation. *Pattern Recognit.* **2009**, *42*, 1017–1028.

19. Wong, A.; Scharcanski, J.; Fieguth, P. Automatic skin lesion segmentation via iterative stochastic region merging. *IEEE Trans. Inform. Technol. Biomed.* **2011**, *15*, 929–936.

20. Celebi, M.E.; Kingravi, H.A.; Iyatomi, H.; Alp Aslandogan, Y.; Stoecker, W.V.; Moss, R.H.; Malters, J.M.; Grichnik, J.M.; Marghoob, A.A.; Rabinovitz, H.S.; et al. Border detection in dermoscopy images using statistical region merging. *Skin Res. Technol.* **2008**, *14*, 347–353.

21. Celebi, M.E.; Wen, Q.; Iyatomi, H.; Shimizu, K.; Zhou, H.; Schaefer, G. A state-of-the-art survey on lesion border detection in dermoscopy images. *Dermoscopy Image Anal.* **2015**, doi:10.1201/b19107-5.

22. Celebi, M.E.; Schaefer, G.; Iyatomi, H.; Stoecker, W.V. Lesion border detection in dermoscopy images. *Comput. Med. Imaging Graph.* **2009**, *33*, 148–153.

23. Maglogiannis, I.; Doukas, C. Overview of advanced computer vision systems for skin lesions characterization. *IEEE Trans. Inform. Technol. Biomed.* **2009**, *13*, 721–733.

24. Celebi, M.; Kingravi, H.A.; Uddin, B.; Iyatomi, H.; Aslandogan, Y.A.; Stoecker, W.V.; Moss, R.H. A methodological approach to the classification of dermoscopy images. *Comput. Med. Imaging Graph.* **2007**, *31*, 362–373.

25. Ng, V.; Fung, B.; Lee, T. Determining the asymmetry of skin lesion with fuzzy borders. *Comput. Biol. Med.* **2005**, *35*, 103–120.

26. She, Z.; Liu, Y.; Damatoa, A. Combination of features from skin pattern and ABCD analysis for lesion classification. *Skin Res. Technol.* **2007**, *13*, 25–33.

27. Bakheet, S.; Al-Hamadi, A. A hybrid cascade approach for human skin segmentation. *Br. J. Math. Comput. Sci.* **2016**, *17*, 1–18.

28. Otsu, N. A threshold selection method from gray-level histograms. *IEEE Trans. Syst. Man Cybern.* **1979**, *9*, 62–66.

29. Vincent, L. Morphological Area Opening and Closing for Grayscale Images. In *Processing NATO Shape in Picture Workshop*; Springer: Driebergen, The Netherlands, 1992; Volume 126, pp. 197–208.

30. Canny, J. A computational approach to edge detection. *IEEE Trans. Pattern Anal. Mach. Intell.* **1986**, *PAMI-8*, 679–698.

31. Dalal, N.; Triggs, B. Histograms of oriented gradients for human detection. *IEEE Conf. Comput. Vis. Pattern Recognit.* **2005**, *1*, 886–893.

32. Sadek, S.; Al-Hamadi, A.; Michaelis, B.; Sayed, U. Human action recognition: A novel scheme using fuzzy log-polar histogram and temporal self-similarity. *EURASIP J. Adv. Signal Proc.* **2011**, *1*, 1–9.

33. Sadek, S.; Al-Hamadi, A.; Michaelis, B.; Sayed, U. An SVM approach for activity recognition based on chord-length-function shape features. In Proceedings of the IEEE International Conference on Image Processing (ICIP'12), Orlando, FL, USA, 30 September–3 October 2012; pp. 767–770.

34. Bakheet, S.; Al-Hamadi, A. A discriminative framework for action recognition using f-HOL Features. *Information* **2016**, *7*, 68.

35. Sadek, S.; Al-Hamadi, A.; Michaelis, B.; Sayed, U. Human Action Recognition via Affine Moment Invariants. In Proceedings of the 21st International Conference on Pattern Recognition (ICPR'12), Tsukuba, Japan, 11–15 November 2012; pp. 218–221.

36. Sadek, S.; Al-Hamadi, A.; Michaelis, B. Toward Real-World Activity Recognition: An SVM Based System Using Fuzzy Directional Features. *WSEAS Trans. Inform. Sci. App.* **2013**, *10*, 116–127.

37. Sadek, S.; Al-Hamadi, A.; Michaelis, B.; Sayed, U. Towards Robust Human Action Retrieval in Video. In Proceedings of the British Machine Vision Conference (BMVC'10), Aberystwyth, UK, 31 August–3 September 2010.

38. Sadek, S.; Al-Hamadi, A.; Michaelis, B.; Sayed, U. Human Activity Recognition: A Scheme Using Multiple Cues. In *Advances in Visual Computing, Proceedings of the International Symposium on Visual Computing (ISVC'10), Las Vegas, NV, USA, 29 November–1 December 2010*; Springer: Berlin/Heidelberg, Germany, 2010; Volume 6454, pp. 574–583.

39. Sadek, S.; Al-Hamadi, A.; Elmezain, M.; Michaelis, B.; Sayed, U. Human Activity Recognition Using Temporal Shape Moments. In Proceedings of the IEEE International Symposium on Signal Processing and Information Technology (ISSPIT'10), Luxor, Egypt, 15–18 December 2010; pp. 79–84.

40. Sumithra, R.; Suhil, M.; Guru, D.S. Segmentation and Classification of Skin Lesions for Disease Diagnosis. *Proc. Comput. Sci.* **2015**, *45*, 76–85.

41. Vapnik, V.N. *The Nature of Statistical Learning Theory*; Springer: New York, NY, USA, 1995.

42. Vapnik, V.N. An overview of statistical learning theory. *IEEE Trans. Neural Netw.* **1999**, *10*, 988–999.

43. Cortes, C.; Vapnik, V. Support-vector networks. *Mach. Learn.* **1995**, *20*, 1–20.

44. Elgamal, M. Automatic Skin Cancer Images Classification. *Int. J. Adv. Comput. Sci. Appl.* **2013**, *4*, 1–8.

45. Sheha, M.A.; Mabrouk, M.S.; Sharawy, A. Automatic detection of melanoma skin cancer using texture analysis. *Int. J. Comput. Appl.* **2012**, *42*, 22–26.

11

Numerical and Computational Analysis of a New Vertical Axis Wind Turbine, Named KIONAS

Eleni Douvi [1,*], Dimitra Douvi [1,*], Dionissios Margaris [1,*] and Ioannis Drosis [2]

[1] Fluid Mechanics Laboratory (FML), Mechanical Engineering and Aeronautics Department, University of Patras, GR-26500 Patras, Greece

[2] Small Wind Turbines Development Manager, 97 Dimitros Street, GR-19200 Elefsina, Greece; giannisdrosis@hotmail.com

[*] Correspondence: douvi@mech.upatras.gr (E.D.); dimdouvi@gmail.com (D.D.); margaris@mech.upatras.gr (D.M.)

Academic Editor: Demos T. Tsahalis

Abstract: This paper concentrates on a new configuration for a wind turbine, named KIONAS. The main purpose is to determine the performance and aerodynamic behavior of KIONAS, which is a vertical axis wind turbine with a stator over the rotor and a special feature in that it can consist of several stages. Notably, the stator is shaped in such a way that it increases the velocity of the air impacting the rotor blades. Moreover, each stage's performance can be increased with the increase of the total number of stages. The effects of wind velocity, the various numbers of inclined rotor blades, the rotor diameter, the stator's shape and the number of stages on the performance of KIONAS were studied. A FORTRAN code was developed in order to predict the power in several cases by solving the equations of continuity and momentum. Subsequently, further knowledge on the flow field was obtained by using a commercial Computational Fluid Dynamics code. Based on the results, it can be concluded that higher wind velocities and a greater number of blades produce more power. Furthermore, higher performance was found for a stator with curved guide vanes and for a KIONAS configuration with more stages.

Keywords: vertical axis wind turbine; stator guide vanes; aerodynamic performance; power output; multi-stage

1. Introduction

Since the reserves of fossil fuels are diminishing, there is increasing interest in renewable energy sources, among which wind energy is included. Wind energy is harnessed by wind turbines, which can be either Horizontal Axis Wind Turbines (HAWT) or Vertical Axis Wind Turbines (VAWT). A considerable amount of literature has been published on HAWTs, because they are more effective than the VAWTs. Recently, there has been growing interest in VAWTs, because of their easy installation, manufacture and maintenance.

A review of various configurations of vertical axis wind turbines, along with their advantages and disadvantages, was first conducted by Aslam Bhutta et al. [1]. The techniques for VAWT design and the flow field over the blades were also reviewed. The results showed that the power coefficient is different for various configurations and can be optimized with tip speed ratio. The impact of structural parameters on the performance, particularly for Savonius wind turbine, is studied by Tang et al. [2]. Their findings revealed that for different structures, the maximum power coefficient can be increased by more than 30%.

Numerous investigations have been conducted to show the effects of guide vanes on vertical axis wind turbine performance. The first systematic study of the effects of guide vanes was reported by

Ejiri et al. [3], in 2006. A computational fluid dynamics (CFD) code was utilized to analyze the flow through the vertical axis cross-flow wind turbine and to propose an improved design configuration in order to achieve better performance, which had two guide vanes outside the turbine.

A year later, in 2007, Takao et al. [4] proposed a straight-bladed vertical axis wind turbine with a directed guide vane row, which was added to enhance its torque. The guide vane row improved the performance of the straight-bladed vertical axis turbine and the experimental results showed that the power coefficient of the proposed wind turbine was approximately 1.5 times higher than that of the original wind turbine which has no guide vane. A further study with more of a focus on the effect of guide vane geometry on the performance of wind turbine was conducted by the same researchers [5]. An experimental investigation was carried out, in order to investigate the effects of distance between the guide vanes and the number of guide vanes on power and torque coefficients. Recently, Shahizare et al. [6] simulated a vertical axis wind turbine with omni-direction guide vanes of eight different shape ratios to determine the effects of guide vanes. It was concluded that all the shape ratios improved the power and torque coefficient.

Kim and Gharib [7] studied the effect on the power output of the vertical axis wind turbine configuration by adding an upstream deflector. They found out that the dimensions and the relative position of the deflector are related to the power output of the VAWT. The optimal design of the wind booster, a device which controls the airflow around a vertical axis wind turbine, was also analyzed lately by Korprasertsak and Leephakpreeda [8]. This device consists of guide vanes mounted around the wind turbine, which not only accelerate but also direct the wind in order to impact the rotor blades at the most effective angle of attack. This results in an increase in the VAWT's angular speed and thus in power.

In order to improve a vertical axis wind turbine's performance, a stator is added around the rotor. The stator significantly increases the wind speed, and as a result it improves the self-starting behavior of the VAWT the power coefficient. The effect of a stator surrounding a vertical-axis wind turbine has been studied both experimental and numerical.

Simulations of a new power-augmented shroud integrated with a vertical axis wind turbine (VAWT) suitable for urban and suburban application were carried out by Wong et al. [9]. The results of the numerical simulation indicated that the new design for the power-augmented shroud is able to increase the coefficient of power significantly for the VAWT, by about 147.1% compared to the bare VAWT. At the same time, Nobile et al. [10] proposed and analyzed a computational investigation of an augmented wind turbine. The results of their study also showed that the introduction of an omnidirectional stator around the wind turbine increases not only the power but also the torque coefficients by around 30%–35% when compared to the open case. They also concluded that for optimum performance, attention needs to be given to the orientation of the stator blades.

Chen et al. [11,12] developed a vortical stator assembly (VSA) surrounding a vertical-axis wind turbine to improve rotor performance. The VSA consisted of six guide vanes, in order to guide the air tangentially into the VSA. The experimental results showed that the VSA significantly increased rotor performance and the rotor starting speed was reduced to approximately 1 m/s. The optimal VSA diameter was found to be approximately 1.82 times the rotor diameter.

The first systematic numerical and experimental study of the operating performance and power output from a vertical axis wind turbine was reported by Pope et al. [13]. They studied the effects of varying VAWT stator vane geometries of a Zephyr vertical axis wind turbine on the turbine's performance at constant and variable rotor velocities. Recently, Burlando et al. [14] have examined with a numerical wind turbine technique the effects of stator vanes on the flow around and inside a multi-stage vertical-axis wind turbine. They developed a numerical model to extend the results obtained by means of the physical model to more general conditions.

So far this type of vertical axis wind turbine has been applied to hybrid energy systems. Tong et al. [15] were the first to introduce a patented wind-solar hybrid renewable energy harvester for urban high rise application. The speed of the high-altitude free-stream wind is increased through fixed or yaw-able power-augmentation-guide-vane (PAGV) before entering the wind turbine at the center portion. The geometry of the PAGV was optimized by computational fluid dynamics (CFD) simulation. The generated power was 1.25 times higher after integrating the PAGV with the VAWT. Chong et al. [16] introduced the Eco-Greenergy™ hybrid wind-solar photovoltaic energy generation system to power LED lights or other appliances. The system consists of a novel omni-direction guide vane with a vertical axis wind turbine and a PV panel mounted on the top surface. The system was found to generate a total of 572.8 kWh of energy per year, and the ODGV increases the annual wind energy output by 438%.

This project was undertaken to describe the design of a new vertical axis wind turbine, named KIONAS, and evaluate its performance using mathematical modelling and its aerodynamic behavior and flow field through Computational Fluid Dynamics (CFD) simulations.

The wind turbine examined in this study is a vertical axis wind turbine, which is named KIONAS. It consists of a rotor which is surrounded by a stator. In the rotors center there is a shaft, where a number of flat blades are mounted on, at an angle. The stator is added in order to increase the wind speed that impacts the rotor blades. The above system is a one-stage wind turbine KIONAS. The main characteristic of this wind turbine is that a multi-stage turbine can be constructed by adding more of the same stages to the first one, directly above it. The basic geometry of a three-stage wind turbine KIONAS is presented in Figure 1.

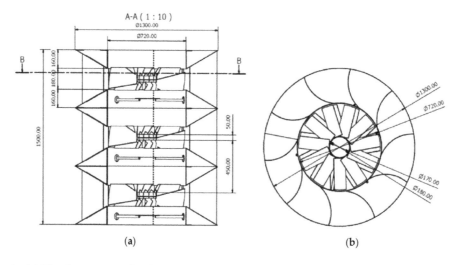

Figure 1. (a) The front view; (b) the top view of the basic geometry of a three-stage wind turbine KIONAS. Units in mm.

The current study contributes to our knowledge by drawing the following important conclusions. First of all, it was found that a multi-stage KIONAS could become advantageous in the long term because the output power per unit weight of the machine is higher as the number of KIONAS stages is increased and simultaneously the power of each individual stage is increased when an extra stage is added. Secondly, from the computational results it was obvious that part of the wind is directed both towards the upper and towards the lower stage for the two-stage KIONAS.

2. Numerical Computation

2.1. Mathematical Study

The first step in the mathematical study is the calculation of the resultant velocity of the air in each of the five sections of the front side of wind turbine KIONAS, Figure 2. The wind speed is considered equal to u_∞ and the average wind speed which enters each stator section, $\bar{u}_{in}$, is

$$\bar{u}_{in} = u_\infty \sin \varphi, \tag{1}$$

where $\varphi = \frac{(2v-1)\pi}{10}$, for $v = 1, 2, 3, 4, 5$. Thus, the average wind speed is:

$$\bar{u}_{in} = u_\infty \sin \frac{(2v-1)\pi}{10} \tag{2}$$

The wind speed that impacts the rotor blades, $\bar{u}$, is calculated by the equation of continuity (3)

$$\bar{u} = \left(\frac{b_1}{b_2}\right)\bar{u}_{in}, \tag{3}$$

where b_1 is the external and b_2 is the internal cross section length between the guide vanes. By substituting $\bar{u}_{in}$ from Equation (2) in the above equation, the following equation emerges:

$$\bar{u} = \left(\frac{b_1}{b_2}\right)u_\infty \sin \frac{(2v-1)\pi}{10}, \tag{4}$$

for $v = 1, 2, 3, 4, 5$. Moreover, each blade has a circumferential velocity, T,

$$T = \Omega R, \tag{5}$$

which is in the x-axis

$$(\Omega R)_x = \Omega R \cos \alpha, \tag{6}$$

and in the y-axis, namely the axis of wind direction,

$$(\Omega R)_y = \Omega R \sin \alpha \tag{7}$$

In the above equations Ω is the rotational velocity of the rotor, R is the rotor's radius and α is the angle of attack. The resultant velocity is in the x-axis

$$u_x = (\Omega R)_x = \Omega R \cos \alpha, \tag{8}$$

and in the y-axis

$$u_y = \bar{u} \pm (\Omega R)_y = \bar{u} \pm \Omega R \sin \alpha, \tag{9}$$

where for the sections denoted by A the quantity $\Omega R \sin \alpha$ is positive while for the sections denoted by B is negative. The resultant velocity is given by Equation (10)

$$u_{res} = \sqrt{u_x^2 + u_y^2} \tag{10}$$

By substituting in the above equation u_x and u_y from Equations (8) and (9) respectively, we get:

$$u_{res} = \sqrt{(\Omega R)_x^2 + (\bar{u} \pm \Omega R \sin \alpha)^2} \Rightarrow \tag{11}$$

$$u_{res} = \sqrt{(\Omega R)^2 \cos^2 \alpha + \bar{u}^2 + (\Omega R)^2 \sin^2 \alpha \pm 2\Omega R \sin \alpha \bar{u}} \Rightarrow \tag{12}$$

$$u_{res} = \sqrt{(\Omega R)^2 (\sin^2 \alpha + \cos^2 \alpha) \pm 2\Omega R \sin \alpha \bar{u} + \bar{u}^2} \Rightarrow \tag{13}$$

$$u_{res} = \sqrt{(\Omega R)^2 \pm 2\Omega R \sin \alpha \bar{u} + \bar{u}^2} \tag{14}$$

The resultant velocity is given by the Equation (15), by substituting $\bar{u}$ from Equation (4) in Equation (14):

$$u_{res} = \sqrt{(\Omega R)^2 \pm 2\Omega R \sin \alpha (b_1/b_2)u_\infty \sin \frac{(2v-1)\pi}{10} + (b_1/b_2)^2 u_\infty^2 \sin^2 \frac{(2v-1)\pi}{10}}, \tag{15}$$

where for the sections denoted by A the quantity $2\Omega R \sin\alpha (b_1/b_2)u_\infty \sin\frac{(2\nu-1)\pi}{10}$ is positive while for the sections denoted by B is negative. In the above equation Ω is the rotational velocity of the rotor, R is the rotor's radius, α is the angle of attack, b_1 is the external and b_2 is the internal cross section length between the guide vanes, u_∞ is the wind speed and ν is the number of each section, i.e., 1, 2, 3, 4 or 5.

Then, the aerodynamic forces of lift and drag that are exerted on the blades can be determined by Equations (16) and (17)

$$L = \frac{1}{2}c_l\rho_{air}u_{res}^2, \tag{16}$$

$$D = \frac{1}{2}c_d\rho_{air}u_{res}^2A, \tag{17}$$

where L is the lift, D is the Drag, c_l and c_d are the lift and drag coefficients respectively, ρ_{air} is the density of the air and A is the blade's area.

The resultant force, F, which is exerted on the blade and can be situated at any position is calculated by Equation (18)

$$F = \frac{1}{2}\rho_{air}u_{res}^2\sqrt{c_d^2+c_l^2}, \tag{18}$$

Then the aerodynamic torque can be estimated by Equation (19):

$$I = \frac{1}{2}\rho_{air}u_{res}^2\sqrt{c_d^2+c_l^2}R, \tag{19}$$

And finally the power output of each blade at each position is given by Equation (20):

$$P = \frac{1}{2}\rho_{air}u_{res}^2\sqrt{c_d^2+c_l^2}\Omega R \tag{20}$$

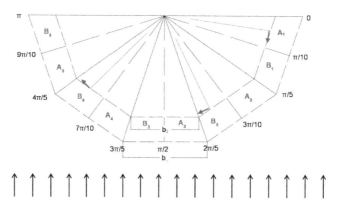

Figure 2. Analysis of the half top view of the stator, in order to calculate the magnitude of velocity inlet and the resultant velocity at various stator sections.

The above equations are solved by the imperative programming language FORTRAN (FORmulae TRANslator), which was originally developed for scientific and engineering applications. The resulting relationships have enabled easy parametric sizing, and so the investigation of the performance of KIONAS on the dimensions of both blades and guide vanes was conducted. Mathematical study is necessary in order to calculate the multi-stage KIONAS power output in less computational time and with less required computational memory compared to the Computational Fluid Dynamics study.

2.2. Computational Fluid Dynamics Study

The commercial Computational Fluid Dynamics code ANSYS Fluent [17] was used in order to show the flow field around the vertical axis wind turbine KIONAS. The first step in the simulation process is the design of the geometries of the various configurations of KIONAS in DesignModeler.

A C-type mesh was constructed; in particular KIONAS is surrounded by a semicircle and a horizontal parallelepiped. The semicircle consists of five parts defined as velocity inlets, with different velocity magnitudes depending on the relative position of the area between stator vanes and the maximum wind speed location. The rotor and the stator are defined as wall boundary conditions, the rear side as a pressure outlet and the remaining sides as symmetry.

First of all, simulations of the flow over the simplest geometry—that is, KIONAS with one stage—were conducted, in which the stator guide vanes are flat. The rotor blades are also flat plates and their inclination is 25° and 45°. After that, simulations were performed for the one-stage KIONAS, with the difference that the stator guide vanes are curved.

Finally, simulations of the flow were performed over the two-stage wind turbine KIONAS with curved stator guide vanes. This type of stator guide vane was found to be more effective and for that reason it was selected for the simulations. The rotor blades inclination was 25°, 30° and 35°. Figure 3 shows the rotor, the stator and the computational domain over the two-stage KIONAS.

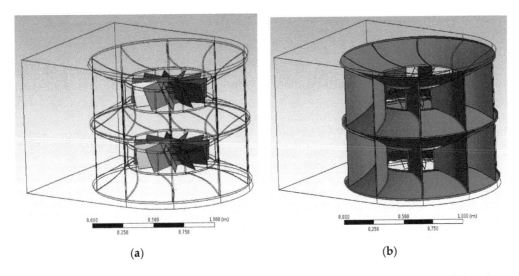

(a)   (b)

Figure 3. (a) Rotor; (b) stator of two-stage wind turbine KIONAS and computational domain.

The grid independence study revealed that a mesh of 1,412,500 cells for the one-stage KIONAS and of 2,825,000 cells for the two-stage KIONAS would be sufficient to establish a grid-independent solution. The mesh was denser near the wind turbine, where changes in the flow occur and thus greater computational accuracy is necessary.

The rotation was simulated by the Moving Reference Frame Model (MRF) [18], a steady-state approximation in which individual cell zones move at different rotational and/or translational speeds, and the most appropriate turbulence model for such simulations is the k-ω shear-stress transport (SST) [19]. In the MRF model, the rotor of KIONAS and the domain surrounding it were defined as a rotating reference frame, while the stator of KIONAS, in other words the flow outside the rotor region, was defined as a stationary frame.

3. Results and Discussion

3.1. Mathematical Results

This section summarizes the results obtained from the mathematical study. Figure 4 presents the total power at each blade's position for wind speeds of 5 m/s and 10 m/s and rotors with various numbers of blades. The results indicate that adding more blades results in higher values of total power for the wind speed that were tested. The results obtained from the analysis of rotors with 2 to 11 blades are summarized in Table 1. The results indicate that there is a significant positive correlation between the numbers of blades and the mean power output of KIONAS. Although most wind turbines achieve an optimized performance with a rotor which consists of three blades, there are plenty smaller scale turbines or at higher speeds, the efficiency of which increases by adding more blades. KIONAS is such a configuration of a vertical axis wind turbine, because not only it is a small scale wind turbine but also its rotor experiences high speeds as the wind velocity is accelerated when it passes through the stator that surrounds the rotor.

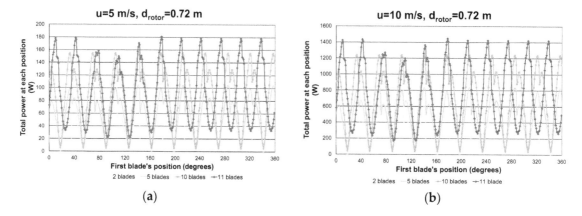

(a)   (b)

Figure 4. Total power at each blade's position for wind velocity (**a**) 5 m/s; (**b**) 10 m/s for various numbers of blades.

Table 1. Mean power output in Watts for wind speed of 5 m/s and 10 m/s for various numbers of blades.

	Wind Speed u = 5 m/s	Wind Speed u = 10 m/s
2 blades	32.9	263.6
3 blades	42.1	336.7
4 blades	50.3	402.1
5 blades	57.8	462.2
6 blades	64.8	440.3
7 blades	71.4	571.5
8 blades	77.8	622.1
9 blades	83.8	670.7
10 blades	89.7	717.6
11 blades	95.4	762.8

An estimation of the power output between KIONAS with blades made of galvanized sheet metal and KIONAS with blades made of aluminum is presented in Figure 5. The greater density of galvanized sheet metal, which means greater weight of the blades, results in lower rotational speed of the rotor and thus less power output.

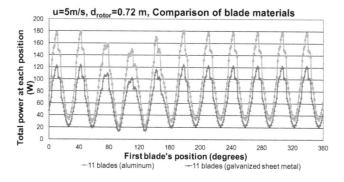

Figure 5. Total power at each blade's position, for eleven rotor blades made of aluminum or galvanized sheet metal.

Figure 6 demonstrates the total power at each blade's position for the same wind speeds and different rotor diameters. The rotor diameter is the diameter that occurs when the stator's diameter increases by 150% and 200%, while its width remains constant. From this data it is obvious that the power of KIONAS increases when increasing the rotor's number of blades and diameter.

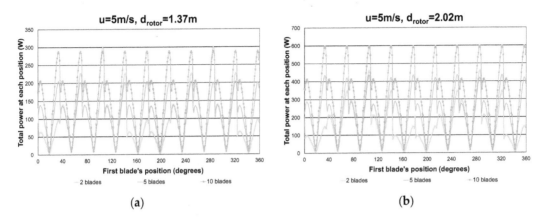

(a)   (b)

Figure 6. Total power at each blade's position for wind velocity 5 m/s, various numbers of blades and rotor's diameter (**a**) 1.37 m; (**b**) 2.02 m.

Table 2 compares the mean power output in Watts for wind speed equal to 5 m/s and the initial rotor diameter of 0.72 m and the new rotor diameters of 1.37 m and 2.02 m. It can be seen from the data that the mean power output of the wind turbine increases as the rotor diameter and number of blades increase.

Table 2. Mean power output in Watts for various rotor diameters and various numbers of blades.

	d_{rotor} = 0.72 m	d_{rotor} = 1.37 m	d_{rotor} = 2.02 m
2 blades	32.9	55.5	81.1
5 blades	57.8	93.5	132.4
10 blades	89.7	141.9	198.3

Figure 7 shows the total power at each blade's position for eleven blades with and without inclination, rotor blade angle of 25 degrees and wind velocity 5 m/s and 10 m/s. It is obvious that the power output is reduced by the inclination of the blades, because it was assumed that the inclined blade has greater length and thus greater weight, and that leads to lower rotational speed.

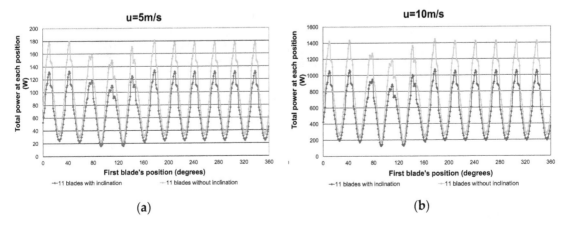

(a)   (b)

Figure 7. Total power at each blade's position for eleven rotor blades with 25° inclination and without inclination and wind velocity (**a**) 5 m/s; (**b**) 10 m/s.

To determine the effects of adding more stages, the total power of different KIONAS types is compared and the results are presented in Figure 8. The results are referred in wind velocity of 5 m/s and diameter of the rotor equal to 0.72 m. There was a significant positive correlation between total power and number of KIONAS stages. Further statistical tests revealed the exact percentage contribution of each stage in the total power of different KIONAS types and Figure 9 shows these results.

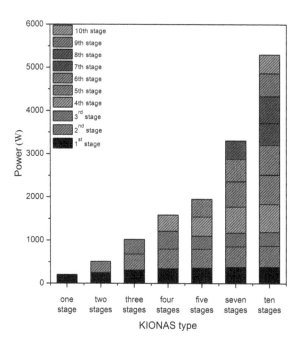

Figure 8. Total power output in Watts for various KIONAS types.

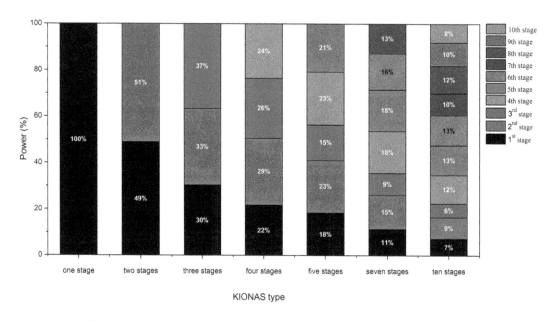

Figure 9. Each stage's contribution in the total power of each KIONAS type.

The percentage increase in power of each stage when it is placed in KIONAS, which has an extra stage, was also investigated and is presented in Figure 10. The most striking result to emerge from the data is that, for example, when the first stage is alone, it has a power of 200.1 W, but when it is placed in a two-stage KIONAS, the first stage power is 249.4 W; in other words, it increases 24.6%. Interestingly, if the first stage is placed in a ten-stage KIONAS, its increase is 91.4%.

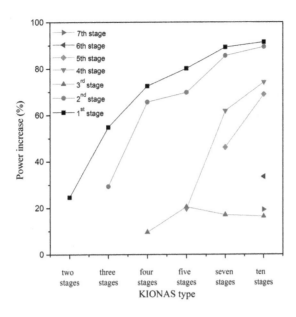

Figure 10. Each stage's increase in power by adding additional stages.

Figure 11 provides the power coefficient versus KIONAS weight and the power per weight unit for various KIONAS types. There is a clear trend of the power coefficient decreasing with KIONAS weight, due to the fact that the power coefficient is inversely proportional to the swept area, which increases by adding more stages because the surface between the stages is included too. Of particular interest is the correlation between power per KIONAS weight and KIONAS type, because despite the increase in the weight of the machine, which means an increase in the cost of construction, the power output is much higher, so a multi-stage KIONAS could become advantageous in the long term.

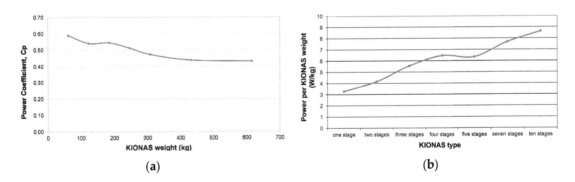

Figure 11. (a) Power coefficient vs KIONAS weight; (b) Power per weight for various KIONAS types.

3.2. Computational Fluid Dynamics Results

In this section, the results obtained from the Computational Fluid Dynamics are summarized. In Figures 12 and 13 the static pressure distribution on the rotor with rotor blades angles of 45° and 25°, respectively, and flat stator guide vanes, which was calculated by ANSYS Fluent, is presented. It is obvious that the contested surface of the rotor has higher values of static pressure and the rotor rotates due to this pressure difference. The values of static pressure on the rotor blades with inclination of 25° are higher than the corresponding values of inclination of 45°.

Simulation of the flow over a one-stage KIONAS with rotor blade angle of 25° and stator with curved guide vanes was also conducted and the results of the static pressure distribution on the rotor are presented in Figure 14. From the comparison between Figures 13 and 14, it is concluded that in the case of curved stator vanes, the static pressure is greater.

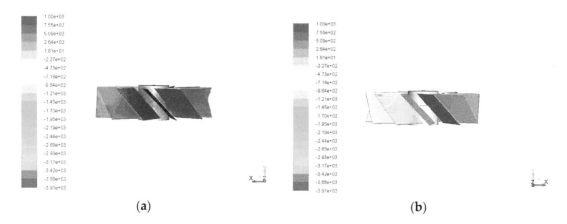

Figure 12. Static pressure (Pa) distribution (**a**) on the contested surface; (**b**) on the non-contested surface of a one-stage KIONAS, rotor blade angle of 45 degrees and stator with flat guide vanes.

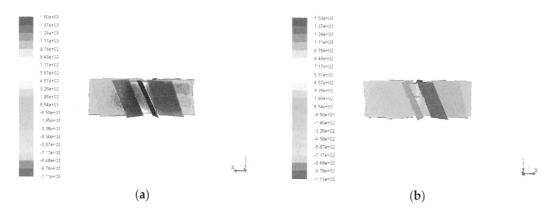

Figure 13. Static pressure (Pa) distribution (**a**) on the contested surface; (**b**) on the non-contested surface of one-stage KIONAS, rotor blade angle of 25 degrees and stator with flat guide vanes.

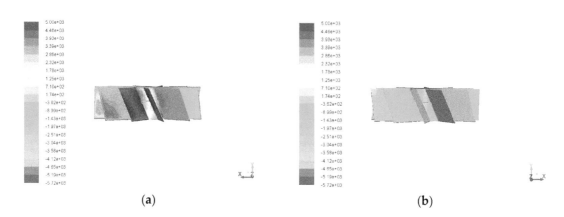

Figure 14. Static pressure (Pa) distribution (**a**) on the contested surface; (**b**) on the non-contested surface of one-stage KIONAS, rotor blade angle of 25 degrees and stator with curved guide vanes.

Figure 15 shows the static pressure distribution on the rotor with a rotor blade angle of 25° and stator with curved guide vanes of two-stage KIONAS. The static pressure is greater on the contested surface of the rotors and on the upper rotor. This result implies that the rotational velocity of the rotor which is located on the upper stage is greater, and thus the power of the upper stage is greater as well. This finding is consistent with Figure 9, where the power of the second stage of a two-stage KIONAS is greater than the power of the first stage.

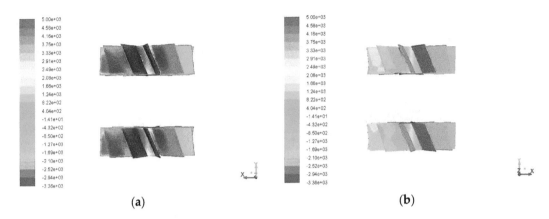

Figure 15. Static pressure (Pa) distribution (**a**) on the contested surface; (**b**) on the non-contested surface of two-stage KIONAS, rotor blade angle of 25 ° and stator with curved guide vanes.

From Figures 16–18 the velocity vectors and the contours of velocity for two-stage KIONAS, stator with curved guide vanes and rotor blade angle of 25°, 30° and 35° are illustrated. The most interesting finding from these Figures is that part of the wind is directed towards the top and towards the lower stage for all the cases that examined, and this move of air mass into KIONAS structure affects the power of each stage when it is placed in KIONAS with an extra stage.

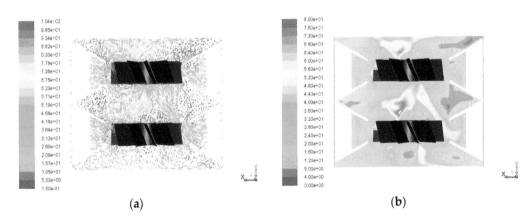

Figure 16. (**a**) Velocity vectors (m/s); (**b**) contours of velocity (m/s) on xy plane and the center of the rotor for two-stage KIONAS, rotor blade angle of 25° and stator with curved guide vanes.

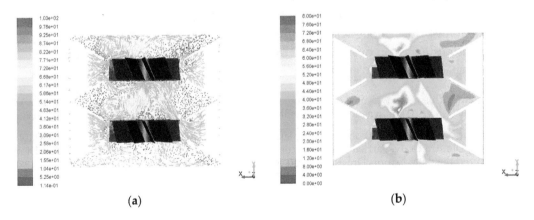

Figure 17. (**a**) Velocity vectors (m/s); (**b**) contours of velocity (m/s) on xy plane and the center of the rotor for two-stage KIONAS, rotor blade angle of 30° and stator with curved guide vanes.

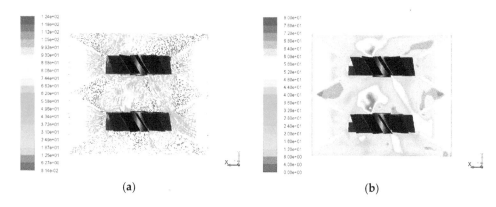

(a) (b)

Figure 18. (a) Velocity vectors (m/s); (b) contours of velocity (m/s) on xy plane and the center of the rotor for two-stage KIONAS, rotor blade angle of 35° and stator with curved guide vanes.

4. Conclusions

This project was undertaken to describe the design and evaluate the aerodynamic performance of the wind turbine KIONAS. This study/research has shown that the power output of the wind turbine increases as the diameter and the number of rotor blades increase. It was also shown that the power output for KIONAS with inclined blades is reduced, due to the increased mass of each blade when it has any inclination. Another major finding was that the curved guide vanes in the stator of KIONAS result in higher power.

The most significant findings to emerge from this study are not only that the power of each individual stage is increased when an extra stage is added but also that the output power per unit weight of the machine is higher as the number of KIONAS stages is increased. That means that a multi-stage KIONAS could become advantageous in the long term.

The results of the computational investigation show that the static pressure is greater in the contested surface of KIONAS and the pressure difference between the front and the rear side of the rotor is responsible for the rotor rotation. The velocity vectors for the two-stage KIONAS indicate that part of the wind is directed both towards the upper and towards the lower stage. Further experimental investigations would be of great help in assessing the actual attitude of KIONAS and this information would help to include more factors affecting the flow in the mathematical analysis.

The evidence from this study suggests that, in general, the present wind turbine cannot compete with the large structures that produce power in the range of 1, 2 and 3 MW, but is a major competitor with the smallest structures of the 5, 10 and 100 kW range. This power may vary with larger diameter dimensions, lighter material, but also with higher wind speeds, in order to cover the needs of individual houses or small settlements. A great benefit of KIONAS is the simple construction of both the guide vanes and the rotor blades, along with its compact shape which can easily be mounted in spaces of small dimensions either on buildings or between them, without creating problems in terms of adaptability in space or public acceptance.

Acknowledgments: This work was part of the project Evaluation and Optimization of Innovation of a Vertical Axis Wind Turbine (ABAKA) and was supported by BIG SOLAR S.A. member of the BITROS Group of Companies.

Author Contributions: Eleni Douvi conducted the simulations for the computational fluid dynamics study and wrote the paper; Dimitra Douvi carried out the mathematical study; Eleni Douvi, Dimitra Douvi and Dionissios Margaris analyzed the data; Ioannis Drosis invented the KIONAS vertical axis wind turbine.

References

1. Aslam Bhutta, M.M.; Hayat, N.; Farooq, A.U.; Ali, Z.; Jamil, S.R.; Hussain, Z. Vertical axis wind turbine—A review of various configurations and design techniques. *J. Renew. Substain. Energy Rev.* **2012**, *16*, 1926–1939. [CrossRef]

2. Tang, Z.; Yao, Y.; Zhou, L.; Yu, B. A review on the new structure of savonius wind turbines. *J. Adv. Mater. Res.* **2013**, *608–609*, 467–478. [CrossRef]

3. Ejiri, E.; Yabe, S.; Hase, S.; Ogiwara, M. Unsteady flow analysis of the vertical axis cross-flow wind turbine. In Proceedings of the ASME Fluids Engineering Division Summer Conference, Miami, FL, USA, 17–20 July 2006.

4. Takao, M.; Maeda, T.; Kamada, Y.; Oki, M.; Kuma, H. A straight-bladed vertical axis wind turbine with a directed guide vane row. In Proceedings of the 5th Joint ASME/JSME Fluids Engineering Summer Conference, San Diego, CA, USA, 30 July–8 August 2007.

5. Takao, M.; Takita, H.; Saito, Y.; Maeda, T.; Kamada, Y.; Toshimitsu, K. Experimental study of a straight-bladed vertical axis wind turbine with a directed guide vane row. In Proceedings of the 28th International Conference on Offshore Mechanics and Arctic Engineering—OMAE, Honolulu, HI, USA, 31 May–5 June 2009.

6. Shahizare, B.; Nik Ghazali, N.N.B.; Chong, W.T.; Tabatabaeikia, S.S.; Izadyar, N. Investigation of the optimal omni-direction-guide-vane design for vertical axis wind turbines based on unsteady flow CFD simulation. *J. Energies* **2016**, *9*, 1–25. [CrossRef]

7. Kim, D.; Gharib, M. Efficiency improvement of straight-bladed vertical-axis wind turbines with an upstream deflector. *J. Wind Eng. Ind. Aerodyn.* **2013**, *115*, 48–52. [CrossRef]

8. Korprasertsak, N.; Leephakpreeda, T. Analysis and Optimal Design of Wind Boosters for Vertical Axis Wind Turbines at Low Wind Speed. *J. Wind Eng. Ind. Aerodyn.* **2016**, *159*, 9–18. [CrossRef]

9. Wong, K.H.; Chong, W.T.; Yap, H.T.; Fazlizan, A.; Omar, W.Z.W.; Poh, S.C.; Hsiao, F.B. The design and flow simulation of a power-augmented shroud for urban wind turbine system. *J. Energy Procedia* **2014**, *61*, 1275–1278. [CrossRef]

10. Nobile, R.; Vahdati, M.; Barlow, J.F.; Mewburn-Crook, A. Unsteady flow simulation of a vertical axis augmented wind turbine: A two-dimensional study. *J. Wind Eng. Ind. Aerodyn.* **2014**, *125*, 168–179. [CrossRef]

11. Chen, T.Y.; Liao, Y.T.; Chen, Y.Y.; Liou, J.L. Application of a vortical stator assembly to augment the rotor performance of drag-type vertical-axis wind turbines. *J. Aeronaut. Astronaut. Aviat. Ser. A* **2015**, *47*, 75–84.

12. Chen, T.Y.; Chen, Y.Y. Developing a Vortical Stator Assembly to Improve the Performance of Drag-Type Vertical-Axis Wind Turbines. *J. Mech.* **2015**, *31*, 693–699. [CrossRef]

13. Pope, K.; Rodrigues, V.; Doyle, R.; Tsopelas, A.; Gravelsins, R.; Naterer, G.F.; Tsang, E. Effects of stator vanes on power coefficients of a zephyr vertical axis wind turbine. *J. Renew. Energy* **2010**, *35*, 1043–1051. [CrossRef]

14. Burlando, M.; Ricci, A.; Freda, A.; Repetto, M.P. Numerical and experimental methods to investigate the behaviour of vertical-axis wind turbines with stators. *J. Wind Eng. Ind. Aerodyn.* **2015**, *144*, 125–133. [CrossRef]

15. Chong, W.T.; Muzammil, W.K.; Fazlizan, A.; Hassan, M.R.; Taheri, H.; Gwani, M.; Kothari, H.; Poh, S.C. Urban Eco-Greenergy™ hybrid wind-solar photovoltaic energy system and its applications. *J. Precis. Eng.* **2015**, *16*, 1263–1268. [CrossRef]

16. Tong, C.W.; Zainon, M.Z.; Chew, P.S.; Kui, S.C.; Keong, W.S.; Chen, P.K. Innovative power-augmentation-guide-vane design of wind-solar hybrid renewable energy harvester for urban high rise application. In Proceedings of the 10th Asian International Conference on Fluid Machinery, Kuala Lumpur, Malaysia, 21–23 October 2010; pp. 507–521.

17. ANSYS® Academic Research, Release 16.0. Available online: http://www.ansys.com/ (accessed on 10 January 2017).

18. Luo, J.Y.; Issa, R.I.; Gosman, A.D. Prediction of Impeller-Induced Flows in Mixing Vessels Using Multiple Frames of Reference. In *IChemE Symposium Series*; The Institution of Chemical Engineers: Rugby, UK, 1994; pp. 549–556.

19. Menter, F.R. Two-Equation Eddy-Viscosity Turbulence Models for Engineering Applications. *AIAA J.* **1994**, *32*, 1598–1605. [CrossRef]

12

Critical Issues in Modelling Lymph Node Physiology

Dmitry Grebennikov [1,5], **Raoul van Loon** [2], **Mario Novkovic** [3], **Lucas Onder** [3], **Rostislav Savinkov** [4,5], **Igor Sazonov** [2], **Rufina Tretyakova** [4,5], **Daniel J. Watson** [2] **and Gennady Bocharov** [5,*]

[1]   Moscow Institute of Physics and Technology (State University), Dolgoprudny 141701 , Moscow Region, Russia; dmitry.ew@gmail.com

[2]   College of Engineering, Swansea University, Swansea SA2 8PP, Wales, UK; r.vanloon@swansea.ac.uk (R.v.L.); i.sazonov@swansea.ac.uk (I.S.); danieljwatson@me.com (D.J.W.)

[3]   Institute of Immunobiology, Kantonsspital St. Gallen, St. Gallen CH-9007, Switzerland; Mario.Novkovic@kssg.ch (M.N.); Lucas.Onder@kssg.ch (L.O.)

[4]   Lomonosov Moscow State University, Moscow 119991, Russia; dr.savinkov@gmail.com (R.S.); rufina3kova@gmail.com (R.T.)

[5]   Institute of Numerical Mathematics of the RAS, Moscow 119333, Russia

*   Correspondence: bocharov@m.inm.ras.ru

Academic Editor: Rainer Breitling

Abstract: In this study, we discuss critical issues in modelling the structure and function of lymph nodes (LNs), with emphasis on how LN physiology is related to its multi-scale structural organization. In addition to macroscopic domains such as B-cell follicles and the T cell zone, there are vascular networks which play a key role in the delivery of information to the inner parts of the LN, i.e., the conduit and blood microvascular networks. We propose object-oriented computational algorithms to model the 3D geometry of the fibroblastic reticular cell (FRC) network and the microvasculature. Assuming that a conduit cylinder is densely packed with collagen fibers, the computational flow study predicted that the diffusion should be a dominating process in mass transport than convective flow. The geometry models are used to analyze the lymph flow properties through the conduit network in unperturbed- and damaged states of the LN. The analysis predicts that elimination of up to 60%–90% of edges is required to stop the lymph flux. This result suggests a high degree of functional robustness of the network.

Keywords: computational model; lymph node; multiscale structure; vascular network; fibroblastic reticular cells; conduit network; lymph flow; destruction of conduits

1. Introduction

The immune system functions to protect the host against various pathogens and tumours. The mammalian immune system is a complex compartmentalized population of different types of humoral factors and cells organized as a body-wide network of interacting lymphoid organs, e.g., bone marrow, thymus, spleen, lymph nodes, gut. Its elements are connected by two vascular systems, i.e., the blood and the lymphatic systems, which enable the immune elements to migrate continuously to or from the compartments during their lifetime. Lymph nodes (LNs) represent the most numerous compartments of the immune system, in which soluble signals and cells are concentrated to enable efficient interaction between them. The structure of a LN is crucial to its function [1]. The development of anatomically correct mathematical models that accurately reproduce the physiological, cellular and molecular processes in LNs remain one of the major challenges for mathematical immunology.

Modelling the lymphatic system and in particular, the lymph flow through LNs is in its infancy [2]. There exist very few computational studies in which the fluid flow through the internal domains of LN was investigated [3,4]. The model is based on an idealized 3D geometry of the LN macro-structures and an approximation of the B-cell follicles, T cell paracortex and medulla as porous regions. The multi-physics description of the lymph flow processes combines the conservation of mass and momentum equations in subcapsular and medullary sinuses (fluidic region) with the conservation of mass and Darcy's law with Brinkman's term for the flow in porous regions. This study can be considered as a milestone for the application of computational fluid dynamics and the whole-organ fluorescent imaging technologies to model the LN physiology.

Lymph nodes are characterized by a highly variable histological appearance. This implies that the development of computational models of the LN structure and function requires (i) an idealization of the structure; (ii) the implementation of a modular approach; and (iii) the analysis of the performance of specific functional LN units in health and disease. The elements of the above framework can be found in [3–7].

LNs are known to present high resistance to lymph flow [3], which results from the internal structure of the LN body comprised of blood microvascular networks, the conduit networks and of domains densely packed with immune cells, i.e., the B cell follicles and T cell zone. In the existing 3D geometry LN models developed for studying the fluid flow, the conduit and blood vascular systems are not structurally described. Meantime, these elements, in particular the conduit system network ensheathed by fibroblastic reticular cell (reticular) network, represent a key system for the delivery of soluble molecules in the paracortex area of the LN. It was estimated in [3] that under normal conditions about 10% of lymph entering the LN through the afferent vessels takes a central path to reach the efferent vessel and high endothelial venules (HEV) via the conduit system and the inner domain of the LN. Under inflammatory conditions and during infections, the conductivity of the conduit system is likely to change dramatically [8], which affects the information delivery (cytokines, hormones, etc.) to the reactive parts of the LN. A fine and elaborate structure of the LN vascular systems requires the development of multi-scale computational models to comprehensively examine the fluid transport in LNs.

In this study we present an overview of the critical issues in modelling the structure and function of LNs and propose some approaches to model the networks of fibroblastic reticular cells, the blood microvasculature and analyze the flow properties of lymph through the conduit network in an unperturbed state and a damaged state with the varying degrees of destruction. We review the major structural elements of LNs in Section 2. The approaches to model the geometry of an a FRC network and the blood microvascular network are presented in Section 3. A fine resolution analysis of the lymph transport through a single conduit are presented in Section 4. The hydraulic conductivity properties of normal and disrupted conduit systems, modelled as 1D topologically equivalent networks are studied in Section 5. Numerical assessment of the percolation robustness of the fibroblastic reticular cell (FRC) network is predicted in Section 6. Further perspectives for application of computational fluid dynamics techniques are discussed in Section 7.

2. Major Structural Elements of a Paradigmatic Lymph Node

Lymph nodes (LNs) are specialized secondary lymphoid organs which are strategically situated at sites where pathogen invasion is likely to occur and where immune responses are induced and maintained [1]. The idealized LN structure can be divided in three major regions: the outer cortex containing the lymph-draining subcapsular sinus (SCS) and B cell follicles, the inner paracortex which constitutes the T cell zone and the medulla containing the efferent lymphatics. Each region contains specialized cellular niches which are critical for the development of adaptive immune responses [9]. B cell follicles are located underneath the SCS where B-cell specific responses take place [10], whilst the inner LN area constitutes the T cell zone where T cells are activated through interaction with antigen-presenting cells, such as dendritic cells (DCs) [11]. Fibroblastic reticular cells (FRCs) form a densely intertwined network that supports T-DC interactions, subsequently leading to generation of immune responses [12–14]. Furthermore, FRCs support lymphocyte migration, retention and survival through expression of chemokines CCL19 and CCL21 [15] and survival factor IL-7 [16,17]. FRCs secrete a basement membrane enwrapping the inner core of LN conduits which consist of collagen fibers and extracellular matrix (ECM) components. The conduit system drains lymph from the SCS through the entire LN T cell zone and the interstitial lymph flow accommodates small molecules and antigen that are <80 kDa in size. Some DCs are capable of extending their cell protrusions into the conduits, enabling them to sample the inner core for foreign antigens [18]. Apart from the lymphatic system in LNs, a specialized blood vascular system permeates through the LN T cell zone, forming high endothelial venules (HEVs) [8,19] which serve as extravasation points for migrating T, B cells and DCs into the LN [20]. Despite technical limitations in terms of rendering difficulties in the assessment of structural information from whole LNs, recent advances in imaging and computational techniques have enabled a comprehensive quantification of e.g., the LN blood vascular network [8,21].

The complexity of the immune system has been recognized in the recent decade as one of its key hallmarks, but also a major challenge for integrative immunological research [22]. Nevertheless, the development of high throughput "-omics" methods [23] and systems biology approaches [24] has made it possible to dissect the spatiotemporal interactions between immune system constituents and reveal functional implications in the context of various diseases. In order to fully utilize systems approaches, it is necessary to integrate available data across multiple biological scales, from lower level processes such as gene expression in different cell populations to higher level processes such as maintenance and regulation of tissue and organ functionality [25]. Finally, the complex dynamics of the immune system can be elaborated from the content-rich observations of these processes.

Increasing computer processing capabilities has made it feasible to design and generate a paradigmatic LN model based on real organ geometry [5]. Such a systems biology approach has allowed us to develop a generalized 3D solid model of the LN, which consists of the following idealized structures: SCS, B cell follicles, trabecular and medullar lymphatic sinuses, blood vasculature and HEVs, the T cell zone and FRC network. An integrated LN model across multiple scales will allow detailed description of global spatiotemporal dynamics of the different cell type interactions and enable us to identify biological parameters that are critical for generation and maintenance of immune responses.

3. Computational Models of FRC- and Blood Vascular Networks of Lymph Nodes

3.1. Cellular Potts Modelling of the FRC Network

In this section we construct a geometrical model of a reticular network using the Cellular Potts Model (CPM). This approach lets us explicitly control the target volume of reticular network, vary properties of each FRC, and directly incorporate the network in further models of cellular immune response. In addition, it is a starting point of modelling reticular network as soft tissue, which would let us explore mechanical properties and behavior of the network in cases of inflammation, T cells depletion or LN fibrosis.

In CPM (reviewed in [26–29]), the cells are defined on a cubic lattice as connected collections of lattice cites (voxels) $v = \{i, j, k\}$ with the same cell id $\sigma(v)$. Each cell can belong to a certain type $\tau(\sigma(v))$. The extracellular medium is defined as a generalized cell with $\sigma = \tau = 0$.

The dynamics of the system are defined with a modified Metropolis algorithm, which models the motion of cells by rearranging the states of the voxels in a stochastic energy minimization manner. It samples random local voxel-copy attempts and accepts them in accordance with provided Boltzman probability acception function $p(\sigma(v_{source}) \rightarrow \sigma(v_{target}))$.

The energy of the system is usually defined as the sum of two terms:

$$E = E_{adhesion} + E_{volume} = \sum_{\substack{\text{neighbors } v_1, v_2: \\ \sigma(v_1) \neq \sigma(v_2)}} J(\tau(\sigma(v_1)), \tau(\sigma(v_2))) + \sum_{\sigma} \lambda(\sigma) \left(V(\sigma) - V_{target}(\sigma)\right)^2 \quad (1)$$

Adhesion term represents the sum of binding energies $J(\tau(\sigma(v_1)), \tau(\sigma(v_2)))$ of molecules located at adjacent pairs of voxels v_1, v_2, which correspond to membranes of different cells $\sigma(v_1), \sigma(v_2)$. The second term describes the ability of the cell to constrain its volume $V(\sigma)$ near the resting volume $V_{target}(\sigma)$ due to the internal pressure. The parameter $\lambda(\sigma)$ is a spring modulus, i.e., the rigidity of the cell to changes of volume. It determines the relative weight of the second energetic term. There are many other possible terms and modifications of the form of energy, E, which allow the modelling of compressibility of cells membranes, chemotaxis, haptotaxis, cell elongation and other properties [26,27,29,30].

The basic form of the probability acceptance function in CPM is given as,

$$p(\sigma(v_{source}) \rightarrow \sigma(v_{target})) = \min\left\{1, \; \exp\left(-\frac{\Delta E}{T}\right)\right\}, \qquad (2)$$

where T is a global parameter representing the amplitude of cells fluctuations, proportional to the probability to accept energetically unfavourable voxel-copy attempts, $\Delta E = E_{after} - E_{before}$ is the change of energy of the system (1) as a result of sampled voxel-copy attempt. If $T = 0$, the simulation is fully determinate and can freeze at local energy minima. As a possible extension of (2), each cell type or each cell can have its own $T(\sigma)$.

The other form of acceptance function, which provides a biologically relevant meaning of parameter $T(\sigma)$—the intrinsic motility of the cell (discussed in detail in [29]), was specified as follows,

$$p(\sigma(v_{source}) \rightarrow \sigma(v_{target})) = \tanh(T_m) \cdot \min\left\{1, \; \exp\left(-\frac{\Delta E}{T_m}\right)\right\}, \qquad (3)$$

where

$$T_m = \begin{cases} T(\sigma(v_{source})), & if \; \sigma(v_{source}) \neq 0 \\ T(\sigma(v_{target})), & if \; \sigma(v_{source}) = 0 \end{cases}$$

is the resultant motility of membrane between $\sigma(v_{source}) \neq \sigma(v_{target})$. Given the tanh-mapping of membrane motility, Function (3) restricts the voxel-copy attempts involving so-called frozen cells (with $T(\sigma) \rightarrow 0$), even if calculated ΔE is significantly negative. This allows us to specify the motility of cells, i.e., their ability to react on external stimuli.

We extend this approach by setting intrinsic motility for each voxel of the cell. By doing this, we can easily model the reticular network, making the ends of protrusions frozen (forming FRC junctional complexes [31]). As a result, there is no need for extra assumptions and extra CPM plugins such as cell elongation or connectivity constraints (which are computationally expensive in 3D [30]), utilized in other models of cellular networks (such as in the study of vasculogenesis [30]).

We initialize cells as thin ($d \sim 1.0$ µm) cylinders along the graph of reticular network topology (constructed in [5]), forming the conduit system (Figure 1a). Protrusions of different cells are connected at the middles of the corresponding edges. For each FRC we define the center of its body $v_c(\sigma)$ at the coordinates of corresponding graph nodes. We define the motility of voxels occupied with cells ($v(\sigma)$) according to the distribution localized around $v_c(\sigma)$:

$$T(v(\sigma)) = T_{max} \cdot \exp\left(-\|v(\sigma) - v_c(\sigma)\|^2 / s^2\right) \qquad (4)$$

By doing this, the voxels, which are far from the center of FRC body $v_c(\sigma)$, have close to zero motility $T(v(\sigma)) \rightarrow 0$. As a result, the ends of FRCs protrusions are linked with each other in accordance with given topology and are not altered during the simulation, resulting in no connectivity issues. The voxels which are closer to centers $v_c(\sigma)$ have more intrinsic motility, thus it is more probable for them to extend to the medium due to internal pressure until the FRCs would reach their target volume $V_{target}(\sigma)$.

Figure 1b illustrates the reticular network, reached it's target volume (4% of the whole volume of lattice [5]). It contains 3374 FRCs in a 177.0 μm × 197.4 μm × 201.0 μm computational domain with $l_{px} = 0.3$ μm length of the voxel resolution. Parameters used in the simulation are listed in Table 1. We set adhesion energies to zero because they are not relevant for the result as there are no other cells in our model. The choice of FRC-FRC adhesion energy doesn't affect the simulation because FRC junctional complexes are modeled by freezing the ends of protrusions. A high value for lamda is chosen ($\lambda(\sigma) \gg 1$) because of rigidity of the reticular networks. The deviation of volume from the target volume for the whole network is less than 1% after 20 Monte-Carlo steps (MCSs) burn-in period.

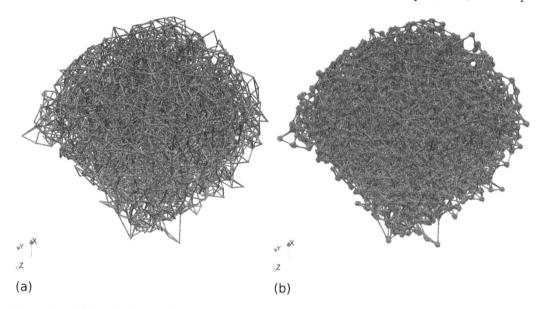

(a)   (b)

Figure 1. (a) The initialized reticular network as the system of conduits of given topology. State of the simulation at MCS = 0; (b) The reticular network reached its target volume. State of the simulation at MCS = 20.

Table 1. Parameters of Cellular Potts Model used to generate the reticular network (a.u.e. stands for arbitrary units of energy).

Parameter	Description	Value
l_{px}	length of the voxel	0.3 μm
$L_x \times L_y \times L_z$	sizes of computational domain	590 px × 658 px × 670 px
$d_{conduit}$	diameter of the conduits	1.0 μm
N_{FRCs}	number of FRCs in domain	3374
$N_{FRCs} V_{target}(FRC)/L^3$	volume fraction of reticular network	4%
$J_{i,j}$	adhesion energies	0 a.u.e.
λ_{FRC}	spring modulus of FRCs	10 a.u.e./px^6
T_{max}	amplitude of intrinsic motility	2 a.u.e.
$2s$	characteristic diameter of FRC body	12 px

The implementation of the model is based on the open-source CompuCell3D application (available at http://compucell3d.org/). We modified the source code of its core C++ library to accomplish voxel-based motility and developed Python scripts to configure the simulation. The computation of the FRC network shown in Figure 1 requires about 10 min real time on Intel Xeon 4-core 3 GHz CPU with 4 Threads based parallelization.

3.2. Modelling Blood Vascular Network

The vascular network of a lymph node is a rather complex construct and is placed inside the internal space of the LN with various items, such as B-cell follicles, FRC network, medullar and trabecular zones. The vascular network provides the delivery of oxygen, nutrients and signal molecules. Lymphatic fluid can leave the LN through the blood vessels due to a pressure difference, hydrostatic and osmotic, between the interstitial pressure in the node and the pressure in the blood vessels [2,3]. The vessels of the blood microvascular network have lots of close intersections with the FRC network, pervading the whole space inside LN, so the vascular network influencesshma many processes in the lymph node. In this way, construction of a 3D model of vascular network provides an insight into the role of the vascular network in processes of tissue homeostasis and pathology.

While constructing the vascular network, we had to solve some problems with intersections of the FRC network, vascular network and internal items of the an LN. The main challenge there was to overcome the differences between the typical sizes of the networks. An FRC network consists of conduits with a diameter range from 0.2 to 2 µm, while the vascular network contains vessels with a diameter range from 5 to 30 µm. We modified the algorithm from [7] to meet these conditions.

3.2.1. Initial Data

We used data from [21] to set the length of the network vessels.

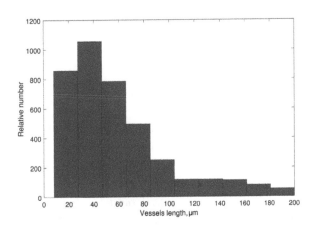

Figure 2. Blood vessels length distribution summarized from [21].

The blood microvascular system is characterized by the length distribution of the vessels as shown in Figure 2 and branch separation from the feeding vessel. The number of capillary vessels was taken from [21] as 40 vessels. It could be approximated as 3 vessels with 5 bifurcations (32 vessels) and 1 vessel with 6 bifurcations (64 vessels), the diameter of input and output vessels was taken as 8 µm.

3.3. Algorithm of Network Graph Generation

The algorithm of vessels network graph construction consists of three main steps:

Step 1. Graph topology organisation. In this step we generate the basis points and edges of connections.

Step 2. Local edge length optimization. In this step we use the algorithm from [7] just for a local (i.e., for neighbouring nodes) adjustment of the mismatch of the model and target graph edges lengths. In this and the next steps, the following parameter from Step 1 is used: **blos** (length of segmentation of the vessels). It's the canonical length of segments of the vessels graph.

Step 3. Global network structure optimization. In this step we use a modified algorithm from [7] for (i) minimization of the edge length deviation from the real data for all neighbouring nodes; (ii) pushing apart disconnected nodes from each other to prevent merger of the vessels; and (iii) shifting the nodes away from the prohibited domains associated with other LN structures.

Pseudocode of Step 1 (graph topology organisation):

```
   // Initialise the data arrays
1  set "length distribution" as real array ld;
2  set {5 5 5 6} as integer array bf;
   // Specify the segmentation accuracy, vessels radius and decreasing, processing zone size
3  set "initial input/output vessels diameter" as real vd;
4  set 4.0 as real blos; // length of segmentation of the vessels, µm
5  set 2^(1/2) as real rf; // coefficient of vessels radius decreasing
6  set "work sphere radius" as R; // simplify the constructing
7  set graph structure t;
   // Attach the input and output vessels
8  insert line "input vessel" and line "output vessel" to t; // simple lines, splitted into 100 segments
9  for (integer j = 1 to NC) begin
       // In this loop, we create new vessels, growing from input and output vessels
10     set real vdl = vd;
11     set real sl = random from ld;
12     sl = sl / blos;
13     set integer sc = sl;
14     sl = sl − sc;
15     if sl > 0.5 then sc = sc + 1;
       // sc defines the number of segments for current generating line
16     set point pin = random point from input vessel;
17     set point pout = random point from output vessel;
18     set point pm11 = random point from sphere with radius R;
19     set point pm12 = random point from sphere with radius R;
20     set point pm21 = random point from sphere with radius R;
21     set point pm22 = random point from sphere with radius R;
       // we used points pmXX to avoid helical structures while the second and
       // third parts of graph construction.
22     init line lx1 that goes from pin to pm12 through pm11 splitted into sc segments;
23     assign vdl as lx1 diameter;
24     insert line lx1 to t;
25     init line lx2 that goes from pout to pm22 through pm21 splitted into sc segments;
26     assign vdl as lx2 diameter;
27     insert line lx2 to t;
28     execute code lines from 18 to 27;
29     integer nbf = random from bf;
30     for (integer i = 1 to nbf) begin
           // In this cycle in each loop we create two sub-vessels for each
           // couple [lx1, lx2], created while previous loop
31         set real vdl = vd/rf^i;
32         set pm12 from lx1 as point pin;
33         set pm22 from lx2 as point pout;
34         if(i < nbf) then execute code lines from 11 to 15, from 18 to 26;
35         if(i = nbf) then begin
               // here we connect the inner and outer parts of vessel
36             execute code lines from 11 to 15;
37             set point pm1 = random point from sphere with radius R;
38             set point pm2 = random point from sphere with radius R;
39             set point pm3 = random point from sphere with radius R;
```

40   *init line* **lx1** *that goes from* **pin** *to* **pout** *through* **pm1, pm2, pm3** *splitted into* **sc** *segments;*

41   *assign* **vdl** *as* **lx1** *diameter;*

42   *insert line* **lx1** *to* **t**;

43   *end*

44   *execute code lines from 34 to 43;*

        // Note : inside cycle for all i > 1 **pm12, pm22** *should be used from previous loop of cycle.*

45   *end*

46 *end*

To avoid the occurence of intersections with internal items of the LN , we attached a set of static points, created via the voxel approximation of the internal items of the LN. Unfortunately, it works only for convex structures, such as B-cell follicles.

The blood microvascular network generated using the developed algorithm is shown in Figure 3.

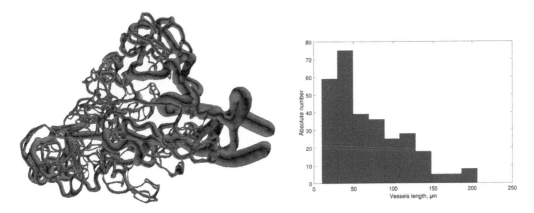

Figure 3. **(left)** An artificially generated 3D blood vessel network (for a sphere with a diameter of about 200 μm); **(right)** Vessels length distribution of the computationally constructed blood microvascular model.

3.4. Integrative Geometric Model of Vascular Networks

To assemble the two networks [FRC + vascular networks] into one 3D geometric model, we used the FRC network constructed with the algorithm from [7] for a sphere with a diameter of about 200 μm as shown in Figure 4.

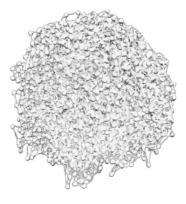

Figure 4. FRC network 3D model (for sphere with a diameter of about 200 μm).

The graph of the network topology and its node-level characteristics are shown in Figure 5.

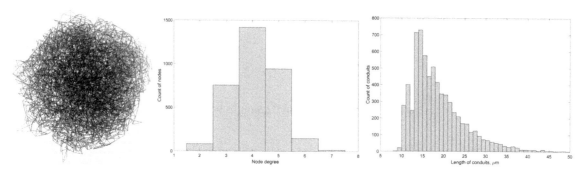

Figure 5. FRC network. (**left**) Network graph; (**center**) Node degree distribution; (**right**) Edges lengths distribution.

The method developed in [7] was further utilized to place two or more network graphs in same domain.

To this end, we placed both graph structures in one structure, unified the length of all edges (we converted them into sets of edges with length about 4 μm) and executed the minimisation of length inconsistencies using a modified version of the algorithm from [7]. Some remaining intersections were removed at the stage of voxel-based approximation of the graphs. The integrated blood microvascular network and the FRC networks are shown in Figure 6.

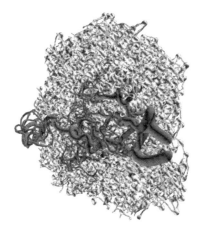

Figure 6. Integrated model of vascular vessels and FRC network (for a sphere of about 200 μm).

The key characteristics of the constructed 3D blood microvascular and FRC network geometric model are listed in Table 2.

Table 2. Constructed 3D models characteristics.

	FRCn	Vascular Network
Surface area	1,131,209 μm^2	61,264 μm^2
Relative volume	7.98%	1.71%

All the algorithms were implemented using C++ language and Microsoft Visual Studio 2015 IDE. Construction of the vascular graph takes about 10 min and 20 Mb of RAM (CPU - Intel Core i7-4700HQ 2.40 GHz), integration of the blood vascular vessels and FRC network takes 20 min, and additional operations (voxel approximation, smoothing of the 3D surface) requires about 2 h CPU time.

4. Lymph Dynamics in Conduit Elements of FRC Network

In this section we examine generic conduit and the FRC network properties.

4.1. Transport Through a Single Conduit

FRC network conduits consist of reticular fibres arranged in bundles encased by FRCs [31]. These conduits have been observed with radii between 200 nm and 3 μm [32], consisting of 10–100 reticular fibres [33] with radii of 20–40 nm [34]. Microscopy of FRC conduits appear to show that the fibres are densely packed [33]. Lagrange found the optimal packing of cylinders is hexagonal with a maximum fibre density of $\phi = \frac{\pi}{2\sqrt{3}}$. There is some justification for the assumption that FRC conduits consist of reticular fibres arranged in such a manner. As the FRCs hold the fibres together it is likely that they exert a force on the fibres pushing them close to one another. The above numbers would suggest that a 200 nm radius conduit would have between 7 and 29 fibres which would appear to approximately agree with values found in literature [33]. A diagram showing the paths between fibres available for flow and the arrangement of the fibres is shown below in Figure 7.

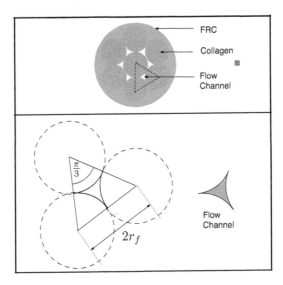

Figure 7. Diagram showing the packaged bed model of an FRC conduit. Reticular fibres are hexagonally close packed and encased in FRCs. r_f is the radius of the fibres.

The cross section of the path available for flow between three fibres is bound by three $\frac{\pi}{3}$ arcs together forming the flow boundary, Γ. The area of the section bound by the fibres is the flow domain, Ω. The area of this domain, A_p, can be found by subtracting the area of the circular sections from the area of the triangle shown in Figure 7.

$$A_p = r_f^2 \left(\sqrt{3} - \frac{\pi}{2} \right) \tag{5}$$

The Navier-Stokes equation for incompressible, steady-state, unidirectional flow of a Newtonian fluid reduces to a Poisson equation and can be written as below.

$$\nabla^2 u = \frac{p_z}{\mu} \tag{6}$$

where u is the velocity, μ the viscosity and p_z is the z axis component of the pressure gradient. Using a finite element solver with a no-slip boundary condition $u(\Gamma) = 0$. An area independent flow parameter, χ, is defined as follows,

$$\chi = \frac{A_p^2}{Q} \frac{p_z}{\mu} \tag{7}$$

A finite element solver was used the find χ for curvilinear triangular domains such as Ω. The area independence of χ was verified and a convergence study performed, the results are tabulated below as presented in Figure 8, left. The computed velocity profile of flow through a curvilinear triangle with area A_p is shown in Figure 8, right.

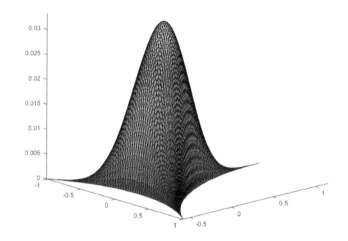

Degree of Freedom	χ
16	49.4300
64	50.1578
256	49.8887
1024	49.7000
4096	49.7130

Figure 8. (left) Table of area independent parameter χ against degrees of freedom in the FEA model; **(right)** Numerically computed velocity profile of flow through a curvilinear triangle with area A_p.

A rearrangement of Equation (7) gives the flow in one of the Ω domains for a given pressure gradient in the form $QR = p_z$ with R defined as ,

$$R = \frac{\chi \mu}{A_p^2} \tag{8}$$

Based on the values found for χ it is observed that the resistance value found for flow through a curvilinear triangular cross-section is twice that through a circular cross-section of the same area. The total resistance, R_{tot}, for a conduit containing multiple fibrils is the reciprocal of the sum of the reciprocal individual resistances provided that $r_c >> r_f$. This leads to $R_{tot} = R/n$, where n is the number of fibres.

4.2. Diffusive Transport in an FRC Conduit

At scales such as these diffusive mass transport can be considerably more significant than fluid flow. The geometry of the channels seems that it will produce large viscous losses whilst still retaining a large cross-sectional area available for transport. Assuming ideal mixtures a relationship (Fick's law) can be constructed for mass diffusion within the conduits in a similar manner,

$$-\mathcal{N} \frac{l}{DA} = \Delta C \tag{9}$$

where ΔC is the difference in molar concentration, $\mathcal{N}$ is the molar flux and D is the diffusivity. Now if we assume a 300 μm long pipe spanning a lymph node with a pressure difference of 6 cm H_2O and a viscosity of 1.5 cp [35] then the Péclet number in a conduit is 0.0388—for diphtheria toxin, see below—suggesting its motion is diffusion dominated. Thus it is reasonable to assume the flow will have an insignificant effect on the concentration of diphtheria toxin allowing these two transport phenomena to be decoupled.

Instead of a 3D fluid solver operating on a void space of the network, a 0D solver can operate on the connectivity and associated properties of the network with a considerable reduction in computational expense. Such a solver was implemented in MATLAB® and a cuboid block of a generated FRC network consisting of 6927 edges and 3374 nodes was subjected to analysis. Contiguous nodes were made co-planar to give a domain of known dimensions, $151 \times 193 \times 187$ µm. Pressure or concentration gradients were placed across the block, a linear system formed and solved for the fluid permeability or diffusive flux using a direct solver. One species often considered in lymphatics is diphtheria toxin with a diffusivity $D = 6.2 \times 10^{-7}$ cm/s [36] and a molecular weight of 58 kDa [37]. For the network under consideration a 2 ng/g imposed gradient across the first axis of the network gave a diffusive flux of 2.68 µg/s. Whilst for an imposed pressure gradient of 6 cm H_2O gives a fluid flux of 0.0214 µm³/s. The fluid flux would have to be ~10 orders higher to have a similar contribution to mass transport as diffusion.

5. Modelling Lymph Flow in Conduit System of FRC Network in Idealized LN

5.1. Normal FRC Network

In order to simulate a steady-state lymph flow in a conduit system of the FRC network model in an idealized LN designed in [7], we applied Poiseuille law as well as mass conservation law. Let's consider the graph of conduit network shown in Figure 4 and denote set of vertices and edges $\mathbf{G} = (\mathbf{V}, \mathbf{E})$. For each edge $e_{ij} \in \mathbf{E}$ we apply the Poiseuille equation and for each vertex $v_i \in V$ we apply the mass conservation law $(i, j = 1, 3694)$.

$$Q_{ij} = \frac{1}{R_{ij}} (P_i - P_j) \qquad \sum_{k_i : ik_i \in \mathbf{E}} Q_{ik_i} = 0 \qquad (10)$$

The variables are the lymph flow Q_{ij} ((µm)³/s), the hydraulic pressure P_i (Pa) and hydraulic resistance, R_{ij}. According the Poiseuille equation, hydraulic resistance for non-elastic tubes is the following: $R = \frac{8\mu l}{\pi r^4}$ The parameter $\mu = 0.0015$ Pa·s is the lymph dynamic viscosity [35]. The radii r_{ij} of all channels are assumed to have a constant value of 1 µm. Channel lengths l_{ij} can be calculated from graph data shown in Figure 4. If we take into consideration reticular fibres densely packed in conduits and use hydraulic resistance defined in Equation (8), the flow through the system will be about 7 orders lower.

$$\frac{Q_{fibres}}{Q_{tube}} = \frac{R_{tube}}{R_{fibres}} = \frac{8\mu / \pi r_c^4}{\mu \chi / (\sqrt{3} - \frac{\pi}{2})^2 r_f^4} \simeq 1.33 \times 10^{-7} \qquad (11)$$

The system (10) needs to be closed by setting boundary conditions. The conduit network is connected to the floor of the subcapsular sinus. In our model implementation, the nodes located at the border of the FRC network graph are connected to the SCS by additional edges. The flow through the system depends on pressures in these vessels. There is no experimental data on the pressure distribution in the SCS. In this study we consider two variants of pressure distribution (see Figure 9). If we set the x-axis in the direction of flow through the LN then boundary vertices with smaller x-coordinate will have higher pressure values. The first variant of pressure distribution is called «Gradient» with a linear decline from $P_{max} = 500$ Pa to $P_{min} = 0$ Pa depending on x-coordinate. The pressure estimates are based on values reported in [3,4,38]. The second variant is referred by term «Constant». If we set a plane normal to the x-axis dividing the LN into two halves of equal length, points in the upper half will have a value of P_{max} and points in the lower half will have P_{min}.

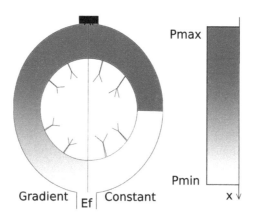

Figure 9. Schematic view of the SCS pressure distribution for two types of pressure boundary conditions (1) gradient and (2) constant. Branches emanating from the inner SCS circle represent the input and output edges of the network.

Having specified the boundary conditions, we build a linear system, excluding the flow variables from Equation (10), and solve it for pressure. The system matrix is sparse but nonsingular so we use UMFPACK solver [39] which provides a direct method for linear sparse systems. The following results have been calculated using the UMFPACK direct method. The inflow and outflow were tested to be equal, the conservation of mass condition is satisfied. A network consisted of 3694 vertices and 7253 edges with the number of input and output vertices 169 to 151 in the gradient case, and 164 to 156 in the constant case.

Figure 10 demonstrates the change of pressure with growth of distance from the afferent lymphatic vessel for all vertices with different boundary conditions. In case of the gradient boundary condition (Figure 10, left) there is an evident linear gradient with a line of boundary points from which others deviate slightly. In case of the constant boundary condition (Figure 10, right) the pressure gradient is obviously higher, but still the pattern is close to linear.

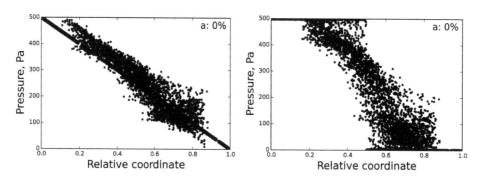

Figure 10. Pressure values depending on coordinate. (**left**) for gradient boundary conditions; (**right**) for constant boundary conditions. Boundary points are highlighted in red.

5.2. Disrupted FRC Network

Viral infections suffered by the immune system can destroy parts of the FRC network and lead to its disruption [8,14]. We applied the model of lymph flow in the conduit system to parameterize the destruction process and study its effect on lymphatic system function. To simulate a disrupted conduit system we delete edges from **E** randomly. If all edges connected to a node are deleted it becomes isolated, with zero pressure. Deletion of edges also leads to broken chains and pendant (or leaf) vertices. Mass conservation law implies that there is no flow into pendant vertex and no flow through broken chains. Some edges which are not removed may have no flow and so disfunction, we call these edges non-functional («n-f edges»). For example, in Figure 11 illustrating the disruption elements vertices 2 and 3 are pendant, edges (1–2) and (3–8) are non-functional, vertex 6—isolated.

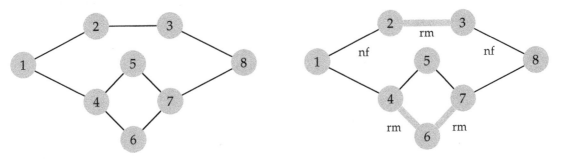

Figure 11. Scheme of network edges deletion from graph. (**left**) Normal network structure; (**right**) Randomly removed (rm) edges are marked in pink and non-functional ones are indicated as (nf).

Degradation of the FRC network through the edge removal is depicted in Table 3 (for constant boundary conditions) and in Table 4 (for gradient boundary conditions). The damage percentage in Tables 3 and 4 is equal to the ratio of removed edges to its original number. We calculated the number of inputs and outputs with nonzero inflow and outflow (inputs and outputs are boundary nodes through which lymph flows in and out of the LN). In the tables only non-isolated nodes are counted, that's why the number of vertices, inputs and outputs decreases. We also calculated the summary flow out of the LN (equal to the flow into the LN) and total flow through all system channels. In the tables we show a fraction of flow through the damaged system to the flow through initial undamaged system.

The results depicted in Tables 3 and 4 reveal the following difference in the output of the flow for two types of pressure boundary conditions. In case of constant boundary condition total flow and outflow are higher, but the degradation rate is high as well. For gradient boundary conditions the flow continues even if 90% of system is destroyed. Pressure gradient on two neighbour boundary nodes allows a small flow between them, and it is not defined whether the boundary vertex is input or output. When 60% of the edges are removed the upper and lower halves of system loose their connectivity, but some small connected components remain. That's why there are less non-functional edges and more inputs and outputs in the «gradient» case than in «constant» case.

Table 3. System degradation for constant boundary conditions.

Damage (%)	Nodes	Edges	n-f Edges	Inputs	Outputs	Relative Outflow	Relative Sum. Flow
0	3694	7253	0	164	156	1.0	1.0
10	3671	6528	29	156	147	0.82	0.84
20	3608	5802	108	143	132	0.615	0.653
30	3454	5077	1792	117	105	0.414	0.386
40	3135	4352	2138	94	78	0.16	0.149
50	2713	3626	2365	55	89	0.044	0.019
60	2202	2901	2443	16	85	0.0	0.0

Table 4. System degradation for gradient boundary conditions.

Damage (%)	Nodes	Edges	n-f Edges	Inputs	Outputs	Relative Outflow	Relative Sum. Flow
0	3694	7253	0	169	151	1.0	1.0
10	3671	6528	27	157	146	0.854	0.845
20	3608	5802	110	140	135	0.678	0.66
30	3454	5077	226	109	113	0.49	0.398
40	3135	4352	346	85	87	0.33	0.23
50	2713	3626	454	68	76	0.26	0.149
60	2202	2901	599	46	55	0.185	0.095
70	1623	2176	512	34	41	0.135	0.074
80	1062	1451	254	13	25	0.072	0.039
90	513	725	76	5	13	0.028	0.013

Figures 12 and 13 demonstrate the difference of pressure-coordinate dependance for graphs with consequently removed edges (pressure in isolated nodes is zero).

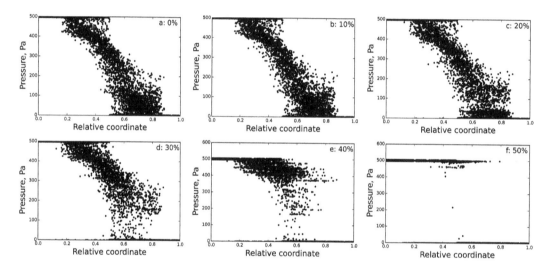

Figure 12. Pressure gradient for (**a–f**) 0%–50% edges removed (constant boundary conditions). Boundary points are highlighted in red.

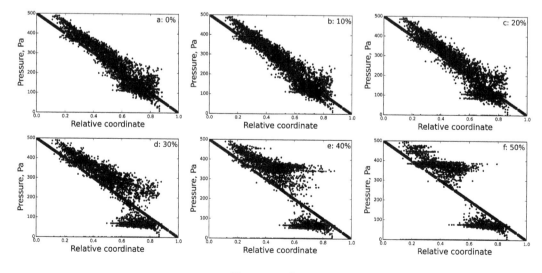

Figure 13. *Cont.*

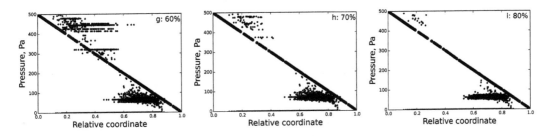

Figure 13. Pressure gradient for (**a–i**) 0%–80% edges removed (gradient boundary conditions). Boundary points are highlighted in red.

6. Percolation Robustness of the FRC Network

6.1. Graph Measures

From graph theory there are several observations and quantitative metrics that can be made of an FRC network that imply aspects of its function. Firstly, hierarchy, which can be defined as the imbalance between the number of nodes of a low degree and the number of nodes of a high degree. A network can have more lower degree nodes than higher degree nodes by adopting "hub and spoke" features where some higher degree "hub" nodes connect to many lower degree nodes. This is indicative of a scale-free network where the degree distribution is approximately that of a power law [40]. Currently, studies of FRC networks have found a Gaussian degree distribution indicating an absence of "hubs". A more formal definition can be used to explore this through two numbers; the mean local clustering coefficient, $\bar{C}$, as defined by Watts-Strogatz and the mean shortest path length $\bar{L}$. C_i can be defined for each node, i, by the number of neighbours of i, $N(i)$, which are also neighbours of each other, $|N(i) \cap N(N(i))|$ and the total number of neighbours, $k(i)$ [41].

$$C_i = \frac{|N(i) \cap N(N(i))|}{k(i)(k(i) - 1)} \tag{12}$$

We can now define $\bar{C}$ as the average of C for all i, i.e., the average occupancy of connections between neighbours. If $L(i, j)$ can be defined as the shortest possible path between two nodes i, j. Then $\bar{L}$ can be defined as,

$$\bar{L} = \frac{1}{n(n-1)} \sum_{i}^{n} \sum_{j \neq i}^{n} L(i, j) \tag{13}$$

where n is the number of nodes in the network. In lattice type networks the mean shortest path length is relatively long compared to random networks as is the clustering coefficient. Small-world networks are defined by their small mean shortest path length whilst still maintaining the high clustering coefficient of a lattice. In order to compare networks dimensionless forms of these numbers are defined.

$$\hat{C} = \frac{\bar{C}}{\overline{C_{ER}}} \quad \text{and} \quad \hat{L} = \frac{\bar{L}}{\overline{L_{ER}}} \tag{14}$$

where the $\overline{L_{ER}}$ and $\overline{C_{ER}}$ forms of $\bar{L}$ and $\bar{C}$ are the quantities calculated on an equivalent Erdös-Rényi random networks. Erdös-Rényi equivalent random networks have the same number of edges on the same vertices, as the network, but with edges having an equal probability of existance between all vertices. From this the small-worldness quantity, σ can be defined as the ratio of the two [41].

$$\sigma = \frac{\hat{C}}{\hat{L}} \tag{15}$$

For the network under consideration the quantities are as follows: $\hat{C} = 67.87$, $\hat{L} = 0.817 \pm 0.0605$ and $\sigma = 83.1 \pm 6.19$. The values suggest that this network has a similar mean shortest path length to a random network but a much greater degree of clustering giving a large small-worldness value indicative of a small-world type network. Analysis of actual FRC networks have shown average small-worldness values of 6.128 across 6 mice [14]. This is of particular relevance to FRC networks given their hypothesised role in maintaining chemokine gradients. A small-world network would be more likely to reduce gradients by spatially homogenising at "hubs" which will connect to a large number of "spokes". Maintenance of gradients between these spokes will be impeded by the "hub" compared to a lattice type network were in the absence of "hubs", a regular structure would exist between the "spokes". More complex gradients can exist across this regular structure than across a "hub", anode with a singular value. A greater understanding of the FRC network and the spatial variance of these quantities could allow more representative FRC networks to be generated.

6.2. Percolation Threshold

If each bond within a network has a probability, p, that it exists then the percolation threshold, p_c, is the value for p below which a spanning tree cannot exist. That is the point at which the networks connectivity is sufficiently damaged that it is not possible to move across the network. At this point the largest spanning tree remaining is a fractal object which scales with the total size of the network according to a power law [42].

The percolation threshold for this network was found to be 0.32 with a standard deviation of 0.0825 which is close to the p_c of a face centred cubic, 0.119. The network under consideration was subjected to a flow solver as described in Section 4.2 in order to study how fluxes change as $p \to p_c$. For each case the flux across the network was calculated, after which an edge was removed. This process was repeated until the flux was zero. 100 cases were run and the range and standard deviation for relative change in flux are shown below in Figure 14.

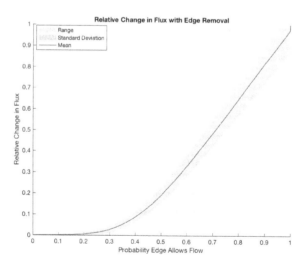

Figure 14. The change in flux as $p \to p_c$.

As both viscous and diffusive effects have the same dependance on length the relationship shown in Figure 14 is true of both diffusion and fluid flux. The high p_c suggests a high degree of topological robustness within the network implying a large difference in the importance of edges to maintenance of flow. The range indicates the minimum and maximum relative fluxes recorded at a given probability. Note that fluxes far below the standard deviation exist for all $p > 0$, which suggests that some edges are of considerable importance to flow. Verifying the existence of these properties in nature and correctly replicating them in artificial networks will be challenging.

7. Discussion

In this study, we developed computational algorithms for modelling the geometry of two transport systems of the LN, i.e., the FRC network and the microvascular network. The first one provides the structure for lymph flow through the internal parts of the LN as well as cell migration. The blood vascular networks provide access for lymphocytes from the circulation to the LN parenchyma. As the remodelling of the networks takes place during infections, it is important to map the dynamic structure of the networks to their function in terms of cellular and information molecules (cytokines, antigens, etc.) transport and distribution within the LN. The application of experimental imaging of internal LN structures is limited in humans. Therefore, computational modeling provides the tools for predicting the relationships between geometric and topological properties of the networks as well as on their performance under homeostatic and pathological conditions.

Capturing the 3-dimensional organization of LNs presents a challenge for existing imaging and analysis systems [21]. Recent studies provide basic information about geometrical and topological properties of the LN vascular systems. We used the data on organ-wide 3D-imaging of the microvascular network in murine LNs [21] to develop a voxel-based algorithm for 3D geometric modelling of the LN blood vascular network consistently with the data on blood vessels length distribution. A Cellular Potts Modelling framework was used to develop the FRC network model meeting the constraints on the volume and properties of FRCs. The blood microvascular- and the FRC network models were embedded into the SCS of the LN modeled as a sphere with the diameter about 200 μm. Taking together these two transport modules can be used to build up structurally complete computational models of the LNs as compared to those presented in [3,4,6]

To our knowledge, this is the first study in which the lymph flow through the conduit network was studied under a range of physiological conditions. The FRC network can be severely destroyed during viral infection leading to immune deficiency [8]. It has been shown recently that an FRC network can tolerate a loss of approximately 50% of their FRCs without substantial impairment of immune cell recruitment, intranodal T cell migration, and dendritic cell-mediated activation of antiviral $CD8^+$ T cells [14]. To evaluate the robustness of the conduit system in terms of the lymph percolation parameter, we have examined the lymph flow through the conduit network for an idealized geometry and under specified boundary conditions. The model based on a steady state Poiseuille equation predicts that the elimination of up to 60%–90% of edges is required to stop the lymph flux. This result suggests a high degree of the functional robustness of the network. We consider an idealised lymph node.

The conduits comprise of collagen fibers rather than being idealized empty cylinders [33]. We examined the impact of the presence of internal collagen fibers in the conduits on the resistance to fluid flow. Calculations, based on values in the literature of fibre size, conduit size and the typical number of fibres observed, seem to confirm that the collagen fibres inside the conduit are densely packed. This would suggest that the FRCs wrap themselves tightly around the collagen fibers. For a scenario of a conduit cylinder densely packed with collagen fibers, the computational flow study suggests that the diffusion would be the dominating process in mass transport as opposed to convective flow. These predictions warrant further experimental analysis. In addition, a more detailed analysis of our artificially generated FRC network showed that this network has a similar mean shortest path length to a random network but a much greater degree of clustering giving a large small-worldness value indicative of a small-world type network, which is qualitatively but not quantitatively matching to what was found experimentally [14].

In our study, we were interested in assessing the small-worldness property of the model network graph embedded into metric space, i.e., having realistic edge lengths distribution according to the real FRC network data. To this end we evaluated the shortest path length to be a real physical path length. Earlier, in [41] it was shown that the small-world parameter scales linearly with network size, for both model and real-world networks. The estimate of small-worldness parameter $\sigma = 6.128$ for murine FRC network data is based on the observed FRC network in T cell zone with about 170 nodes. In the model network for the entire lymph node the number of nodes is 3374, i.e., about 20-fold larger. The increase in the network size (the number of nodes) results in a proportional increase in the value small-world parameter, i.e., up to 83.1, consistently with the demonstration of the above cited study. These differences and their implications for flow and transport require further investigation. Finally, in an earlier study [43] it has been shown that fluid flow in turn regulates the reticular cell network, suggesting that models of the LN fluid homeostasis should consider elaborate feedbacks. LNs are characterized by complex multi-scale structures which represent critical issues in computational modelling of the LN physiology. Here we presented a consistent approach to integrating the blood microvascular- and the conduit network models within a confined space of the LN that will be used to study how the lymph-borne information is distributed to various parts of the lymph node under normal conditions and during an immune response. Further analysis should focus on studying the fluid-structure interactions for the vascular systems in conjunction with the cellular and chemical reactions taking place in live LNs. Finally, as it was stressed by W.E. Paul [44] "...It is to the quantitative prediction of the outcome of given perturbations in the immune system that we envisage our mathematical/modeling colleagues will apply themselves".

Acknowledgments: The research was funded by the Russian Science Foundation (Grants 14-31-00024 and 15-11-00029 (Section 3.1)).

Author Contributions: Conceived and designed the study: R.v.L., I.S., G.B.; Performed the wet experiments and analyzed the data: M.N., L.O.; Developed the models and performed the computations: D.G. (Section 3.1), R.S. (Section 3.2), R.T. (Section 5), R.v.L., I.S., D.W. (Sections 4 and 6); Wrote the paper D.G., R.v.L., M.N., R.S., I.S., R.T., D.W., G.B.

Abbreviations

The following abbreviations are used in this manuscript:

FRC   Fibroblastic reticular cell
SCS   Subcapsular sinus
LN   lymph node

References

1.   Junt, T.; Scandella, E.; Ludewig, B. Form follows function: Lymphoid tissue microarchitecture in antimicrobial immune defence. *Nat. Rev. Immunol.* **2008**, *8*, 764–775.

2.   Margaris, K.N.; Black, R.A. Modelling the lymphatic system: Challenges and opportunities. *J. R. Soc. Interface* **2014**, *9*, 601–612.

3.   Jafarnejad, M.; Woodruff, M.C.; Zawieja, D.C.; Carroll, M.C.; Moore, J.E., Jr. Modeling lymph flow and fluid exchange with blood vessels in lymph nodes. *Lymphat. Res. Biol.* **2015**, *13*, 234–247.

4.   Cooper, L.J.; Heppell, J.P.; Clough, G.F.; Ganapathisubramani, B.; Roose, T. An Image-Based Model of Fluid Flow Through Lymph Nodes. *Bull. Math. Biol.* **2016**, *78*, 52–71.

5.   Kislitsyn, A.; Savinkov, R.; Novkovic, M.; Onder, L.; Bocharov, G. Computational Approach to 3D Modeling of the Lymph Node Geometry. *Computation* **2015**, *3*, 222–234.

6.   Bocharov, G.; Danilov, A.; Vassilevski, Y.; Marchuk, G.I.; Chereshnev, V.A.; Ludewig, B. Reaction-diffusion modelling of interferon distribution in secondary lymphoid organs. *Math. Model. Nat. Phenom.* **2011**, *6*, 13–26.

7.   Savinkov, R.; Kislitsyn, A.; Watson, D.J.; van Loon, R.; Sazonov, I.; Novkovic, M.; Onder, L.; Bocharov, G. Data-driven modelling of the FRC network for studying the fluid flow in the conduit system. *Eng. Appl. Artif. Intell.* **2016**, doi:10.1016/j.engappai.2016.10.007.

8.   Kumar, V.; Scandella, E.; Danuser, R.; Onder, L.; Nitschke, M.; Fukui, Y.; Halin, C.; Ludewig, B.; Stein, J.V. Global lymphoid tissue remodelling during a viral infection is orchestrated by a B cell-lymphotoxin-dependent pathway. *Blood* **2010**, *115*, 4725–4733.

9.   Malhotra, D.; Fletcher, A.L.; Turley, S.J. Stromal and hematopoietic cells in secondary lymphoid organs: Partners in immunity. *Immunol. Rev.* **2013**, *251*, 160–176.

10. Cremasco, V.; Woodruff, M.C.; Onder, L.; Cupovic, J.; Nieves-Bonilla, J.M.; Schildberg, F.A.; Chang, J.; Cremasco, F.; Harvey, C.J.; Wucherpfennig, K.; et al. B cell homeostasis and follicle confines are governed by fibroblastic reticular cells. *Nat. Immunol.* **2014**, *15*, 973–981.

11. Chang, J.E.; Turley, S.J. Stromal infrastructure of the lymph node and coordination of immunity. *Trends Immunol.* **2015**, *36*, 30–39.

12. Chai, Q.; Onder, L.; Scandella, E.; Gil-Cruz, C.; Perez-Shibayama, C.; Cupovic, J.; Danuser, R.; Sparwasser, T.; Luther, S.A.; Thiel, V.; et al. Maturation of lymph node fibroblastic reticular cells from myofibroblastic precursors is critical for antiviral immunity. *Immunity* **2013**, *38*, 1013–1024.

13. Fletcher, A.L.; Acton, S.E.; Knoblich, K. Lymph node fibroblastic reticular cells in health and disease. *Nat. Rev. Immunol.* **2015**, *15*, 350–361.

14. Novkovic, M.; Onder, L.; Cupovic, J.; Abe, J.; Bomze, D.; Cremasco, V.; Scandella, E.; Stein, J.V.; Bocharov, G.; Turley, S.J.; et al. Topological Small-World Organization of the Fibroblastic Reticular Cell Network Determines Lymph Node Functionality. *PLoS Biol.* **2016**, *14*, e1002515.

15. Luther, S.A.; Tang, H.L.; Hyman, P.L.; Farr, A.G.; Cyster, J.G. Coexpression of the chemokines ELC and SLC by T zone stromal cells and deletion of the ELC gene in the plt/plt mouse. *Proc. Natl. Acad. Sci. USA* **2000**, *97*, 12694–12699.

16. Link, A.; Vogt, T.K.; Favre, S.; Britschgi, M.R.; Acha-Orbea, H.; Hinz, B.; Cyster, J.G.; Luther, S.A. Fibroblastic reticular cells in lymph nodes regulate the homeostasis of naive T cells. *Nat. Immunol.* **2007**, *8*, 1255–1265.

17. Mueller, S.N.; Germain, R.N. Stromal cell contributions to the homeostasis and functionality of the immune system. *Nat. Rev. Immunol.* **2009**, *9*, 618–629.

18. Sixt, M.; Kanazawa, N.; Selg, M.; Samson, T.; Roos, G.; Reinhardt, D.P.; Pabst, R.; Lutz, M.B.; Sorokin, L. The conduit system transports soluble antigens from the afferent lymph to resident dendritic cells in the T cell area of the lymph node. *Immunity* **2005**, *22*, 19–29.

19. Onder, L.; Danuser, R.; Scandella, E.; Firner, S.; Chai, Q.; Hehlgans, T.; Stein, J.V.; Ludewig, B. Endothelial cell-specific lymphotoxin-β receptor signaling is critical for lymph node and high endothelial venule formation. *J. Exp. Med.* **2013**, *210*, 465–473.

20. Girard, J.P.; Moussion, C.; Förster, R. HEVs, lymphatics and homeostatic immune cell trafficking in lymph nodes. *Nat. Rev. Immunol.* **2012**, *12*, 762–773.

21. Kelch, I.D.; Bogle, G.; Sands, G.B.; Phillips, A.R.; LeGrice, I.J.; Dunbar, P.R. Organ-wide 3D-imaging and topological analysis of the continuous microvascular network in a murine lymph node. *Sci. Rep.* **2015**, *5*, 16534.

22. Subramanian, N.; Torabi-Parizi, P.; Gottschalk, R.A.; Germain, R.N.; Dutta, B. Network representations of immune system complexity. *Wiley Interdiscip. Rev. Syst. Biol. Med.* **2015**, *7*, 13–38.

23. Heng, T.S.; Painter, M.W. Immunological Genome Project Consortium. The Immunological Genome Project: Networks of gene expression in immune cells. *Nat. Immunol.* **2008**, *9*, 1091–1094.

24. Kitano, H. Systems Biology: A brief overview. *Science* **2002**, *295*, 1662–1664.

25. Ludewig, B.; Stein, J.V.; Sharpe, J.; Cervantes-Barragan, L.; Thiel, V.; Bocharov, G. A global "imaging" view on systems approaches in immunology. *Eur. J. Immunol.* **2012**, *42*, 3116–3125.

26. Glazier, J.A.; Balter, A.; Poplawski, N.J. Magnetization to morphogenesis: A brief history of the Glazier-Graner-Hogeweg model. In *Single-Cell-Based Models in Biology and Medicine*; Anderson, A.R.A., Chaplain, M.A.J., Rejniak, K.A., Eds.; Mathematics and Biosciences in Interactions, Birkaüser: Basel, Switzerland, 2007; pp. 79–106.

27. Balter, A.; Merks, R.M.H.; Poplawski, N.J.; Swat, M.; Glazier, J.A. The Glazier-Graner-Hogeweg model: Extensions, future directions, and opportunities for further study. In *Single-Cell-Based Models in Biology and Medicine*; Anderson, A.R.A., Chaplain, M.A.J., Rejniak, K.A., Eds.; Mathematics and Biosciences in Interactions, Birkaüser: Basel, Switzerland, 2007; pp. 151–167.

28. Marée, A.F.M.; Grieneisen, V.A.; Hogeweg, P. The Cellular Potts Model and biophysical properties of cells, tissues and morphogenesis. In *Single-Cell-Based Models in Biology and Medicine*; Anderson, A.R.A., Chaplain, M.A.J., Rejniak, K.A., Eds.; Mathematics and Biosciences in Interactions, Birkaüser: Basel, Switzerland, 2007; pp. 107–136.

29. Scianna, M.S.; Preziosi, L.P. Multiscale Developments of the Cellular Potts Model. *SIAM J. Multiscale Model. Simul.* **2012**, *10*, 1–43.

30. Merks, R.M.; Brodsky, S.V.; Goligorksy, M.S.; Newman, S.A.; Glazier, J.A. Cell elongation is key to in silico replication of in vitro vasculogenesis and subsequent remodeling. *Dev. Biol.* **2006**, *289*, 44–54.

31. Roozendaal, R.; Mebius, R.E.; Kraal, G. The conduit system of the lymph node. *Int. Immunol.* **2008**, *20*, 1483–1487.

32. Delves, P.; Martin, S.; Burton, D.; Roitt, I. *Roitt's Essential Immunology*; Wiley: Somerset, UK, 2011; p. 239.

33. Gertz, J.E.; Anderson, A.O.; Shaw, S. Cords, channels, corridors, conduits: Critical architectural elements facilitating cell interaction in the lymph node cortex. *Immunol. Rev.* **1997**, *156*, 11–24.

34. Ushiki, T. Collagen Fibers, Reticular Fibers and Elastic Fibers. A Comprehensive Understanding from a Morphological Viewpoint. *Arch. Histol .Cytol.* **2002**, *65*, 109–206.

35. Swartz, M.A.; Fleury, M.E. Interstitial flow and its effects in soft tissues. *Annu. Rev. Biomed. Eng.* **2007**, *9*, 229–256.

36. Pappenheimer, A.M., Jr.; Lundgren, H.P.; Williams, J.W. Studies on the Molecular Weight of Diphtheria Toxin, Antitoxin and their Reaction Products. *J. Exp. Med.* **1939**, *71*, 247–262.

37. Wolffa, C.; Wattiezb, R.; Jean-Marie Ruysschaerta, J.; Cabiauxa, V. Characterization of diphtheria toxins catalytic domain interaction with lipid membranes. *Biochim. Biophys. Acta* **2004**, *1611*, 166–177.

38. Bouta, E.M.; Wood, R.W.; Brown, E.B.; Rahimi, H.; Ritchlin, C.T.; Schwarz, E.M. In vivo quantification of lymph viscosity and pressure in lymphatic vessels and draining lymph nodes of arthritic joints in mice. *J. Physiol.* **2014**, *92*, 1213–1223.

39. UMFPACK. Available online: http://faculty.cse.tamu.edu/davis/suitesparse.html (accessed on 20 August 2016).

40. Rodrigue, J.P.; Comtis, C.; Slack, B. *The Geography of Transport Systems*; Hofstra University Press: Hempstead, NY, USA, 2013; pp. 60–70.

41. Humphries, M.D.; Gurney, K. Network 'Small-World-Ness': A Quantitative Method for Determining Canonical Network Equivalence. *PLoS ONE* **2008**, *3*, e0002051.

42. Stauffer, D.; Aharony, A. *Introduction to Percolation Theory*; CRC Press: Boca Raton, FL, USA, 1994.

43. Tomei, A.A.; Siegert, S.; Britschgi, M.R.; Luther, S.A.; Swartz, M.A. Fluid flow regulates stromal cell organization and CCL21 expression in a tissue-engineered lymph node microenvironment. *J. Immunol.* **2009**, *183*, 4273–4283.

44. Paul, W.E. The immune system—Complexity exemplified. *Math. Model. Nat. Phenom.* **2012**, *7*, 4–6.

Permissions

List of Contributors

Reem Yassine, Faten Salman, Ali Al Shaer and Mohammad Hammoud
Department of Mechanical Engineering, Lebanese International University, 146404 Mazraa, Beirut, Lebanon

Denis Duhamel
Laboratoire Navier — UMR 8205 (Ecole des Ponts Paris Tech — IFSTTAR — CNRS), Cité Descartes — Champs-sur-Marne, Université Paris-Est, 77455 Marne-la-Vallée Cedex 2, France

Young-Moo Byun and Carsten A. Ullrich
Department of Physics and Astronomy, University of Missouri, Columbia, MO 65211, USA

Michaela Elmatzoglou and Aris Avdelas
School of Civil Engineering, Aristotle University, GR-541 24 Thessaloniki, Greece

Dimitra C. Douvi, Dionissios P. Margaris and Aristeidis E. Davaris
Fluid Mechanics Laboratory (FML), Mechanical Engineering and Aeronautics Department, University of Patras, GR-26500 Patras, Greece

Anass Bouchnita
Institut Camille Jordan, UMR 5208 CNRS, University Lyon 1, Villeurbanne 69622, France
Laboratoire de Biométrie et Biologie Evolutive, UMR 5558 CNRS, University Lyon 1, Villeurbanne 69622, France
Mohammadia School of Engineering, Université Mohamed V, Rabat 10080, Morocco

Vitaly Volpert
Institut Camille Jordan, UMR 5208 CNRS, University Lyon 1, Villeurbanne 69622, France
Institute of Numerical Mathematics, Russian Academy of Sciences, Moscow 119333, Russia
INRIA Team Dracula, INRIA Lyon La Doua, Villeurbanne 60603, France

Fatima-Ezzahra Belmaati and Rajae Aboulaich
Mohammadia School of Engineering, Université Mohamed V, Rabat 10080, Morocco

Mark J. Koury
Vanderbilt University Medical Center, Nashville, TN 37232-6307, USA

Theodore D. Katsilieris, George P. Latsas, Hector E. Nistazakis and George S. Tombras
Department of Electronics, Computers, Telecommunications and Control, Faculty of Physics, National and Kapodistrian University of Athens, Athens 15784, Greece

Martin Geier and Martin Schönherr
Institute for Computational Modeling in Civil Engineering, TU Braunschweig, 38106 Braunschweig, Germany

Aristidis G. Vrahatis, Andreas Kanavos and Athanasios Tsakalidis
Department of Computer Engineering and Informatics, University of Patras, Patras 26500, Greece

Konstantina Dimitrakopoulou
Centre for Cancer Biomarkers CCBIO and Computational Biology Unit, Department of Informatics, University of Bergen, Bergen 5020, Norway

Spyros Sioutas
Department of Informatics, Ionian University Corfu, Corfu 49100, Greece

Amir Masoud Abdol and Jaap A. Kaandorp
Computational Science Lab, University of Amsterdam, Science Park 904, 1098XH Amsterdam, The Netherlands

Damjan Cicin-Sain
EMBL/CRG Systems Biology Research Unit, Centre for Genomic Regulation (CRG), The Barcelona Institute of Science and Technology, 08003 Barcelona, Spain
Universitat Pompeu Fabra (UPF), 08003 Barcelona, Spain

Anton Crombach
EMBL/CRG Systems Biology Research Unit, Centre for Genomic Regulation (CRG), The Barcelona Institute of Science and Technology, 08003 Barcelona, Spain
Universitat Pompeu Fabra (UPF), 08003 Barcelona, Spain
Centre for Interdisciplinary Research in Biology, College de France, CNRS, INSERM, PSL Research University, 75231 Paris, France

Samy Bakheet
Department of Mathematics and Computer Science, Faculty of Science, Sohag University, 82524 Sohag, Egypt

Institute for Information Technology and Communications, Otto-von-Guericke-University Magdeburg, P.O. Box 4120, 39016 Magdeburg, Germany

Eleni Douvi, Dimitra Douvi and Dionissios Margaris
Fluid Mechanics Laboratory (FML), Mechanical Engineering and Aeronautics Department, University of Patras, GR-26500 Patras, Greece

Ioannis Drosis
Small Wind Turbines Development Manager, 97 Dimitros Street, GR-19200 Elefsina, Greece

Dmitry Grebennikov
 Moscow Institute of Physics and Technology (State University), Dolgoprudny 141701 , Moscow Region, Russia
Institute of Numerical Mathematics of the RAS, Moscow 119333, Russia

Raoul van Loon, Igor Sazonov and Daniel J. Watson
College of Engineering, Swansea University, Swansea SA2 8PP, Wales, UK

Mario Novkovic and Lucas Onder
Institute of Immunobiology, Kantonsspital St. Gallen, St. Gallen CH-9007, Switzerland

Rostislav Savinkov and Rufina Tretyakova
Lomonosov Moscow State University, Moscow 119991, Russia
Institute of Numerical Mathematics of the RAS, Moscow 119333, Russia

Gennady Bocharov
Institute of Numerical Mathematics of the RAS, Moscow 119333, Russia

Index

Printed in the USA
CPSIA information can be obtained
at www.ICGtesting.com
JSHW051443221024
72173JS00006B/1559